On the Theory of Chinese Ideology

On the Theory of Chinese Ideology

Tony Kosuge

FOCALPOINT
LONDON

First published in Great Britain 2012
by Focalpoint Press Ltd
135 Northfield Avenue
London W13 9QT
Copyright © Tony Kosuge 2012

All rights reserved. This book is sold subject to the condition that it shall not by way of trade or otherwise, be lent, resold, hired out, or otherwise circulated without the publisher's prior consent in any form of binding or cover other than that in which it is published and without a similar condition, including this condition, being imposed on the purchaser.

Tony Kosuge has asserted his right under the Copyright, Designs and Patents Act 1988 to be identified as author of this work. A CIP catalogue record for this book is available from the British Library

ISBN 978-0-9571991-0-1

Typeset by Windrush Publishing Services, Gloucestershire, Great Britain
Printed and bound in Great Britain by MPG Books Group,
Bodmin and King's Lynn

CONTENTS

List of Maps and Illustrations	9
Introduction – Debacle in East Asia	11

PART ONE – THE THEORY

Is this an 'Everlasting' Economy?	19
The Need for a Comprehensive Political Analysis	22
The Chinese Model for Expansion	25
A Centralized Regime and the Economic Cycle	30
The Prototype – Yin-Zhou 'Revolution'	36
The Political Core	44
What is Arch-Bureaucracy?	50
The Original Chinese Pattern	55
The Korean Pattern	59
The Japanese Pattern and 'Toynbee's Orbit'	66
Two Colliding Civilizations	76
The Political Core Trap	81
Control by Human Networks	84
The Fragmentation of Power	87
The Areal Concept	92
The End of Expansion	96

PART TWO – THE PRACTICAL TREND

I – *China and the Chinese Economic Area*

The Adjusted System	101
Problems of a Socialist Market Economy	107
An 'Advanced' Arch-Bureaucracy	112
A Chinese Democracy in Taiwan	117
The Altering Status of Hong Kong	121
Colonial Power in Singapore	124
Successful Immigration to South East Asia	128

CONTENTS

II – South Korea

Faltering Idealism	135
Catching up with the Japanese Economy	138
Emerging Democracy	142

III – North Korea

The Failure of Autocracy	147
The 'Fall' of the People's Democracy	153
An Existing Deterrent in the Peninsula	157
Defeatism as a Major Stumbling Block	161

PART THREE – JAPAN IN CRISIS

I – *The System*

Democracy Adrift	167
The Decisive Role of the Emperor	172
'Hijacked' by Bureaucracy	176
The 'Liberty' of the Press	181
Opinion Leaders as Propagandists	184
'Fair-minded' Business Leaders?	188
An Underground World in Daylight	191
The Opposition and the Anti-American Wrangle	194
Eroded Sovereignty	198
The 'Assault' of the 'Land Standard'	201

II – *The Origin of the Deflationary Spiral*

The Bubble that Failed to be Defined	207
An Ideological Problem inside its Economy	210
Banking Bureaucracy – Welch vs. Miyazawa	214
A Quicksand of Deterioration	218
The 'Big Bang' without the Infrastructure	222
The Ministry of 'Irrelevant' Finance	226
The Mechanism of the Zero Interest Rate	230
Global Capitalism in Danger	233

III – An Impossible Reform

The Mandate Given	237
The Yasukuni Shrine and Chinese Anger	240
Surprise Visit to Pyongyang	245
Manifestos for Delay and No Decisions	248
The Road Corporation Fiasco	250
The Farce of the Postal Corporation 'Reform'	254
The 'Main Castle' Intact	257
Conflicts amongst Chinese Ideological States	260
Japan as the Cornerstone of Global Democracy	262

PART FOUR – THE CHANGE

Sun Yat-sen and the Political Base of Modern China	269
The Resurgence of Shintoism	272
A Sense of Crisis	276
The Land of Human Gods	284
The Roman Empire and Christianity	288
European Expansion	292
American Growth	298
Misunderstanding of Max Weber	302
No Valid Social Science	308
When Japan has the Presidency?	314
Implications for Chinese Politics	317
Disintegrated State Power	321
On the Road We Were Before	332
Only Alternative to Abysmal Breakdown	335
NOTES	343
BIBLIOGRAPHY	365
INDEX	381

LIST OF MAPS AND ILLUSTRATIONS

1	China at the time of the Yin-Zhou Revolution	37
2	Korea: From Three Kingdoms to a Peninsula State in the late sixth century	63
3	Ancient Japan: Expansion after the Taika Reform	69
4	The Treble Ball of Rational Politics	310
5	The Superiority of Rational Politics versus Irrational Politics	311

INTRODUCTION – DEBACLE IN EAST ASIA

It happens as an implosion. A process unknown until recently to the western world. As the major economies face potential risk of a financial meltdown, however, the West and the rest of the world could also find themselves suddenly experiencing a similar implosion in their economies. It should have meant a time for reflection on a situation that was the consequence of an unprecedented western expansion toward the East whereby all its major indigenous economies were integrated without the necessary political adjustments.

The pre-war Great Depression suffered by the United States was a deflationary spiral – the same one that Japan is struggling with today. Without any doubt the American experience was a grave economic disaster at that time which certainly affected subsequent various political events on a global scale with horrendous magnitude. But it took only four years for the striving Americans to return to growth again. Just to remind you, we are already entering into a third decade following the burst of the Japanese bubble. During this period of 'Hyper-Great Depression' in Japan, the actual economic life of an ordinary Japanese citizen has constantly deteriorated as individual debts became uncontrollable.

In terms of income, Japan came twentieth among the industrialised nations at a GDP per capita of $32,018 as of 2009 (OECD). In terms of debt, however, each Japanese national (including babies!) had the heaviest burden bearing $93,153 ($1/Y82) of government debt by the end of 2010 (MOFJ). The balance of these two figures shows without a doubt that the Japanese taxpayer is the world's poorest, bearing a burden of minus of $61,135, but this fact and its repercussions have been constantly neglected in the world's economic forums. The West was luckily immune from such figures of Negative Gross National Public Debt, until Greece, then Ireland, were suddenly trapped in 2010. And even some major Western economies may also be dragged into this dire situation if the current global economic 'road' unexpectedly becomes more treacherous.

In Japan, moreover, this ratio is rapidly enlarging in terms of the politically-concealed actual enormous sums. It should include various undisclosed bad debts from numerous state banks, public corporations, quangos and public business schemes (or their loans) and other forms of given credit toward all these uneconomic entities both at state and regional levels. We should further extend the scope to many of the ex-government businesses that are now declared as belonging to the private sector, or all Japanese quasi-state controlled 'private' banks and corporations depending on their risks for government guarantees or cheaply-calculated public insurance policies and so forth.

Some would imagine rightly, even if things change 'modestly' in the coming decade continuing the levels that have been witnessed in the last ten years, that nobody in the world, including the Japanese taxpayers, can finance or give aid to repay this astronomical debt. At least fourteen years ago in the late 1990s, there was no such enormous debt burden on Japanese public finance as this indicator was then in a positive position. This situation is an on-going new global politico-economic phenomenon, to which we should perhaps pay more attention to in our interdependent society.

To begin with, it would be worthwhile for all of us to ask why such an economic mess had to be experienced in the East. You might have never thought about it before, but you do not require any specialist knowledge to understand it. It was first born as a side-effect of unprecedented western capitalistic expansion and a subsequent power shift from the once prosperous East to the rising West.

How would you act if you had to get involved in this game of geopolitical expansion? Whoever does so, the principle applicable

INTRODUCTION

would be the same, which is to achieve an easier or better target (or simply the ones situated closer to you) first and to enhance your power base and strength. And to keep the strongest targets for a future final showdown until you have become confident enough to crack this last hardest nut. Somehow, this was exactly what happened in history. The West had to wait for more than five centuries to set up a presence in East Asia, which could not be ignored either militarily or economically. What patience? No, the West just had no other choice.

It may sound implausible but more than three-quarters of a century ago, a Chinese man thought about this issue seriously. He was a professor of philosophy and religion at National Beijing University and his name was Hu Shih. Having studied in America and read all the Chinese classics, he concluded that there was no equivalent in the Chinese hemisphere to prevailing western philosophical and political values. Confident of his academic belief, he worried about the future of the fellow Chinese nations:

'East Asia is the meeting point of all the three routes of this aggressive civilization,' he predicted on the future shape of the Western expansion. 'Thus far it has met with no serious resistance. It is in East Asia that the grand finale of this drama of world-conquest is to be staged. For it is here that the civilization of the West is brought into direct contact and conflict with the two principal centres of the civilization of the East: the continental empire of China and the island empire of Japan. Upon the final Westernisation of these two empires depends the completion of the world-conquest of this new civilization.'[1] What he could not foresee, however, was the resilience of Eastern politics. With his clear-eyed awareness and great political sensitivity and perhaps because of his prematurely-released warning, he had to face the wrath of his Chinese audiences.[2] No matter what philosophical defects they had, they were certainly not ready to give up the principles of their politics or their traditions without a bitter fight.

In the current world of nuclear deterrence, information technology and much other know-how, the United States, Britain and Europe seem to control the world economy through the financial centres of

London, New York and elsewhere, despite a recent loss of confidence in their systems. East Asia had no option but to join their trading and financial links once they lost their own military and economic superiority. East Asia tried to gain a stronger position within this 'borrowed' system but the basic pattern of incompatibility never abated.

Above all, East Asia had to accept the political status quo and the incoming global values from the West which were imposed upon them. How did East Asia react to the new situation? Even a secondary company who gave up a lion's share in the global market could still try to survive in a niche market. Everybody tries to survive somehow. The only place that could match up to doing such deals was inside their own East Asian territories. There, and only there, the old eastern states could bargain with the West on all economic fronts without compromising their own political identity.

The current policy applied by the East has been the virtual rejection of Western or global principles in the region. Many people tried and are still trying to explain that there should be a 'paradise' called a 'middle ground'. And it is true in some insignificant cases that it is possible to achieve a compromise. Ultimately, however, this gap will continue to grow and a decision must be made. In the end, the differences come down to political systems.

The first country to be hit by this sort of debacle in East Asia was Japan, just after the First World War, as its economy reached a peak and then entered into decline. Up to that point, the world had been amazed by the degree and speed of Japanese modernisation but the success proved to be short-lived. Why did neither ancient Japan nor China experience this implosion? Put simply, East Asia was then enjoying its own traditional non-industrialised economy. In the era of agrarian economy, the people in East Asia did not care about Western values. There was only the East Asian standard on the streets and they experienced the explosive events of internal conflicts or war.

Finally, the West needs to be aware of another important point. Due to their passive stance, the East will outwardly do nothing while

INTRODUCTION

vigorously disputing in secret. And the West may encounter a certain diplomatic impasse as things get rough. By setting your face against those non-participative 'procrastinating' tactics, it has always been up to the West in the past, and will be again in the future, to take the initiative to finish this false and disastrous process for the sake of everybody concerned.

Could there be another military conflict in East Asia? There must be another way to approach the problem, which is both proactive and peaceful. I will now try to explain all about this particular strategy.

PART ONE
THE THEORY

IS THIS AN 'EVERLASTING' ECONOMY?

Great powers have a relatively short history when we look back at them. Today's superpower, the United States, would be a typical example. After many hindrances, George Washington finally managed to accept the surrender of Lord Cornwallis at Yorktown to end the war for its independence from Britain and to secure its own development. It is hard to imagine today, but the victory was attained by the indispensable help of the tricolour-flagged navy and army from the then European 'superpower', France.

Around two hundred years before this spectacular historic event in the West, a Russian expeditionary army under the orders of the newly titled Tsar, Ivan IV or the Terrible, had advanced to Siberia for the first time to assure expansion on its vast eastern territory, which was to eventually reach to the Pacific Ocean. Astonishingly, three centuries earlier than this, Russia was groaning under the tyranny of Mongolian conquerors, when its existence as a unified nation was in danger. How can we correlate this moment to Khrushchev's threatening diplomacy during the Cuban Missile Crisis? Then the world was trembling on the brink of collapse.

And how about the massive global expansion of such a small country as Portugal? Most of these strong national states were shaped by modern political ideas only in the last millennium – which is a short period in terms of human history. In this context, China is an exception. Some might argue, as many people have difficulty in accepting a changing reality, that China could not be counted as a great power in the first place. But in addition to its permanent UN

Security Council seat, China has advanced rapidly with modernised military capability and, as it became the world's second largest economy by the end of 2010, vigorously chasing only America as the next target, it is now certain that fewer and fewer people would dispute that China is a strengthening global power.

For long periods, however, China seemed to be exotic, gigantic, confusing or sometimes unimaginable for the West. This sentiment is recognisable in cultural terms where most people tend to see China as a different world, somewhat irrelevant to their own lives (except Chinese take-aways, of course!). With this sort of prevailing indifference, the nature of its history or language was rarely studied even in intellectual circles. We must admit that, without easily available information, the reality of something like the Egyptian Empire surviving into the twenty-first century would indeed be difficult to understand as a political entity.

For the Chinese, their unparalleled history has been always a major source of burning national pride. If you have ever stayed in one of the Chinese speaking-countries, perhaps you would have heard this popular Chinese saying – 'Yes, it may take a hundred years for the Chinese but it will be done.' By this saying, the Chinese are indicating to you that no matter what happens in the world, China would remain the same. When the Chinese thought of their country, they always believed the assumption that this vast and populated economy would last forever, regardless of what might happen in the outside world. In other words, whatever world changes occur, they will be ephemeral in nature, and their influence is limited for the Chinese nations... no matter how far from reality this assumption is.

The current state name for China is *Zhongguo* or *Zhonghua* in Chinese. It is translated in English usually as 'China', but in fact, its meaning is rather different in the original context as those two Chinese characters connote 'the centre of the world'. And this Chinese meaning is directly connected to its old dynastical political principles which survived under traditional ideology. On the other hand, its name in English and most of Europe – 'China' – was deduced merely from the name of its first historical empire, Qin,

PART ONE – THE THEORY

without any specific political significance attached to it, like England or France.

Some would say that Chinese communists abolished the traditional principles of the old Chinese world. It was certainly not too radical when they put this name on their new state, compared to the Russians who at the time of their own revolution had shaken off their ancient name in favour of a fresh beginning with the Soviet Union. All modern Chinese states always chose to be called 'China' or rather, 'Zhonghua' including Sun Yat-sen's first republic. What was repeatedly confirmed was that the Chinese leaders had no other choice but to embrace this name in order to appeal to all ordinary Chinese, by deliberately recalling thousands of years of the prosperous Chinese past. But in doing so, perhaps they hung on to the dangers of its old political philosophy.

I am not suggesting here, of course, that nations should forget about their own past. What we need to acknowledge, however, is that the importance of specific historical interpretation, which is now firmly adhered to by the Chinese, has come from a historical link to previous affluent times. The philosophy of 'Zhonghua' is nothing related to that of communism. No old Chinese dynasties ever used this name. It was unnecessary to emphasise this political principle embedded in the centre of dynastical politics. The fact was that modern communist China needed to keep its own traditional political identity even as it adopted a stream of new political ideas and changes from the West and all the confusion coming out of this.

There were many reasons for the Chinese or Japanese to stick to their own tradition, culture, and above all, political behaviour, or more precisely, their own political ideology. But it also depended on how their economy could cope with future challenges. As Karl Marx rightly defined it, although no one stated it in Britain but they all instinctively understood, 'Politics is based on its economic infrastructure.'

Regarding the nature of political ideology, Aristotle once made an important remark on how to define it, 'Observation tells us that every state is an association, and that every association is formed with a view to some good purpose. I say "good", because in all their actions all men do in fact aim at what they think good.'³ He argued a simple, but essential point, that every political system is the result of a good political idea accepted by the people who originally formed an association defined as a state.

Unless we can prove otherwise, therefore, we should assume that the political ideology created by the ancient Chinese was also formed for a good purpose like all other states, while judgement on whether it was good or bad could be changed depending on the circumstance, or more precisely, the political environment. Hence, if it was bad, China should have already rejected it. We also have to recognise that the objective and the political idea of implementing the ideology, was essential for the development of the Chinese economy. In order to continue, 'good' must have meant 'economically good'.

This ancient ideology became invisible on the surface, after many successful years of historical evolution but it is firmly affiliated in China's social customs, people's mentality, and above all, as the basis of political behaviour.

THE NEED FOR A COMPREHENSIVE POLITICAL ANALYSIS

Let us have a brief look at the eastern state of Japan again. So far, all global economists have failed to provide a convincing solution for the ailing Japanese economy. Among them, however, I would like to introduce one of the most carefully-crafted comments from Lester Thurow. This top American economist concluded that Japan had no economical problem! Japan's problem is instead political; therefore, Japan lacks, in his words, an 'economic environment' which could provide a new course of growth or political will to improve it.

He therefore refused to go into details of an economic policy package for the failing Japan. What could be the sense of providing the country with an economic solution, if the problem was political in nature? He affirmed his idea with modesty, 'I do not see the point of explaining to the Japanese the details of the required policies for

PART ONE – THE THEORY

Japan. Any Japanese would know what has to be done.' Indeed. And the solutions would be rather basic. Most of the other economists crossed this boundary and did not hesitate to risk their reputations. Of course, we can tolerate watching more economists lose their reputations by smashing into an intellectual dead-end, but the world cannot afford to watch some of its key national economies go into bankruptcy while the leading economists are busy occupying themselves with pointless arguments.

Perhaps we should listen to Thurow's opinion more carefully, '…There would be no remedy if this disease of deflation started worldwide. To prevent deflation, we must focus on Japan. If the Japanese economy could come back to its growth trend quickly, there would be no danger of worldwide deflation happening. If the Japanese economy could not come back to growth, however, most certainly, the world economy will enter into deflation…'[4] In the last decade of the financial bubble, we could comfortably ignore this early warning, taking a global perspective on Japan's problems, but today it unfortunately sounds all too real.

To assess the indigenous politics of the Japanese, particularly its peculiarities from a western viewpoint, so-called 'revisionists' appeared in the West. This seemed to be a move in the right direction. Karel van Wolferen, a Dutch journalist, keeping his country's traditional dominance over Japanese affairs, produced a controversial book *The Enigma of Japanese Power*. In his conclusion, he focused on the bureaucratic system which existed in pre-war Japan. By paying attention to the extraordinary presence and strength of bureaucrats, he focused on similar political movements visible in post-war Japan.

He struggled, however, to show the concept behind his analysis, 'And where must one look for the beginnings of what is most essential in Chinese culture? To the state, or to the philosophy that justified it? Such "chicken and egg" situations are less applicable to Japan. Looking back over its history, it is clear that political arrangements have been a major factor in determining the development of Japanese culture.'[5] While he was correct in raising the matter, he could not differentiate the fine line between Chinese and Japanese 'political arrangements'. Although his assertion was a powerful one and he grabbed the right target, he failed to nail it down, and exposed the limit of his subsequent arguments. His targeted object was huge, disguised and it was not visible from this angle.

In simplifying his analysis, he concentrated virtually on one thing: Japanese modern history, leaving the principal issue unexamined. From this viewpoint, he focused on the pre-war bureaucratic control of the Cabinet Planning Board as the major cause of the Japanese failure. I agree with him that the case study on pre-war Japan in general is indispensable and is where we can find all the related politics of current Japanese problems, but it did not just suddenly arise in this period.

In Japan, his argument rather provided a relief to 'opinion leaders'. They modified it with a new version of 'The year 1940 system' to explain and limit the problem to this relatively short period of modern history for the cause of the current setback. Wolferen's view coincided with the Japanese politics of convenience which protect current 'modern' politics where all problems are seen to be caused by hackneyed policy failures that can be fixed by a new general election.

Another revisionist, Chalmers Johnson, tried to enlarge his scope to cover the whole of East Asia in his *Japan: Who Governs?* But, he too, was drawn into a general argument where he exposed his weakness, 'Most of the theorists who allege a link between Asian economic dynamism and "creative Confucianism" are actually not interested in Weber but nationalistic, ideological, or journalistic motives. They want to explain Asia's competitiveness as due to primordial characteristics in order to get their own governments to protect them from it…'

As long as such inherited characteristics remain positive, we certainly do not need to argue about them. Despite Johnson's multiple and pre-emptive thinking, what he did not include in his survey was the negative side of 'primordial characteristics'. If just one or only a few people are causing the problem, we can definitely avoid analysing those political characteristics or 'very complex socio-economic development'. But as he successfully depicted in his book with his outstanding knowledge of Japanese politics, Japan's case was very distinct from common practices of modern politics.

By failing to address the nature of the Japanese political entity, his conclusion was only partially true and rather bleak, 'It may well turn out that the two (the US and Japan) different states – the one military and regulatory and other economic and developmental – cannot overcome their differences.'[6] Again, we cannot underestimate his warning when world politics as a whole are currently moving into his projection, consciously or unconsciously. But we all have to take a breath here in thinking about what he overlooked or thought unimportant, i.e., the origin of this political power.

Above all, America needs to know about its 'enemy' and their strategy to assess America's real power, as the ancient Chinese military strategist, Sunzi, insisted. And as the former US ambassador, Mike Mansfield, once argued in Tokyo, we certainly should draw a conclusion on the future direction of US–Japan politics in view of 'the world's most important bilateral relationship', which is pivotal for East Asia and the entire world.

Rather than ending the subject on a superficial note, like someone who lived in the twentieth century would have preferred, or satisfying oneself with a nineteenth-century view of national interests, we in the twenty-first should be required to go beyond this drastic solution, in dealing with today's nuclear-armed East Asia. Furthermore, with this apparent political breakdown in sight, it is vitally important for the West to create a theoretical formula based on the critical facts whereby it is possible to solve each specific problem in East Asia, but only if there is the political will to do so. To understand its political entity, however, we need to dig further into East Asian history.

THE CHINESE MODEL FOR EXPANSION

Unlike the European expansion mode of thought on the equilibrium of power, the Chinese rudimentary model adhered to the idea of a single centralised power – Dayitong. While there were periods when states were divided in Chinese history, these 'broken-up' eras, no matter how long their time span, could be interpreted as a temporary transitional process to form another expanded centrifugal power structure.

In this mode, China has never slept, or it is wrong to assume, as Napoleon Bonaparte once did, 'When China wakes, it will shake the world.' For China indeed has been incessantly shaking the world... its own world of East Asia. With continuous economic growth since ancient times, China expanded on a recognisable political path. But this basic pattern of expansion was different from one of western origin.

Historically, the Chinese themselves often tried to depict China as an exemplar of the greatest empire of absolute rule that prospered because of all the technologies and resources developed within their own world. But this depiction merely comes from traditional diplomatic posturing, and was categorically incorrect. For instance, China had no iron technology in its early days when most of the ancient western world already enjoyed the power of an iron age. It was very likely finally brought into China from India, yet Chinese records never mention how this important technological transfer was made.

How did the process of divided states become important for China's subsequent active expansion as another new and greater power? To expand the Chinese economy, colonisation, immigration and development had to be encouraged as a fundamental political tool. This basic mode for expansion continued even when no powerful central regime existed in China. A Chinese-armed colonising group or sometimes migrating refugees could initially carry out this movement to the adjacent territory. And when the official Chinese army joined them, the territory became forever a part of the Chinese realm. Even for unconquered lands, they produced a Chinese 'myth' attached to each place so that they could invade the land with a bit of 'legitimacy' in the future, when the military balance turned in their favour.

The first empire of China, Qin (*c.*221-206 BC), which was situated in the far west of China, was born as a colonialist state. Qin expanded to the south, to the modern province of Sichuan, that was extraneous to the original China. In addition, the area was probably a point of contact with a superior Indian civilization that had built its first Mauryan Empire around forty years prior to the rise of the Qin.

As we all know, the idea of an ancient imperial system originated in West Asia, where the mighty empire of Persia was born. At one time in the mid-sixth century BC, it became so powerful that all surrounding states including Greece and Egypt had to pay a forced tribute to the Persian emperor. This movement influenced India, and then China. In this context, the annexation of far western provinces was a necessary step for the Qin to establish the Chinese imperial system. But it was not until the Shu (or Shu Han) regime (221-263) that the province was thoroughly assimilated and expansion to areas further south was initiated. The Tang dynasty (618-907) would not later have enjoyed its power and glory without this successful colonisation of the Qin/Sichuan province.

Similar massive colonisations occurred during the period of the Five Dynasties and Ten Kingdoms (902-970), when a larger region, south of the Yangtze River, was developed, including the area of the modern Guangdong province, while the majority of this territory was declared to have been conquered militarily by China much earlier during the mighty Han dynasty (206 BC-AD 220). The work of integration was only completed by the time of the Song dynasty (960-1279). From then on, the newly-developed regions could provide a strong economic basis for the subsequent dynasties as the richest agricultural territory among the Chinese provinces.

China was a dynamic society, always keen to grow aggressively, with a thirst for new technologies. Konan Naito, a singular Japanese Sinologist, once envisaged this dynamic of Chinese politics and he tried to characterise the entire story of Chinese history as the movement of 'Action and Reaction'.[7] I absolutely agree with him on the existence of this historical mechanism. But perhaps we should modify it as 'Expansion and Integration' to make it more appropriate in today's terminology. At the time of Chinese expansion, many other people joined in the Chinese world, either voluntarily or by force. In fact, there was no alternative force to confront this new rising power in East Asia, as analogous to a similar situation which emerged in the seventh century in the Islamic Arabian Peninsula.

I would classify these expansionist Chinese states as Zhou, Qin, Former Han (206 BC-AD 8), Sui, Tang, Yuan and Qing. Between these dynasties, there were always the dynasties, or the period of divided states, whose aim seemed to be the consolidation of the previous expansion such as Eastern Zhou (770-453 BC), Later Han (25-220) or Han, Three Kingdoms, Song and Ming. As a contrast, the former seem to be colourful and bright, while the latter's image looks sober and solemn. Comparatively, the expansionist states were vital, imbued with foreign culture, challenging and imaginative, while the integrating states were traditionally more indigenously Chinese, conservative and tightly-administered.

In world history, the Chinese state that underwent most expansion was the Tang dynasty. It had the deepest boundary to the westward. Jacques Gernet focused on this vital historical moment, 'In 648 General Wang Hsuan-ts'e organized an expedition to the Patna area of northern India, doubtless with Nepalese and Tibetan troops, in order to settle to China's advantage the succession to the throne of the little kingdom of Magadha… In 662 China intervened in the internal affairs of the Sassanid dynasty at Ctesiphon on the Tigris, just at the very time when the Persian empire was threatened by the advance of the Omeyyad Arabs.'[8] The Sassanian Empire of Persia emerged at one time as an influential state in the region, trying to expand into Roman territory and Arabia when Islam was about to be born. Patna or Pataliputna, once the capital of Emperor Asoka's vast empire, was a renowned location as the principal centre of the iron industry in India.

One could even argue, therefore, that China was the first global power connected to both East and West. Korea and Japan also entered wholly into the Chinese world in this magnificent period of glory and prosperity. The new political system of the Tang dynasty finally emerged to control all of East Asia for the first time, with Indian-born Buddhism and the finest iron technology as the source of its new military powers.

Michio Tanigawa astutely captured this critical political movement, 'The vassalage system would explain the Chinese emperor and vassal relationships between the Tang and East Asian states. As the ruling class of the Tang government were all aristocrats, it could be regarded that the ruling class of a vassal state equally belonged to this aristocratic group…Japanese ruling class who had a tributary relationship with the Tang was also inside of this group.' This was a vital link to the further evolution of the Japanese politics. His final conclusions on the historical importance of this event are, 'It would be more appropriate to consider that but for Chinese civilization; Japan could not form a unified state.'[9]

As the Chinese empire expanded, many foreigners came into its society to take advantage of its inside power and economic privileges. Particularly as the new aggressive political philosophies and technological bases were firmly established in China, bolstering its military strength, economic prosperity and political importance, neighbouring nations in East Asia found it difficult to remain outside China's hegemony. This was a credible reason for the Korean and Japanese leaders to accept these new Chinese political principles with enthusiasm.

Only by voluntarily adopting the more advanced Chinese civilization and its various new political ideas voluntarily, could Japan and Korea keep their independence by fortifying their political systems. In this narrative, it is important to acknowledge that China or Chinese was not originally a racial concept, despite the fact that the Chinese assimilated others living in this vast area by promoting a racial concept under a single political ideology.

The westward expansion of these newly-born East Asiatic global forces suffered a severe blow when the strong army of the Tang, led by a Korean General, Gao Xianzhi, was defeated by a rising new global power, the advanced Abbasids Arabs, at the battle of Talas River basin (near modern Tashkent) in 751. It was an omen for the crumbling great empire in the golden age of Tang.

In this process of Chinese expansion, the Chinese system and people always showed their remarkable resilience to outside invaders. For instance, Mongolians invaded China in the thirteenth century and then the Sinicised-Mongolians established the Yuen dynasty (1234-1368) in China as a part of their vast Eurasian empire. Unlike others, however, they eventually retreated to their grass homeland to preserve their own identity when their power declined. It took another three hundred years for China to expand into this land of the mighty Genghis Khan. But the formidable Chinese system finally made it as a proof of the effectiveness of its traditional politics.

As Arabian merchants went out to the sea, Canton, with its natural advantages, emerged as a port city for the tea trade. By the thirteenth century, it became the centre of Chinese and Islamic overseas trade. Again, China had no problem in continuing to absorb new technology from the rest of the world and further using its benefits and strengthening its own economy. China demonstrated extraordinary maritime progress when Emperor Yong Lu of the Ming Dynasty (1368-1643) sanctioned the navigation of a huge Chinese fleet led by the Muslim general, Zheng He, which travelled as far as Africa in the fifteenth century. It made it possible for China to expand subsequent colonisation to overseas territories such as Taiwan, and soon Chinese mass immigration to South East Asia was launched.

A CENTRALIZED REGIME AND THE ECONOMIC CYCLE

Why, or based on what mechanism, could the Chinese economy expand in the age of the old dynasties? Looking into this subject, one notices that there was a notable characteristic in the old Chinese economic growth patterns. In the rise and fall of the dynasties, particularly after the Han dynasty which organized production of iron and thereby established a solid national economy in China, the changes constituted not only political upheavals but also represented a single, long-term economic cycle of very roughly a period of between a hundred to three hundred years.

PART ONE – THE THEORY

The political change heralded by the downfall of each different dynasty arrived as if it was necessary for a new economic cycle to begin, and it was called in Chinese '*Geming*', the word usually translated in Chinese as 'revolution' as for the French revolution or the Chinese communist revolution. But we need to be careful about this usage, because it did not mean always revolution with new democratic ideas as in the western sense but merely denoted 'change of (dynastical) regime' in the old Chinese terminology.

Jin Guantao and Liu Qingfeng tried to explain this particular Chinese process, 'Why did such a law of diminishing returns on reforms emerge? The key to this answer is…in order to reform, the Chinese dynasty can rely only on its bureaucratic system… Especially, in the dynasty's final period…to try to clean up a rotten bureaucracy by corrupted bureaucrats would be just like pouring oil on the fire.'

There was, however, a rational solution for this irrational process, as they continue, 'This disruptive power in organizations cannot be contained and nothing could stop it in Chinese ancient society… No, when a decayed outdated form of politics reached to its maximum extent, society would provide the traditional antidote. A full-scale peasant rebellion began to arise all over the country…The disruptive power in the old system ceased to exist by swords and fire!'[10] In the Chinese 'revolution', as they argued here, the focus had always to be given always to the power itself.

The inherent characteristics of a Chinese 'revolution' would appear as the removal of a political barrier by force. In fact, a sort of power politics based on the same logic was also recognisable on the side of 'revolutionary power'. What was lacking in this confrontation of East Asian politics was any rational criteria, whereby both parties could acknowledge that reform should move in a better direction. In other words, the Chinese 'revolution' appeared not as a logical clarification of political differences but actually as the end of political arguments.

The 'revolution' in ancient China was often accompanied by hyperinflation and violent destruction for long periods. In the age of agrarian economy, the initial signs for 'revolution' in China often began with a large-scale natural disaster. When a dynasty was still young and flexible, it could overcome these difficulties, but for an old and ailing regime, it ignited the process of economic stagnation, which emerged as an unstoppable decline in the long-term. This repeated process was exacerbated by inflexible economic policies which culminated with a grave political crisis in an increasing jobless population both in the cities and elsewhere at a time of growing economic failure.

There is no credible data on these events but a large number of the Chinese population were just wiped out in this ruinous cycle, which regularly arrived at the final stages of even mighty dynasties with horrible consequences for humanity. Looking at it from a different aspect, however, this Chinese traditional revolution could be described as a 'scrap and build' process which terminated an outdated old economy and generated the power for the next expansion boom.

In this process, many of the Chinese dynasties wanted its predecessor's signs of grandeur, together with its records and often their technologies as well, to be wiped out completely. A typical example, after the fall of the Qin, was that its capital city, Xianyang, was set on fire by the opposition's general, Xiangyu. It was believed that the city burned for three months until all its gigantic structures, built by the first Chinese emperor, Shi Huangdi, were completely reduced to ashes in 206 BC. Even discounting for exaggeration, we have to acknowledge that the city vanished completely, although the renowned Qin dynasty was exceptionally short-lived in Chinese terms.

The long-lived Han's capital was also thoroughly destroyed by rebels as a result of deteriorating politics. The end of the once glorious Tang dynasty was likewise appalling; people endured widespread starvation and an upsurge in all kinds of atrocity and destruction. These 'revolutions' were as devastating as plague in medieval Europe but were caused by human hands each time one of these transitional periods occurred, as if this seems to be an innate function of the system.

PART ONE – THE THEORY

There were also smooth transitions of power in Chinese history. But politically, these changes did not function effectively. It was known as Shanrang and a typical example of it is demonstrated when General Zhao Kuangyin seized the power of the Song (or Northern Song) dynasty in 960 in the hope that he could unite China. But he failed to do so and China had to wait another two hundred years for the arrival of the fresh blood of the Mongols for unification.

The last dynastic power of the Manchu, whose homeland was in Manchuria, joined China in 1644 by establishing the Qing dynasty. Although seventeenth-century Manchuria was strategically important for China, it did not add a sufficient economic base, compared to the growing expansion of the West to every corner of the world at that time. It must be noted, however, that the Qing dynasty became the most geographically extended Chinese state when it conquered Mongolia in the late seventeenth century and subsequently expanded into the southern and western territories. Like the Russian Tsars' expansion, the Chinese dynastic system ended when the system could apparently no longer cope with further territorial growth.

And the nature of this growth was always quantitative. Mark Elvin wondered, 'Reading in the literature of the China two or three centuries before the modern age, there are moments when it is hard to believe that an industrial revolution had not begun...' He saw the continuation and the pattern of Chinese growth on its growing population, 'For it was the expansion of the population which produced that combination of *high-level* farming and transportation technology with a *low* per capita income which perceptive economists since Adam Smith have recognized as the distinctive characteristic of China in the seventeenth and eighteenth centuries.'

It was not only economic factors that brought about this evolution but, as he noticed, a peculiarity in China's internal politics, 'We have therefore to ask how far government policy and government shortcomings are likely to have blocked a modern type of economic growth.' where he marked on a 'symbiosis between bureaucrats and businessmen.' There was certainly an ideological aspect to this, 'A technology is the expression of man's working relationship with the natural world, the point at which environment and society meet and shape each other. His tools, his medicines and his weapons are the physical form of his conceptions, their effectiveness a matter of life and death.'[11]

In Europe, a new invention would be quickly disseminated throughout the continent.

For instance, the printing machine invented in Germany in the mid-fifteenth century, was introduced all over Europe within a few years. Or when an American conceived of an iron ship, within a year all of Europe's major powers were starting to compete to copy the design and the mechanism of this new invention. Notably, these sort of multiple technological transfers did not happened among the Chinese or East Asian states. The Industrial Revolution took place only in a competitive environment that was not present in China.

Why did a once mighty China become so backward? To understand the reasons behind this, it is important to acknowledge the simple fact that China, a success for more than a thousand years, was over-confident of being able to absorb new technology and catch up or even overtake advanced outsiders by their own self-belief in their power base. This did work perfectly in China at first. The adoption of Western technology was considerable throughout the Ming era (1368-1644) and the early period of the Qing (1644-1911). With its advanced metallurgical sector and weapons, China thrived right up to the eighteenth century, never conscious of any backwardness in relation to the rest of the world. We often forget how important the Industrial Revolution was. This huge historical phenomenon caused by new iron technology changed the shape of global trade and communications completely as the production of iron soared, igniting a new form of global economic expansion.

This economic change forced emergence of new power bases. Eighteenth-century London was not only the English capital but also became the centre of the British Empire and its entire global economy. This global dominance was also applicable to the other European powers albeit to a lesser extent. In other words, the

European global empires expanded outside the frame of the Chinese continental or East Asiatic regional empires which were simply not even in competition.

Nineteenth-century China failed to adapt to these massive revolutionary changes in the western world. For the first time in its history, the Chinese felt its 'regional' empire left behind. And the globally expanded West surpassed China in its size as well. The Chinese economy lost its status along with a rapid economic decline as its wealth was still based mainly on agriculture rather than on industry.

Where should we place communist China today? When Gorbachev received the news of the then hardliner, or the last pal of Brezhnev, Chernenko's death, Russia's Perestroika – 'restructuring' – was to begin in every part of the European side of the communist bloc.[12] The Soviet *nomenklatura* system that had been introduced in China should have collapsed at the same time it did in Eastern Europe. But during this turbulent era for communism, China was completely indifferent to this movement and did not identify with the political revolution in Russia and Eastern Europe.

Chinese communists apparently had their own agenda. Wang Gungwu saw this self-sufficiency of the Chinese mindset visible in the founder of the communist regime, Mao Zedong, '...He was effortlessly and supremely confident about being Chinese...and never suffered the agonies and self-doubts, which paralysed so many Chinese of his generation. And it was this freedom from genteel sensitivities that gave him the single-mindedness to bring Marxism-Leninism to the Chinese people as if it were the most natural thing for him to do.'[13] So, what is Chineseness or the distinctive shape of Chinese political behaviour?

For hundreds of years, we all preferred to mothball this question. People do not care what others think or do as long as it will not disturb them. In the old era of disengagement, one could live with plausible explanations which were not necessarily based on facts. But those days are definitely over today. It is time perhaps to investigate this issue of a separate Chinese political entity as the volume of new

Chinese economic expansion and its political influence starts to increase aggressively on a global scale. In focusing on this point, we will be surprised to discover that so many current problems can be linked to China's original political model, despite the immense period of its historical evolution.

THE PROTOTYPE – YIN-ZHOU 'REVOLUTION'

Every powerful state had its historical turning point. In Europe and America, it coincided with the birth of a national state. In the case of China, we usually apply the word 'tradition', which implies it is not possible to trace this or there is no need to pursue it. In this specific evolution, where the state has endured and survived such a long time as a rare example in history, we would be required to look back to the great Bronze Age of China in order to find out the origin of its political model. This is not an utterly impossible task, as we can always confirm how even in the present, China's 'DNA' is stamped firmly.

The Yin (also known as the Shang, which means 'trade' in Chinese) period (*c.*1600-*c.*1050 BC) was the cradle of Chinese civilization. Some Chinese historians insist upon the existence of the legendary Xia or an even earlier myth as the first dynasty but these were not distinctively Chinese. The critical point is that the existence of a recognisable Chinese political element became visible under the Yin rule, or more precisely, in the late Yin period.

To start in our search, we need to be aware that historical facts and incidents were manipulated, such as reporting that events happened earlier than the actual date, or even making it up or omitting them, in accordance with political convenience. This was a common practice in ancient East Asia. For instance, Bronze technology might have spread to China from West Asia where the Sumerians in Mesopotamia ('the land between two rivers' according to the Greeks) first invented this technology by 3,300 BC. The Yin people subsequently emerged as masters of the technology in East

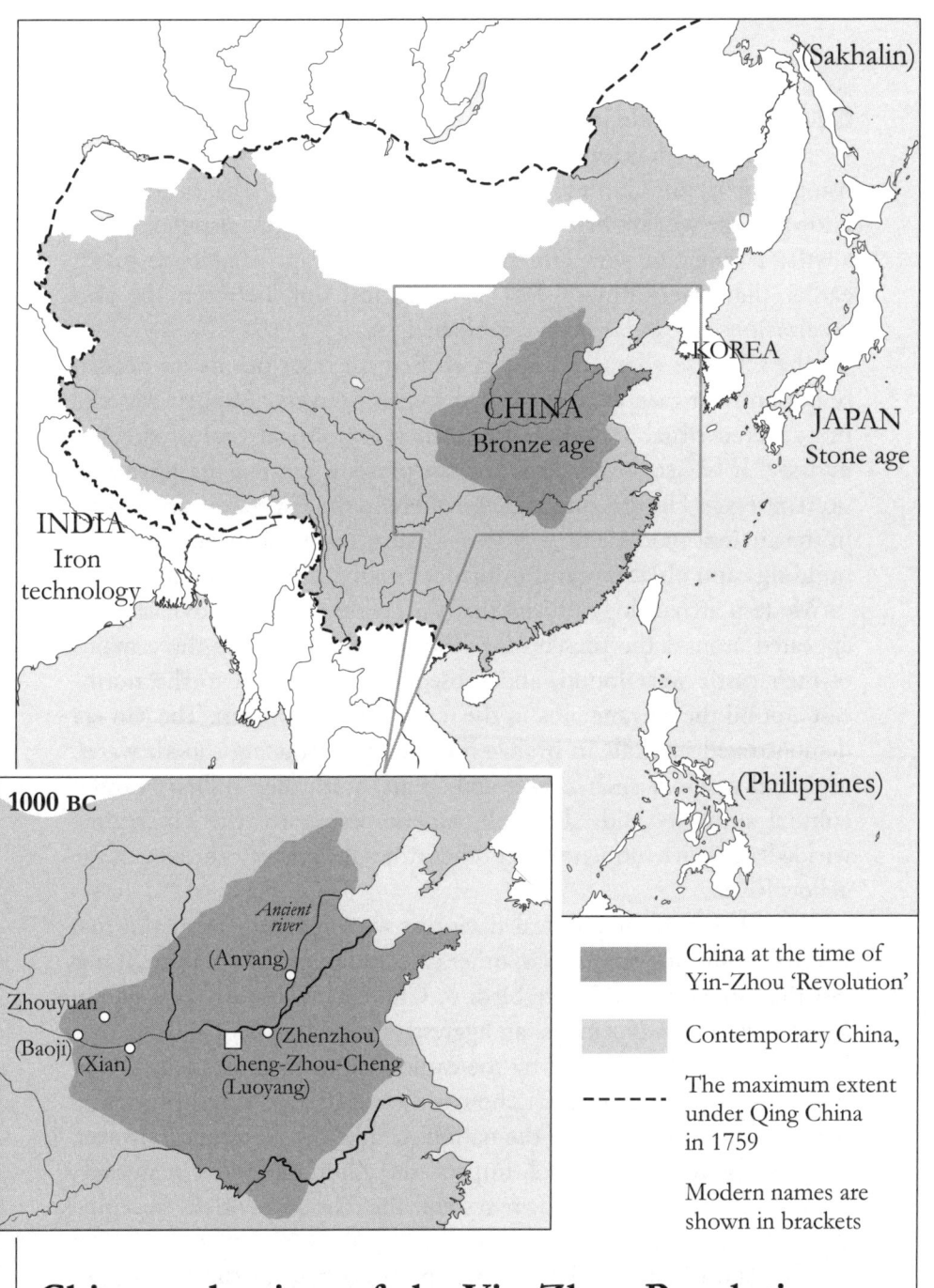

China at the time of the Yin-Zhou Revolution

Asia, together with Egyptians and Indians, but did not acknowledge their debt to outside influences.

The Yin also developed the Chinese language and writing system, using han-zi, or Chinese characters. Incidentally, the Sumerians, known as the world's first civilized people and traders, also developed a written language with cuneiform and pictograph characters much earlier than the Chinese, but no historical link between the two civilizations has so far been established.

The Chinese characters appeared first on inscriptions on animal bones and tortoise carapaces used by soothsayers. Augury was the most sacred ritual as well as the principal political tool of the Yin dynasty. It has survived down to the present, among the glittering skyscrapers in Hong Kong and elsewhere in the Chinese community, in the ancient practice of *feng shui* – using auspicious signs to orient buildings and objects – and influences many other social customs.

Modern archaeology proved that the centre of the Yin dynasty first appeared around the present-day Zhengzhou area where the remains of their castle were found, and subsequently it moved to the northeast around the Anyang area in the (ancient) downstream. The Yin era demonstrated its skills in bronze metallurgy, producing superb wares, tools and weapons such as axes and spears. With their military power, cultural authority and, above all, superior economy, the Yin regime wielded a decisive influence over other tribes throughout the area of the Yellow River.

But what kind of political decisions were made to form the first Chinese political system? As in other cases of national formation, it was not the Yin alone, who gave birth to Chinese civilization. Just like in Britain where the Normans, an aggressive maritime people, gave new life to the island populated by the earlier Anglo-Saxon settlers, so too in China, the Zhou people (Zhou period, *c.*1050-770 BC) brought a wealth of new influences to the nation. Unlike the Normans, however, who had perhaps a 'paternal' impact, the Zhou's role was 'maternal'. Instead of imposing their own system, the Zhou essentially accepted the Yin's principles.

The Zhou first established their political base in the far west of the Yin territory at a place later named as *Zhouyuan* – Zhou's Land – on the hillside near the east of today's Baoji in Shaanxi province, overlooking the fertile Wei River valley. As the Yin's supremacy grew, their territory spread to occupy all the Huabei plains and beyond, forming the biggest mass of agricultural land in the Chinese continent. Gradually, the Zhou, whose antecedents most likely differed from those of the Yin people, accepted the hegemony of the Yin while subjugating other tribes in nearby lands.

The Zhou dynasty had a nomadic element but emerged without a doubt as a military state.[14] Was it easy for foreign tribes to become Chinese? Probably not, but a superior civilization has always attracted people towards it. In this case, only China had a writing system while the tribes of herdsmen in East Asia had no means of record. This would have provided a great incentive for what we would call now Sinicization – the assimilation of Chinese language and culture. Above all, the Zhou absorbed all the three major political achievements of the Yin: 1) the practice of augury; 2) Chinese writing as their political instrument; 3) bronze metallurgy in the form of military hardware such as arrowheads. The Zhou simply took advantage of the affluent resources of the Yin, their rich tradition and economy, and progressed it further.

The Yin's expansion continued for a while but eventually it began to decline. Historians estimate that around 1,050 BC, the Zhou finally advanced to the Yin capital and destroyed the central regime after a decisive battle. In order to control the entire old Yin's territory, the Zhou dynasty built a new capital and walled city named as *Cheng-Zhou-Cheng* – the Castle of the Established Zhou – in the suburb of today's Luoyang situated around midway between the old capitals of the Zhou and the Yin. But despite this terrific military success, the total conquest of the Yin seemed no easy task. Pockets of Yin resistance held out in many parts of their vast territory.

In this situation, the Zhou tried to complete the task of conquering the Yin remnants by gradually establishing sorts of feudal or *fengjian* principalities within the conquered lands, utilising one of the world's oldest official ranking systems. This was a successful policy. The

Zhou soon built the most powerful, prosperous and expanded state which ever flourished on this fertile land. This first change of central regime is identified as the Yin-Zhou 'revolution' in Chinese history.

The first Chinese *Yixing* – change of the divine order – revolution was thus made. It represented a complete change of the dynastic bureaucratic system as a dynamic political tool. We must recognise that this ancient Chinese concept was an unusually flexible political system, as an unknown foreigner or peasant could become an all-mighty emperor of China, if he only had the power, or more precisely, if he was capable enough to get it, subject to his acceptance of the Chinese way of life. In terms of degrees of political power shifts, the US presidential system was certainly not the first one to appear in history. Ancient China survived on this flexibility, social mobility and dynamism.

The importance of the Yin-Zhou 'revolution' is that it was the prototype of all the subsequent Chinese political systems, and it laid down the pattern of Chinese economic expansion. It also represented the birth of Chinese ideology, which is the principal political philosophy of the Chinese political movement and has survived over millennia since that time. The important mechanism here was that the Zhou and other peripheral tribes who voluntarily joined the Yin's political order and participated in its economic power thereby extended the boundaries and hegemony of the Chinese nations as a whole.

Ever since, throughout Chinese dynastical history, this pattern has remained the same. The Chinese political system always offered open access to any peoples who subscribed to the Yin-Zhou ideology and acknowledged the legitimacy of this political system. All the ancient Chinese canons were conceived in this Zhou era or elaborated soon afterwards, and by the time this era ended, these principles, together with Chinese writing, had been adopted by most people within the vast Chinese empire.

It is inaccurate, therefore, to say as many influential western political analysts do, including Samuel Huntington in his article 'The Clash of Civilizations?', to describe Confucianism as the prime functioning political philosophy of the Chinese, or still carry out a debate on China in 'Confucian' terms.[15] The heart of Chinese ideology is as Arnold Toynbee emphatically argued, '... The flame of militarism which burnt itself out in the post-Confucian age was already alight before the great philosopher took his measure of human affairs.'[16] Toynbee was absolutely right to have focused on this historical turning point – what I call his first proposition – as essential for identifying this political entity.

Confucius, who lived some five hundred years after the Yin-Zhou 'revolution', regarded the Zhou era as the ideal Chinese world, and he greatly admired the political thought of the Chinese canons which date from that era. Confucius' biggest contribution to the Chinese political system is that of the clan system known as Zongfa, the significance of which will be reviewed later in detail. He played an indispensable role in subsequent Chinese social movements. In *Lunyu* – Confucius' dialogue – he, as a most famous Chinese philosopher or religious leader, avoided all metaphysical questions:

> Chilu (his follower) asked how the spirits of the dead and the gods should be served. The Master said, 'You are not able to serve man. How can you serve the spirits?'
> 'May I ask about death?'
> 'You do not understand even life. How can you understand death?'[17]

Confucius was by no means a religious leader in the western sense. He was nothing but a genuine Chinese ideologist, rather than a simple secularist. Because of his merit, he was acknowledged in Chinese politics as the 'philosophical' leader. But he was not interested in subjects that existed beyond Chinese borders or anything global. He simply accepted the Zhou's traditional principles without any criticism, and developed them further with enthusiasm.

The early Han dynasty officially adopted these inherited Chinese Five Canons or Classics.[18] Later, they became the essential subjects for public examinations and education together with the four classic works of Confucianism. In my opinion, only two among those canons are relevant for understanding the political aspects of Chinese ideology.

The first one is *Yijing*, or *Book of Changes*. This sets out the principles of augury and covers metaphysical matters such as the nature of the universe, the principle of *Yin* and *Yang* (negative and positive basically, but it could be any opposite force) as cosmic dual forces. We notice another link to western Asia here. The dualistic theology itself appeared first with Zoroastrianism, which was subsequently adopted as the state religion for the Persian Empire.

Yijing was supposed to be only understood by sages, the stratagem being that all these 'sages' were allowed to flourish without serious criticism within the Chinese political power structure. We could find here the origins of Chinese authoritarianism. No Chinese person would use the *Book of Changes* as a political tool today but its philosophy and political methodology are still firmly entrenched in the form of social rituals, customs, religion and Confucian belief in East Asia at the present time.

The other important Chinese classic is *Shijing*, or *Book of Songs*. In essence, Shijing is a collection of poems from each region of the Chinese realm, from the Yellow River valley to the Huabei plains as well as lands away to the north and south, from the vast combined territory of the Yin and the Zhou at its maximum extent. My interpretation of this political tool is that the Chinese dynasties used this book to claim legitimacy over this vital land mass.

In the course of accumulating the largest agricultural landmass in East Asia, named as *Zhongyuan*, or 'centre of the world', the Zhou established their innovatory order based on fiefdoms and bureaucratic officials that both underlined the power of the new regime and bolstered governmental integrity, forging a broad alliance among the Chinese nations. The other Chinese canon as *Liji* or *Book of Rituals & Ranks* for such purposes is also inventive but it is just not as distinctively Chinese compared to those other two canons.

The Yin-Zhou 'revolution' and its new political ideas put China in a leading position among the people of East Asia. At the time when the Yin alone ruled, the word 'Chinese' would have denoted something that was in essence merely racial or tribal. In this process, at least two races, one in the remote west, and one which controlled the central and the eastern regions of the Chinese continent were amalgamated, under a single political belief. This fusion of peoples was repeated many times later, but first the Zhou had to be Sinicised or Yin-ised.

Once the Yin-Zhou 'revolution' had taken place, therefore, 'Chinese' became an ideology, a peculiar East Asiatic political belief that set the stage for the long-term expansion of the nation outwards to its peripheral regions. The Zhou blazed the trail for expansion and people hailed their political thoughts simply because there was such ample potential for new ventures in this vast continent.

The Chinese called themselves *Hanren* – Han's people – or the Chinese characters as *Hanzi* – Han's letters – as the Han dynasty played a decisive role in furnishing Chinese political tradition with added sophistication for its subsequent expansion. But the Han did not create this spirit of political venture; they just endorsed it with their own newly-obtained substantial power, which, in its turn, was further extended by the new technology of mastering iron.

Fortified by their new political ideology, the Chinese tried to place themselves in the centre of the lucrative agrarian world that they were developing and expanding for their survival. Inside the Chinese boundary, the territory was named the 'civilized world' or simply 'world'. As this Chinese concept was elaborated, China called the outside non-Chinese world *Huawai,* which denotes 'outside of the civilized world' or 'barbarian's world'. The Chinese suzerainty system began with this particular political concept that civilized China should expand towards the barbaric lands on its periphery. The non-Chinese lands were there only to be conquered. Ever since that ancient era, this unique political ideology has controlled all the major political systems without interruption in the East Asiatic world.

On the Theory of Chinese Ideology

THE POLITICAL CORE

Toynbee tried to name this political entity of Chinese expansionism as the 'Sinic' or 'Far Eastern' civilization. Science and Art are necessary conditions for creating civilization. But they are not sufficient conditions in themselves to keep it going. Political decisions are paramount in deciding the outcome of a nation as sometimes even a substantial civilization with the finest culture has been obliterated. For further discussion purposes, therefore, I would prefer to describe the political process of this Chinese-style mode of expansion simply as 'Chinese ideology'.

As stated, this unique political ideology was transplanted to the major parts of East Asia but failed to attain global universality. Since this particular political ideology was invented in China, even though it was imported subsequently to Vietnam, Korea and Japan, for identification purposes it is appropriate that the name should be classified by applying it to its country of origin.

What, then does this political core of the East Asiatic polity mean in precise terms? To extract the essence of Chinese expansion, John K. Fairbank tried to analyse the entity by concentrating on a genetic approach by pulling out fifteen essential political features. But when he said, '...As cavalry from the inner Asian grassland gradually became the final arbiter of battle in East Asia, it became an established practice that in eras of Chinese weakness non-Chinese rulers could become actual emperors of China, Sons of Heaven at the apex of the structure.' In my opinion, this is just one facet of Chinese expansion and not a definitive analysis.

I agree with him, however, on his first assertion, 'The Chinese world originated as an agrarian-based culture island.'[19] This natural advantage was indispensable for the birth of Chinese civilization. It was not born as a maritime commercial state like Greece or Rome. Instead of the sea, the control of rivers and nearby land masses was a driving factor. To explain these historical truths, which are still visible in East Asia, I would apply the following four hypotheses as the vital elements for the evolution of the Chinese political core.

PART ONE – THE THEORY

First came the existence of a huge agrarian asset occupying a vast area in the eastern part of the Asian continent with substantial river and later canal networks. This was the largest water system in East Asia. China, and only China, had two enormous rivers: the Huang He (Yellow River) and Chang Jiang (Yangtze). We can assume that the Chinese situation was even stronger than the Egyptian civilization that had only one similar gigantic river basin in its territory. In addition, unlike Europe which sits next to North Africa and the Middle East and is surrounded by sea from three directions, China had a rather isolated geographical base. This natural environment seemed indispensable for the birth of this particular political ideology and for its subsequent expansion.

The Chinese land mass acquired by the Yin was the largest in East Asia right from the beginning – the Yin emerged as the first Chinese state after they occupied this huge land mass and adopted a new political strategy backed up with superior bronze technology. These core assets travelled to adjacent territories creating an enormous economy as new land was constantly conquered. This critical land mass would also make China impregnable to invaders. In this context, to expand was to defend. Based on this economy, the Chinese rulers became indisputably the richest in East Asia, and from this point, the desire for a larger, and eventually for the largest, state was born.

In the age of the Korean Three Kingdoms, when Koguryo Korea challenged Yangdi of the Sui dynasty over Chinese hegemony in 612, a determined Chinese emperor was ready to crush the inferior and far fewer Korean troops. To assemble a massive army and the resources required for this Korean expedition, he even developed canal networks in the south with great feats of civil engineering to aid the logistics of this campaign. Against all odds, however, a Korean general, Ulchi Mundok, destroyed China's massive invading army and navy of around 300,000 men. It was a disastrous campaign as only 10 to 20 per cent of Sui soldiers returned to the Chinese homeland.[20]

The failed emperor was assassinated and the Sui dynasty fell as a result of this shambolic defeat. But subsequent Chinese leaders never gave up on his venture as his historical enterprise chimed with their own ideals. Having learned from the failure of the Sui's high-handed approach, and being similarly unsuccessful in initial attempts to conquer the Koreans themselves, the Tang dynasty were more cautious. Instead of directly attacking Koguryo, the Tang waited for an opportunity to arise, which arrived as a request from the Silla to join an alliance against Koguryo/Paekche under the Korean Three Kingdoms. The alliance first defeated Paekche in 660 who had then tied up with Japan.

After isolating Koguryo on the diplomatic front, the victorious combined force of the Tang and Silla finally entered Pyongyang, the capital of Koguryo in 668. This meant Koguryo and the concept of Korean Manchuria or the 'Greater Korea' policy ceased to exist on this earth. From this incident, it can be seen that the process and fate of this conflict was eventually decided by the largest economic power on the Chinese continent, in which China alone could be the champion.

From this viewpoint, it is not surprising that the Chinese New Year is still being celebrated today as its roots connect to the traditional agricultural calendar. The largest agrarian economy was a matter of pride for the people, a symbol of the most powerful and wealthiest Chinese society since its launch as a nation. We need to remind ourselves that all the world's principal economic activities belonged to the agrarian sector until some two hundred years ago.

The second indispensable Chinese ideological characteristic was the development of written Chinese characters, which remain as a unique form of writing. Many dynasties tried to change some characters to suit themselves and their volume was constantly increased. To move forward economically, China required these artificial political tools to bring cohesion to their empire. The invention of the Chinese characters played an important role in this – even in the formation of Chinese family units as people gathered under a specific surname that carried political and traditional significance.

There is no doubt that Chinese characters established essential communication among the people with its thousand conveniences and advantages. Despite this function, there was a problem in the complexity of this writing system, which, combined with the exclusive right of interpretation on meaning by the authorities, tended to divide the people into those who rule and those who are ruled. To pass the lengthy process of the Chinese bureaucratic examinations, the one instituted by the Sui dynasty, applicants had to memorise the Nine Chinese Classics, which consisted of 431,286 characters.[21] The combination of this complicated writing structure together with a secretive and opaque political system always posed the danger that anyone who had mastered these characters and classics, however evil or unworthy they were, could still rise to a ruling position or use state power for their own purposes.

The harmful effect of this writing system was not paid attention to until the early twentieth century in China. A renowned novelist in communist China, Lu Xun, offered his condemnation of the old writing system's danger to democracy, 'Because of the difficulties of Chinese characters, most people are barred from access to advanced civilization. They are also unable to be intelligent or to clarify the essence of suppression and exploitation which they are facing. Therefore, they cannot understand the nature of our crisis that is presenting itself over the entire nation.'[22] At the time, the Chinese literacy rate was only 20 per cent of the total population and was causing a serious educational problem. Mao Zedong agreed on a radical change and applied the current simplified form of writing and *pinyin* alphabetisation.

Again, unlike a phonetic language, most Chinese characters have meaning. People subconsciously treat these artificial parts of the language as something important, vital or supernatural, converting the characters unwittingly into an instrument of prejudice. Once this notion is engaged, no logic will shake this impression. Lu Xun was aware of this fatal defect. To make it more complicated, some Chinese characters had no meaning or the meaning was arcane and hidden. Characters also provided a sort of magical charm element and their evil genius appeared in the Chinese classic writings such as the *Book of Changes* or subsequently produced Chinese

On the Theory of Chinese Ideology

Buddhist scriptures like *Sutra for wisdom, borejing*, or, hannyakyo, in Japanese.

The third element in the Chinese equation would be the use of military power plus a police force as its affiliate which were required to control this agrarian wealth. I put it third in order of sequence but it is of prime importance in terms of the structure of East Asiatic power politics. Underpinning any successful state, military power is essential from the beginning and will stand as the final arbiter to settle any political disputes. In this sense, Toynbee was correct in defining this old Chinese polity as 'militarism'. Military power was the origin, the ruling classes' political power, and this concept was the cradle of the entire political system. All the sub-divisions under the bureaucracy of the state were, therefore, only responsible to this upper echelon in the hierarchy.

The military leaders in old China occupied a position superior to the ordinary legal system and people. In ancient China, wars were fought on an enormous scale. It is believed that in the Warring States (453-221 BC) era, an army of around 100,000 to 200,000 men fought and were destroyed in a major battle among twelve divided Chinese states. The renowned strategist, Sunzi, whose real name is unknown, lived in this era. His (or their) fascinating analysis on military strategy and tactics was created from abundant observations during frequent and costly actual war experiences in ancient China.

Despite the diplomatic stance that China later adopted that claimed China was a civilian-led state with its civil servants chosen through state examinations based on literature, China has been, since its origin, a military state. The proven risk of this structure was that those who controlled power behind the scenes could also manipulate politics. At one stage in the Han or Ming dynasty, unknown relatives or court eunuchs actually directed the politics of this once successful dynasty, manipulating the power of the secret police in the name of the emperor.

From this political process, we can assume that the actual political core under Chinese ideology was run by constantly changing political powers. The essential nature of Chinese power politics can be defined as a continual process of a pure power struggle. And this power struggle itself was the ultimate purpose of politics. This is sometimes visible in the history of the West too, but in East Asia the struggle never ceased.

The fourth element of the Chinese political core is the nature of the administrative set-up which serves this supreme political power. This elite corps of administrators was only accountable to the military rulers. But since military campaigns were costly affairs, they were used only in the last resort and instead, mandarins emerged as the actual executors of Chinese rule.

The administrators of East Asia had a distinctive character, which related directly to political ideology and should not be confused with Western bureaucracy. To avoid confusion, we need to distinguish between the Chinese style or East Asiatic bureaucracy and modern bureaucracy in English, as it could be the same entity but, at the same time, it could be completely different. I would suggest, therefore, naming this Chinese-style administrative system as 'arch-bureaucracy' for the purpose of differentiation. In modern Japanese or Chinese, the respective word for bureaucracy is *kan* or *guan,* and it existed a long time before the modern concept of bureaucracy was introduced to the region, under the English words 'civil service'.

Those four political elements were the basis of Chinese ideology and can be defined as its 'political core', in other words, the rudiments of specific East Asiatic political thought. And this has remained as the *modus operandi* of the East Asiatic nations ever since.

Latecomers like Koreans and Japanese had to modify the original Chinese model in accordance with their own political environment to preserve their own identity. Before we analyse these specific types, perhaps, we need to clarify how this important political organ of arch-bureaucracy functioned in East Asian society and why it is so different from modern western bureaucracy.

On the Theory of Chinese Ideology

WHAT IS ARCH-BUREAUCRACY?

Bureaucracy, a modern instrument of government, caused unexpected problems in the West by constantly suppressing the economy of the private sector. C. Northcote Parkinson warned about the growing bureaucracy for the first time when he analysed the British Admiralty statistics between 1914 and 1928. While its capital ships in commission decreased from sixty-two to twenty during this period, 'a magnificent navy on land', dockyard officials and clerks were increased by forty per cent and Admiralty officials were increased even more to seventy-eight per cent plus. He tried to measure this bureaucratic tendency of enlargement by using a mathematical formula. No doubt, Parkinson's Law would be also observed in East Asia where it caused similar problems.[23] But when we discuss the problem of arch-bureaucracy in the context of East Asiatic political characteristics, we need to put additional and more serious questions about their nature.

Many western scholars, including Parkinson, were confused by the Chinese system of selecting bureaucrats through a written examination, as it sounded rather advanced. We must not be bewildered by face value here. The problem lay in the subjects selected and the method of appraisal. In the West, people envisage written papers being based on appropriate subjects related to a profession. But the old Chinese assessments for bureaucrats were completely different.

Ichisada Miyazaki studied the issue thoroughly and he concluded, 'The Examination System for the bureaucrats in ancient China – *Keju* – was a continued process of competitions (there were once twelve exams to the final degree) which candidates had to endure spiritually and physically by completely sacrificing themselves for this hardship.'[24]

To offset the candidates' personal sacrifices, the states in East Asia had to provide, in return, distinct political privileges to those who were successfully selected. The East Asiatic bureaucrats shared in supreme political power. They enter the government to rule, rather than to serve. Even in Japanese modern history, the system did not create civil servants to act on behalf of the people but an elite cadre to rule and preside over people instead.

Another important aspect was that the state bureaucracy at the top of this polity operated as the source for all other political factions in East Asiatic society. With an overwhelming and incontestable legitimacy, it acted as the supreme organ and final backer of the politics of factionalism, and kept aloof and apart from ordinary people. It promoted the proliferation of other factions in the process of its own expansion within society.

One sheer difference between 'modern' arch-bureaucracy from a western bureaucracy would be recognised in its unusual mechanism whereby it controls lawyers, prosecutors, judges, courts and the entire legal system politically, in addition to all religious and social activities. Even in East Asia today, this is the fundamental reason why lawyers work without real independence except where the British ex-colonial system still pertains in Hong Kong or Singapore. From the beginning, this was an essential political function of arch-bureaucracy. The two social functions, the rule of law and arch-bureaucratic control, are in conflict with each other, and cannot work in parallel.

Again, without an appropriate political philosophy, the habit of an old arch-bureaucratic country cannot be guided by legal rationale. And of course, in practice, arch-bureaucracy with its political antennae fully working would make sure that there would be no second wheel 'threateningly' driving in front of them. Under these circumstance, lawyers in Japan or China are required only to serve as the means to drive an unfair and often erratic political agenda under a political double standard. So, where does rational law exist? Everywhere, they say, as long as it does not conflict with the upper echelons of politics. But in its true sense, it does not exist at all.

In the West, bureaucracy emerged as a modern political tool. French ministerial bureaucracy appeared for the first time during the French revolution. France was then a most vibrant state in the heartland of Europe together with its global empire.

Clive Church observed that the growth of personnel in central government jumped from under seven hundred before the Revolution to about six thousand, an 850 per cent increase in 1788. But the problem of its growth had to be rectified, 'The Restoration then did not fundamentally question the existence of the bureaucracy. Rather it exposed the bureaucracy to new political currents...' and the numbers decreased again to less than three thousand by 1830.[25] Since then, bureaucratic reform appears as a constant political issue in which today's elected politicians regularly struggle to gain control.

As we saw earlier, arch-bureaucracy was born as the unit of central administrative power of Chinese militarism. The process of its expansion, therefore, could be defined as the ultimate form of Chinese politics. Hans Bielenstein claimed, 'The total size of the bureaucracy, from the Chancellor down to the Accessory Clerks, is recorded as being 130,285 men in 5 BC.'[26] This reflected the scale of Chinese power and the consequences of favouritism and nepotism practised by powerful rulers. More importantly, when the modern concept of bureaucracy arrived in East Asia, arch-bureaucracy was already sitting there with its abundance of experience but existing as a completely different political entity.

The bureaucracy had to be expanded naturally, as Gwyn Harries-Jenkins asserted, 'I have hitherto stressed the point that bureaucracies will persist and, indeed, flourish because the dominant elites can conceal their exercise of personal preferences under the guise of implementing bureaucratic rationality, technical expertise, and impartiality. I would also argue that the bureaucratic mode of organization is attractive to elites because, by emphasizing the innate efficiency of the bureaucracy, they can further validate and justify decisions which have been made.'[27] This is, however, the background of modern bureaucracy. In the eastern world of arch-bureaucracy, we should not forget that not only their bosses, from cabinet ministers to all elected politicians, but also the bureaucrats themselves are the exclusive 'elites' and participants in a quite different decision-making process from those in the West. The problem is, under this self-perpetuating structure, it would be impossible for an East Asiatic arch-bureaucrat to maintain rationality or impartiality, regardless of his individual capacity, due to the existence of its own 'sacred' factionalism.

Since arch-bureaucracy was born as the servant of autocratic power, it could not survive under a democracy of any kind. Democracy needs continual striving to change the dual direction of power. In this scenario, modern bureaucracy, which should be impartial in implementing decisions, cannot be found in the East.

Whether it performed well or badly, arch-bureaucracy existed without having to react to political change. In modern political terms, any change to the elected administration or shift of power could not be processed for effective democratic control because arch-bureaucracy itself constitutes the supreme authority. In the case of Japan, the changes caused by elections were effectively made only to the tip of the iceberg. To correct this 'foreign' element, the remaining 'submerged' part of the iceberg, or, more precisely speaking, the arch-bureaucracy, was always there to adjust this 'rogue' element.

Why does bureaucratic reform have to be continued? David Mitchell explains on this point, 'In many institutions or organizations, there is little tendency to wander from a course, once it is set. The forces at work within it may act naturally to discourage change. There may seem to be a lot of little men, as in *Gulliver's Travels*, attempting to tie the whole organisation down.'[28] The mechanism he depicted here was also applicable to Eastern arch-bureaucracy. But it is happening not as a hypothesis but as a definite reality.

And we must be aware of another troublesome facet of arch-bureaucracy. Arch-bureaucracy does not co-exist with private sector enterprises like the western public sector; instead arch-bureaucracy expands to control the entire society from the top down to the private sectors at the bottom, both horizontally and vertically. In the social hierarchy, it eventually reaches up to political leaders and down to all sub-organisations in politicising public, private or even family bureaucracies. The private sector, the vital part of capitalism, therefore, is bound to be arch-bureaucratised sooner or later (especially, as it grows significantly), as it also needs to operate in a strictly controlled market in this political environment.

The reason why reform is impossible in the East Asiatic political scene actually comes from its mode of constant expansion. In difficult times, the weak links of arch-bureaucracy suffer but the core unit and the system as a whole continue to expand even disguising their shape in order to gain a stronger grip in unusual, disorderly and critical conditions. A stronger activation of the state control had to come forward because in those Chinese ideological states, arch-bureaucracy is only the means to strengthen social cohesion. In order to fortify it physically, not rationally, however, they have to enter the whole 'body' like a blood vessel.

Arch-bureaucracy controls even private enterprises by regulatory measures, establishing the links to factions and other social means of political guidance. One of these practices which appears in Japan is known as *Amakudari* – descent from 'Heaven' – that is sending retired officials to the private sector. I shall refrain from boring you to death by explaining the various techniques applied by them, but the arch-bureaucrats finally dominate the whole of society including the private business sector. This was the ultimate goal of arch-bureaucracy – to make sure that this 'perfection' was reached!

As arch-bureaucracy expanded to all corners of society with its controlling power, when the dead-end finally appeared, it arrived not in one particular 'organ' but in its 'entire body'. This was the reason why no internal reform was possible across the board from ancient China to modern Japanese politics. Like Britons who would put a market value on anything and anybody, the Japanese would try to distinguish an arch-bureaucratic rank in everybody and everything.

In East Asia, all arch-bureaucrats were there to protect the traditional state structure, to which they belong, and aimed for full social amalgamation to include all the religious authorities and their activities. These legitimised 'legal' movements at the supreme state power level in society were hyper-resilient, and therefore arch-bureaucracy would survive until the fall of a regime. But the state could not avoid its own self-destruction because of the constant rigidity and inflexibility of arch-bureaucratic movements inside its make-up.

PART ONE – THE THEORY

THE ORIGINAL CHINESE PATTERN

Chinese ideology with its accumulated sophistication expanded steadily over the traditional Chinese area and beyond. The ancient Silk Road which extended from China, via Central Asia and West Asia, to Rome (or vice versa) played its part as the main transport link of Chinese imperial expansion whereby many people joined the rising Eastern Empire. The decisive turning point, however, arrived in the eighth century, as western tribes' participation in this Chinese political world looked increasingly fragile with a surge of Islamic power.

Various nomadic ethnic groups which were spread in a wide area of northern Central Asia now decided to relocate to a new living space by learning their own written phonetic language and Arabic. In this new migration, they gradually started to settle down in cities. Since the ninth century, imported Turkic military slaves from Central Asia even rose to become generals to the caliphs and ministers in Islamic courts, until finally they controlled some states in the region as rulers.[29] They were no longer interested in joining Chinese ideology as a main 'component' of China's western expansion. The Chinese capitals soon moved from the glorious history of western Chang-an to the eastern cities.

Since then, China had to thrive as part of an amalgamated state of East Asian nations in mainly heading south and north for a new successful expansion. In this political shift, the only thing that the people had to observe was loyalty to the supreme political values of Chinese ideology. New immigrants were encouraged to take a Chinese name as the declaration of a bond with a Chinese clan. Family units were regarded as an important factor of society from the realistic viewpoint that state power could not always be reliable in the extended territories of China. In this flexible system, a tribesman hopping around in the mountains could be accommodated as an authentic Chinese in just a few decades.

This vibrant mode of Chinese expansion, even when the level of state controls collapsed because of an outside invasion or internal disturbances, meant that rural life and the economic activities in villages had to go on. For this specific purpose, the Chinese agricultural community was built as a strongly kinship-based community where 'all in one and one for all' Confucian principles were established. All the inhabitants shared the same surname in some villages but usually there were a few of them. These groups could be mobile units and a whole village could even move to another remote location, if required.

In enemy territory, villages were often walled and armed to repel the 'invaders'. They certainly required a strong motivation for living under such circumstances. Only nationalistic Confucianism could provide a backbone for this Chinese spirit albeit with strict political limits. In a clan which carried the same surname, people worshipped the same ancestral lineages, who were enshrined in their temple.

The key message of Confucius was to protect the legacy of the glorious Zhou no matter what happened, and to further expand his idea of Chinese family values in this indisputably rich country of China. But it was also to the disadvantage of Chinese society, because of its heavily tradition-oriented thinking which tended to lean only towards the past, despite the nature of its inherent aggressively and dynamic society.

For the purpose of social cohesion on the Chinese model, stringent family customs were introduced. In order to link different kinship societies, marriages within the same clan were forbidden. Chinese society had to be built firmly on principles of traditional social rules. Filial piety towards one's parent was also extended to one's ancestors. A village elder influenced the name of a newborn baby as a 'religious' ritual, by bestowing him or her with some important Chinese characters that he deemed appropriate. Often brothers had one common Chinese character for their first name.

The blood and family birth ties were given social priority as they created a solid foundation of factionalism. Confucius laid down strict rules to protect and maintain Chinese family ties. For instance, he explained, 'In serving your father and mother, you ought to dissuade them from doing wrong in the gentlest way. If you see your advice being ignored, you should not become disobedient but should remain reverent. You should not complain even if you are distressed.'[30] Nothing is wrong in respecting seniority, but in the field of politics, numerous similar restrictions were used to protect the establishment and the old rules based on pedigree and sectarianism, and the future, freedoms and adventurous spirit of younger generations were often neglected.

In return for their deference, parents looked after their sons and, to a lesser extent, daughters by giving a sort of full lifetime protection to all their descendants. The essential family asset usually meant farmland in China. In this regard, the rules of family or clan often took precedence over legal rights, and sometime local laws had to conform to clan rule that depended on factional economic benefits.

With Confucianism, the original Chinese pattern, therefore, could be defined as a double structural system of state and village. As a general tendency, Chinese villages were self-governing. When state control somehow collapsed, village rules were always there like a back-up generator, as independent political sub-units for the upkeep of the rural economy and the Chinese economic infrastructure remained intact. Confucianism certainly gave Chinese society extra strength and resilience.

As an exception, however, Qin Shi Huangdi (Qin period, 221-206 BC), the first Chinese imperial ruler, was to ban Confucianism and ordered all the books related to Confucius in his empire to be burnt. Having conquered most of extended China at the time, he might have thought his extended territory should be enough. He wanted stronger powers concentrated within the state and tried to promote a political school called *fajia* – legalists – or simply, arch-bureaucracy, which relied solely on state decrees. Qin was also the one who started to construct the Great Wall project.

The Chinese majority, however, did not agree with him. Because of this policy, his regime weakened in the long-term, even though his empire emerged as an enormous one by previous standards. This might be the main reason that his dynasty was short-lived, because it lacked solid support from the people.

The far-western Qin emerged with strong influences from West Asia and Shi Huangdi was by no means a traditional Chinese. Proof of the prosperity enjoyed under the Qin's initiative, possibly bolstered by its use of iron technology, still remains today in an ancient irrigation system from the Minjiang River in Sichuan Province.

While Qin's way of thinking did not attract Chinese attention, the Japanese way was almost identical, relying on firm state control as originally conceived by him.

In appreciation of the merit of traditional politics, the next Han dynasty quickly restored Confucianism as the official basis for the principal rules of society, its educational system, and in particular, state bureaucracy. At the same time, the Han did not forget to strengthen the Qin's established arch-bureaucratic networks that covered the whole empire.

This successful empire lasted more than four hundred years with a short interruption by a usurper – Wang Mang's Xin dynasty ruled from AD 8 to 23. No subsequent dynasties survived longer than the Han. It was a time for both expansion and integration under tighter Chinese controls continually preparing for future growth. The Chinese political foundation made by the Zhou was intensified and further strengthened, by creating a national mould.

Buddhism, Daoism or other religions, at one time or another, flourished in China but these 'religions' were never able to supplant the importance of Confucianism, which provided the basic political needs for the realm under the umbrella of Chinese ideology. All religions had to be Sinicised as subordinate political organs. In other words, the role of those sub-concepts, including Confucianism, were allowed to exist only to 'fortify' the supreme principles of Chinese ideology. Under this political mode, merchant and industrialists prospered in a booming economy but the dynastical governments never seriously protected them, as their vital interests were always to maintain the empire's main 'engine' – the agrarian economy.

PART ONE – THE THEORY

THE KOREAN PATTERN

As various barbarians from the north attacked the Roman Empire in Europe, a very similar situation arose for the Chinese Empire. While there was inevitably a time gap between these separate historical events, the movements of these nomadic tribes which began from the north of China, and from Central Asia to Eastern Europe were interrelated, as many historians have claimed.

The barbarians first appeared at a time of unparalleled stagnation in the once great Han Empire, which was shortly to fall. During this period, a political complex based on the rise of a new people's power, specific politics defined as a 'Sino-barbarian synthesis', was emerging in northern China. This trend lasted actively for around four hundred years in the East. Like the Germanic tribes in Europe, some of these 'barbarians' built up their strength as they were employed as mercenaries of the Han emperors in remote regions. The difference was that 'barbarians' could become emperors in the Chinese dynastical system and they actually took the opportunity to do so.

In Chinese history, this age began in the third century when Wei (220-263) under the Three Kingdoms, representing a Sino-barbarian synthesis, occupied northern China and abolished the traditional Han dynasty. There were also decisive movements toward Japan. The Chinese recorded information for the first time about the Japanese islanders, naming them as *Wo-ren* a who lived in various eastern small islands, and paid a tribute to the Han emperor. It was the *Chronicle of Wei,* edited by Chen Shou (233-297), which tried to depict more details about the indigenous Japanese who again sent a tribute to Emperor Mingdi (239). With much exaggerations, Japan was described as a huge island archipelago divided into more than thirty countries with ample potential lands, in conflict with each other and ruled by a female, *Himiko*. Frankly speaking, the *Chronicle* sounded like it was setting up Japan as a prime target for invasion from the advanced continent.

In the same way that Europe and its civilization was under siege, many new tribes around China were circling the empire's established wealth. Broadly speaking, ancestors of modern Koreans and Japanese were one of these tribal clans whose language belonged to the Altaic group and differed from those of Chinese origin. The Chinese language belongs to the Sino-Tibetan group, which covers Thai, Burmese and others. In the opinions of linguists, Turkic, Mongolic, Tungusic, Korean and Japanese languages can all be linked.[31]

These were all horse-riding tribes or people who knew how to use horses for military purposes. The historians' view, which converged recently, is that powerful, very Sinicised, various Altaic-origin groups have invaded and controlled China ever since this era began, partly by accepting Buddhism. This led all the way up to the establishment of the Tang dynasty in 618, a moment which could be regarded as the pinnacle of this Sino-barbarian synthesis in Chinese politics.[32]

The Tang's capital city, *Chang-an,* was an international city like Rome, connecting East Asia and Central Asia, and beyond. There were Korean generals, Japanese bureaucrats, Turkic soldiers, Persian merchants, Indian monks, European entertainers, Mongolian nomads, Tungusic politicians, their mixed races and variety of peoples from the Tang's huge territory all communicating in Chinese. In other words, this newly expanded East Asiatic ideology openly ruled the East by this period as a single Asiatic world. Enormous and powerful links began to spread outside the empire.

The first unitary Korean state, Silla (The unified Silla period: 668-918), appeared as a peninsular kingdom like today's Korea after the fall of Koguryo as we have already seen. While the Koreans lost their former territory in Manchuria, its national power was strengthened and the peninsula better defended. In its new political formation, the Koreans constantly expanded their influence to Japan.

Simultaneously, another principal movement in this rather entangled evolution, was the reversed impact from Japan towards the Korean peninsula. According to Chinese historical documents, during the Five Kings of Wo period (*c.* 369-502), Japan demanded various Chinese official titles in the Korean peninsula such as 'General of Eastern Territory' in addition to 'King of Japan' from the

Chinese dynasties and kept a base in the area of the small Kaya states along the sides of the Naktong River and its tributaries, opened to the sea, sandwiched by the Korean states of Paekche and Silla.

Under its last Great King Wu – *Bu* or likely to be *Wakatakeru* in Japanese – it is believed that the Wo's hegemony was established from the Kawachi area (roughly in modern-day Nara and Osaka) as its centre, to Kyushu, and to the Kanto plains, judging from archaeological evidence garnered from the fifth-century burial mounds.[33] On the other hand, the influence of Silla – the newest among the Three Kingdoms of Korea founded almost in the same period as the Wo – in Japan was, at the time, getting stronger on the Sea of Japan's southern coastal side (including today's Izumo). In the diplomatic relationships among the ancient states in East Asia, it was normal practice to 'subjugate' the weaker ones.[34]

The basis of such a *modus vivendi* within the Korean Peninsula drastically changed when Silla tried to integrate its diplomacy with its most reliable and equally formidable ally, the Tang. Silla feared the stronger power of Paekche who allied itself with Japan and started to expand against them, after Silla had absorbed all the strategic Kaya states. Silla's policy was realistic. The new diplomacy of Silla could be defined as the Small Korea policy that set a precedent for this peninsular state in avoiding major confrontation with China. Without an 'active' Korea, however, Japan's ties to the western world were also cut off and the situation worsened, as the Tang's global Chinese empire declined, and as China shifted to inward-looking politics. In this situation, the Silk Road was disappearing and West Asia and East Asia begun to move on different paths.

In this political change, Chinese ideology in Korea was only formed gradually. The pattern of the Korean political core appeared to differ from the original Chinese one. To understand how and why, we need to look at the specific geopolitical environments of Korea and the constant political influences exerted by its powerful and volatile neighbours. As the Koreans faced direct and strong pressure from the Chinese empire, they had greater need for cooperation with China, and were therefore, more receptive (than the Japanese) towards the Chinese original pattern.

Confucianism was thoroughly accepted in Korean society. Soon after Silla came to power, the Royal Confucian Academy was established in 682 and furnished a systematic education to aristocratic youths. Its curriculum included Confucian classics and history. A Chinese-style state examination for entering the bureaucracy was also introduced to Korea in 788.[35] Those two measures contributed to the subsequent assimilation of Confucianism into the Korean peninsula.

Chinese-style kinship ties also became pivotal in Korea, although there was a basic difference between the two systems, which was called *bongwan* in Korea in contrast to the Chinese *zongfa* system. The major difference is that the Korean system imposed conditions on the locality of kinship. For example, the Yi family from the Chonju region would be regarded as a member of a different clan from a Yi family from another region even though they carried the same surname. By this alteration, it might be argued that the Korean model lacks the strength of the Chinese original but it is more stable.

In the Chinese system, by contrast, the Li family or clan are regarded as one kinship regardless of the native land of their ancestors. For instance, whether a Chinese Mr Li came from Sichuan or Fujian made no difference. In Korea, where there was a smaller population and fewer surnames, the direct importation of the Chinese clan system would have caused a social problem, as their rules on intermarriage would have forbidden marriages among the same clan.

Some Japanese have calculated the number of surnames in Korea, China and Japan! It is said that there are roughly around two hundred in Korea, around two thousand in China and over a hundred thousand in Japan. It is true that I can still, from time to time, meet a Japanese person whose surname I have never heard before whereas it would rarely happen in Korea. The existence of fewer surnames in Korea arrived directly from this specific clan system.

The strength of the clan community was also critical in Korea, when the country sometimes lost its centralised regime. In the Korean

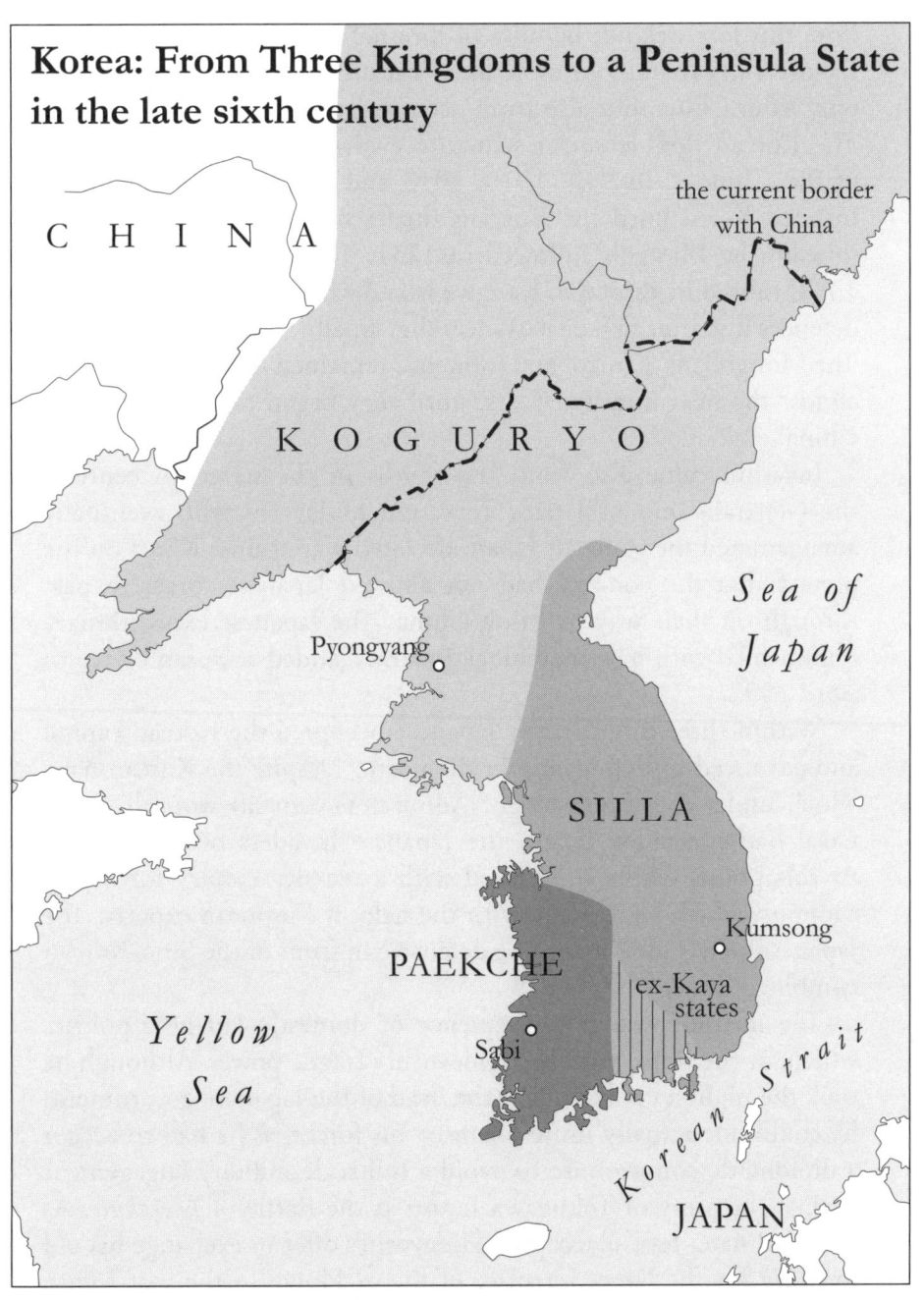

case, this loss was not because of internal upheavals resulting from the drive to expand, but more likely because of foreign invasion, not only from China, but also from occupiers on its northern frontiers. The Korean double social structure evolved differently from that of the Chinese. In 993, 1010, 1013 and 1018, Liao (or Khitan) invaded Korea until the Koreans finally repelled them. The fatal invasion by Mongols followed in 1231. The Koryo dynasty (935-1392) moved its capital to Kangwa Island where it deployed its naval defences but after fierce resistance, they finally surrendered in 1259. The Mongolians' control and influence remained strong in Korea for almost the next hundred years, until they began to lose control in China.

Invasion came also from the south. In the sixteenth century, the Generalissimo of Japan, Toyotomi Hideyoshi who eventually amalgamated the states of Japan, declared war against Korea on the pretext that the country had not allowed Japanese forces to pass through on their way to Ming China. The Japanese expeditionary force armed with new matchlock firearms landed at Pusan by sea in April 1592.

Within three months, the Japanese occupied the Korean capital and advanced to Pyongyang in the north. Despite the Korean navy which under the leadership of Admiral Yi Sun-sin won all major naval battles against Japan, the Japanese invaders overran Korea. At this point, China intervened with a massive cavalry force plus cannons, which were made with the help of European experts. The Japanese were suddenly on the defensive in front of the Sino-Korean combined force.

The invasion was a consequence of domestic Japanese politics which, at the time, reflected Hideyoshi's fragile power. Although he took the highest court rank as the head of the Japanese government, he could not actually unite Japan by his forces, as he had to accept a diplomatic compromise to avoid a full-scale military engagement against the army of Tokugawa Ieyasu at the Battle of *Nagakute*. As a subordinate, Ieyasu accepted Hideyoshi's offer to exchange his old territory for the larger territory of the ex-Hojyo in the vast Kanto plains with its capital and castle of *Edo* (today's Tokyo). Although Ieyasu endorsed Hideyoshi's venture to Korea, his army did not participate in this expedition. By not taking the risk, however, they lost the kudos of showing samurai bravery to the western Japanese warlords such as Shimazu or Mori who fought vigorously under the Japanese flag and won a few battles in this war. The Mori's main army helped by a renowned warrior, Tachibana Muneshige of Chikuzen/western Fukuoka, defeated the Chinese army of Li Rusong at the battle of Pyeoktchegwan near Seoul in 1593.[36] The long seven-year campaigns finally ended with the sudden death of Hideyoshi. Throughout the hostilities, both sides had reconfirmed their strong national identities.

But the real tragedy for Koreans arrived thirty-five years after this war. The Manchu (Qing), who had gradually regained their power over the whole of Manchuria, emerged as a strong military state just as the Ming's military might in Korea was greatly diminished by the war against Japan. The Manchu invaders attacked Korea in 1627 and returned to make a full assault again in 1636-37 against the exhausted Koreans. The Qing's aim was total subjugation of Korea as preparation for the coming war with the Ming who were still clinging to power in southern China. Within two months after the second invasion, the Koreans were forced into surrender to this authoritarian Qing regime. Korean subjugation to this foreign power lasted for 258 years until the Japanese defeated the Qing dynasty in 1895.

In this political tragedy, Confucianism flourished in Korea. The Koreans tried to believe as an indication of their 'superiority' that the philosophy of Confucianism reached its pinnacle in Korea. In the midst of their hopeless situation, a strange way of thinking prevailed among the Korean ruling class: that this small peninsula was 'the centre of the world'. It was the birth of a concept, which could be described as mini-Zhonghua-ism. They even harboured a belief that the authentic Koreans, not the Manchu of Qing China, were the real successors to genuine Chinese traditions. Thus, the strictest interpretation of Confucianism was applied and admired in Korea, to a level unknown even to the Chinese. In fact, this disguised nationalism was a passive force compared with their super-heavyweight neighbour who seemed invincible.

After 1905, Korea remained as a Japanese protectorate and colony for almost forty years. Under Japanese rule, Korea was an industrialised colony. As agreed by the major western powers, the Japanese annexation of Korea in 1910 arguably seemed at the time the only way to spur its modernisation by officially ruling out the tenacious old ruling class. Japan relied heavily on Korea as a major heavy industrial centre for its continental expansion and soon Korean industrial output surpassed its agrarian sector.[37] For instance, an imperial university was established in Seoul in 1924, even earlier than the one in Osaka.

Here the two Chinese ideologies clashed. Did the Japanese political model influence Korean politics? In this brief period, Japan with its modern western technologies rocked the old regimes in East Asia. The ancient strict Confucianism political system with its tight arch-bureaucratic grip was no exception to this. With the advent of technology, Korea's mindset never returned to the past after independence in 1945. But its political core remained intact; after all, as it was nothing but the same old Chinese ideology.

THE JAPANESE PATTERN AND 'TOYNBEE'S ORBIT'

Namio Egami noted that the ruling clans of Japan initially came from the Korean peninsula as invaders from horse-riding tribes armed with the use of iron weaponry.[38] Judging from the various archaeological and documentary evidence, this process of immigration was gradual and multiple, constantly mixing with the native Japanese through marriage and employment. It began from the period of the third century and was consolidated right up to the ninth century. In the sixth century, a new movement for political centralisation began to evolve with an economic bang.

After various developments and struggles, Japanese rulers finally completed the country's adaptation of the Chinese ideology by Taika

Reform – *Taika no Kaishin* – in 645. This reform was executed as a *coup d'etat* in the imperial court led by Prince Naka-no Ooe (later Emperor Tenji) and his confidant Nakatomi-no Kamako (later Fujiwara-no Kamatari) against the power of the leading Soga clan.

Soga-no Umako was the astute head of the influential family first as a public financier; he then took power by controlling the imperial throne backed up by continental links, in particular, with the Chinese Sui dynasty. He seemed to have produced the first history of Japanese emperors and Japan, together with a constitution. He was instrumental in a massive promotion of Buddhism via China into the imperial court together with China's finest technologies, symbolised by the architecturally magnificent Horyu Temple (607).

According to the *Sui's Writings* edited by Wei Zheng (580-643), Umako seemed to try to claim Japan's equal status to China by renaming Japan as the country of the Rising Sun, and applying the word for the Japanese emperor – *Tianzi* – or the Son of Heaven, a Chinese word thus far used only for the Chinese emperor. He passed away in 626, after which the Japanese economy seemed to gradually decline. Meanwhile, the successors to the Sui, the Tang dynasty's superiority was assured in China during the course of the 630s, an early era known as *Zhenguan* and admired as the pinnacle of peace and prosperity by Chinese historians.

The Japanised Chinese ideology reinstated the supreme dominance of state Shintoism. As in China, it was then decided to subjugate Buddhism to be only a secondary religion regulated by strict state guidance. The new regime adopted a Tang-style powerful political system based on its military power, the Chinese chronology of imperial periods, and an arch-bureaucracy regulated by ranks and honours in the gift of the imperial court. Furthermore, everything that the Japanese today see as traditions were introduced under the new diplomatic link with Tang China.

The effect of this political reform was thorough and decisive. The newly planned capital of Nara was modelled on the superb original Tang's capital of Chang-an and advanced and centralised governmental organs were instituted. Japan now enjoyed various imported technologies, a single state bureaucracy and a large-scale combined economy via an effective tax system which were introduced to enable new economic expansion as Wado-Kaichin, the first form of legal coinage, was circulated in 710, following Chinese financial practice.

Arnold Toynbee asserted 'Japan never gave birth to an independent civilization but was occupied by an offshoot of a continental civilization that had emerged in the interior of China.'[39] His globally comprehensive analysis in *A Study of History* understood this critical historical moment for Japan – the existence of an essential link between Japanese and Chinese political systems. This is what I call Toynbee's second proposition, understanding of which is prerequisite to deduce the form of this political entity.

The influence of Chinese ideology was finally confirmed by this extraordinary scholar equipped with the most advanced western 'radar', with a clarity that outshone eastern historians. Toynbee's thinking grew from his outstanding studies facilitated by complete freedom of speech in Britain. It was a great leap forward in Political Science, and of course, his findings are more important than ever for assessing today's global politics and economics.

To understand this seventh-century political decision together with its implications is the key to grasping the nature of Japanese power, just as Toynbee perceived it. If we ignore this link, our study would be based on a false assumption, and consequently, it would lead to a wrong or inaccurate conclusion. And this is basically all that the various analysts today, including the native Japanese experts, have been doing so far. In other words, they have been all out of 'Toynbee's orbit', and therefore, they fail to capture the nature of Japan's political mechanism.

Although Japanese rulers enthusiastically embraced the Chinese methods of governance, they paid only scant attention to Confucianism. This never meant that Japan invented another political ideology. Rather, its political environments were different from China, and therefore, its *mode d'emploi* had to be adjusted. Above all, the mechanisms of Confucianism, especially kinship society, were not easily adaptable to an island nation that had

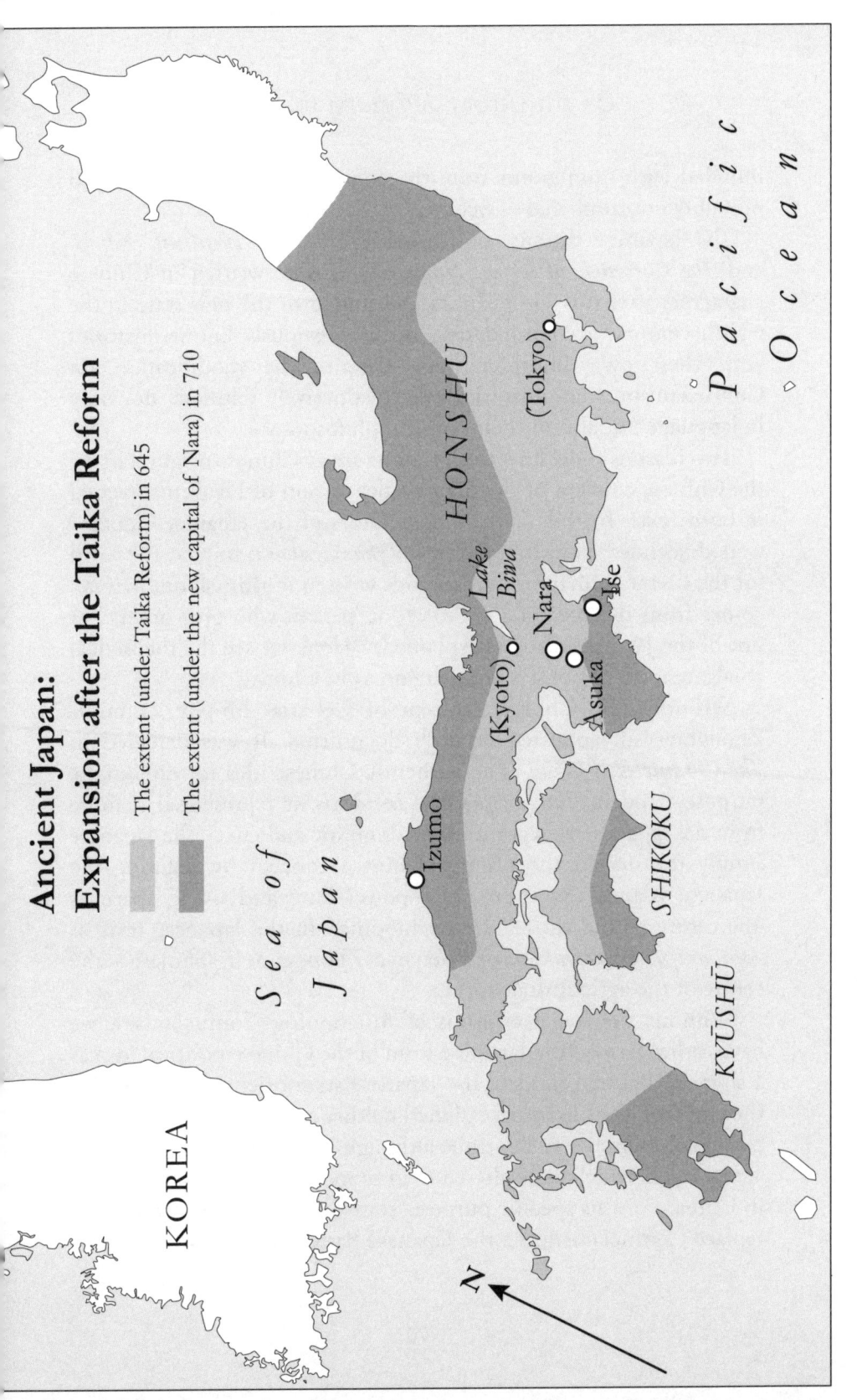

mingled with immigrants from the continent and the natives who probably outnumbered newcomers.

The Japanese canons, both *Tales of the Old Incidents, Kojiki,* and *The Chronicle of Japan, Nihon-Shoki,* were written in Chinese characters after this successful establishment of the new state in the eighth century, accommodating all the previously known histories with their own interpretations. Despite the modification on Confucianism, these histories were distinctively Chinese, not only in language but also in their political philosophy.

Two reasons show how these canons are of Chinese origin. Firstly, the Chinese concept of the divine ruler or Son of Heaven appeared in both texts. In this myth, the ancestors of the Japanese emperor were descended from the heaven – *Takamagahara*. In fact, the word for the divine human or human gods written in this canon, *Mikoto,* comes from the meaning of 'ruler' or 'person who give orders', as one of the Japanese experts explained.[40] Here, we see the theoretical amalgamation of politics and religion as in China.

Secondly, the Chinese concept of Celestial Empire or mini-Zhonghua-ism appeared in both documents. It was depicted in *The Chronicles of Japan* as an authentic Chinese idea for diplomatic purposes, and in *Tales of the Old Incidents*, it represented it more from the Japanese viewpoint for its domestic audience. The Japanese simply transferred the original Chinese concept by defining the Japanese islands that were their power base and living space as 'the centre of the world'. It was modified in the Japanese texts as *Ashihara-no-Nakatsukuni* or 'Weiyuan-Zhongguo' in Chinese – the centre of the agricultural world.

Without the social customs of functioning Confucianism, we have earlier termed the Japanese form of the Chinese political idea as a single-structured model. The Japanese state-oriented system with the emperor as its head necessitated neither a peasant rebellion nor a change of dynasties to continue although it still required changes of actual rulers which were altered even more frequently than was seen in China. For this specific purpose, state Shintoism was invented to replace Confucianism. As the Japanese pattern is concentrated only on a state level, when it collapses, there is no back-up structure.

In the island state of Japan, however, ancient invaders could be repulsed, in theory at least, at the shore and were in practice after this 'revolution'. In other words, unlike its two East Asiatic neighbours, Japan had a clear geographical limit as an island nation. But this had to be balanced with stronger state control of Shintoism. Because of this structure, the Japanese form developed as an isolated concept compared to the dynamic Chinese model. But it was still ambitious for its time as a large chunk of present-day Japan was still occupied by 'barbarians'.

On the other hand, Japan was capable of thorough adaptation within its boundaries as a counterpoint to outside change. As an example of this, Japanese aristocrats including the court ladies, the only intellectuals at the time, invented the phonetic alphabets – *kana* – by the ninth century which was the first one within the area of Chinese civilization.[41] Perhaps this creation was only possible in the modified political core of Japan. This easy-to-learn writing had a great impact on Japanese education and literature as a whole.

With the implantation of a Chinese-style political core into Japanese political soil, however, Japan was laid open to the same pattern of an economic cycle which would arise from its inevitable political processes. The first economic cycle was to last a relatively long time, presumably because the new Japanese state was still expanding its agricultural basis by conquering additional farming lands and native people.

To annexe and administer all the regions took hundreds of years of Japanisation. For instance, a nine-year rebellion led by the native warlord, Abe-no Yoritoki and his son, Sadatou, of the Mutsu country in the North East region – *Tohoku* – was subdued in 1062. But this victory was only grasped by the indispensable help of another mighty indigenous leader, Kiyohara-no Takenori, who ruled the adjacent country of Dewa (Western Tohoku). The two independent regions were renowned for agricultural abundance, good horses and gold mines. The control of the region appeared crucial for a unified Japanese state. The Genji clan responsible for the eastern (or north-eastern) expansion, however, was too weak to withstand the rival Heike clan which monopolised power in central government for almost a quarter of century. Suddenly, the situation changed as the capable chief of Heike, Taira-no Kiyomori, died hearing the news of the Genji revolt.

After securing the region under his direct control, Minamoto-no Yoritomo, the chief of the Genji, finally established the first centralised Shogunate – the government of Shogun or *Bakufu* – by moving the capital to Kamakura in 1192 in order to ensure that the process of integrating this newly extended and unified Japan could continue. His formidable military power was based on cavalry equipped with light longbows and sharp swords and this enabled Yoritomo to govern the whole country effectively.

At the same time, when the charismatic Yoritomo passed away, the privileged samurai leaders and administrators in Kamakura became vulnerable to interventions from traditional politics at the imperial court in Kyoto. By that time, the Genji's power was firmly established in the Kanto district. His widow's family, the Hojyos, were determined to continue the legacy of Yoritomo and to counter the imperial decree issued against them. They were perfectly aware that only their military might could rule this newly extended state.

A civil war ensued in the Jokyu era in 1221 but without any significant battles. The victorious Kamakura government severely punished their adversaries including the young emperor who was then only four years old but the authority of the imperial court at Kyoto itself remained intact, as the Hojyos required it to give them the legitimacy to rule. It reconfirmed a reality that actual political power in Japan did not belong to the emperor but to those who run the arch-bureaucracy.

In 1270, the Mongolian-Chinese emperor, Khubilai Khan, ordered his expeditionary force of around thirty thousand men in nine hundred ships to invade Japan from Korea. The Mongolians fought during the day but they did not sleep on the Japanese shore, fearing a night attack. Then, a seasonal typhoon unexpectedly hit the fleet. More than one-third of China's forces perished in this first attempt.

After the subjugation of Southern Song in mainland China, the mighty Mongolian emperor decided again to crush Japan. This time, the majority of the unprecedented number of invasion forces were dispatched from the Chinese mainland. In 1281, a huge Chinese and Korean Armada of over four thousand ships with 140,000 soldiers and sailors filled up Hakata Bay by the southern island of Kyushu. But as another Kamikaze – divine wind – struck, only a few hundred of those ships managed to return home. Japan was miraculously saved again.

The Japanese were preparing for a third invasion by fortifying their beach defences, but Emperor Khubilai cancelled a further attempt by an imperial edict in 1286, saying that the Japanese were no more than 'island barbarians in a remote region' it was, therefore, unjustified to 'overburden the imperial subjects with another expedition.'[42] The Chinese had found themselves fighting against their own political system so successfully implanted in the Japanese islands. But Japan had been exhausted by this war, and afterward, the economy visibly declined.

Towards the end of this first economic cycle, Japanese politics lapsed into anarchy despite the efforts made by the Kyoto-based Ashikaga Shogunate (1335-1467) who reopened trade with China. Japan was thrown into a period of riot and rebellion. This *Ge-koku-jo* – insurrection from the lower class – was led by rural warlords, many of them ascended from a lower rank and their rise was based purely on merit. Eventually, independent warlords divided up Japan and tried to revitalise the economy as the central government was completely crippled. The first cycle ended at this point.

In 1543, shipwrecked Portuguese navigators arrived at the southern island of Tanegashima with two matchlock firearms, and taught the natives how to use and replicate them. The Japanese studied this new weaponry avidly and other European technologies such as metallurgy, shipbuilding, civil engineering and construction, as only these new ideas could renew the economy. European know-how arrived in Japan like a light after a long dark tunnel.

After the arrival of a Jesuit priest, Francisco Xavier, in 1549, many Japanese, including the ruling class, accepted Christianity. The emerging Japanese supreme power holder, Oda Nobunaga, welcomed the Portuguese to ensure that new western ideas could be expanded in Japan. He seized this opportunity, as he realised that Japan could only be reunified by this unknown science and technology.

As religious wars intensified in Europe, both the Spanish and Dutch soon aggressively joined in the colonial expansion to East Asia. Despite the new religious environment created by Nobunaga, however, the Japanese rulers who followed him returned to a traditional isolationist policy to secure power by compromising with the establishment. Tokugawa Ieyasu and his son, Hidetada, strictly banned Christianity, and showed a determined hostility towards the numbers of Japanese Christians which grew steadily, undeterred by the ban. In spite of the death of Nobunaga in 1582 and the subsequent various persecutions against Christianity, it is estimated at least seven hundred thousand or seven per cent of the total population in the early seventeenth century in Japan converted to Christianity.

In 1635, despite the newly attained economic progress, the third Shogun, Iemitsu, applied an extreme policy of seclusion by prohibiting all foreign trade and immigration in and out of Japan. All overseas Japanese were deserted with the sole exception of a small trading outpost – *Dejima* – in Nagasaki harbour licensed only for a few selected Dutch and Chinese traders. The long-term trend of Japanese backwardness was sealed by this illicit act.

In 1637, the people of Shimabara and Amakusa in the once quasi-Christian island of Kyushu, headed by the fifteen-year-old brave samurai, Amakusa Shiro-Tokisada, took refuge in the old deserted castle of Hara to affirm their faith against forcible and violent conversion to Chinese ideology. After a four-month devastating siege, a massive besieging force slaughtered around thirty-five thousand Christians including women and children in the cruellest way possible. In this battle, government forces were aided by Dutch battleships, allies of the Tokugawa Shogunate which bombarded the castle for almost fourteen days.

The early Edo era in the seventeenth century was approaching the peak of the second economic cycle, as a large quantity of land all over Japan was cultivated by applying various new technologies. The population of Japan increased to a new and previously unseen level under the Tokugawa government (1603-1868). It increased from ten million in the early Tokugawa era to thirty million by its end. But by 1836 when the great famine of Tempo struck, the decline of Japan's second economic cycle was plain for all to see. Various reform movements were never successful in halting the gradual slide of the economy as it hit rock bottom.

Why did the Japanese rulers keep to their political posture of isolationism? One of the most convincing reasons for this uncompromising political attitude would be that China under the Ming – and the subsequent Qing dynasty – was growing its long-term economy including its trade activities at full momentum. In other words, Chinese ideology as a whole was still intact. In this era, although the influence of European powers was not negligible elsewhere in East Asia, it was not yet strong enough to claim a firm position in the region. For instance, the Netherlands had to hand over their colony of Taiwan in 1662 to a stronger Chinese force led by Zheng Chenggong, the remaining admiral of the fallen Ming navy. Even Imperial Russia entered into a defensive mode in the East after the Treaty of Nerchinsk with China in 1689.

A notable dispute occurred in the eighteenth century when a Japanese ideologue, Motoori Norinaga, blamed his rival philosopher and novelist, Ueda Akinari, of lacking Japaneseness. Ueda replied to the accusation, 'If the Japanese spirit – *Yamato damashii* – becomes too extreme, it will become equal to the Chinese spirit – *Karabumi gokoro.*'[43] It was an early recognition that Japan could be trapped into a mini-China philosophy. Ueda as a Japanese intellectual recognised this ethos and the danger attached to it.

A gifted Japanese novelist, Ryunosuke Akutagawa, in the twentieth century later depicted this critical moment in his short story 'Smile of gods':

Padre Organtino…returned to the old folding screen pictured three centuries ago…you are here walking on the shore of Japan with your colleagues looking at a huge foreign ship flagged high in gold-painted mist. Whether Deus wins or the (Japanese) Sun-Goddess prevails – it may not yet be easily decided. But our enterprise will determine the matter in the future. Until then, please watch us from that past shore quietly. Even if you were completely forgotten… someday, the sounds of guns on our black ship shall awake you from your old dream. So Good-bye, Padre Organtino…Good-bye![44]

TWO COLLIDING CIVILIZATIONS

After Europe's industrial expansion accelerated, the great powers were ready to take on the old civilization of China once again. The first sign of their aggressive tactics appeared as a matter of a diplomatic protocol over performing a kowtow in front of the Chinese emperor. In 1793, Lord McCartney, the first British envoy, managed to escape this practice and yet saw the emperor in close proximity, which astonished Chinese mandarins who regarded his behaviour as proof of the 'obstinacy' of the British! Alain Peyrefitte skilfully wrote about this embarrassing practice of kowtowing: 'from their own point of view, the logic of the Chinese was flawless. Nothing was more natural than kowtowing to the emperor, a daily habit with centuries of history behind it. But no one had ever seen a Chinese bow to another monarch.'[45]

There was, however, another way to approach China. Even under similar official Chinese intransigence, the Portuguese colony of Macao started to thrive. This trading outpost had been established around 1554 after 'informal' negotiations with the local authorities and the harbourmasters of all the ports of Xiangshan district that Macao belonged to.[46] After being halted in its expansion in East Asia by the Qing's unstoppable forces in the seventeenth century, Russia was also trying to reactivate its trading interests to China with its new naval power.

In order to open up trade with China, the British had to identify a major import, which was not hard to do. Tea imports to Britain started slowly but soon built up to a rapid pace. On the other hand, it was difficult to find goods for export to China, since Chinese consumers believed that they had everything they needed to maintain their own traditional life style. Only the illegal drug trade could offset this trade deficit as the Chinese government continued to discourage imports from the British Empire. Consequently, illicit opium took its place as the only item available to trade with China. As Chinese tea exports grew, so the drug traffic thrived. Soon a steep rise in the opium trade began to cause serious social and financial problems in China. As the Chinese emperor appointed Lin Zexu in 1839 as an imperial commissioner with full power to stop this drug dealing, the collision against the British became inevitable. By 1830, the opium trade revenue in China was linked to more than ten per cent of the British revenue from India.[47]

The British steam battleships dispatched from Indian waters were the symbol of a new and aggressively expanding industrial power. Refusing to change their own system, the Chinese dynasty finally made up their mind to exercise their 'invincible' army, believing in its strength as there was no record of being defeated by a western naval power. But the emperor failed to recognise the real power difference between the two nations, which had substantially changed before this unfortunate Chinese encounter.

The British were no longer ready to be dictated to by the Chinese emperor or to be treated as 'barbarians' by them. And the British armed forces were confident that they had finally developed sufficient new power that could rock this outdated realm. The opposition leader, Gladstone, protested that the war over opium would remain as a moment of shame for British history, but the young rising industrial nation could not help but take on the world's largest and richest nation for decades, to move up to a different dimension of glory.

Modern warfare was somewhat surprising to the Chinese. The British attacked Amoy (now Xiamen) first. Discovering that it was strongly defended, they swiftly switched to attack Dinghai, which was lightly defended, and occupied it. From this strategic location in the Zhoushan islands, the British fleet could easily reach Tianjin, the principal port of the Chinese capital. The imperial court was thrown into a panic, and amid this uproar, the emperor dismissed his defence chief, Lin Zexu.

After diplomatic negotiation failed, the fierce battle spread to the Chinese stronghold of Canton. When modern British reinforcements arrived, however, the Chinese government had no choice but to accept the treaty drafted by the British in order to avoid more destruction and humiliation. The Nanjing Treaty in 1842, signed by British and Chinese envoys on board the HMS *Cornwallis*, was virtually the first international agreement made between China and a nation of equal status.

This astonishing news of the collapse of the once-invincible Chinese world order arrived as a terrifying reality to the rest of East Asia. Next, it was the turn of the United States to tackle another ailing power in the region. When the American fleet under the command of Commodore Matthew Perry cautiously arrived at Kurihama in Tokyo Bay in 1853, the Japanese Shogunate government had no alternative but to open up the country for overseas trade. The closed-door policy once established by the force of the mighty samurais now had to be nullified with the realisation of a new and unimaginable external strength demonstrated by the hundred gun shots which sounded like 'thunder' off Yokohama. After a lapse of two centuries of scientific progress under the influence of a renewal of Chinese ideology and closed-off minds, Japan's status in the world had been visibly degraded.

The Chinese and the Japanese now had to pay the price for their retrogression during the period of rejection and isolation in a quite humiliating manner, by making strenuous efforts to catch up. Soon the clan union of western Japan, the houses of Shimazu (Satsuma clan) and Mori (Choshu clan), emerged with British back-up in opposition to the Shogunate government who were supported by the French. Finally, the Satsuma-Choshu joint force prevailed. The 'architect' of the new Meiji government was Toshimichi Okubo of the ex-Satsuma clan. After his removal, Hirobumi Ito of the ex-Choshu clan, who had studied in London, managed to follow up

PART ONE – THE THEORY

Okubo's foundation in a time of fragile divisive politics, with the government's diplomatic objectives clearly set by the British. During this period, the Japanese were more receptive to such external influences than the Chinese.

In this race to the future, Japan appeared as the first 'modern' state in the region after their victory over China in the Sino-Japanese War of 1895. As a result of this war, Japanese influence extended over Korea and Taiwan as Japan's new war machine was now duly established. As Japan's rivalry with the expanding Russian Empire, whose interests were also directed to the Korean peninsula, was enhanced, war between the two seemed inevitable.

In 8 February 1904, after an ultimatum but two days before the declaration of war, the Japanese navy attacked Russian naval forces in Port Arthur and off Inchon, in a convincing display of similar naval tactics that had been used by Britain at the Battle of Copenhagen (1801), and the Russo-Japanese War broke out.

The Russian Tsar had his own Achilles' heel at home. The revolutionary movement sparked by the Bloody Sunday incident intensified first in 1905 in St Petersburg. The change, supported by the workers, started to spread to the whole empire and the Tsar had finally to concede the establishment of the first ever Duma. The situation in Finland was also alarming after the governor-general was assassinated in 1904 and the Russians also faced increasing political dilemmas in Poland.

The victory of the Russo-Japanese War could be regarded as the pinnacle of the Japanese Empire. But this glorious victory left Japan with a legacy for self-admiration, indulgence and a lethal military influence on subsequent governments. On the other hand, for Russia, this unbelievable defeat meant the beginning of the end of one of the world's most successful imperial dynasties.

Japan's exceptional adaptability seemed to be working as Japanese industry expanded further and Japan was soon counted as one of the world's industrial powers. As the First World War begun in 1914, Japan swiftly entered the war in accordance with the Anglo-Japanese Alliance. The Japanese army occupied the German colony of Qingdao and the navy quickly took the German Pacific islands.

During the war, the Japanese government under Prime Minister Shigenobu Okuma in 1915 demanded negotiation of Japanese rights and interests in China, most importantly in Manchuria, which was later criticised as the 'Twenty-One Demands'. Sun Yat-sen's new republic was faltering and in great confusion, Japan unilaterally seized its opportunity. Alarmingly, a powerful faction of the Japanese military was behind this move.

With new industrial expansion sustained by an export boom during the devastating war in Europe, the Japanese economy advanced as an industrial and capital exporting nation, based on its textile, machine, electric, shipbuilding and iron industries, which reached their peak in Japan's third long-term cycle of expansion. With this prosperity came the recognition of a fragile democratic movement. But it was impossible for the Japanese to keep up the momentum as a crack in its economic policy had already appeared with rice riots in 1918. On the diplomatic front, the Japanese government was also suffering from excessive involvement in Siberia. In participating with the Allied effort to help the Russian counter-revolutionary forces, Japan had occupied a large area in Siberia and Northern Sakhalin but without a defined objective, which raised suspicions in the West.

On the other hand, Britain, as her sole ally, was expecting Japan to send troops to the European front like the Americans, Canadians, Australians and others had. The Japanese military-led government repeatedly declined the requests although the navy did eventually send a small fleet to protect the Allied sea-lane. A British expert on the Anglo-Japanese Alliance, Ian Nish, explained the situation with a mild reproof, 'The British judged Japan's failure to contribute wholeheartedly to the European war effort over-harshly in the heat of battle. The officials therefore spoke of "the present hollow friendship" and said that the alliance was at its nadir.'[48] The British government soon notified their Japanese counterparts in May 1921 that Britain would neither extend nor renegotiate the Alliance.

Part One – The Theory

THE POLITICAL CORE TRAP

It is worth noting that, in previous Japanese economic cycles, as soon as a once politically isolated Japan regained fresh power and influence in the world with a new open-door policy, its domestic politics moved back to the 'usual' closed-door policy of isolation in a reverse direction. Japan was driven by a political phenomenon, which could be defined as a 'political core trap', as if the nation always had to go back to its old politics of hidden autarky. And this happened even after a visibly successful diplomatic outcome in co-operation with the West, or despite the introductions of various science breakthroughs and technologies under a stronger international dialogue.

Talking about a balance sheet for Japan, one would notice that within domestic politics, there have been shifting movements between success or prosperity on the positive 'credit' side and power struggles to share the fruit of this on the negative 'debit' side of the equation. In East Asiatic Japan, newly obtained success was not passed on towards a new cycle of prosperity but as soon as it hit its peak, the long-term cycle eventually declined, exactly as before.

From a different angle, the modernisation or 'westernisation' of Japan was always insufficient and stopped short of functioning effectively. In other words, external-factored success always had to be processed by the established interests based on Chinese ideological conflicts which produced the same old political consequences. In this situation, only diplomacy became the key to Japan forging forward and sustaining the right political course. And when this failed, Japanese politics had to returned to its own indigenous instinct and patterns like a kite that suddenly lost its string.

When the global recession blew Japanese politics away in 1932, Prime Minister Tsuyoshi Inukai was shot dead at his official residence by a group of young naval officers and military cadets, who then shouted symbolically, 'No need of arguments!' – *'Mondo Muyo'*. This was called the 5.15 incident after its date. He was the last pre-war politician in this post. Thereafter, only members of the military, bureaucrats or aristocrats were elected to steer the nation as Japan fell headlong into an abyss.

Gradually, Japanese army officers were split into two major factions and the frictions between the two inter-factional rivalries increased. The *Kodoha* – Emperor's Way Group – showed no hesitation in assassinating Major General Tetsuzan Nagata, then the leader of *Toseiha* – Control Group – at the Ministry of Army building in 1935. The former advocated links with newly established military business groups while the latter wanted to tie up with traditional businesses – *Zaibatsu* – as well. Monies 'flew' among members and supporters. Only a power struggle without rationale dominated Japanese politics.

On a snowy day in the following year, the *Kodoha* launched a military rebellion by killing several politicians including the finance minister, Korekiyo Takahashi, and the interior minister, Minoru Saito, but just missed the prime minister, Keisuke Okada, and failed to secure their prime target, the imperial palace. It was called the 2.26 incident. The Japanese emperor emphatically condemned this madness and the *Kodoha* lost control of politics, paving the way for the rise of the *Toseiha* movement who were to lead Japan into war.

What were the Japanese trying to achieve with these inexplicable acts? In this context, Takeshi Hamashita was correct when he observed a basic trend in pre-war Japanese politics, 'When we try to define the modernisation of Asia based on Chinese concepts, we can deem that the process of modernisation for Japan was nothing but trying to control China…the objective of Japan's modernisation was, therefore, to obtain the exclusive monopoly over regional trading networks in East Asia, which were once attained by the tributary trade practices of the Chinese dynasties.'[49]

Furthermore, his historical hypothesis is important in two ways from the Chinese ideological viewpoint. Firstly, despite the modernisation of East Asia, the process of political modernisation is not yet over, even today. Secondly, therefore, this pattern can be recognised in the current economic situation in East Asia. It could perhaps explain the Japanese trade pattern with China, which emerged after 2007 as the largest trading partner of Japan, and overtook its trade with the US.

This recurrence to the old ideology was neither recognised nor confronted because the Chinese and the Japanese as state, individuals, companies or even nations carried it in their blood stream. It emerged because even in the process of their modernisation and the massive social changes attached to this, their ancient political core remained intact and unchanged. In this political environment, Chinese ideology functions as the only existing 'force' available in the politics of East Asia.

But why did these fanatics always win in Japanese society? As these recurrences to the old ideology finally got the upper hand, independent individuals became weak and vulnerable targets. If you were a capable individual, this meant you would be in eventual conflict with strong factions and become an 'outcast' in a power crash where your reason and logic had no role. To avoid annihilation, most people felt the need to join some faction or other to protect themselves.

Suppose everybody ended up belonging to a certain faction in tough times. Because factions could never be run by rational rules, the important criteria for selecting your particular faction would be if it was perceived as stronger in the Japanese ranking system, i.e. sufficiently powerful to confront another menacing sect. As a concrete example, suppose you were an apathetic student in pre-war Japan who belonged to a Karate circle. If you left the group by your own volition, as a customary rule, you could expect violent gang bullying by the other members. To protect yourself from this outcome, you would have to declare that you were now a member of a stronger faction such as the Cheering squad – *Ouendan*. To leave this untenable position once again, you might end up belonging to the Patriotic Student Union. You were safe but you had become an extremist!

Here fanaticism has the edge for either defending your sect (and you) or attacking another group (or person), as things get rough in the approach to the final process of implosion under Chinese ideology. The degree of this entrenched and entangled social element increased so that in the political arena only fanaticism remained as a controlling force, no matter how irrational it was and even if it could only represent the reflection of weakness in despair.

This prevalent social movement was one of the reasons why previously admired western social sciences were quickly forgotten in Japan. In order to show off your Japanese extremism, you would certainly be playing safe if you quoted Motoori Norinaga or some Japanese Buddhists, rather than, say John Stuart Mill, to protect your political position, or more immediately to secure your job, or to 'excel' in society. (He did not give you much insight on factional politics, did he?)

In the race for modernisation, Japan dramatically emerged as a rising master of western technologies and sciences but it was failing rapidly again due to its internal political conflicts which the fanatics were bound to win. Could this political phenomenon also explain why North Koreans became so extreme?

CONTROL BY HUMAN NETWORKS

There would be no society without human relationships. Yet, East Asian society is peculiar as it lacks the sort of open social relationships that westerners commonly enjoy in the form of parties, social events, gatherings or congregations. Instead, East Asians tend to mingle only with people with a common background who are an extension of family and business relationships. These human networks played a principal role in traditional East Asiatic politics.

Professor Miyazaki of Kyoto University explained the true nature of these networks politics in his *Yandi of Sui* showing how the Sui dynasty was actually run by a group of people called the *Wuchuangzhen* clan. He reminded us why a faction worked for their self-preservation: 'factions should not exist at all but in reality they could achieve a great deal. The Mikawa/eastern Aichi Samurai group in fact constituted the Tokugawa Shogunate. The new Meiji government was built on the power of the factions of Satsuma/Kagoshima and Choshu/Yamaguchi.' He then gives an acute analysis as to the relationship between such factional politics and the rule of law, 'They committed many crimes but a faction would emerge as a sort of necessary evil when the rule of a society is not yet established. If this situation continues too long, it would be troublesome as it prevents society from instituting a fair rule.'[50] The rule of factions created a social injustice that constantly increased.

Another important point we need to be aware of was that the politics of human networking was not only an eastern invention. It also ruled most of traditional western politics all the way up to the initiation of the western global expansion, and it is still alive even today as a potentially threatening factor for national (or multinationals such as the EU) politics and society. In other words, it never died away in Western society, and one can never rule out the human element of favouritism and nepotism, one can only seek to contain it.

In feudal Japan, most samurai warlords were supposed to belong to the *Genji* or *Heike* Clan. In official lineages, both clans were declared as descendants of the Japanese emperor. In the later days of the sixteenth century when the authority of the central government collapsed, actual power became more important than pedigree. But the concept never died away.

For instance, Toyotomi Hideyoshi came from an unknown but vibrant peasant family. As soon as he acquired political power, however, he claimed himself as of 'Heike' descent. Nobody, of course, wanted to dispute it with him as he signed off official documents for the Chinese emperor as Taira-no (Heike) Hideyoshi. Similarly, Tokugawa Ieyasu falsified his family lineage, changing his old name of Matsudaira to Tokugawa of 'Genji' in order to get the official status of *Mikawa-no-Kami* – the governor of Mikawa region – so he could act as a major player in Japanese politics. These political leaders endorsed by the imperial court were above the normal laws in Japan.

Chinese ideology was most strictly adopted in ancient Korea but it was only used to hamper the intellectual progress of this once thrusting nation, by creating a privileged and arrogant ruling class. Once they gained their prerogative position, it would be most unlikely that they would consider the fate of ordinary people who did not belong to their class or faction. In order to bridge this gap, the Chinese invented the concept of *De* or 'virtue' whereby all these rulers should have a degree of high morality. But unfortunately, this did not enjoy universal application. Autocrats enjoyed power without merit and often committed illegal acts, but they could not be removed in this strictly past-oriented society.

In the old clan's rule, the interest of its members came first, they were protected over outsiders and stood above general law. If a clan member committed an offence against another member, he would be punished by clan rule. What would happen if a clan member committed an offence or crime against ordinary people? The clan would ignore or permit a crime against outsiders. Of course, in a modern Chinese or Japanese community, this would be no longer the case but this was the mental attitude of a 'good' clan member. The clan rule and its spirit covered the entire society in East Asia. Its ethos still appears in Japan, as corporate executives tend to break or ignore laws willingly in order to protect their 'sacred' company.

In ancient East Asia, the law was never conceived as common law, or as a means to solve disputes among people of equal rights. It existed as an order which came from the ruling arch-bureaucratic organisation, or in other words, a controlling powerful faction, to subdue subordinate factions. A privileged legal status for the ruler was a part of normal life. Afterwards, it emerged as a principle that had to be adopted under Chinese ideology.

In Japan, the samurai class could kill an ordinary merchant or peasant with a plausible excuse whenever he deemed it appropriate under the Tokugawa Shogunate rule. In those days, there was a strict class rule similar to the Indian caste system. First class was the samurai and included nobles and monks. The second class was made up of peasants because they cultivated farmland in the vital agricultural sector. The third was the people who manufactured goods. The fourth was the merchant class. They were regarded just as exploiters of somebody else's produced wealth and goods by trade and without hard labour in pre-capitalistic Japan.

And each class was further subdivided. Altogether, there were more than twenty classes which could only be changed by marriage in Japan. There was also the lowest class, Eta, which was not included even in official ranks. An irrational explanation was given for this differentiation. For instance, people who dealt with animal skins were all included in this lowest class. Regardless of merit, the Japanese rulers of the old system tried to control the population with these artificial social and family ranks, and severely punished those who stood up against these false rules.

Under this social environment, there was a prejudice against commercial wealth. Many wealthy merchants in China or in Japan could not protect their accumulated private assets as a solid long-term business and their own wealth could be abruptly confiscated by the will of the ruling class. The life of merchants was unstable and unpredictable, as the law could not defend their properties or private monies solidly in pre-capitalistic East Asia. Even though this sort of danger did not often arise, it was almost certain to occur with every declining economic cycle of the 'revolution'.

THE FRAGMENTATION OF POWER

Another notable feature of the Chinese ideological system appears in the structure of political power. Under the Chinese political core, arch-bureaucrats have to rely on their subordinate functions to execute their orders by using human networks (i.e., its civil service operates without any modern ideas). If we examine this process carefully, this is actually a process of delegating the state (or emperor's) power to a subordinate organization which in turn orders a lower unit or individual to take charge. On the other hand, there is no integrated dialogue upwards from a lower section to the decision-making organ of a state (or dynasty). All the remaining power has been already divided into sections somewhere at the bottom of the heap. The inevitable consequence of this process is the fragmentation of state power. In this situation, state power and its grasp on political control can be lost from the centre of the government.

In August 1939, the Japanese army took the initiative for preparing a premeditated attack on the Soviet forces at the Mongolian and Manchurian border with one of its best-equipped army divisions. The 23rd Division was under the command of Lieutenant General Michitaro Komatsubara and acted as the main thrust to finalise the border dispute once and for all. It was known as the Nomonhan Incident (in Japan) or the Undeclared War at Khalkhin-Gol (in Russia). Many influential Japanese leaders took the view at the time that Mongolia together with Manchuria was not part of China proper, and was therefore a legitimate target for Japanese colonisation.

Since the military confrontation began in May, the Russians seemed to discern Japanese intentions, taking immediate action to transfer undetected its best officers, artillery, airplanes, pilots and mechanised army from European Russia before the decisive battle began. Although they were facing the threat of German invasion, the Soviet leaders knew that it was essential to stop the Japanese advance with a proactive force as strong as possible so that the Japanese would refrain from future aggression towards Mongolia and the Soviet Union.

It was the intelligence capability of the two sides which made all the difference in this conflict. The Japanese assault plan was ruined when its 'unrivalled' air force failed to take control of the air space.[51] It soon became apparent that this was a complete disaster for Japanese forces, as the Soviet heavy artillery and new mechanised army of BT-7 tanks supported by I-16 fighters slaughtered well over ten thousand unprepared Japanese soldiers in this open battlefield.

The Soviet Union conducted the first *Blitzkrieg* in modern warfare – a concept invented by the Germans and one which the Russians learned from them and used to devastating effect, whereas Japan had existed in a state of diplomatic isolation produced by their own impervious mentality. Japanese arch-bureaucrats under on-going economic implosion were incapable of developing armaments with new technology such as heavy tanks, anti-tank guns, missile weapons and anti-tank aircraft, which rapidly became common in the US, France, Britain, Germany and Russia during the 1930s.

The incident was a critical factor for the Japanese military's subsequent policies – not only in the field of war, but also in domestic politics. Facing an imminent threat from Russia, the army (or army faction) wanted a stronger alliance with Germany than the previously signed Anti-Comintern Pact between the two countries (1936), as this seemed the only remaining option to counter the enormous power gap Japan faced.

Foreign Minister Yosuke Matsuoka joined the Tripartite Alliance with Germany and Italy in November 1940. In April of the following year, he flew to Moscow to conclude a neutrality pact with the Soviet Union to buy some time, or as he later confessed 'pressurising the United States for peace'. Berlin protested and in the Kremlin, Stalin proposed a toast to the Japanese delegations, shouting, 'To the southward advance of Japan!'[52]

Soon afterwards, Adolf Hitler launched Operation Barbarossa and asked Japan to enter into the war against Soviet Russia based on their alliance. The Japanese army in Manchuria was ordered to manoeuvre its entire force, which had increased from 350,000 to 750,000, to the Russian border (This astonishing military manoeuvre was known as *Kan-Toku-En*) with secret permission to attack, if there was an opportunity to advance. The Japanese emperor, who had the prerogative of the supreme command under the Meiji constitution, strenuously protested against the plan. The Japanese army stayed put because the Soviet military formation along the border was intact, despite massive German attacks and losses on the western front. Again, Soviet intelligence had detected the intentions of Japan and prepared for it.

The Japanese army gave up the initiative in a war against Russia but advanced further into China to extend their power under the form of another undeclared war. Finally, it was the 'world's finest' navy's turn to take the initiative by shifting attention to South-East

Asia. Some naval sectarian leaders believed that a war against the US was a better option than being drawn into a war by the army with the Soviet Union. After the economic blockade against Japan, Admiral Osami Nagano, the naval commander for operations, who supported the Pacific war against the United States, thought at the time, 'If Japan does not stand up now, the nation will die out. Even if Japan is defeated, the nation could be revived again.'[53]

In the deteriorating crisis, some politicians sought reform but there was no real power left to act on because state power had been fragmented. Political power was submerged in the hands of hundreds of arch-bureaucrats whose only interest was to protect and enlarge it for their own benefit. Within this political structure, Japanese politics was completely rotten but empty debates continued in the Japanese Diet as if some action was possible. The power of the state was subdivided, and then again, and again, as if nobody could control this failed venture. No clear objective for fighting a war could be defined by the Japanese military who manipulated state power as politicians in disguise.

The Russian commander, Georgi Zhukov, the architect of all the major Soviet military counter-offensives during the Second World War, who had planned and led the Red Army against the Japanese at the Mongolian border, seemed intuitively to recognise the strange weaknesses of his enemy and its operating structure.

He admired his adversary, 'Japanese soldiers who fought against us on the Khalkhin-Gol are well-trained, especially for fighting at close quarters. They are well disciplined, diligent, dogged in combat, especially in defence. Junior commanding officers are well trained and fanatically persistent in battle. As a rule they do not surrender.' He could not, however, help but criticise the Japanese commanding officers harshly, 'Officers, especially senior and high-ranked officers, are not sufficiently-prepared, lacking initiative, and are apt to act only in a stereotyped way.'[54] Curiously, the phenomenon, which he saw then, is still visible in today's Japan, especially in governmental organizations or big corporations.

As he realised, most of the high-ranking Japanese military were not professionals but arch-bureaucratic experts who belonged to the exclusive elite corps and owed their positions to factional connections and passing exams. Strictly speaking, they were merely political appointments based on the power balance within the organisation rather than based on expertise or merit.

They were adept at covering up the extent of their defeats in this battle and this is one reason why Japan lost the war. In the Japanese political environment, if revealing the truth would expose a shameful reality or an insurmountable hopelessness, many Japanese preferred to conceal it to avoid further disastrous consequences and to keep morale intact for their next move. Again, this obsession for short-term solutions and complete negligence for long-term objectives visibly survives in post-war Japan.

In addition, the position and designated power of Japanese commanders were very different from their Soviet counterparts. Jiro Tokuyama, who led the various think-tanks including that of the Defence Agency in post-war Japan, lamented the nature of this anti-Soviet military campaign, about which most people were unaware. He revealed a situation where the Japanese generals on the battlefield were actually forced to carry out this ill-advised attempt by Colonel Masanobu Tsuji, the chief of staff of the Kwangtung Army Headquarters in Manchuria, who refused to take the responsibility for this devastating defeat. Not only that, he was allowed to repeat other ill-planned operations including Guadalcanal, Attu, Kiska, China and Burma until the total defeat of Japan's military powers. Subsequently, just after the war, he was even elected as a member of the new Japanese parliament.[55] There was an irreconcilable gap between the power of officers and the ranks.

John Owen Haley, a British legal expert who studied post-war Japanese law intensively, encountered this specific phenomenon. He noticed the visible division of power in the Japanese legal system, 'What has been described as the paradox of Japan as a society rests above all on the dichotomy of authority and power. Because in English these terms are so often used interchangeably, the German distinction between *Authorität* and *Macht* may be more useful to delineate these two concepts. By authority or *Authorität*, I mean the legitimacy or socially recognized entitlement to command and to be obeyed; by power or *Macht*, the capacity to coerce others to do something they would not otherwise do.'

He detected that this came directly from the top political hierarchy, 'No characteristic of Japanese political life seems more remarkable or intrinsic than the separation of authority from power…this separation is represented at the highest political level by the imperial institution. It is also evident in everyday affairs of contemporary Japan, in the relative weakness of most forms of law enforcement. Japan is thus a society in which in terms of authority to act and intervene, the jurisdictional mandate as it were, government or state seems pervasive yet its capacity to coerce and compel is remarkably weak.'[56] The Japanese legal system was indeed very different in nature from a European one. As he noticed, any reform or democratic control would require consolidated power under a single authority as a prerequisite condition but this was exactly what was lacking in Japan under Chinese ideology.

THE AREAL CONCEPT

Without any modesty, Chinese dynastic rhetoric claimed that they were the masters of the world notwithstanding the fact that somebody else controlled most parts of the globe. As mentioned already, China limits the boundary of its political world to the Chinese territory of *Zhonghua*, which is supposed to be constantly expanding. In the case of pre-modern Japan, political perspective was limited at its maximum extent to China – *Kara* – included its peripheries, South-East Asia, and India – *Tenjiku* – at its far west. Both countries tried to expand within this traditional area and no further.

In the sixteenth century, Europe expanded out to sea. Ferdinand Magellan set out to sail round the world with his five little ships. After a two year voyage of hardship during which Magellan named the Pacific Ocean, the great Portuguese navigator was killed by native warriors in an island near Cebu, in the Philippines. But one of his ships, the *Victoria*, returned to Spain in 1522 after completing his goal. It was this spirit of adventure, which was to shape the future global economy. There were no such aspirations on the Chinese side, despite the fact that China was certainly far richer than Spain at one stage.

The concept of areal limitation in the Chinese ideology came from the reality that its agrarian economy could only be expanded to its peripheries. The industry-driven European world put no such limitations on its global reach. As an example, Peyrefitte noted that when China heard about Napoleon's defeat at Waterloo, the Chinese response was complete indifference, 'Your Majesty's kingdom is at a remote distance beyond the seas, but is observant of its duties and obedient to our law, beholding from afar the glory of our Empire and respectfully admiring the perfection of our Government.'[57] Of course, China never applied this kind of political indifference to an East Asiatic state, which it might threaten or demand tribute from or intend to control its trading network or, in the worst case, plan an invasion.

This concept of territorial cut-off works as a driving factor for an East Asiatic double standard, in a sense that people do not feel mentally constrained in their limited cultural living space under the influence of Chinese ideology. And they tend to apply different standards to anything beyond their own 'world'. While this Chinese economic perspective was gradually expanded to include the larger outside world, or even where the Japanese or Chinese economy was rapidly gaining a vital global network, this geographical and conceptual political restraint still seems to exist as before in a Chinese or Japanese mind.

It is also important to remember that each Chinese ideological state in East Asia had its own political interests and myths. The political links among those nations became weaker in spite of the existence of their shared ideology because each state was and is fiercely nationalistic within its own boundaries and its desire to expand these.

On the Theory of Chinese Ideology

The assimilation or modification of this nationalism is only possible through military conquest in East Asia. In this political matrix where any sense of 'fraternity' was lost at the beginning, common ground for political manoeuvres is actually quite limited. Under the influence of such mini-*Zhonghua*-ism, Japan once adopted its own extreme interpretation of this idea and even closed the country by banning communication and transportation to 'protect' Japan from 'foreign evils'.

The concept of geographical restrictions has never altered in modern Japan. Ryuzo Sejima, who served as an elite army staff member in pre-war Manchuria, and was detained by the Soviet Union after the war in a Siberian prisoner-of-war camp, then became a vice chairman of a major trading corporation, and also an influential leader in the Japanese governmental organizations, expressed this sentiment not too long ago. He insisted that his reason for calling the Second World War a 'Great East Asian War' in the pre-war Japanese way was correct. A solid historical text was prepared with the help of some Japanese academics for his lecture at Harvard University in which he defined the Second World War as, 'simply the war fought in the area of East Asia', by which he meant, 'East to Burma, North to Lake Baikal and West to Marshal Islands approximately, excluding India and Australia.'[58]

Was this the only sphere for Japanese military advance? Although I do not know how the American audiences reacted to his lecture, I presume that it might have sounded strange to them, particularly as Japan had tried to move into India, Australia and the United States only to be repulsed by the Allied powers. I found it amazing because it confirmed Japanese mentality and political thinking have not changed even in post-war Japan.

Politically, Japanese were taught to be interested only in their own territory, just as the Chicago mafia were in the roaring twenties. In this case, he simply presented the view of his compatriots' 'natural' sentiment as the Japanese prefer to put it. For him, how the outside world of the United States or Europe would regard his viewpoint was immaterial. After all, he was living in a society with this particular idea in which he enjoyed a powerful position. What was really important for him was how Japanese audiences would appraise his comments although they were made in front of foreign intellectuals and outside of Japan's territory.

At the same time, it indicates how difficult it is for Japanese to cope with both external and domestic matters, under the current global political and business realities that are constantly penetrating every street of Japanese towns and cities without giving people any place to hide, while their 'leaders' see the world with such limited vision.

In Japan, of course, there are many internationally experienced people, classified by the Japanese press as *Kokusaiha* (incidentally, the Japanese literal translation for this word would be 'International-faction'!) in the world of bureaucracy and business. As soon as they returned from a long assignment abroad, they would undergo a special 'treatment' called *Rihabiri* – rehabilitation – so they could be accommodated safely again back in Japan and embrace its indigenous standards, or more precisely, to make sure any 'dangerous' political ideas from foreign influences are properly eliminated. Overall, they are given a sort of secondary status from which they are supposed to assist the domestically brewed elite group.

It is perhaps because of this traditional political behaviour that the Japanese or Chinese cannot have any real sympathy for grievances existing outside of their world or any determination to understand the 'foreign' system unless they are naturalised there. Although they have, of course, common feelings as human beings, but expressing these sympathies or experiences is somehow not politically encouraged. This tendency simply comes from the fact that the outside world is excluded from their political core. This ceiling on political thinking caused problems as it could evolve at various decision-making levels in society. With this defect, the Meiji state of Japan struggled to master western imperialism.

Above all, Japan's major success in the Russo-Japanese War (1904-05) did not mean that the Japanese had mastered modern imperialism successfully as Japan had no true global spirit. It was merely attained by Japan's role as an agent of British imperialism in East Asia. When Japan hit its peak in fulfilling this role but then failed to act independently, the system collapsed.

After the Second World War, the United States emerged as the most powerful western state in the region. But a new question must be asked: 'What was the nature of post-war Japan's success?' Has Japan acquired its capitalistic success by its own merit, or was that status attained merely as an agent of American capitalism in East Asia? If the latter is the answer, we all need to be careful.

THE END OF EXPANSION

Today, East Asian-originated culture and goods, including arts or foods with their distinctive characteristics, are increasingly popular in the West. And there would be absolutely no need to abolish any of these wonderful products, practices or skills achieved from past greatness. So then, what is wrong with our traditions? – some would ask in East Asia.

Only now does adhering to an ancient political ideology become critical for those nations, when their politics and related social practices still operate despite their becoming obsolete and outdated. In thinking about this issue, we realise that our judgement needs to be focused on one point after all, i.e. whether this quantitative (or any other forms of) long-term growth, which was the whole purpose of this original political concept, is approaching its limits of expansion in the foreseeable future or not.

We have to conclude that this crucial test is unfortunately compellingly negative. Firstly, by economic reasoning. The industrial economy of East Asia grew more rapidly than one could have imagined in recent years after China's accession to WTO membership in 2003. Japan, Taiwan, Korea and finally China became true industrial states. As the centre of East Asia, China's progress was rather remarkable. On the back of this change, service industries supported by the financial business sector expanded in East Asia.

All the profitable flows of industrial and other businesses had to be managed as national social assets in the Chinese financial centres of Shanghai and Hong Kong. For today's economic reality, therefore, we now have to acknowledge that China has already departed from reliance on its agrarian economy, which constituted the supreme objective of its old political system and the foundation of its wealth. The fundamental economic base, which sustained the old Chinese political concept, therefore, is vanishing. In other words, China now needs to navigate into uncharted territory.

Secondly, we must consider the military aspect. The emergence of nuclear weapons in terms of the degree of their destructive force and their responsible use changed the traditional Clausewitz-style theory of 'War as an extension of politics', and this old way of thinking had to be absolutely revised in East Asia.[59] In this new political environment, international boundaries are given legitimacy by international law and no powerful nation or politicians can change it by force without facing intolerable consequences in today's global community. While China is the sole nuclear power acknowledged in East Asia, this only has an effective significance in its defensive deterrence power.

As for the coming Chinese 'revolution' in the old economic cycle, the modern Chinese internationally recognised central government with its nuclear capability cannot be overthrown by a peasant rebellion or any kind of force. That is to say, the old military mechanism, a prerequisite for the 'revolution', could no longer function as any Chinese military insurgents would not be allowed to cause mass-destruction in China under international law. Similarly, the Chinese government could not use its superior nuclear power against its own people or its East Asian neighbours without first risking cutting its 'lifeline' to its quasi-capitalist economy. As a prerequisite condition for survival, therefore, it must find peaceful means such as democratic elections, even if this seems utterly impossible today.

Thirdly and finally, is the reality of historical 'revolution' mechanisms inside China's expansion mode, which have run the country for more than three thousand years. The problem is that communist China could not be classified as an external tribal state in the context of Chinese history, like the Qing, Yuan or Tang dynasties, which played key roles in the state's traditional expansion. Communist China should instead be categorised as the latest integrating type of state since the time of the Ming dynasty. As for new Chinese expansion in post-communist China, it must be another state's turn to take up the next growth cycle. But where could China find a partner for traditional expansion in Asia? With on-going social and economic problems, China's influence and fundamental power, beside its East Asiatic neighbouring states, are expected to disappear with a steep downward trend.

As we saw earlier, participation in Chinese politics was first curtailed in the eighth century by westerners such as the Turkic people. In this aspect, fellow eastern nations through full industrialisation now decisively apply the same policy. In Chinese history, it would appear that the Manchu people were the last nation to have willingly joined this old type of expansion in East Asia. In the age of global capitalism, there will be no eastern nations ready to join in old Chinese quantitative expansion as the world must now pay urgent attention to the spectre of global warming and increasing energy consumption. In terms of Chinese ideology, this means that there will be no more 'coal' to fire up the engine.

With this new political change, therefore, we have to now conclude that the pattern of physical Chinese expansion has became irrational as the historical rationale for Chinese ideology has thus been lost. China and Japan, as archetypal arch-bureaucratic states, have to find a way to reform their politics. For the first time in history, the end of Chinese expansion is approaching in East Asia. Hence, alternative political mechanisms must be brought into the region as a whole as soon as possible, before it becomes too late.

PART TWO
THE PRACTICAL TREND

I – CHINA AND THE CHINESE ECONOMIC AREA

THE ADJUSTED SYSTEM

How can we apply our theory on Chinese ideology to current Chinese politics? The first conclusion to draw when discussing the challenge facing Chinese people today is that Chinese dynastical politics ended – or Chinese modern politics began – as part of the typical process in the old Chinese economic cycle, regardless of the modern revolutions occurring in the rest of the world. Arthur Cotterell described the situation in brief, 'The Sino-Japanese War of 1894-5 was of major importance because it revealed the full extent of the Qing dynasty's collapse and set off a scramble among the European powers for territory and markets on mainland East Asia.'[60] In this new political environment, by giving up the 'only ticket' for industrialisation in East Asia to Japan, China was able to refrain from becoming an 'imperialist' state and could move on to the next traditional cycle of an agrarian economy.

In other words, pre-China avoided expanding into an industrial economy, thereby distancing it from the West's constant diplomatic pressure. China 'escaped' from modern political power play and did not experience the eventual implosion caused by East Asiatic double political standards such as Japan was to undergo in this 'modern' era. For this reason, in spite of the abolition of the dynastical system, the progress of 'modern' Chinese politics was rather slow as, unlike Japan, China still had tangible resources and potential agricultural wealth, and was therefore less ready to embrace a shift to industrial power.

The Chinese communists exploited this old remaining power base by successfully raising agricultural productivity even beyond the post-war period. Mao Zedong focused on the peasants and villages. And when he stipulated that, 'Unless the peasants participate in this national revolution and help it, the national revolution could never succeed...'[61] – he was talking about exactly the same principle as Liu Bang, the founder of the Han dynasty, who conducted 'revolution' for his new regime had done slightly more than two thousand two hundred years ago.

'The People's Republic of China has been inaugurated! – *Zhonghua Renmin Gongheguo Chenglile*' Chairman Mao declared solemnly in front of some 300,000 people packed in Tiananmen Square in 1949. A second later, there was a burst of joy from all the people present as everyone enthusiastically endorsed his 'traditional' policy with its new face. But among those masses who were smiling, only a very few would have been sure of this outcome, say, a few years before this, when powerful nationalist forces renewed their onslaught against Japanese invaders.

The sudden advance by the Soviet Red Army to Manchuria and then to North Korea in pursuit of the Japanese Kwangtung army in 1945 made a decisive impact on the course of Chinese domestic conflicts. To Chinese eyes, it seemed impossible for the Kuomintang – the Chinese Nationalist Party – to survive without Soviet help in ex-Japanese Manchuria.

As a new Chinese ruler, Mao Zedong was well aware of the importance of military power just as all the Chinese emperors had been. He was amazingly pragmatic and clever in dealing with the issue. His global vision was sometimes lacking but this was not a disadvantage in Chinese domestic politics rather it contributed to his charisma. The process of this 'revolution' was always a purely internal Chinese affair.

Why did he employ rather 'non-Marxist' methods in China? Put simply, there was no modern political infrastructure in China to support a Marxist platform. Initially, not all party activists were convinced that this was the right way forward. Li Lisan, one of Mao's predecessors as the leader of the Chinese Communist Party (CCP), actually tried a Soviet-style uprising which began with general strikes in the cities with the full support of the Comintern and the Chinese intelligentsia in 1930 and then failed so miserably that even Moscow had to desert him. After similar setbacks, communism in China was in danger of an imminent collapse. Only Mao Zedong with his political instincts, a son of peasants and the soil, could provide an alternative.

After the birth of the CCP, he firmly established his leadership by applying traditional strategies, and finally by undertaking the famous Long March (1934-36). The marchers moved first westward to Yunnan and then northward to Wuqizhen, gathering support from the peasant population, changing the communists' military movement from quasi-rout to a solid defence under the clear objective of fighting against Japanese 'imperialists'. During this period, the foundation of the People's Liberation Army as a new military group was put firmly in place. This historical march was later regarded as 'sacred' among the early Chinese communists as its participants played a notable role in subsequent Chinese politics.

All the Chinese political leaders in the early days of communist rule belonged to this group of veterans. Not only prominent figures in world politics such as Zhou Enlai and Deng Xiaoping, but also key domestic political figures such as Ye Jianying, the chief of general staff of the People's Liberation Army who subsequently played a decisive role in Deng's sensational comeback just after the stormy Cultural Revolution.

In fact, the Long March veterans acted as the first leading powers in traditional Chinese factional politics. Li Peng, the adopted son of Zhou Enlai and influential as a long-serving premier, could be regarded as representing this group's second generation. On the other hand, the power base of this Chinese political circle was to end with general secretariat appointments of technocrats like Hu Yaobang, or from the new party cadres where figures like Jiang Zemin came to prominence and were ready to form a new ruling group.

In order to avoid a 'strong military man' coming to power in the Chinese tradition, the CCP constitution made it clear that the People's Liberation Army (or armed forces) had to accept the leadership of the Party and the constitution of the People's Republic of China. The chairman of the CCP is also the commander of the armed forces.[62] The general secretary of the party usually holds this post concurrently. So although it seemed that solid civilian control was established – something very difficult to adhere to in East Asian politics – any appraisal of Chinese communism should analyse its military power base, which used new technology to expand but was firmly linked with old political ideology.

In addition to conventional weaponry, Mao Zedong was keen to introduce nuclear armaments by saying, 'China will produce an atomic bomb even if we don't make underpants!' And his rather embarrassing determination was apparently the cause of the diplomatic rift with Soviet Russia who had supported communist China from the beginning. On this point, Roy Medvedev observed, 'Differences between China and the Soviet Union in 1957-8' were mainly due to this contrary military view, and 'Economic relations between the Soviet Union and China were virtually broken off altogether in 1963.'[63] In the following year, faster than any outsiders had estimated, China successfully detonated its first nuclear explosion in the Xinjiang desert. A resolute Mao caught everybody by surprise.

From the Sinicised political ideology of communism to the newest atomic weapons, China was successful in steadily introducing all of these innovations from the western world. And no critic could win any argument that said the Chinese communists did not modernise China on a tremendous scale. Yet this was achieved by very traditional methods, frankly, the same old politics. And of course, Mao Zedong chose the orthodox Chinese way of quantitative expansion with his newly acquired power, without any modern concept of economics in view. Nothing has been changed since the era of the Kuomintang. As Trotsky once felt about those who led an autonomous traditional existence beyond the existence of the classes that they embraced, one could say of the Chinese communists, 'The classes come and go but the continuity of the Kuomintang [or Chinese Communists indeed] goes on forever.'[64]

This was how Chinese communism was firmly launched to build 'modern' China. Chairman Mao tried to fortify the theory of Chinese communism in quite an impressive fashion by introducing a Chinese interpretation to communism's vocabulary but he could not contribute anything new to it. To be more precise, he simply adopted the Chinese double standard of politics. Communism could provide a new model for Chinese political power with the expansion of its vital agrarian economy upon which the Chinese nation relied so heavily – it was the only available asset in front of them.

Mao Zedong made a realistic decision for subsequent Chinese policies. He knew how to chart a course for modern China and for this agrarian economy in a way which would appeal to the ordinary Chinese. His basic and essential concern always matched their needs, 'How to eat – *Chifande wenti*.' He was successful in solving this problem but he could not provide more. But a modern China desperately needed more than these basic provisions, as he himself would have known.

The application of the Soviet economic model under the Mao administration as the only method available at the time initially appeared successful. It soon encountered difficulties as Tony Saich explained, 'It was not long before the kind of problems that have plagued other Soviet systems also began to emerge in China. The concentration on heavy industries soon led to the creation of bottlenecks in the system as well as imbalance in the economy.'[65] The Chinese communists might have identified this potential crisis just after criticism of Stalin began in Soviet Russia in 1956 after the dictator's death – but they could not alter Mao's economic policy.

With Mao Zedong's fundamental weakness in modern economics, the policy which appeared under his name as the 'Great Leap Forward' was even more disastrous. Once a young compassionate idealist, Comrade Mao turned into an old and suspicious politician and all the legacies of traditional Chinese power politics remained wholly visible during his reign. All his 'rivals', among them Peng Dehuai, Liu Shaoqi, Lin Biao or Zhou Enlai, faced stern and bitter criticism over their disagreements on Mao's policy, which often cost them their lives, as if the Chinese political tradition of serving the 'emperor' was exacerbated by a Stalinist influence. The situation worsened as the supreme Chinese leader tried to cling on to power until the very last minute.

When Deng Xiaoping finally inherited this outdated regime from Mao Zedong, he had few choices. He had to rebuild the base of the economy and restart Chinese industrial power which now proved to be desperately backward. What he inherited from his predecessor was a massive increase in the population and worn-out and neglected industrial development. The population of China was 540 million in 1949. It surpassed 1 billion in 1981.[66] And without any new technological input, China's steel and other major industries were ailing.

Arising out of political turmoil and Mao's legacy, Deng emerged as the first Chinese communist leader who had been educated in the West, initially in France, and later in Russia.[67] His view was therefore quite different from other contemporary Chinese politicians who lived only on indigenous soils. When he thought of improving the quality of the Chinese economy, the enlarged population was identified as a major obstacle for development and he adopted the infamous 'single child' policy to stop its momentum.

His first task seemed to expose the obsolescence of China as a grim reality. Deng had agreed to move the 'mighty' Chinese army against its former ally, Vietnam, 'to punish' them in 1979. Incidentally, the Japanese militarists used the same rhetoric when they invaded Northern China in 1937. However, Deng Xiaoping was more astute than those past Japanese mediocrities as he ordered a withdrawal after only seventeen days. By that time, it was quite obvious that China, and the Chinese army in particular, required serious modernisation. Even the military hardliners now had to listen to him while a possible stronger intervention from the Soviet Union was another factor in his decision.[68]

Part Two – The Practical Trend

Deng Xiaoping's political slogan of Chinese supreme power, 'Practical experience is the only criterion by which we can verify the truth', was indeed of western origin. He boosted Chinese diplomatic relationships with the West, which had been initiated by Zhou Enlai, his old mentor, and set a course for China to practise their own brand of 'capitalism' by saying, 'White cat or black cat, a cat that catches a rat is a good cat.'

His eyes were focused on a Japanese, Singaporean or Hong Kong style manufacturing economy which could be adapted for China. In 1980, he appointed the radical technocrats Hu Yaobang and Zhao Ziyang as the general secretary and premier respectively to lead this breakthrough and set the course forward for the current Chinese economy. All three Chinese leaders, Deng, Hu and Zhao, were keen to visit Japan for factory inspections. Agrarian China had also to modernise its economy for future political change. But the only realistic policy they could adopt was to pursue the Chinese political path set out by Mao Zedong. By shifting the country's course to industrialisation and subsequent export prosperity, however, Deng Xiaoping actually enhanced the evils – in other words, by increasing its 'contradiction' or *maodun* in both more Marxist and authentic Chinese expression – of the Chinese double standard.

PROBLEMS OF A SOCIALIST MARKET ECONOMY

The anti-communism revolutionary process was gaining momentum in Europe and reached its height in 1989 when the Berlin Wall was finally dismantled. Just like the original revolution, Russian political reform initially started rather slowly. Mikhail Gorbachev was in the spotlight and took a similar role to that of Aleksandr Kerensky in an earlier era. Both perhaps lacked the radicalism required for this drastic political change and power shift over their huge 'empire'.

In the former revolution, Vladimir Lenin immediately stopped the war against Germany and the Central Powers with the Brest-

On the Theory of Chinese Ideology

Litovsk Treaty and declared in 1918, 'in six months we will have built socialism.' This time, it was Boris Yeltsin who asserted in 1991, 'A one-time change over to market prices is a difficult and forced measure, but a necessary one, but then prices will fall, the consumer market will be filled with goods, and by the autumn of 1992 there will be economic stabilization and a gradual improvement in people's lives.'[69]

At both historical turning points, priority was given to revolutionary political reforms all over Russia and the Russian-controlled republics. For this new political change, multiple party systems were instantly introduced as the West offered their assistance for this nascent Russian capitalism. Russia restructured its own presidential system based on the French model as did new regimes in all other Eastern European countries in a domino effect. In this process, it was revealed that any government called a People's Republic or People's Democratic Republic was nothing but an autocracy or a failed state management system.

The Chinese method of attaining phenomenal changes from communism was in great contrast to the Russian and East European pattern. At first, the change began modestly by expanding zones of enterprise autonomy. It started, much earlier than Russia, without any visible political reforms. In October 1978, Zhao Ziyang, then the first secretary of the Sichuan party committee, granted more autonomy to six enterprise zones (later to be increased to a hundred) on a trial basis. This experiment yielded excellent results and won an enthusiastic response in many other provinces.[70] Following this success to its manufacturing economy, and by establishing a Special Economic Zone for Shenzhen and Xiamen, the opening up of other coastal cities began to encourage foreign trade and investment. The success from this open-door policy was then accelerated to the entire mainland and the Chinese economy was gradually lifted up to another dimension.

In a new ambitious economic plan, Shanghai, once designated the 'Paris of the East', declared itself again as the economic capital of China with its financial centre in the newly developed Pudong district as its heart. This project was a symbol of the strength of China's political ambition and became one of the most intensive reshapings of a modern city in the world, as if China wanted to construct its own New York completely from scratch. Notably, again without any basic political change, communist-controlled China tried to revamp its economic system.

Gradually, political differences emerged within the top Chinese hierarchy concerning this economic progress. It started with the sudden death of the much-admired Hu Yaobang in April 1989 when students and young workers in Beijing who supported more democracy and freedom gathered at Tiananmen Square. Many people joined their protest and occupied the square in May. Day by day over a period of several weeks, this demonstration became more serious and it was finally undermining the power of the authorities as the police were unable to disperse the crowds. After a long standoff and negotiations, party leaders were suddenly alarmed when the general secretary, Zhao Ziyang, appeared at the square to demonstrate his sympathy with the growing numbers of protesters.

As the demonstration turned into a real political protest, Premier Li Peng without any reservations ordered a mechanised division of the People's Liberation Army to intervene. Their forcible removal of the protesting students and workers from the square caused shocking bloodshed in the centre of the Chinese capital. The televised 'incident' confirmed to the world that China was in no way close to Russian-style political reform. Deng Xiaoping replaced Zhao Ziyang with Jiang Zemin, who was then a politburo member and the mayor of Shanghai. And so China's real 'could-be Gorbachev' was politically eliminated and 'glasnost' was denied in China.

'Colonial governors, like the Sumatran rhinoceros, the Florida manatee and the Politburo of the Chinese Communist Party, are an almost extinct species' wrote the last governor of Hong Kong, Chris Patten with his unique formula of bitterness and charm.[71] But Deng Xiaoping was not even a politburo member. The 'Patriarch' ruled over the whole event but this did not mean he enjoyed absolute power as Mao Zedong had. And even Mao's seemingly emperor-like power had recognisable limits comparable to a modern leaders in the West. The warning signal to the Chinese leaders was that Zhao Ziyang's 'liberal' view could have led China into political confusion and chaos. And this was never acceptable to the CCP cadres. Nobody, including Deng Xiaoping, could have opposed this clear majority view, and therefore he did not hesitate to act firmly, relying on their indisputable support.

How could China take such a completely different path compared to their 'comrade' states in Europe? One credible reason was that, unlike Russia, China was able to retain its old politics and still grow in every economic dimension. Russia and China were both communist states but when the communist system faltered, Russia realised that she was after all a European state albeit one with its economy collapsing and without any credible western links. Failed communist states in Eastern Europe knew that they could not survive without maintaining this vital political 'pipeline' from the West and they had to change to save their skins, while China had another option with their own examples in East Asia. 'Successful' Japan was almost exclusively controlled by the same old politics despite the existence of bi-party elections. And only nationalists ruled Taiwan at the time. So, what was wrong with continuing the system?

In this context, Joseph Fewsmith questioned the role of Zhu Rongji as China's economic tsar, 'Zhu has often been referred to as "China's Gorbachev" by the Western press (and by his domestic enemies as well), but there is little in his economic thinking, much less political position, to suggest that he either desires or can play such a role in China... Zhu's approach to economic reform and political control appears modelled after that of Park Chung-hee or Lee Kuan Yew, favouring strong state control combined with a marketized economy.'[72] The system was defined by some others as 'developmental authoritarianism'.

There was a price to pay for this economic reform but no other option was available for China. Deng Xiaoping's 'audacious' economic challenge paid off as the growth in Chinese foreign investment and export gained momentum soon after this period. We must admit

Part Two – The Practical Trend

that since 1992, the Socialist Market Economy (SME) of China, as endorsed by Jiang Zemin, was immensely successful in raising the Chinese people's living and technological standards that had once fallen to rock bottom.

At the same time, we need to realise that the Chinese idea of SME was nothing new, but a reassertion of old political values to bridge a gap between the established socialist (or traditional) regime and a changing new economic reality. With rapidly growing global activities at the centre of its economy, China had to accept her own role as a part of the international community, as the Chinese economy, with its supply chains and markets, had to be reconnected with the global economy.

Beneath the unprecedented prosperity, however, a social chasm was also constantly enlarging as the new economy advanced and met all sort of difficulties, which needed solutions that only modern political states can provide; but those social innovations were never naturally forthcoming. As a colossal environmental disaster is under way, it would appear that China should have equipped itself with modern social tools from legal infrastructure to welfare systems to counter this. What a towering responsibility Chinese leaders risk to face the coming crisis in the world's possibly largest unbalanced state.

The following anecdote that has appeared in Beijing hits the nail on the head, 'When Li Peng and Jiang Zemin went out they met a donkey on the road. The donkey blocked their path and showed no sign of backing down. Li Peng got angry and shouted, "If you don't get out of our way, I shall order the People's Liberation Army to shoot you!" But the donkey ignored him and still refused to move. Having seen his failure, Jiang Zemin approached the donkey and whispered, "My dear donkey, if you don't want to go away, should I give you my post as the General Secretary of the Chinese Communist Party?" The astonished donkey ran away immediately.'[73]

Premier Li made a speech on the Chinese economy at the UN Security Council on 31 January 1992, 'In contrast to a turbulent Europe, the Asia-Pacific region enjoys relative stability.' He further boasted of its progress, 'Quite a few countries in the Asia-Pacific region have enjoyed a rather high economic growth rate thanks to political stability at home. This region has now become a dynamic and promising region in world economic development.'[74] But today, it seems as if he made this comment prematurely.

The political turmoil ended (but the economic turmoil has only just started!) in most of Eastern Europe as the EU continued to enlarge. Meanwhile, despite occasional political spats with the West, Russia's economic reform began to spread from Moscow to other rural cities, gradually matching Chinese success – while a turbulent period could yet be seen in China.

AN 'ADVANCED' ARCH-BUREAUCRACY

Why can such an arch-bureaucracy continue to lead China? Just imagine if there was a similar level of 'autocracy' in the western world. Only a conspicuous political movement and radical upheaval could bring the West to the same point. The leaders in East Asia did not particularly promote this course as it was just there, like an old peach tree in China or apple tree in Japan, for them to take advantage of. This lack of awareness was also the reason why the situation was never considered as a critically alarming factor in the West. The effect of this traditional and supreme political entity was overwhelming and quite uninterrupted as it continued to control religions, economy, laws and all social functions of the state.

From this perspective, the observations of a prominent Chinese sociologist, Wang Hui, regarding the people's democracy in China are pertinent and highlight the crucial failures of East Asian politics. Wang Hui detected this, without analysing the reasons for it, seeing it as nothing but a normal part of daily political life, 'China's level of democracy is quite low as people do not exercise their right as the master…to elect a people's representative; they just circle the name of a candidate on the ballot paper. This attitude was formed over a long period of history. There are problems about the credibility of the people's representatives or people's congress itself, of course, however, the biggest problem lies in the fact that our nations were accustomed to relax even in the situation whereby a few people have total control and power and act on their behalf as their master.'[75]

After the Second World War, democratic states – or rather nominally states representing the people – emerged at least as an official system in East Asia. Larger nations such as China or Japan, however, never functioned as democracies because the inherited political behaviour of those nations was utterly incompatible with modern democratic systems. People do not change their solid political attitudes even if they are told that they are now obsolete, or just given a general explanation on the necessity of global democracy. Firstly, they have to be convinced that the new idea is for the better and realise the bad effects of their old ideas, then they need to reconfirm this as a national political decision, before they can even begin to move on it.

This phenomenal change is perhaps equal to the situation of the ancient tribes which once occurred in western Central Asia where people regarded horses only as domestic animals with the same uses as cattle rather than for riding. People fought on foot just like their fathers and grandfathers did, until somebody developed a bit to control the animal, and at this point the real power of horses was discovered and a horse-mounted man appeared.

The difference was not the discovery of the bit itself. It was about the variance of a foot soldier with a formidable mobile cavalry, or about the contrasting life of a small and secluded farm and an open larger economy whereby a superior force could carry their preserved milk and meat with them. More importantly, it amalgamated a world beyond previous traditional boundaries, and the world became symbiotic. According to Herodotus, Scythians entered into the area around the north of the Black Sea from Central Asia in the sixth century BC. Eventually, the old practices had to be recognised as inferior to ensure dramatic change – unless they wanted to be submerged under a superior civilization. Perhaps, East Asia is yet to find the real power of a 'horse'.

Let us listen to another grim 'cry' from the East. Jing Huang explained the presence of factional politics in China, 'Factionalism in Chinese Communist Party politics cannot be eliminated because it is innate to the system. The excessive factional struggles for power, however, can lead to an explosion that will undermine not only stability but also the supreme leader's position, given that his dominance is essentially based on his control of various mountaintops. Thus, it is in his best interest to keep factional activities under control.'[76] The existence of this factionalism in the Chinese top political echelon is by no means astonishing as the same political phenomenon is visible in Korea, Taiwan, and above all, in Japan and it constitutes the essence of its politics. We can plainly see that this political 'disease' came from the same 'virus'.

Another important characteristic of modern Chinese politics is that segmentation of power as a major feature of Chinese traditional ideology is still recognisable today. The argument between centralism and decentralism occasionally appeared in and outside of China. The decentralisation of China could lead to more democracy like US federalism. But historically China experienced many self-governing and uncontrollable regions and had realised that the delegation of power had to be carefully balanced, as otherwise it could appear simply as a more troublesome and another ineffective faction.

An experienced Chinese journalist, Chao Wendou, warned of the danger of this kind of divided state, once wished for by many Chinese politicians including the young Mao, by paying attention to what had happened in the South, 'For instance, the Guangdong regional government decided to approve the free exchange of US and Hong Kong dollars in Guangdong province in 1980. Simultaneously, they issued the large Renminbi bank note of a hundred Yuan with a unilateral decision in 1983. Such a misguided act is not possible even in the United States, which has a federal system... It is unimaginable that these things happened in a country regarded as highly centralised.' While the Chinese central government eventually acted by removing the leaders of Guandong province in a 'gentle' manner, Chao Wendou's caution remains valid, as a similar political mentality exists at various levels in China and cannot be easily eliminated.

He also observed rightly that the nature of Chinese society even under the communist state was a continuation of traditional farming society. As Liu Shaoqi once remarked, the ideal life of a Chinese man was, 'to own 30 Mu (200a or 5 acres) land and a cow to raise a family'; to protect this was the most important point of the Chinese revolution.[77] This aspiration remained as part of the major political element in post-war Chinese society as a whole.

The recent massive economic upheaval, however, brought unexpected problems to a Chinese society where this old agrarian dream became no longer valid in this newly emerging economic reality, as the Chinese urban population surpassed rural dwellers by 2010. In this demographic change, China's economy and society were rapidly transforming to capitalism but this change occurred only on the surface, as communist politics remained inflexible and rock solid with the unshakeable power of the state's armed forces ever present. More worryingly, the strengthening of arch-bureaucratic control exacerbated problems 'under the radar' even in times of prosperity. Like Japan, China refused, or more precisely, was unable to change its political direction to meet the new economic challenges.

Under these political and economic trends, China's new leaders headed by Hu Jintao were elected in a smooth succession process, or, that is to say, without any radical reform, through long summer holiday discussions among the party cadres at the exclusive Beidaihe seaside resort in 2002. In previous years, it seemed that Chinese leaders were selected who would focus on Shanghai development, the national project in the 1990s. As a new trend, President Hu and his number two, Premier Wen Jiabao, both had working experience in Gansu Province. Hu Jintao was regarded as an expert on the inner provinces with experience of further restructuring the government in Guizhou Province and the Tibet Autonomous Region.

In the first term of the Hu administration, the 'anchor' seemed to be Zeng Qinghong. The deputy premier had served as ex-bureau chief of Jiang Zemin in Shanghai but he stepped down from the post for Hu Jintao's second term. The re-elected president promoted 'scientific development' at the party congress in 2007, and 'meritocracy' of younger comrades. We should not overlook the fact, however, that the real power behind all these appointments was still firmly based on the old system of factionalism. What else can Chinese politicians rely on?

Despite lacking the charisma of his predecessors, Jiang Zemin remained as a conservative figurehead and the senior ex-head of state in the Chinese arch-bureaucracy. To develop the inner regions using the same successful tactics as in Shanghai, however, would be quite an uphill task for China as a policy of extending developments to other regions could face a risk of over-capacity. Can this 'advanced' arch-bureaucracy manage the direction of a Chinese power shift when it is required? The answer would unfortunately be 'No'.

Like every other successful nation, a sound service industry should have been created in order to meet the requirements of controlling newly created personal wealth and to balance expanded development. This basic economic situation was extremely similar to what has been happening in Japan during the 1980s and beyond. And those structures cannot be developed without political will even in this information age in which China has emerged as the world's largest internet user.

In the last sixty years or more, China has made enterprising ventures with growing confidence. Mao Zedong once declared he would 'liquidate all the ancient philosophical inheritance.' While he actually delved into such an arena and tried to change it, he could not succeed in altering Chinese traditional politics, which has survived in the form of people's mind-set. We do not require another militaristic revolution but we certainly need a stronger radical change than even this most powerful Chinese revolutionary achieved, across the politics of East Asia, to avoid a collision course under the current automatically applied double standard where arch-bureaucratisation inevitably proliferates and becomes uncontrollable.

The recent economic growth pattern in China showed that problems were accumulating in China's economic irregularities in the corporate sector including the inadequate infrastructure of its investment market. It is critical to analyse the process of the Chinese bubble, the cause of the Chinese economic crisis, and to seek its eventual reform. Assessing the real issues from a historical and current political perspective should be a subject assigned for a native Chinese expert. So we must leave a solution to this still unidentified person. The only certainty is that until somebody finds the solution and it is successfully implemented, economic implosion will fester under current Chinese politics, and the world needs to prepare for this outcome.

A CHINESE DEMOCRACY IN TAIWAN

'Taiwan is a paradise which is not yet tainted by communism,' wrote the Nationalist leader, Chiang Kai-shek, in his diary after he had inspected Taiwan for the first time in 1946. He was highly impressed with the status of this 'island fortress' with its extended infrastructure including railways, roads and an educational system all developed under the Japanese colonial government of the previous fifty years. From that day on, his subsequent strategy, until his final retreat from the continent in 1949, was to include Taiwan in his plans. As the tension with the communists grew, President Truman sanctioned the dispatch of the US 7th Fleet to dissuade a planned Chinese invasion from the mainland. Since then, there has existed a 'non-negotiable disagreement' between China and the United States over the issues of the Taiwan Strait.[78]

The strong military connection between the United States and Taiwan was extended to economic cooperation. With advice from US economic experts, the Taiwanese government applied a flexible policy towards foreign capital. In 1966 the Kaoshung Export Processing Zone was set up, an industrial development scheme for export destined mainly for the US and Japan. During this period, the power of the state sector was constantly diminished. For instance, in 1952, when all the former Japanese companies were nationalised, the public sector contribution to industrial production was around 56 per cent but this ratio was reduced to 13 per cent by 1973.[79] Under this steady economic trend, Taiwan exports grew by twenty times in thirteen years from 1959 to 1972.[80]

From this economic base, in order to reduce a heavy trade dependence on the United States and Japan, the government led the way in diversifying and finding new partners. In order to open new markets in Western Europe, Taiwan liberalised imports first from Western Europe, and later in 1979 abolished the ban on trade with Eastern Europe. By 1980, Europe emerged as Taiwan's second largest export market.[81]

As Taiwanese manufacturing capacity steadily improved, its trading account surplus increased further resulting in a booming economy in the late 1980s. With this solid progress, its economic ties with mainland China were strengthened. From November 1987, Taiwanese tourists were allowed to travel to the mainland via Hong Kong. In this new business environment, the thirty-eight years of martial law in Taiwan ended, and the Taiwanese trade and investment activities with mainland Chinese received a boost. Just as the Cantonese dialect-speaking Hong Kong had 'allied' with Guandong province, Fukienese dialect-speaking Taiwanese became deeply committed to developments in Fujian province and set up a special economic zone in Xiamen and introduced other investment projects.

Looking at this steady economic progress, in 1985, the Reagan administration recommended that Taiwan should democratise its politics. The Democratic Progress Party was formed in the following year under martial law. The Nationalists (the Kuomintang) had to recognise the new political party by the extraordinary order of President Chiang Ching-kuo under strong pressure from the US government. Finally, Lee Teng-hui, a vigorous Taiwanise reformer, who studied in Japan and the United States, was re-endorsed to continue as the President of the Republic in the first-ever Chinese democratic election in 1996. The election result was that his Nationalist Party won a majority with 103 seats but the Democratic

PART TWO – THE PRACTICAL TREND

Progress Party managed to win 52 seats and declared this as a 'victory'.

While the US and China had agreed on a diplomatic line giving the People's Republic of China legitimacy that led to Taiwan's expulsion from the United Nations in 1971, the Lee administration began to concentrate its own efforts on achieving independent political status for Taiwan in the international community. In 1995, President Lee met officials from Jordan and the United Arab Emirates, despite fierce protests from China. Since then Lee Teng-hui has extended his mission to other countries in the hope of gaining recognition for independent Taiwanese political status. It was obvious that Taiwan had here a most courageous modern Chinese politician, as no other individual was ever criticised so vehemently, constantly and threateningly by the Chinese state-owned press.

Despite these tensions with mainland China, the country's democracy moved further forward under the initiative of this strong Taiwanese leader by overtaking the Japanese at the functioning level of accountability in East Asia, together with South Korea. The people's awareness on the real political issues in Taiwan was hugely improved as the ratio of the Taiwanese members in the Central Committee of Kuomintang was increased to 52 per cent under the Lee administration by 1988.[82]

During the election campaign in 2000, Chinese officials harshly criticised Chen Shui-bian, the candidate for the opposition Democratic Progress Party, whom they claimed was leading the movement for eventual Taiwanese independence from the mainland. Having, however, been embarrassed by global criticism on their previous conduct, this time China refrained from shooting missiles in the Taiwanese Sea. The result of this election was somewhat similar to the US presidential election in 1992 in which Bill Clinton was running against George Bush senior. In Taiwan, James Soong was running as an independent candidate, just like Ross Perot, and split the Nationalists' vote. The final result was that Chen Shui-bian defeated his native Taiwanese opponent, Lien Chan, of the ruling Nationalist Party.

Thus, despite all the criticism from mainland China, for the first time in Chinese history, the people of Taiwan elected a leader from the newly created opposition party with their own free will using a democratic electoral system. But many East Asiatic political problems remained. Factional confrontation and corruption were rife in Taiwanese party politics and overall, its democracy was still fragile.

Compared to China, Taiwan is after all only a small island. Yet unlike Singapore or Hong Kong, it had a solid critical mass of over twenty million people as an independent state. Despite all the militant and narrow 'traditional' Chinese views, the existence of Taiwan benefited China tremendously, bringing its technologies and audacious entrepreneurial spirit to the mainland through its economic development model.

So, ahead of Chinese economic development in East Asia, were the two creditor nations of Taiwan and Japan. Without these nations, China's smooth entry to the global economy would have been doubtful. Today China has become the biggest creditor nation ever. But who on earth could be sure that a similar situation of Chinese poverty would never come up again? In any case, Taiwan seems to be the strongest candidate in the modern economic survival game among the three nations due to its flexible private sector economy and its transparency, and now retains an important position in East Asia. A sensible Chinese government would conclude that China still has need of this pleasant capitalistic island as an insurance policy.

Meanwhile, in Taiwanese society, influence from the Chinese mainland (including Hong Kong) was constantly increasing in terms of its work force and business activities. China emerged as its top trading partner in 2004, surpassing the US for Taiwanese exports. Despite a massive increase in China's military capability and this growing economic tie, to unite the two nations politically under the doctrine of the Chinese Communist Party – the old dream of the Red Guards that has somehow firmly survived in the mind of the mainland top cadres – seems unlikely even if the two successful economies converge.

The subsequent improvement in the country's relationship with mainland China under a Hong Kong born Nationalist President Ma

PART TWO – THE PRACTICAL TREND

Ying-jeou since 2008 marks another challenge for the Taiwanese people in advancing its politics and economy. Realistically, however, to fully accomplish a functioning democracy of its own, Taiwan will have to wait for an eventual political change on the other side of the strait.

THE ALTERING STATUS OF HONG KONG

Shortly after the British handover of sovereignty to China in July 1997, Hong Kong was suddenly stricken by the Asian financial crisis, which started initially with the depreciation of the Thai baht. By October, its contagion spread to Taiwan as the New Taiwan dollar took a tumble. Then a huge amount of speculative funds were placed on the Hong Kong dollar and its stock market in expectation of the break-up with its links to the US dollar. In this economic turmoil, the overnight Inter-bank rate of the Hong Kong dollar shot up by 280 per cent.[83] It was a critical moment for the government of Hong Kong under its newly established Chinese sovereignty.

Facing up to this challenging task in the new administration, the Hong Kong Monetary Authority and Financial Secretary, Donald Tsang, stood firm to protect its US dollar link, which he (and the British) deemed vital for the stability of Hong Kong and its economy. Fortunately, there was a sufficient amount of foreign currency reserves in Hong Kong by 1997 to counter this speculation. But the Hong Kong currency board system managed its own affairs without appealing to the British government, and apparently without any significant help from China.[84] How important was that? Well, eight years later, Donald Tsang emerged as the only candidate who could succeed to the chief executive's post in the eyes of Beijing.

On this occasion, the Hong Kong government impressed on the world that the efficiency of its bureaucracy which it inherited from the British political tradition did not alter even under Chinese rule. Unlike other East Asian bureaucracies, the Hong Kong government appointed its senior bureaucrats on the principle of merit, 'The claims of officers for promotion will be considered on the basis of official qualifications, experience and merit' – (*Colonial Regulation 24*).[85] Hong Kong also assumed the most extensive rule of law in East Asian society and a transparent business system under the British administration. This 'inherited asset' played a critical role even after the Chinese takeover of Hong Kong.

At first, Margaret Thatcher was relieved when Deng Xiaoping indicated to her that two economic systems could exist in one country, as she wrote, 'I found his analysis basically reassuring, if not persuasive.' Her astute observation was of a Briton with common sense. She also analysed the issue further, 'The Chinese belief that the benefits of a liberal economic system can be had without a liberal political system seems to me false in the long term.'[86] The British legacy in Hong Kong has been the creation and continuing existence of modern technocrats to bridge this gap.

With an efficient modern bureaucracy intact, a good sort of economic compromise could be achieved as all the systems were already in place. What China had to do was just to follow the 'British' rule and leave it to the Tung Chee-hwa's capable administration to handle matters independently. Hong Kong itself never had a democracy in a strict sense even under British rule but its legislative council was connected to the democratic UK government, as was its legal system to the High Court in London. The major British business groups and its equally experienced local businesses could easily run the city-state's economy with its population of around six million.

In other words, the new task was not to launch a satellite by rocket but rather to continue a flight on an established orbit. China went along with its required passive role rather well during this initial period. Following the major industrial boom in southern China that took place prior to Chinese rule, Hong Kong's role as the gateway to China, its capitalist stance and the attraction of its service infrastructure were not diminished by global financial industries, and China could enjoy Hong Kong's further prosperity despite its inherited market volatilities. On the other hand, no matter that it was invisible, we need to assume that Hong Kong's sinicisation (by Chinese ideology) started from Day One under Chinese sovereignty.

Hong Kong's economy as a British financial centre was always vulnerable to the political changes in China. Even when China's own 'market' economic policy was firmly on course and its influence expanded in Hong Kong, this factor did not decrease but became more prevalent. In this regard, economic factors from China including the movements of shares of the Chinese major business groups listed on the Hong Kong stock market became a somewhat sensitive issue to the stability of this former British colony, which existed with its own social network quite independently from the City of London.

As a key movement to this new economic environment in Hong Kong, the Chinese export market relied more and more on America. The US Department of Commerce announced that the increasing trade deficit with China in 2005 renewed its status as the largest record among US trading partners including the EU and Japan, at $201 billion, a 24.5 per cent increase on a year by year basis. It represented 27.7 per cent of the US total trade deficit of $726 billion. At least half of this amount was earned by foreign subsidiaries in China, but as more of Hong Kong became dependent on positive Chinese economic trends, the risk of a negative impact from the Chinese export economy also grew.

On the back of this economic trend, China's foreign currency reserve surged to US$1.9 trillion and left the 'silver medallist' Japan under the US$1 trillion mark by September 2008, just after the successful Beijing Olympic Games. This abnormal currency flow affected the structure of various financial business markets including the price of commodities in the West and became a major cause of the subsequent global financial bubble.

Against US demands to curb this excessive increase on Chinese imports, China responded negatively by giving priority to its export competitiveness exactly as the Japanese government had once behaved, while saying that they would not repeat the Japanese mistakes. These happened even with a stronger currency and other financial controls available for a state-driven economy but China tried to stick to its high growth target firmly based on exports. Without any dramatic events taking place, the reality was that Hong Kong was caught in the middle of this dispute.

No doubt Hong Kong's renowned efficiency and comparative advantages, which were once the best in the Chinese-speaking world, will remain as a key element for establishing an eventual Chinese democracy in the long term although Hong Kong needs to improve its own independent economy in a changing environment. There could be a rough period again in Hong Kong if the US-China economic relations become a politically confrontational issue, or if the Chinese bubble bursts unexpectedly.

COLONIAL POWER IN SINGAPORE

'Here all is life and activity; and it would be difficult to name a place on the face of the globe with brighter prospects or more pleasant satisfaction,' Thomas Stamford Raffles wrote to the Duchess of Somerset in 1822.[87] The British East India Company knew the importance of Singapore's strategic location amongst the richest Dutch colonial islands in Indonesia. And it was due to new British naval superiority gained after the Napoleonic wars that made this enterprise sustainable.

Originally, the island was almost uninhabited and so the Singaporean economy started purely as a British venture. Backed by Eastern trade, Singapore's rapid growth seemed to be assured as soon as it was established as a free port by 1823. Since then the population of Singapore and its ratio of Chinese immigrants have constantly risen.

This was a rare example of a British colony, which was taken over, not by the indigenous population, but by Chinese immigrants. Why did this situation evolve? Overall, it was achieved by Chinese resilience. The many small European traders lost business to the industrious Chinese merchants who controlled not only the local market but also a broader regional business with its trading networks in South East Asia and China. When Singapore broke away from the federation of Malaysia to become an independent republic in 1965, over 70 per cent of the population were of Chinese extraction, immigrants originally from other Chinese trading spots in East Asia including mainland China.

From this background, one could conclude that Singaporeans are the most internationally oriented Chinese people. It is simple to assess this mind-set if you ask a Singaporean, 'Where are you from?' If you ask this question of a Hong Konger, most of them would answer, 'I am Chinese.' But a Singaporean would reply, 'I am Singaporean.' They are fully aware that their country is a state made up of immigrants like the United States, although on a much smaller scale, and with a completely different political perspective.

But it doesn't mean Singaporeans are less concerned about their Chinese origin. On the contrary, Singaporeans have a burning sense of pride in their Chinese identity, equal to any other group in the Chinese economic area. They constantly had to struggle in a foreign and harsh environment. It seems that this sort of fighting spirit came from their ancestors' resolve not to mix with indigenous people and lose their own bloodlines or to become submerged in the native soil. This sense of identity was bolstered by many folk tales and social traditions, and by their confidence that the existence of a strong Confucianistic philosophy and spiritual links would uphold their success.

The founder of the state and Cambridge law graduate, Lee Kuan Yew's political philosophy was surprisingly Chinese when he made speeches. But the well-balanced leader never gave in to a Chinese-style leadership when he made a move to politics. One's heart might belong to China but the brain always thinks of its own pocket! Some say that it is wrong to conceive of Singapore as a state. It should be considered merely as a conglomerate of businesses. From this political base, Singapore's situation at the crossroads of Chinese culture and trade was indeed politically difficult to handle in a multi-racial society and we must recognise the extraordinary progress made under his leadership.

Lee's political career could be traced back to his London days just after the Second World War. An organization known as the Malaya Forum, established with his lieutenants, Goh Keng Swee and Abdul Razak, brought them together to discuss the kind of society and government that would replace British Malaya.[88] In Singapore, the Chinese political system was contained by the adoption of the English language and British commercial and administrative practices including its legal system.

But, at the beginning, even his realistic policies aroused confusion and resistance among Chinese conservative groups. When this confrontation was at its height, an unfortunate incident took place as three journalists on the *Nanyang Sing Pao*, a then-prominent Chinese-language newspaper, were arrested and the paper had to be closed down after it had vehemently criticised the government, in particular its policy on education with respect to Chinese language and culture. The pragmatic nature of Singaporeans was required to overcome this incident and Lee Kuan Yew was bold enough to stand firm on his course for this former colonial outpost.

After Singapore was given autonomy from Britain in 1959, the road to full independence was a turbulent one. The critical moment arrived when, in 1963, Lee Kuan Yew, as the leader of the People's Action Party, decided to join the Federation of Malaysia where more than half the population was also made up of Chinese descendants.

Eventually, however, disagreements between Singaporeans and the administration in Kuala Lumpur, plus an uncertain economic climate, led to Singapore's departure from the federation in 1965. As a leader of Chinese immigrants, it was not an easy separation. He could not stop crying when he declared his secession in front of world reporters. There was an actual danger that the Malaysian military would act against the Singaporeans on the ground of treason, but the British government intervened to stop Malaysia, thereby saving Singapore.[89]

This experience of being part of the Malayan Federation was, after all, not entirely fruitless particularly for Singapore and Prime Minister Lee himself. Having been in the federation, he had learnt a great deal and emerged with increased confidence as a realistic and determined political leader of this small but vibrant city-state.

In 1967, a major economic change arrived in Singapore when Harold Wilson's Labour government announced the withdrawal of all the British garrisons from east of Suez. The economic base of British colonial policy had to be adjusted with the rise of the United States as a global economic power. A revolutionary change to military perspectives was to be followed by the emergence of the subsequent superpowers. For instance, the US Arms Lending Act to India was signed directly without British involvement in 1943, and was a first sign of this forthcoming global change.[90] To Singapore, however, the new British policy shift meant a loss of 13 per cent of its GNP and 40,000 jobs.[91]

Singapore took the change as an opportunity. The demise of British involvement was to be compensated by incoming oil-refineries, for which Singapore was a perfect location. Bukum Island and other sites were designated to construct gigantic oil-refining facilities with a production capacity of 800,000 barrels a day. This investment came from major American and British oil companies. Massive foreign investment also poured into the petroleum-related sector and spread into other industrial sectors. The Jurong industrial complex was built on reclaimed swampland to accommodate these requirements. Multinational corporations from North America, Europe and Japan gradually occupied the complex. The change also provided a boost to Singapore's cargo-handling business, which subsequently became the largest port in Asia.

In addition to these 'legacy of Raffles' businesses, Lee Kuan Yew wanted to employ town planning of an international standard to turn Singapore into a 'garden city', set in a leafy environment, which would be not only a pleasant place to live but also an attractive tourist and business destination. Using his economic achievements, he wanted Singapore to also exercise a regional influence. He made Singapore's regional role clear in a speech to the French National Employers' Federation in Paris in May 1990, 'Singapore was fortunate to have made the right economic choices and by linking up with Europe, the US and Japan, had played a crucial ancillary role that had ensured its survival. It had made itself a desirable base from which multinationals could extend into other developing countries. The next key role was for Singapore to help accelerate the development of the region, for as its neighbours grew, it would grow too.'[92]

Having set up all the political foundations, he appointed his deputy prime minister and trained economist, Goh Chok Tong to be prime minister in 1990, and as the party leader in 1992, as an 'interim' administration before handing over to his son, Lee Hsien Loong, who had earlier experienced health problems. This 'dynastic' change was actually made in August 2004 after fourteen prolonged years of the Goh administration. His critics opposed such East Asiatic thinking as undemocratic nepotism.

Democracy in Singapore is not of an advanced nature despite its growing economic presence in the region. But the country is not in a hurry to change under the Lee family's beneficial form of control and the last thing Singapore needs is political instability. As long as Singapore remains at this level, a sort of Swiss-style major multi-national corporation, more democratic systems may not be expected from this island. With solid economic progress, Singapore's unique position as an active business location in South East Asia will continue with its accumulated wealth and good management although the uncertainty over global financial markets in general could affect its overall capacity. The island state can probably afford to wait for change until other nations in East Asia catch up to its economic vantage point.

SUCCESSFUL IMMIGRATION TO SOUTH EAST ASIA

A noticeable movement prior to Chinese and the subsequent European expansion to South East Asia was the arrival from the eleventh century onwards of a significant number of Islamic traders initially from the Arabian Peninsula. But the Islamisation of the region only began in the thirteenth century, almost parallel with its expansion in India. The most influential people in this development were the merchants of the Indian subcontinent who spread their influence to the region with the benefits of a lucrative trade with India, Arabia and beyond.[93] Islam soon became the major local religion in Malaya, Indonesia, southern Thailand and southern Philippines, and a solid religious base was established in other countries in South East Asia.

By the early sixteenth century, when the first European sea power, Portugal, seized Malacca, these systems of Islamic and Chinese maritime business networks and immigration throughout all of South East Asia were already thriving. For the European colonial governments and traders, it was vital that they used this link to succeed. In this particular place, the power of the Chinese immigrants played a decisive role for the Portuguese against the larger local Sultan's force in Malacca in August 1511.[94] The vanguard of this new Chinese 'colonisation' was helped by hard-working characters of the *Hakka* people with their own dialect and customs, who had originally colonised Southern China from their native Northern China with determination and tenacity.

As urban centres were set up after the European arrivals, it created constant new demands for immigration from China to the region. The access to a vast Chinese consumer market for local goods and agricultural products, including rice, was a major strength for the Chinese merchants and farmers wherever they settled in South East Asia. Only Chinese could provide the European colonial powers as suppliers, or 'comprador' as they were then called, of various articles of merchandise and as a reliable labour force.

The Chinese model of immigration meant that people from various parts of China could participate in this venture, using the Chinese *Bang* – kinship network. Wherever you went, Confucian temples and the kinship society were there to help new arrivals and to facilitate their economic independence. It was a different form of Chinese expansion outside their traditional boundaries. Generally speaking, the numbers of immigrants grew rapidly whenever there was an economic crisis in the homeland. But there was another factor as well. For instance, when gold was discovered in Pontianac,

Western Borneo in 1740, there were less than one hundred Chinese immigrants. By the 1770s, the population had increased to over twenty thousand. Later they formed an independent communal union, which paid tribute to the Qing dynasty.[95]

The Philippines was another place which experienced massive Chinese immigration. Here the Chinese residents were confronted by a leading European power. In the Spanish Philippines, when the Chinese population hit a level of fifteen thousand in Manila in 1621, which was a third of the entire population then in the Filipino capital, the Spanish colonial government tried to control and oppress Chinese immigration. The immigrants were arriving in fleets of junks from China and often penetrated into society carrying out illegal activities. A further political development affecting the Spanish immigration policy towards the Chinese was during the Seven Years War (French and Indian War 1756-63) which broke out in Europe. The indigenous population stood side by side with Spain but the Chinese supported the British. In this political environment, the Spanish officials thought Chinese immigration growth too rapid and that it was possibly endangering the stability of their colony.[96]

There were obvious differences from the situation in Malaya partly due to the Philippines' proximity to mainland China, plus most of the local population had converted to Christianity in the northern and central Philippines. Against the government's policy of suppression, many Chinese had to assimilate and adopt Spanish or other indigenous names and become Christians. It was therefore statistically impossible to calculate an accurate number of Chinese immigrants. Despite the Spanish policies of oppression, Chinese immigrants managed to control the economy of the Philippines including the southern island of Mindanao where the dominant population are Muslim.

The Chinese descendants of the original immigrants also made inroads into the country's politics, unlike in other parts of the region. They included most influential politicians such as the Marcos and Aquino families and others who became completely assimilated into the indigenous population. The Filipino-Chinese run many of the big and local businesses and there is no doubt they are the largest influential ethnic group in the Philippines' economy.

In Thailand, the business leaders who are of Chinese origin also predominate as the largest influential corporate group. In a similar situation to the Philippines, they were absorbed into the mainstream and most of them are difficult to differentiate from the ethnic Thais. The most influential kinship group among the Chinese immigrants came from Chiuchow (or Chaozhou), in northern Guangdong province and they originally controlled the rice trade in and out of Thailand. Chinese merchants expanded the trade with new investments by setting up vital depots for all the necessary goods. In the early days of industrialisation, they quickly established their businesses as agents of the various Japanese and western companies that moved into the country.

The Thais are considered to originate from an area in today's southern China. There were distinguishable cultural similarities, including the use of a sensitively tone-based language between the Thais and the southern Chinese from this historical link. Thais seemed generally receptive to Chinese culture as long as they followed Thai customs. The ethnic Chinese were also represented in the politics of Thailand. But they seemed to stay away from the sources of military power after a Chinese descendant military leader and later a king, Taaksin or Zheng Zhao, was assassinated in the eighteenth century, as he tried to challenge the supreme political authority. Since then, the only area where Chinese influence was almost non-existent or rather 'off limits' was Thailand's military services.

It is interesting to note that Japanese immigrants to South East Asia never thrived in this way. It was recorded that there was once a Japanese town in Ayutthaya in Thailand where they worked as the king's guards or in Davao in the Philippines where they were employed in the jute trade, or sizeable communities in Manila or Jakarta. Gradually, all those immigrants were eventually assimilated by the local and Chinese populations and disappeared as a racial group without any trace. The few Japanese who had moved or 'deserted' their country becoming eventually disconnected with their single-mode ideology without Confucianism; they seemed to become rootless among local people and unable to make human connections amongst themselves in societies where perhaps the rule of law was weak.

A new wave of Chinese immigrants came into the Mekong delta area. Their biggest contribution was to cultivate the huge rice field and since the eighteenth century became the dominant economic power in southern Vietnam. After the Vietnam War, the central government in Hanoi persecuted the Chinese population including the largest community in Ho Chi Minh City, and many ethnic Chinese 'boat people' fled to other countries. This was the main cause for the subsequent Chinese military intervention in Vietnam.

Historically, the Han dynasty annexed Vietnam in the first century. The Vietnamese were forced to adopt Chinese ideology and accepted the usage of Chinese characters – the only indigenous nation to embrace it in South East Asia. But the Vietnamese were asked to forsake the old practice including its writing system under new French colonial rule which started in 1862.

Chinese immigrants also kept a major commercial critical mass in Cambodia. In Phnom Penh, like in Thailand, the Chiuchow-Chinese were most active in retail business in this rapidly developing nation's economy after a long absence in the violent era of the Khmer Rouge.

Myanmar (Burma) was another country where significant Chinese immigrants ended up. There were more than 500,000 Chinese, second only to the Indian population in the country. This may be one of the reasons for the Chinese government's friendly posture towards the military government in Myanmar and its controversial record on human rights.

The largest Chinese population among South East Asian countries is in Indonesia. The estimate varies from 3.6 to 7.2 millions.[97] The country was built up mainly by Dutch colonialism, in the sense that no past Indonesian historical empire reached to its current expanded boundary. As soon as Achmed Sukarno took over the newly independent country of Indonesia from Japan after the Second World War, he had to start with fresh ideas.[98] He succeeded in the immense task of keeping this large nation together with a new spirit of Indonesian nationalism, linked strongly with modern Malaysia via the island of Sumatra. In this new movement, many Chinese became naturalised by taking Indonesian surnames to avoid persecution. Under Thojib Suharto's following regime, Chinese businesses strengthened with industrial and urban developments. Chinese descendants were politically passive and stayed away from the military establishment which enjoyed special political status under the country's constitution.

In Malaysia, many ethnic Chinese kept their traditional identities in contrast to the indigenous Malay native *bumiputra*, 'son of the soil'. With the country's abundant natural resources, Malays became rich and powerful as the age of the global economy arrived. But some frictions appeared as the Chinese inhabitants used their power to seize the opportunities of this new economic expansion. They are the country's largest ethnic group, making up almost half of the population.

Key state and related major corporations were kept out of Chinese hands. But the Chinese business community had a strong presence in retailing, trading, property, and some banking and service sectors, following in the footsteps of their ancestor, Yap Ah Loy, who enjoyed remarkable success despite arriving without a penny later owned half of the land in Kuala Lumpur in the 1860s.[99] Only a few Chinese seemed to convert to Islam although China had a long tradition of peaceful co-existence with Islam, in particular in its western and southern regions.

The power of these overseas Chinese businesses, including companies from Taiwan, Hong Kong, Singapore and mainland China, and its business network in South East Asia, leapt after the rapid industrialisation of the 1980s. The flow of investments from these overseas Chinese settlements to China and to other countries were indispensable for successful development in the region. Many overseas Chinese companies took advantage of the tax haven status of Hong Kong and moved into its capital market. For example, the amalgamated Chinese (Taiwan, China, Hong Kong and Singapore) investments in the Philippines had already by 1987 surpassed those of the US and Japan combined, and a similar trend prevailed throughout the region.[100] It would be fair to say, therefore, that the power of the Chinese business communities in the region as a whole is so great that future economic developments in South East Asia cannot be achieved without their contributions.

II – SOUTH KOREA

A FALTERING IDEALISM

Korean Christian martyrdom inspired by Bishop Imbert of France first took place in 1839. Since then the Christian church in Korea has continued to appear as a sort of pressure group under Japanese rule. Among the repressive measures taken by the Japanese against the Korean Christians was a massacre in the village of Cheamni, near Suwon in April 1919. Rev. Herbert Welch, a bishop of the Methodist Episcopal Church in Korea, visited Tokyo to discuss this tragedy with the Japanese government.

The Japanese prime minister replied, 'I desire to assure you that the report of abuses committed by agents of the Japanese government in Korea has engaged my most serious attention.' Following the prime minister's recommendation, shortly afterwards, the Japanese emperor officially appointed the 'milder' Admiral Saito as the new governor-general for Korea.[101] Japan was in already shaky, but still relatively good shape, and the Japanese prime minister at the time was Takashi Davide Hara.[102]

Takashi (also pronounced as Kei) Hara through his career as journalist, diplomat and businessman, struggled against the growing militarism of Japanese politics. He was one of the very few Japanese politicians who understood the importance of democratic values.[103] Two years later, after a landslide election victory, he was assassinated by a political thug at Tokyo station before being able to carry through his political reforms. Korea then became the focus of false-Japanese imperialism in this cycle of Chinese ideological expansion.

To replace the disastrous Japanese colonial regime, Rhee Syngman, then aged seventy-three, seemed to be an ideal and sufficiently mature man to face this challenging moment in Korean history by establishing a modern democracy in the newly born South Korean state in 1948. Everything looked perfect from his career – various academic achievements, long experience of living in the US, together with his Korean background etc… A year later, however, many people realised that his mentality and posture belonged to the same old anachronic ruling class of Korea known as *Yangban*.

The economic situation in the South Korea was initially unstable, and the Rhee regime was not progressing on this vital front, despite a newly developed favourable political base. In this rather discouraging environment, underground activists from the North successfully penetrated into some Southern cities where they were causing constant problems. A worrying signal was that some might have also entered into the heart of the South Korean army.

In this volatile atmosphere, the Korean War was brewing. As many historians have already argued, it is still a mystery, why in the US Secretary of State, Dean Acheson's speech at the National Press Club in Washington, did he exclude South Korea from the US defence perimeter? Gary Donaldson thought that 'Acheson's speech certainly reflected the administration's budget considerations.' He further explained, 'Congress and the president in this period were under great pressure from the electorate to cut spending and move toward a balanced budget, and it was on military spending that the budget axe was falling the hardest.'[104] But in a larger picture, some believed that there was a 'poker game' element to this US move. Under these circumstances, the Americans decided to unilaterally remove all the US combat troops from South Korea in June 1949, leaving only a few hundred military advisers behind, and therefore, the country was left virtually unguarded.

The fact was that when the North Korean Army invaded the South military conditions became hopeless in South Korea but the political situation improved in an equally drastic manner. Truman might not have been so excited about this news as much as Churchill was when he heard about the Japanese attack on Pearl Harbor but he certainly rose to the challenge.

At the same time, the viability of the Rhee regime was confirmed as strong anti-communist sentiments emerged with the outbreak of war from the North which publicly exposed evil and cruelty in various incidents during the invasion. The majority of people in South Korea were now convinced that the North was not a reliable ally after all. Finally, an immense force from the US was directed to South Korea to win the war and to restore the country after its wartime destruction.

Even after peace was restored, however, President Rhee continued to demonstrate his old oppressive, dogmatic and rogue nature to the people including the practice of election rigging. Frustrated student demonstrators clashed with the police in the capital. As more professors and ordinary citizens joined an enlarged protest against him, South Korean politics became confused and lost its direction. Rhee also applied his hostile diplomacy towards Japan. With his newly acquired naval power, he set up the 'Rhee Syng-man Line' by force, declaring the uninhabited island of Takeshima (Liancourt Rocks or Tok-to in Korean) to be in Korea's inside zone and suddenly declared it as Korean territory in 1952.

Despite all this political turbulence, Rhee Syng-man's era and the subsequent rule of President Yun Po-son, were without a doubt meaningful to the people of Korea, and for South Korean democracy. Korean people learned that true democracy would be difficult to attain. But the South Koreans accepted the presidency system and progressed it by their own volition with American advice.[105] They realised that political decisions were vital for the survival for the nation.

In this era of hardship for the Koreans, the foundation of Korean democracy was laid but it was still fragile and, as in the French Revolution, there was military intervention afterwards but it only strengthened the Korean determination.

On the Theory of Chinese Ideology

CATCHING UP WITH THE JAPANESE ECONOMY

The Korean War had an impact on Japan in two ways. Firstly, it was an immense impetus for growth in the war-wrecked and still fragile Japanese economy. Secondly, the American effort to establish a democracy through trial and error in Japan had to be declared as 'completed', as soon as the alarming hostilities in the Korean peninsula were witnessed. In other words, the US efforts, which could be linked to American idealism, had to be now changed to a more pragmatic realisation that saw Japan as a solid base in the war against communism.

In return, the Japanese economic 'miracle' in the 1960s began to affect South Korea in a reverse direction. The new relationship between the two countries remained at its lowest ebb with Japanese embarrassed indifference on one side and residual Korean anger as a result of historical Japanese aggression in the peninsula. It was particularly important for the South Korean economy to co-operate with Japanese manufacturing businesses in this newly developed economic environment. US anti-communist policy, which was again firing up over Vietnam, required a *rapprochement* between the two 'allies' as a necessary step to enhance the free nations' camp in East Asia.

In South Korea, revolutionary political change in this direction was made possible by the *coup d'etat* led by Park Chung-hee in 1961. It was inevitable that the 'fully-invested' Korean army, navy and air force with 650,000 soldiers and sailors would emerge as the most powerful element in society after the Korean War. Just before the war, Park Chung-hee had been wrongly arrested on the suspicion of a communist link under 'Korean McCarthyism'. He might have been convinced that his life was utterly unpredictable as regarding politics, and decided to chance all.

As an experienced professional soldier, his military career was his greatest asset. Throughout his time in various army posts, he nurtured significant support from young officers who were gradually promoted to the highest hierarchy in the Korean military. Finally, an opportunity seemed to arrive. By this time, the forty-three-year-old was secretly confident that by relying on this growing military power now under his control, he could take the country on a better course. All the factors indicated to him that it was a case of 'now or never' to take a stand against the evidently unpopular government of Prime Minister Chang Myon and President Yun Po-son, which laboured with economic difficulties but could not reach a compromise with the Japanese.

Park Chung-hee could not speak English well but he spoke impeccable Japanese as a result of his time as a Japanese military academy cadet and later as an infantry officer in the Manchurian state army in the pre-war Japanese Empire. As a typical commoner, he was quite different from the previous leaders of South Korea who had a wealthy family background and a western education. In Korean history, revolts emanating from the lower peasant class had always saved the country in a time of crisis. Korean political struggles needed a strong leader rather than a weak aristocrat. Major General Park was certainly equipped to fit the bill.

His confidence was based on his capability to deal with the Japanese. In Japan, many ex-Manchurian bureaucrats including former Prime Minister Nobusuke Kishi influenced its early economic policy. Broadly speaking, Park belonged to this group. As a brilliant military officer, he also knew the importance of intelligence, having seen the Japanese failures in Manchuria. For practical decision-making, therefore, he was keen to establish an intelligence agency, the KCIA, modelled on American lines, which began his anti-communism campaign.

After his sudden accession to power, the US government, having previously helped South Korea, now had to control the country from a distance, like a cowboy would have done to a strayed cow by 'roping'. Upon renewed pressure from the US administration, Park Chung-hee, as Chairman of the Supreme Council for National Reconstruction, had to set forth explicit details of how and when the transfer of the government to civilian rule was to be accomplished. He declared a new constitution was to be established prior to March

1963, and political activities to resume in preparation for the general election in October 1963.[106]

As soon as he was elected to be the president of the Korean Republic, Park approached the Japanese government to normalise their relationship despite fierce opposition from the former President Yun's party. In 1965, the historical treaty between Japan and South Korea was signed on his initiative. Japan agreed to pay and lend US$800 million to South Korea. Because of this agreement, many Japanese companies established business relationships with their Korean counterparts.

The result of this policy shift produced a visible impact on the South Korean economy. For instance, the Pohang Steel Company (Posco) built world-class steel mills with an annual production capacity of 9m tons through Japanese know-how, and various other technologies were transferred from Japan to South Korea to form the basis of Korea's own subsequent economic revolution.

Double digit growth was assured in the late sixties as the war in Vietnam gave a momentum to the South Korean economy. This helped to establish a solid Japanese-style export-oriented economy in South Korea. On the diplomatic front, President Park sent its elite 'Tiger' division of forty thousand to Vietnam following a US request. This news pleased even the liberals in the United States who were critical of South Korea's military regime. But under the Park regime, the pace of the Korean democratic movement slowed down. After all, he was not a believer in democracy. In a booming economy, however, this was not an issue as he won a second term of office in the May 1967 election.

In 1969, President Park and his party successfully amended the constitution so he could serve a third term – something that had been prohibited by the previous constitution. Some worried that this could be an ominous sign of his problematic desire to cling on to power. The South Korean people endorsed him in November 1972 on his *Yushin* government and the National Conference for Unification, and removed restrictions on the terms of office for the president as political uncertainty emerged in South Korea with the visit of President Nixon to China.

The subsequent global economic turbulence from rising oil prices embroiled his regime in late 1973 although the South Korean economy was able to withstand this, despite constant threats from the North, and grew at a terrific pace. On the other hand, Park's discredited policies were already apparent in 1973 when he ordered the KCIA to kidnap the opposition leader, Kim Dae-Jung, while he was staying in Tokyo.

In December 1977, President Park triumphed at the celebration party held in Seoul stadium when Korean exports finally exceeded US$10 billion, and boasted of his and his county's achievements, '… Fifteen years ago, our exports were a tiny US$55 million when we planned the first economic development plan for five years. Today, we have achieved our objective of US$10 billion, four years earlier than our plan. It took eleven years for the great economic power of West Germany to reach its target from US$1 billion to US$10 billion. It took sixteen years for Japan. We have made it in seven years. We attained it in an environment where we had to face the jingoists in our divided country and a global depression. Exports of US$10 billion have a great significance to us as it shows the limitless power and potential of our nation.'[107]

After the election in 1978, the student demonstrations surged as the labour unions begun to dispute his policy with violent protests. More harsh measures were required to avoid further social confusion in a changing economic environment. Then, in a dramatic and sudden dispute, the president was shot dead by his director of the KCIA at a presidential hideout. The longest-serving South Korean president's reign abruptly ended in October 1979.

Throughout the period of political uncertainty, the ambitious General Chun Doo-hwan moved to take over the presidency in 1980, disregarding all requests for democracy. He belonged to the leading military junta, which had supported Park Chung-hee's original uprising. The Korean economy continued to advance even under these political setbacks.

In October 1987, Roh Tae-woo, as presidential candidate

supported by the Chun's military faction, accepted the opposition's demand for a direct presidential election. Overall, he seemed to be much more balanced than his predecessor and gained popularity through this act. In 1988, elected President Roh opened the Seoul Olympics. Having successfully established diplomatic relationships with Russia, South Korea became a member of the United Nations together with North Korea in 1991 and its diplomatic relationship with China was restored in 1992. The Koreans were ready to advance as a rare example of a democratic nation in East Asia as its military leaderships ended in a sort of self-destruction process, losing their force in a declining economy.

EMERGING DEMOCRACY

The Koreans enthusiastically welcomed a civilian president, Kim Young-sam, after a long absence when many years of military rule ended in February 1993. Shortly afterwards, Chun Doo-hwan and Roh Tae-woo were arrested on charges of corruption as public opinion was eager for harsh retaliation to the dark legacy left by the military regimes. By prosecuting the former presidents from the Korean military, and by shaming their memory, the president hoped that he could eradicate forever the possibility of a military coup in Korea's political future.

In fact, he was rather good at destruction, but sometimes he went too far. He demolished the former Japanese governor's office which was being used as a history museum and was the only western classical building in Seoul designed by a German architect. It was also the site of the inauguration ceremony of the Republic of Korea. Was this really a necessary step for Korean democracy?

Sung-hwa Cheong explained the background behind this kind of political manipulation, 'In considering anti-Japanese sentiment in Korea, it is important to analyse not only the issues that provoked anti-Japanese feeling but also the political environment in South Korea.' And he pointed out, 'Most political groups in the Republic of Korea exploited the latent hatred of the Korean populace toward Japan for their own political purpose.'[108] Perhaps, this unabated rigid mentality remains as the last hurdle for Koreans (and for Japanese too) to clear for establishing their own democracy.

On the contrary, Kim Young-sam was unable to launch his creative policies during his tenure, especially, for running the economy. At the end of 1992, just before President Kim was elected, Korean foreign debt was $42.8 billion. This figure enlarged to $164.3 billion by 1996. This was partially a consequence of Korea joining the OECD as an open economy and the deregulations that resulted in an outflow of foreign currency.[109] As Kim was not well prepared for identifying and solving such difficulties, South Korea was soon bound to be caught in a serious economic crisis.

The inflow of foreign direct investment (FDI) continued to be low: $1.9 billion in 1995 and $3.2 billion in 1996. Facing this situation, Kim Young-sam announced the formation of a presidential commission consisting of thirty-one members drawn from the industrial and financial sectors and academic circles to hammer out counter-measures in January 1997. But it was too little and too late. Later, as the economy improved with IMF reforms, those figures increased to $6.97 billion in 1997 and $8.85 billion in 1998 while Korea's ratio of FDI to GDP remained among the lowest both in Asia and among the OECD nations.[110]

Meanwhile, the Asian financial crisis gradually spread into South Korea. As the country's financial turmoil deepened, South Korea had to seek a bailout loan from the IMF which meant that Kim Young-sam's chance to run for the following year's presidential election was over. In the 1998 presidential election, overshadowed by the economic environment, Kim Dae-jung rose like a phoenix.

Kim Dae-jung was originally from Cholla province in the southwest of the peninsula which, although the richest in agriculture, lacked industrial power. The reason why Kim Dae-jung could not win the previous elections was largely related to regional and factional politics in Korea, which were, as already noted, rooted in ancient historical and Confucianism elements.

For him, it was vital to focus on the Seoul district and the Kyongsang and Chungchong provinces in order to win the election. Carl Saxer explained, 'Kim Dae-jung only won the election because… he had acted to expand his voter base by going into a coalition with another regionally based politician.' It was a narrow victory but one with political significance and he finally made it. And 'the election resulted for the first time in a power alternation with an opposition candidate winning the presidency, and as such it constituted an important step on the road towards democratic consolidation in Korea.'[111] Kim Dae-jung seemed to have accumulated his political knowledge when he had to lie low while in opposition and spent some time as an academic in the United States and in Britain before dealing with this international crisis in Korea.

A set of radical reforms in South Korea focused on both the financial and industrial sectors where *Chaebol* – a sort of Japanese-style conglomerate – was abolished and state-owned enterprises were privatised while flexibility in the labour market was preserved. And this was vigorously implemented under his leadership. Among the big four Chaebol, Daewoo collapsed and Hyundai disintegrated. The others were forced to sell their non-core businesses. In this economic crisis, South Korea showed amazing political resilience in tackling its problems, and transparency in the Korean economy was hugely improved. Above all, it appeared as a historical victory for Korean democracy and capitalism.

President Kim also took the initiative on the diplomatic front by visiting North Korea to see Kim Jong-il, as the state head of South Korea for the first time, in June 2000. His 'Sunshine policy' or the policy of engagement toward the North was not an easy task to complete. But the importance of South Korea's offering help to the people of the North who were struggling in a depleting economy was perhaps an overwhelming reason for his move.

On the other hand, the secluded Northern leader had his own strictly domestic agenda, and in most cases, he found only difficulty in keeping his promises. For instance, Kim Jong-il could neither reciprocate a visit to the Southern capital nor unfortunately take bold steps for further progress. Despite a political breakthrough and the subsequent calmer relationship, economic co-operation between the two brother nations stalled. The Mt Kumgang sightseeing project which was originally financed by the Hyundai group and the development of the Kaesong industrial park barely survived – or were deemed as quasi-dead – and various difficulties and scepticism gradually deepened on both sides.

Kim Dae-jung tried to renew the relationship with Japan for future co-operation of these two developed Asian nations. Lifting the ban on the import of Japanese music CDs and films, he visited Japan to convey this change soon after his inauguration in 1998. For the first time, the Japanese saw an impressive leader from South Korea and some might have wondered what was wrong with their own politicians. To many of the people of Japan, it was obvious that South Korea under Kim Dae-jung seemed to surpass Japan in terms of being a functioning democracy, in particular, on its decisive economic reforms. What was completely different in his political stance was that he refused to be trapped by populism and boldly applied a mix of fair policies to the troubled areas including the renewal of diplomatic relations with Japan. It was nothing magical in itself but was executed with his magical resolve.

A chilling threat blocking South Korea's democratic goals and economic prosperity was, however, the constant militaristic noises and conduct from the North, with its development of long-range missiles and nuclear weapons. This kind of inter-relationship between the South and the North could be described as the 'Korean dilemma' in which the South's dazzling progress has to be somewhat offset by a dangerous uncertainty in the North. In this fluid situation, it would be difficult to assume South Korea can generate the 'engine's' role for the further evolution of East Asia as long as this Korean dilemma continues.

To make matters worse, as the new leadership in North Korea is losing its diplomatic calibre after the death of Kim Jong-il in December 2011, South Korea's fortunes are an unpredictable political risk rather than a calculable economic one. For political reform in the East Asian politics, we need to focus, therefore, most reluctantly, on the situation in Japan where the same 'old sick man' is in danger of slipping out from the edge of the international community again.

III – NORTH KOREA

THE FAILURE OF AUTOCRACY

In August 1949, Soviet Russia successfully tested its first atomic bomb at a secret location in Kazakhstan. The news arrived quickly, creating a kind of enthusiasm in communist East Asia. In mid-December 1949, Mao Zedong left China for the first time in his life, heading a large and imposing Chinese delegation to the Soviet Union.

In the company of leaders of the other communist parties, he took part in the celebration of Stalin's seventieth birthday. Mao and his delegation greeted the incoming New Year there, but it was not until the middle of February 1950 that a treaty of friendship, union and mutual assistance, to last thirty years, was signed between the USSR and the People's Republic of China (PRC). Before departing from Moscow, he gave a farewell address at Yaroslav station, 'People can see that the unity of two great nations, China and the Soviet Union, reinforced by the treaty, will be eternal, indestructible, and that nobody will ever be able to tear us apart.'[112]

Kim Il-sung too made trips to the Kremlin in this era. But the main purpose of his stay in Moscow seemed to get Stalin's support for his planned invasion of the South. He was confident of the North's military superiority enhanced by equipment and supplies from Soviet Russia. In fact, North Korea was stronger economically than the South in the initial stages of post-war Korea.

Under Japanese rule, investments and developments for Korean industrialisation were concentrated on the North. Consequently, the requisition of the former Japanese military-industrial assets was much bigger in North Korea. The best of those facilities were those of the ex-Chosen Chisso's (Korean Nitrogen's) several power plants and military complex alongside the Yalu and Tumen Rivers. In 1944, electricity capacity of two million kilowatts in total had been achieved in this plant under Japanese management, and it remained intact during the war. This foundation gave a huge advantage to the North to launch and to sustain its communist regime.[113]

Meanwhile, Kim Il-sung gathered from his intelligence agents who had penetrated deeply into the South that morale under the Rhee Syng-man regime was particularly low, under the threat of impending economic difficulty. He might have further thought that if he could enter into the South as a liberator, the people in the South would join him in constructing a unified state.

At first, Stalin was apparently not convinced. He also knew that Russia should not confront the US when it was the sole possessor of atomic weapons. North Korea's leader was now encouraged that this major obstacle was at last removed when the Soviets joined the nuclear club. Russia seemed finally to be caving in to his demands.

But what Kim Il-sung failed to understand, or perhaps tried to forget, was that crossing the border with South Korea also meant cutting across America's 'unofficial' commitment line. Would the Americans really remain there like sitting ducks? One could only assume he was ready to take chances equipped with his brand new armaments received not too long ago from Russia. His confidence increased so much that he completely misinterpreted the real intentions of the US. It was too much for this young ambitious ex-partisan to resist, although his reckless attitude was always covered up under an impressive smile.

In the end, the decision was in the hands of North Korea. China was not only ready but eager to support this war for its own purposes. The Chinese military desperately needed Soviet technologies, which could give a boost to Chinese military industrial power following the agreement with Soviet Russia. Finally, Stalin was ready to give a nod to his 'comrades' in East Asia. Sometime in early 1950, therefore, the communist side were all more or less happy with Kim's ambition to invade the South.

As we have already mentioned, the US military forces had virtually withdrawn from the Korean peninsula in 1949. As the result of this US policy, South Korea had no mechanised division. Only four under-equipped forces of 38,000 men guarded the entire South without military discipline or high morale – dangerously weak against the superior military might of the North.

At 04:00 on 25 June 1950, a rainy Sunday morning, the North Korean heavy artilleries started to open fire on the South. Soon after the bombardments, its 150 new Soviet-made T-34 tanks advanced, firing into the battlefield followed by a force 89,000 strong with a further 23,000 soldiers in reserve. The communist onslaught began with six major thrusts plus two amphibious landings on the peninsula's west coast.[114]

Faced with this massive sudden push of well-trained forces, the South Korean army was soon routed and in confusion. The major target of this unstoppable, advancing army was the capital, Seoul. It took only three days for the North Koreans to subjugate the city. It was exactly the terrific victory that Kim Il-sung could have wished for. In his most optimistic scenario, Kim Il-sung might have expected that he, like 'Napoleon in Germany', would see the South surrendering with people in many cities and villages welcoming the compatriot 'liberators'. But perhaps to his hidden disappointment, this expectation was not fulfilled. Instead, it soon turned out to be a rather 'Napoleon in Moscow' situation.

To counter this sudden aggression from the North, the US and South Korea successfully secured the United Nations' backing for military intervention at the Security Council despite the abstention of the Soviet delegation. The reason for this Soviet diplomatic tactic was officially in protest against the UN's failure to admit the People's Republic of China. But the Russians were put in an awkward position and the situation was too sensitive to challenge the major powers without risking Soviet credibility. It was, after all, a clear case of blatant military invasion. And this false cause was to cost the North Korean leader dearly.

Military success was quickly turning into becoming a grave political blunder for Kim Il-sung. The North Korean army advanced further, dangerously extending its line of logistics to the South, then to the direction of Pusan to finish off the job. In facing this massive advance, South Koreans and Americans decided to dig in to defend this area. Despite the push of North Koreans, the area had a stable supply line supported by the sea. Eventually, American air superiority began to tell and halted North Korea's military advance.

As a massive contingency force, including new US tank battalions, arrived by ship at Pusan port, it was the turn of Kim Il-song to worry about the static front line. Demonstrating his brilliant military leadership once again, General MacArthur took the initiative with a surprise amphibious landing at Inchon, to the west of Seoul, which left the southern North Korean forces isolated.

'It was a moment of crisis, and the threat of catastrophe was hanging over North Korea itself,' as Khrushchev recalled. As he suggested to Stalin that Russia should help North Korea, Stalin snapped back at him; 'It's too dangerous to keep our advisors there. They might be taken prisoner. We don't want there to be evidence for accusing us of taking part in this business. It's Kim Il-sung's affair.'[115] But this was not the end of the story. Russia was determined to supply the necessary reinforcement of armaments, ammunition and other necessary materials to North Korea. Secretly, the general secretary of the Soviet Union was also to order Soviet veteran jet pilots to act as the North Korean air force to guard its air space from the American air raids.

If the US and UN forces refrained from crossing the 38th parallel north to his territory, Kim's misfortune would not turn out to be a complete nightmare. Premier Zhou Enlai had already made it clear through diplomatic channels that if the Americans entered North Korea, this would force the Chinese to intervene in the war. But his warning was never taken seriously.

Part Two – The Practical Trend

Backed by the UN, Rhee Syng-man now became belligerent and intransigent, as if he had been struck by the same illusion as that of Kim Il-sung, that he could unite the nation by force. As the old man started shouting the odds in the South, the young novice in the North was rapidly losing both his temper and power. In its victorious pursuit of the enemy, US forces decided to cross the border. Failing to get full support from the Soviet Union, North Korea now had to rely entirely on Chinese help to secure his own state, just like all the old Korean dynasties.

It turned out not to be an easy advance for the Americans as the winter weather deteriorated but they were near to the North Korean and Chinese border by the end of November. The Americans demonstrated their superiority in logistics by celebrating a traditional Thanksgiving dinner even in this remote mountainous area before they attempted one more push in the hope of the army returning home by Christmas.

The presence of the US or any enemy force on the other side of their border was, however, as intolerable to communist China as it had been for the Ming dynasty in June 1592. The Chinese waited for the right moment to launch their counter-attack, holding back until the enemy advanced to an optimum point where the 'invaders', supply line was most stretched, and therefore, vulnerable. Mao Zedong had boldly decided to dispatch 300,000 soldiers of the People's Liberation Army led by General Peng Dehuai as 'Volunteers'. The Chinese army crossed the Yalu River and successfully penetrated undetected into North Korea.

Finally, an American reconnaissance plane belatedly identified that the snowy ridges were filled up with Chinese soldiers, most of them armed with automatic weapons, moving towards the US forces. The largest weapons they had were mortars but the force was highly mobile and the attack was vicious. Outnumbered more than three to one, the US, South Korean and UN armies were soon in full retreat. Why was the overwhelming Chinese army so determined despite the immense losses it had incurred initially from this 'human wave' tactic? In the Chinese army, 'The familiar communist organizational device of dual political and military authority was employed down to and including company level,' Alexander George observed.[116] The commanders instigated this strategy and were ready to pay the 'price'.

In the face of this military disaster, MacArthur, as a fully decorated general, was contemplating a new counter-offensive. His favoured plan, 'provided for a naval blockade of Red China, air reconnaissance and bombing of the Chinese mainland, use of Chiang's Nationalist force in Korea and the atomic bomb, 'if tactically appropriate."[117]

'I became increasingly anxious over the situation in Korea,' thought the then British Prime Minister, Clement Attlee. He recognised the 'curious relationship between Government and a General' and flew to Washington immediately. He gave his opinion to President Harry Truman that 'the Far Eastern War should be confined to Korea.'[118] In a television interview, Nikolai Fedorenko, then a Russian diplomat in China and later the Soviet ambassador to Japan, disclosed that a secret assurance was given to China that in case of MacArthur's scenario of using an atomic bomb against the Chinese, Russia would use their atomic weapon in retaliation against the Americans. Whatever the truth was, it was a dangerous scenario.

This was the background of Truman's historical decision, which stunned the Japanese who believed in the general almost as a god. In April 1951, President Truman dismissed Douglas MacArthur as the UN commander and the commander of US forces in the Far East and replaced him with General Matthew Ridgway while the fighting around the 38th Parallel continued. It should have been a moment to realise the true meaning of democracy.

Death tolls were rising on both sides. In South Korea, the estimated figures were the largest, numbering about 1,300,000 most of them civilians. A significant numbers of Chinese, $c.110,000$ had perished. In 2010, Chinese sources revised this figures upwards to 180,000 by checking regional records in detail. North Korea suffered similar casualties. The US and UN troops lost around 40,000 lives between them.

To end the war, the newly elected President Dwight Eisenhower decided to grasp the initiative on 16 April 1953. Joseph Stalin had passed away by that time and Eisenhower proposed that the new Soviet leadership would seize the 'chance for peace' and join in the opportunity to help 'turn the black tide of events.'[119] But China and North Korea were not yet ready to listen.

Peter Lowe adroitly explained the situation, 'Eisenhower used the National Security council to express his opinions and frustrations to much greater extent than his predecessor. He believed that relentless economic pressure on China, plus encouragement of fear among the Chinese and North Koreans that he might approve the selective use of nuclear weapons, could convince the communist states that an armistice should be signed.'[120] Under these circumstances, Kim Il-sung, perhaps regrettably, ended up with the worse possible situation whereby he faced a much stronger Chinese influence upon his regime and his military machine. It was the same old situation which all the previous historical Korean leaders had tried to avoid… in vain.

THE 'FALL' OF THE PEOPLE'S DEMOCRACY

To commemorate the twenty-fifth anniversary of the founding of the Democratic People's Republic of Korea, Kim Il-sung boasted of the achievements of North Korean politics on 9 September 1973, 'for the past twenty-five years (1948-73), our country has been fundamentally transformed. The society has been restructured, the people have been reformed.' Thus, he lauded a quarter century of social, economic, cultural and political progress in North Korea.[121] In the same year, he applied tighter controls on the people's freedom by strengthening the security police.[122] In reality, the North Korean economy had visibly started to decline.

A simple question might be, 'What went wrong with this "reform" under the Kim regime?' Was it the lack of freedom or democracy? We can point out one critical factor as his fatal error. And it is perhaps still applicable to all of the East Asiatic states while its degree varies. He just applied it the most rigidly. In North Korea under Kim Il-sung, the concepts of 'freedom' and 'democracy' existed. In fact, he used these words more than any other words in his speeches.

But one thing he denounced was individualism. He often allied this word to egoism or selfishness. He explained his views at a seminar for propagandists of the National, City and Village commissions in November 1958, 'Individualism or egoism hampers socialistic ownership, in other words, it undermines collective ownership and people's ownership. In the future, it will become the obstacle for us in establishing communistic and people's ownership as a whole.' He further insisted, 'The assets of cooperative association are more important than one's private assets.' He denounced individualism as 'an old capitalistic poison'.[123]

'Freedom' in North Korea was used only for the state or community's benefit. There was no freedom or democratic right at an individual level, which was, under his instigation, categorically denied in this country. Consequently, usage of this word was strictly limited for the North Korean factions, whose nominal leader was the Kim family. A democratic political party meant not democratically elected but merely representing the people nominally, as so insisted on by all the old Korean dynasties. In this context, the word 'people' is no different from the state, or in, other form of his rhetoric, 'nations', that were controlled by his military clan.

Now we can clearly see that Kim Il-sung's regime was probably not based on communism or any sort of modern idea but on a traditional form of Chinese ideology similar to that existing in historical Korean dynasties. Like the old regimes, therefore, he needed a myth for self-aggrandisement. Kim Il-sung's birthplace of Mangyondae (near Pyongyang) was made a spiritual shrine in honour of the great Korean 'revolution'. North Korea's strictly state-controlled media boasted that millions of pilgrims visited it from inside the country and that they also came from every corner of the world – facts that completely disregarded reality.

He carefully prepared a myth for his eldest son as well. It was officially declared that Kim Jong-il was born in a secret hideout at Mt Paektu, near the Manchurian border where, according to the traditional Korean myth, *Hwanung*, a descendant of a god, founded the first Korean nation and a divine city some four thousand years ago (it must be older than China, even just a little bit!). In the memorial wooden house, a wooden-made handgun and a pair of binoculars were exhibited – purportedly used by Kim Jong-il in his childhood. However, as testified by a Russian correspondent, Aleksandr Zhebin, he was actually born near Khabarovsk when his father was in training for the Red Army.[124] But by creating these myths, two leaders were elevated to the status of a 'human god' figure.

In this political system, most North Koreans had no effective individual defence under these ancient concepts which controlled the legal system, as Kim Il-sung and his followers had sufficient power and military means to implement his preferred factional policies. His economic policy of *Chollima* (Flying horse) forced the Korean people into terms of slavery similar to life under ancient oppressive regimes. The aim of his dogmatic policy of *Chuche* – which could be translated as 'the Koreans as the principal entity', was to completely isolate the Korean nation from the outside world.

Although this external world was meant to refer to capitalistic nations, it also implicated the two 'big brothers' who were always trying to intervene in this small country's affairs because of its 'strategic' location. An American North Korea watcher, Donald Zagoria observed, 'By skilfully exploiting the Sino-Soviet conflict that developed in the late 1950s and early 1960s, he began to balance between Moscow and Beijing in order to maintain North Korea's independence. His signing of friendship treaties with both Russia and China in 1961 was an early and significant stage in the balancing act that he has continued ever since.'[125] But what were his diplomatic objectives other than that?

The deepening of North Korea's economic plight occurred in parallel with the end of the Cold War in Europe. During the 1970s, Soviet Russia's military strength against the US continued to grow as it developed more powerful ballistic missiles with larger warheads. Entering into the 1980s, however, the balance of power visibly shifted in the US's favour with the arrival of computerised advanced nuclear armaments such as multiple independently targeted re-entry vehicles (MIRV) under the Reagan administration. Capitalism, once declared a dying force, had been re-vitalised as the backbone of this strong military force. By the mid-1980s, like a marathon runner in mid-race who suddenly changed pace, the disadvantage to Soviet politics and its economic system was there for all to see in the midst of this fierce armament competition.

In a declining economic cycle, North Korea's diplomacy seemed to become quite unpredictable and desperate as demonstrated by their execution of a terrorist time-bomb attack directed at the South Korean delegation in Rangoon that took the lives of seventeen South Korean officials including the vice prime minister in October 1983. It occurred shortly after Soviet Russia had shot down a South Korean passenger airliner killing all 269 people on board which had accidentally entered Soviet air space in September.

After basic changes to the political environment, the dictatorships in Soviet Russia and Eastern Europe were collapsing but North Korea kept to its hard-line form of communism and solid dictatorship. Again, the hypothesis for this East Asiatic movement would be exactly the same as what took place in 'communist' China: that this Kim's 'dynasty' was launched on its upkeep of traditional Chinese ideology. It appeared even more stringent and isolated and clung to the past Korean pattern of arch-bureaucracy.

Moreover, there is a noticeable similarity between North Korea and, in particular, pre-war Japan. The people of pre-war Japan became at one stage hungry, miserable and without any hope, but nobody revolted, fearing retribution and being outcast from a society so tightly controlled by the military regime. Despite a similar kind of oppression, so far, no alternative force has been recognised in North Korea, exactly as in pre-war Japan.

Because of the downturn of the socialist economy in Europe, North Korea could no longer rely on Soviet Russia. Only China was there to close the economic gap of the Democratic People's Republic of Korea. In this situation, China's influence on North Korea grew further. By 2003, it was estimated that China supplied about a half of North Korea's minimum needs of energy and foods and the trend was increasing. In return, North Korea exported its rich mineral resources like iron ore, lead and zinc to China. This lucrative trade for North Korea increased in output as the Chinese economy accelerated its pace of growth.

Back in 1990, the elder Kim launched his first diplomatic initiative towards Japan, by inviting the Japanese politicians, Shin Kanemaru and later Ichiro Ozawa, to visit the country in a desperate attempt to balance the hopeless situation of North Korea. Kanemaru was shown a huge mass display of fifty thousand people which ended up as human letters spelling out, 'Welcome, Mr Kanemaru' in the stadium as another fifty thousand in the city welcomed him. Soon afterwards, he lost his 'cutting edge' in Japanese politics and the attempt at rapprochement appeared completely futile.[126] It is still difficult to assess if this was a miserable last resort for the survival of an aging dictator, or the final desperate endeavour of an experienced politician trying to find a way out of the country's future acute decline.

Having failed on this, Kim Il-sung invited the former US president Jimmy Carter to a surprise meeting in Pyongyang, carefully arranged through diplomatic channels in 1994. He used the nuclear weapons programme as a trump card in his negotiation with the US. It remains unknown if Kim Il-sung wanted to change the course of North Korean politics fundamentally or not, as he passed away in the course of this uncompleted negotiation.

AN EXISTING DETERRENT IN THE PENINSULA

To arm the Korean peninsula with a nuclear weapon was not only the North's idea. President Park of South Korea tried to pursue it once in the 1970s but his ambitions were dissuaded by the US government's fear that it would affect the denuclearisation of the Korean peninsula, Japan and Taiwan, and be detrimental to the stability and peace of East Asia.

The nuclear programme, together with its use for energy purposes, was activated in North Korea during the 1980s. Under mounting global scepticism about its nuclear weapons programme, however, in 1991, North Korea began negotiating a safeguard agreement with the International Atomic Energy Agency together with an agreement with South Korea to ban the possession, basing and manufacture of nuclear arms, including a ban on reprocessing. As regarding the true intentions of the North Korean leadership under Kim Il-sung, Leon Sigal assessed that they 'saw a potentially far graver threat to its survival, one that nuclear arms could not forestall – economic stagnation.'[127]

Despite the official insistence of North Korea that they had to develop a nuclear weapon against possible US aggression, nuclear deterrence already existed in the peninsula under a Chinese or Russian umbrella. We must assume that deterrence is not the true purpose of North Korea's new nuclear programme vis-à-vis the West. But it is understandable that under a Chinese ideological viewpoint, it wants to keep this military option open for its own regime's protection vis-à-vis China or even South Korea.

The two separate issues of defence and economy, however, cannot in reality be combined. A success story of North Korean diplomacy was first claimed in 1994 as a sort of promissory note obtained from Bill Clinton by Kim Jong-il affirming the US responsibility for realizing the $4.5 billion LWR – light water reactor – project, upon which 'Pyongyang heralded the letter and the Agreed Framework as a great diplomatic achievement.'[128] But there was always an immense risk for this secretive regime in embracing an open-door policy which included South Korea. It might bring in a 'Trojan horse', which could expose the reality of its own political defects to the people and thereby increase its internal instability. Consequently, North Korea had to renege on this agreement and other promises.

In 1991, Kim Il-sung made his son, Jong-il, the commander-in-chief of the people's army by allowing him to reach the top echelon of this military state that, until then, had been kept only for himself. Kim Jong-il, with his father's back-up, had already affirmed his power in the army since the 1980s but then he got directly involved as the leader of the supreme North Korean military faction. It was obvious that western ideas of diplomatic strategy were not applicable in this kind of regime.

In this situation, each country that tried negotiating with North Korea had a different diplomatic position and wish-list. With the nuclear arsenal of China protecting North Korea, US military options are extremely limited. Since North Korea notified the US that it had activated its nuclear programme on the pretext of President Bush's 'axis of evil' remark in 2002, the US government has been disturbed by the North's constant violation of diplomatic protocols, human rights and its foreign policies, in particular, possible arms exports to South-west Asia.

The South Korean government believed in its policy of engagement and dialogue with its northern 'brothers' despite its constant 'provocation' on its frontline. The risk always existed of the North taking advantage of this and using it for further oppressive politics against its people or for the developments of its nuclear armament and conventional force, which could be directed against the South. South Koreans are also anxious about the further strengthening of Chinese influence on the Northern economy, leading to subsequent political control.

Another border state, Russia, was also concerned with the North's nuclear programme and the overall unstable situation caused by its unpredictable neighbour. Together with China, Russia kept up a cordial relationship with North Korea long after the Soviet era and declared many times its willingness to offer a nuclear umbrella of its own if the North renounced its nuclear programme. Kim Jong-il visited Moscow and Khabarovsk in his special train in the summer of 2002, and Ulan Ude in 2011. Russia's diplomatic options were few, despite its occasional warning to the North about its nuclear programme. Above all, Russians refrained from any aggressive diplomatic initiative towards the peninsula from the West.

China's posture was somewhat more mixed, presumably reflecting factional differences on the issue inside the leadership. Robert Scalapino gave an insight on this entangled situation, 'China's position on the basic issues is relatively clear. The PRC does not want a collapsed DPRK, a nuclear DPRK, or another conflict. Hence, it favours the status quo continuing, meanwhile encouraging the North to pursue an evolutionary process that would preserve "socialism"...'[129] But this policy was getting more and more difficult as China's economic ties and its diplomatic co-operation with the rest of the world expanded further.

Despite its own shift to a socialist market economy, China seems not to particularly encourage North Korea to take a similar course in open-door economic development. For this to happen, however, there is another issue where even China can do little to help this isolated regime. Before any sorts of sizeable international investments are made, the North has to equip its social infrastructure, in particular, to uphold a minimum degree of lawfulness in the country, which would be hard to obtain bearing in mind the previous appalling conduct of this rogue state.

North Korea paid the price for its outdated diplomacy as US sanctions on its overseas financial activities were suddenly implemented. As an indication of North Korea's pain, the North Korea's number two (or one of number twos) Kim Yon-nam told Japan's Kyodo News Agency that this was the reason for their tougher action including a new nuclear test reported on just before the interview. Soon afterwards, North Korean officials 'pledged' to close the controversial Yongbyon reactor programme in February 2007 if they could get full access to the $25m frozen account at Banco Delta Asia in Macao, which was subsequently remitted back to North Korea via Russia. But North Korean leaders should have realised that their country's economy should have been worth more than this extremely modest sum.

Since then, however, the US stance on the current six-country talks in Beijing has become problematic, as in reality, any offer of further substantial aid to North Korea could not solve the fundamental issue. It is analogous to giving a state pension to a healthy young man who stays at home and refuses to work, which is not sustainable as a long-term solution. Any agreement or sanction would contain explicitly or implicitly a policy of coercion with tighter economic sanctions. But North Korea has already proved many times that they could at least survive under such punitive measures from the West, relying on economic aid from China.

In this situation, North Korea has no other choice but to repeat the basic policy of the Yi dynasty (1392-1910) who lived as Chinese vassals under their extreme interpretation of Chinese ideology and stopped the progress of the Korean people for almost five hundred years so that the ruling class would survive and enjoy power. What is now ensuing in North Korea is a politico-economic implosion despite appearances to the contrary and any solution must focus on the cause. The only reasonable form of politics for the solid future of North Koreans would appear to be unification with the South on a credible legal basis. Then, the status of non-nuclear status in the peninsula could be maintained, if the Koreans agree to dispose of any nuclear weapons in the North under international supervision at the time of unification. And of course, another important factor here is that Japan, with its on-going economic mess, would be powerless to act or play any meaningful role in negotiations on this vital diplomatic issue.

DEFEATISM AS A MAJOR STUMBLING BLOCK

It is important to acknowledge that neither Kim Jong-il, nor his youngest son, Kim Jong-un, created this military sect, nor entered into this camp of his own free will, unlike other modern dictators. It was just there when he was born. In other words, he was a victim in this distorted, often even criminal, and above all, fanatical world of the North Korean arch-bureaucracy. He had to act 'appropriately' to take the initiative in this power game but that did not change the nature of his political starting point.

And no matter how human rights are violated, or that the standard of living plummets as long as its military might is intact, there will be no people's revolt or revolution in North Korea. This kind of a resistance from the people's side or lower hierarchies has never developed as an effectual political movement in 'modern' East Asia.

With the current devastating economic implosion in North Korea, nobody could deny that its fanatical leader is a major problem but a genuine political solution will not be found within North Korea. The fundamental issue here is that this type of regime is still allowed to lead a sizeable state with visibly outdated political tools under the region's old ideology which is still alive and well. Without identifying this as a political entity, a real solution cannot be found in East Asia.

Social coercion in East Asiatic society is led by an arch-bureaucracy without any visible defined goals other than the expansion of its own power, and its reach is much stronger and more penetrating than in a western society which treasures individualism and where the overall social dynamism is always given priority. For instance, even in Nazi Germany, the notorious secret police, the *Gestapo,* could not prevent a revolt inside the powerful military state. But the pre-war Japanese Special Police, *Tokko,* successfully eliminated all dissidents before they could even start to think about such a thing.

The Solidarity movement conducted by Lech Walesa united the Polish people. The East Germans supported the people's disobedience against a brutal and shattered regime. In Russia, the people in Moscow surrounded their leader, Boris Yeltsin, to support the new revolution. And the same took place in Czechoslovakia, Hungary, Ukraine and elsewhere in Europe. From the American Revolution to the recent European movements, it was difficult to see defeatism on the side of people in western politics.

It was not because their East Asian counterparts were not brave enough. Once there was a courageous young man who confronted the advancing tanks in Tiananmen Square just with empty hands, but one personal feat could not change the tide of Chinese politics. The fundamental issue was that the people in East Asia could not unite over their boundaries of village, business or various factions. They could not form a spiritual solidarity as a nation. The state could be only amalgamated by arch-bureaucratic power where the system inevitably divided the people into the rulers and the ruled. And the truth would never surface under such strict factional rules which stretch over the entire society where people tend to escape from politics in various forms of apathy.

This vacant spirit was once vividly depicted by Lu Xun, in his *Aqiu Zhengchuan – The Real Story of Ah Q –* a man who refuses to recognize his actual inferior status in society but always finds some excuse to be content with his own situation and try to remain as a victor in his subjective world. Poor Ah Q was finally executed on a false charge. But what Lu Xun really criticised was the indifference of public opinion that judged Ah Q as guilty, 'He must be wrong because he was executed.'[130]

The Tokugawa Shogunate ruled Japan for almost two hundred and sixty years in isolation prior to the birth of 'modern' Japan and its history is still valid to the current Japanese way of thinking. It administered the country with a principle of *Tami wa yorashimu-beshi shirashimu-bekarazu:* 'People have to be dependant (on the state) and not informed (of state affairs).'[131] In recent years, this Japanese defeatism has been constantly reinforced with yet more indifference to any political rationale and by showing inexplicable fear of superior power thanks to daily propaganda by the entire media and on-going social practices.

In the present information age, it would not be too difficult to form new policy packages for the required reform for each country in East Asia. But it is likely that such a political solution would be rejected by this diehard defeatism among its own people which would instantly attack its real motives and values. The predominant western idea of abolishing a woeful regime or people's revolution, therefore, would be insufficient here. Even if we could successfully remove an old East Asiatic regime which is visibly failing, there would be only the million groups of raw self-interest and confusion. The only thing you cannot find would be an emancipated individual which is the ultimate goal for modern democracy.

So what can be the essential political factor for overcoming this problem? In a famous funeral oration recorded by Thucydides, Pericles explained the principle of democracy in 431 BC, 'We give our obedience to those whom we put in positions of authority, and they obey the laws themselves, especially those which are for the protection of the oppressed... We regard wealth as something to be properly used, rather than as something to boast about... Here each individual is interested not only in his own affairs but in the affairs of the states as well: even those who are mostly occupied with their own business are extremely well informed on general politics – this is a peculiarity of ours: we do not say a man who takes no interest in politics is a man who minds his own business: we say that he has no business here at all.'[132] Nobody has ever made this point clearer. As Pericles emphasised, our constant efforts to strengthen general political knowledge with the help of all other science and art, at both individual and national levels, must be the key element of our democracy.

To beat this reactionary system, it would appear that people's mental attitude, including his or her morals, is the hardest hurdle to clear for any new regime in East Asia. Again, it is not a simple matter of demolishing something, as might be generally believed in the West. It is rather about creating or implanting something that does not currently exist, as democracy always needs to be accompanied by individual rational judgements. Without this political philosophy put in place among the people of East Asia, any democracy is bound to be defunct.

PART THREE
JAPAN IN CRISIS

I - THE SYSTEM

DEMOCRACY ADRIFT

The most important political change ever introduced in post-war Japan came in the form of a new constitution. John Dower, an American expert on modern Japan affairs, focused on a peculiar obstacle in the making of the Japanese constitution, 'To be known as an anglophile or "old liberal," however, did not mean that one was also strongly pro-American or deeply knowledgeable about the United States.' The fact was that the Japanese people could not write their own modern constitution when asked by the Allied powers due to their lack of understanding of American, or rather western politics, as a whole.

The project had to be abandoned because the Japanese government's draft was little different from the previous one from the Meiji constitution, which stated that 'sovereign power belongs to the emperor'. This obvious anachronism met only with international condemnation as the vivid memory of an atrocious war was still burning. The Matsumoto committee had to go – ending up 'in history's dustbin largely because the civilian elites remained autocratic and antidemocratic, whereas a great many ordinary men and women were proving receptive to the sort of democracy the American were promoting.'[133]

The new constitution adopted a constitutional monarchy similar to that of Britain taking into account the existence of the Japanese emperor. Article 1 regarding the emperor was elaborated, '...deriving his position from the will of the people with whom resides sovereign power.' The Japanese *Kokutai* – State Structure – should have changed from its pre-war state bureaucracy under the divine emperor to a modern democracy. But the Shinto-Japanese Buddhism complexities that played a decisive political role in the old state structure were untouched. They were instead protected by the principle of freedom of 'religion' as stipulated in the new constitution. Modern western politics of secularisation produced a completely unexpected result in Japan from that intended by the drafters of the constitution.

After all, Japanese democracy started irregularly, not from the aspirations of the people, but from external forces. What was desperately missing for the Japanese in this new constitution – without an Oliver Cromwell or George Washington – was the spirit of democracy, which cannot be easily imported into a political environment that was already established. And so 'democracy' just evolved in Japan as there was no other form of political power which could actually function, other than the same old political instruments. But everything had to be done 'behind the scenes' under a new double standard put in place without much effort, one for an officially claimed nominal democracy, and the other for arch-bureaucracy controlling the real expression of politics.

Launching the post-war political system, the constituency method that had been proven in the pre-war period was the key element. It was known as a 'medium constituency' as opposed to the single constituency of the British democratic tradition for radical political changes. An influential leader of the Choshu faction, Aritomo Yamagata, publicly emphasised its importance as, 'the need to give urban voters fair and equal representation in the Diet'. His objective, however, was focused on this one point. It was effective in protecting the seats of bureaucratic candidates by relying on factional voting. Yamagata actually experienced the dangers of single constituency elections in 1920 when they had once been adopted in Japan under the Hara administration, the results of which devastated his party to such an extent, that the phrase, 'Lenin is in west while Hara is in east' arose.

PART THREE – JAPAN IN CRISIS

A Japanese expert, Haruhiro Fukui, comes straight to the point, 'This represented a critical point of take-off in the process of the adaptation, or Japanisation, of the European model, setting a precedent for the so-called medium-sized constituency system of three to five members per district that would become the norm after 1925.'[134] Factional politics flourished under this old 'specifically designed' election system in Japan. The Americans first agreed to the Japanese request for a 'major constituency' system as applied by some European states just as the working relationship between the two countries was being established. Not knowing what lay at the root of these issues and despite the initial reluctance and the subsequent objection of his advisors who did not approve of it, General MacArthur was persuaded in 1947 by the then prime minister, Shigeru Yoshida, in a face-to-face meeting to agree to this electoral change.[135]

Therefore, despite all these new superficial changes, the essential political elements were ruined under the same old arch-bureaucracy system, which just a decade previously had pushed the nation to a global-scale disaster, the responsibility for which could not be easily found – even during the allied investigation at the Tokyo Tribunal in 1946. Tokyo University was now relied on to supply the required 'elites' for recruitment to the bureaucracy, virtually as a sole source, instead of the pre-war troika system with the army and naval academies.

The monopolisation of the state university education had actually occurred a long time ago in 1881 by the so-called *Meiji Jyuyonen no Seihen* – the political coup of the Meiji fourteenth year – when the Japanese government decided to expel and boycott all private university graduates from joining the state's bureaucracy out of fear of democratic movements arising. In its entire history since then, pre-war Tokyo Imperial University has produced only one liberal professor in social sciences. An excellent academic, Eijiro Kawai, died in agony as he had been accused by the authorities of the ridiculously unfounded charge of harbouring 'dangerous political thought'.

But what were the differences with L'Ecole Nationale de

l'Administration in France, for instance? Many of the French *énarques* moved to the private sector after their experiences in public service just as in Japan, but certainly not after retirement. They had joined as management professionals like business school graduates in the US quite separate from the French legal system. Post-graduate candidates are selected on merit and no tenacious sectarianism, as in Japan, is seen in French ministries; also the *grande école* kept a dominant political reputation in France by producing two presidents and seven prime ministers.[136] Furthermore, although nothing was wrong with the good students and professors from Tokyo University as individuals, the problem was that Japan's arch-bureaucracy as an iron rule used the university as the sole provider of graduates to employ in the leading factions of the top hierarchies of the key government ministries.

In this political environment, Ian Neary noted, 'Between 1945 and 2000 the USA had ten presidents, the UK eleven prime ministers and Japan twenty-five prime ministers.'[137] It doesn't sound too bad! But among those Japanese prime ministers, Shigeru Yoshida served for six years in the early days. Eisaku Sato, ex-top transport bureaucrat, recorded as the longest-serving prime minister in Japan who established bureaucratic controls and supervising the US handover of Okinawa, served from 1964 to 1972. If these long-surviving leaders' years are removed from the list, the frequency of new heads of government in Japan compared to that of the US or UK can be seen more clearly. In fact, the majority of Japanese premiers served only a year or less and struggled to attain any political achievement.

The Japanese political party system was structured to meet the requirements of the 'real master'. In the Lower House (term: four years) or *Shugi-in* – the House of Representatives – there was a clear division between the Cabinet and the Political Party. The heads of the LDP were elected for three-year terms! The Shadow Cabinet was unworkable, as factional politics were always given priority. As such, there was no equivalent of a party conference to unite the political party and administration in an open manner although it did exist as a ritual in Japan. Cabinet meetings (without a conference table!)

were merely a place to make already-decided matters official rather than holding a decision-making process in discussing the details of a specific policy. Questioning in the Japanese parliament is completely different to the British parliamentary scene, in that there is neither creative logic nor a sense of humour in the exchanges of debates. Why are they so different? As any Japanese reporter would tell you, most Japanese politicians have to read out his or her 'opinion' with complete concentration as their brief is written by bureaucrats, sometimes in impenetrable jargon, and perhaps on a little-known subject as well!

As political parties were further split by the power struggles of internal sects, much energy is wasted in this divisive and camouflaged political game of factional politics. The Japanese press reports detailing which individual politician belongs to which group, or how many times he was elected, are essential information in this game. All modern political tools operate in disguise and are used for a completely different purpose from those in western democracy.

In Japan, politicians and the system itself are not scrutinised by the media or other organs tenaciously and constantly as to their character, capability, integrity, and above all, responsibility over specific political decisions. There is virtually no central governing body which selects candidates on the basis of merit through open competition or by completely changing the constituency. The world of parliamentary activities in Japan is very much an insider's business, with everything decided within political circles which then manipulate public opinion.

The major problem is that both people and politicians do not regard a political party as an important public organ despite the fact that Japanese parliamentarians are not expected to be idle under the constitution. Parliament does have power, as Article 62 states: 'Each House may conduct investigations in relation to government, and may demand the testimony of witnesses, and the production of records.' This fundamental right to change the course of any failed policy of modern government, however, is completely ignored by the indigenous political ideology.

In this reality, therefore, modern Japanese politics does not provide a challenging profession where one can function at maximum strength, as even the most controversial short-lived, politically meaningless, or even, harmful, ex-prime ministers can still remain as factional group leaders. Instead of fighting to be effective politicians, all procrastinate, working to the slowest pace possible, killing most of their time on non-policy issues and intrigues, keeping the lid on the vital, predetermined and hidden factional interests and agenda, and leaving all actual state policies to the equally problematic bureaucracy to run on their behalf.

THE DECISIVE ROLE OF THE EMPEROR

A prominent Japanese scholar who specialised in Japanese classic canons, Saukichi Tsuda, once commented on the mechanism of Japanese state supremacy just after the war, 'State supremacy is wrong, therefore, one would think that a control power above the state is necessary and this could be obtained only from the supreme authority of Christianity as happened in Europe and America. But it is doubtful that Japan could adopt this.' In the scheme depicted by him, unlike modern European monarchies, the Japanese emperor exists as the core of Japanese state power. Professor Tsuda suggested that contemporary Japanese people who 'accepted the scientific spirit' should try to find supreme authority by other means without specifying what it might be.[138] But he failed to clarify the dangers of subordinate religions which were totally controlled by the state.

In the declining years of imperial Japan, most politicians or members of the military did not pay much attention to the emperor's powers as stipulated in the Meiji constitution, which had been created by copying the German constitutional monarchy under the Second Reich (1871-1918), according to the drafter, Hirobumi Ito. But in Japan the reality which emerged was quite opposite to any western ideas; above all, the stipulated, absolute power of the emperor could never properly function due to the existence of the arch-bureaucracy. For instance, matters like the forced resignation of Chancellor Bismarck by Kaiser Wilhelm II in 1890 which enabled the Kaiser to direct the German foreign policy by himself was utterly impossible in Japan.

The balance of power between the Japanese emperor and the arch-bureaucracy is most easily envisaged, if one thinks of the role of parliament and monarchy in medieval England. At that time, the sovereign king had executive power. He could decide whatever he and his advisors wanted as long as the country flourished and the parliament or barons acted or intervened only when matters were going seriously wrong, or damaging the common interests. In Japan, the relationship was completely in the opposite direction. It was the emperor's role to deal with any crisis that arose.

At the end of the Second World War, the situation arrived when Japan had to terminate its bitter struggle, as the future of the state was again in danger. At this point, the emperor temporarily overrode the executive powers of the arch-bureaucracy by his declaration of surrender via his broadcast to the public. As people listened to the emperor's voice on the radio announcing the Japanese defeat, only some fanatics were still ready to fight. But the hyper-nationalistic irrational folly at the centre of Japanese political power instantly died down afterwards.

By this act, all legal legitimacy was removed from the arch-bureaucracy as if the entire mechanics of the political system had lost its 'power generator'. Japan spoke only once and it was necessary for everybody, in particular for the American military, that Japan surrendered in an orderly manner. The political act of the emperor was decisive and final. Historically, Japan could change the entire situation by this single political move solely due to the existence of the Japanese emperor whose solemn duty was to unify the nation with legitimacy at the time of a grave national crisis.

It was the second imperial endorsement in Japanese modern history. The first one was the Meiji Restoration in 1867 when the Tokugawa Shogunate had lost all political and military credibility and decided to submit itself to *Taisei-Hokan* or 'returning of the executive power to the emperor'. In both cases, it is important to note that neither powerful politicians nor capable bureaucrats could perform this critical and extraordinary role in Japan.

After the war, Emperor Hirohito was ready to undertake new duties by visiting people all over Japan in a completely different political environment. His personality and dedication to be a new kind of emperor impressed many Japanese but the question remained in and outside of Japan, 'Was he really not responsible for the war?' Some authors tried to prove that he had been actually leading the war. In some cases, it was probably quite true that as a human being he made mistakes. But one of the many crucial facts was that the Japanese emperor did not even know there was a plan for action until the Japanese army suddenly invaded Manchuria. He volunteered to take all the responsibility for the war on behalf of the Japanese people when it became necessary – but America and Britain knew that this was not justifiable.

Charles Sheldon expressed his astute view on this issue, 'What was at fault was not the Emperor but the Emperor system which permitted the abuse by the power-holder of a power greatly enhanced by the general emotional commitment to the myth-laden imperial institution as a focus for loyalty and patriotism, with its potential for both good and evil.'[139] He was absolutely right.

So far, however, the argument in Japan evolved as a choice between the existence of the emperor and the abolition of the emperor but in doing so, people mixed up the emperor and the emperor system, or more precisely, the status of the emperor and the political ideology behind the old Japanese imperial system. For instance, Iwasaburo Takano, then a professor of Tokyo University, publicised his view on scrapping the emperor system just after the war.[140] His intention was to introduce an East Asiatic people's democracy into Japan that was categorically unacceptable to the Americans or anybody else.

Unlike this extreme view, Joseph Grew, the long-serving US ambassador to pre-war Japan, counselled caution when he said, '[the Japanese] had better keep the throne as the one stabilizing influence.' His assessment was vital in the 1940s. On the other hand, his view was too optimistic when he continued, 'The old feudalistic system can best be destroyed by breaking up the *Zaibatsu* (the Japanese-style conglomerate) and ensuring the farmers a new deal and higher standard of living. The evils of state Shintoism will largely disappear once the militarists are out of the way. All that is purely an artificial growth...'[141] More importantly, his interpretation coincided with what actually happened to post-war Japan under the rule of US occupation.

The Japanese emperor as an individual was virtually controlled by the infamous Imperial Household Agency, or, if you look at the larger picture, by an arch-bureaucracy whose identities are quite unknown to ordinary Japanese people. These secretive bureaucrats can intrude into the private life of the imperial family. This was confirmed again in 2005 when the crown prince made a most unusual remark in a protest on their excessive restrictions on his family life. The Japanese press preferred to use the expression of 'Chrysanthemum curtain'. But the reason why these political cliques still have strength is attributable to the fact that Japanese political ideology and supreme power itself are completely hidden from public view.

In these power politics, nobody except the emperor can take the nominal responsibility for all the experiences of Japanese history. In Japanese festivals, people usually bring in a traditional portable shrine known as a *Mikoshi* to processions. Young energetic men carry it on their shoulders with much excitement, often feeling the effects of binge drinking – sometimes chaos ensues resulting in broken shop windows or the upsetting of street stalls. People usually just stand and observe until the shrine goes on to another location and do not complain about the bad behaviour as this is regarded as an act of 'religious' intoxication. The worst that might happen is that somebody may get hurt or the Mikoshi itself might be broken. The Japanese emperor seems a little like this bumpy portable shrine on the 'International Road' of Japan.

Emperor Hirohito luckily avoided the Mikoshi option before it was crushed in a frenzy of elated extremism. Stalin had a plan to occupy the northern part of Japan at the end of the Second World War. In the worst-case scenario, no Japanese arch-bureaucrats could have stopped the destruction of the Japanese imperial throne. Only the US and Britain disagreed with Stalin's idea. The Japanese political fanatics, like the young men in the festivals, never care about the result of their own crazes, which are completely disconnected from the interests of the Japanese people.

The powerful arch-bureaucrats, as a whole, constantly abused the role of the Japanese emperor. The faction who protected the emperor actually tried to use him to further their own political objectives. Yet, the system has so far prevented Japan from breaking up as a nation. Even for these arch-bureaucrats pretending to function under the principles of modern democracy, the only way they can insist on their legitimacy is to convince the Japanese people that they have received their exclusive administrative power from the authentic emperor, according to 'sacred' Japanese tradition.

The fate of Japanese modernisation, therefore, eventually depends on one point – if the Japanese can ever modernise its emperor system, which is still revered as an autocratic and religious myth that can control the course of the country's politics and economy. Klaus Antoni, a German Japanologist, warned, 'Through constitutional change and the post-war political development, the *Kokutai* ideology became obsolete outside of the national-Shintoistic circle. However, it remains to be seen in the future, if a newly-awakened sensitivity for overall mysterious identity (of the Japanese emperor) would mean a fresh indication of being ready for the possible rebirth of an Japanese Utopia by her *Nationalwesen* or not.'[142] As he realised, this tendency has never abated and continues to be strengthened in post-war Japan.

'HIJACKED' BY BUREAUCRACY

The new post-war Japan had the right technological base for an industrial nation and at that time was the only one of its kind in East Asia. But we cannot ignore two key economic gifts from the West - technology and a peaceful diplomatic environment – which were indispensable for Japan's miraculous recovery. Firstly, these were vitally necessary for the development of new technologies, and secondly, Japan's export market opened up under the new political environment as the country became a new member of the international community. Its former foes, America and Britain treated Japan with mercy as a peaceful ally and were willing to help. Under these fresh auspices, Soichiro Honda, Konosuke Matsushita and many others, flourished as the first generation of Japanese entrepreneurs able to boost the economy to grow and expand hugely by the end of the 1960s.

In South East Asia, Japan was accepted as an industrial nation based on the principle of free trade and all its markets became accessible to Japanese companies. This regional status could never have been enjoyed by pre-war Japan under the advocated order of *Hakko-Ichiu* – East Asia under the single (Japanese) command. From the American point of view, the essence of this so-called Yoshida Doctrine in successful post-war Japan was, 'one nestled under America's wings, military on the one side and economic on the other, and concentrated – not on democracy, not on diplomacy, not on rearmament, certainly not on global leadership and statesmanlike initiatives – but on economic growth.'[143]

Underneath this new prosperity, however, the old political movement was firmly set in every governmental organisation as Japan evolved in its own form of politics at full speed. Actually, what happened was, once the Japanese economy took off, arch-bureaucracy was ready to move in to 'hijack', in a quite irregular and dramatic way in a modern state, the economic concerns of the new Japan. They locked the 'cockpit' without making an announcement even to the 'passengers' who had recently become the owner of this 'aeroplane' as well.

And so the original American concept of the respective balance between the three powers of legislative, executive and judiciary had to be altered to converge upon the sole power belonging to Japanese arch-bureaucracy. By this change, unified democratic power under the new constitution somewhat evaporated. Nobody was aware exactly of what was happening in Japan but everybody was conscious in which direction the country was heading and what each one had to do.

As we have already reviewed in Part One, the state bureaucrats were supposed to extend control to every corner of the society under the old Japanese political system. And Japan's 'heavily structured' regional governments soon followed this example in accommodating US advice that was made with completely different political motives. The effects were thorough and complete, as the upper half of the working society in the public and private sectors were irreversibly bound together, and their form of control began to saturate into society. Just as you would expect to see a Catholic *boulanger* in a rural village of Charente-Maritime, or a Baptist taxi-driver in North Little Rock, you could see a pure Japanese bureaucratic mind at a barbershop in Yonezawa.

How was it different from western bureaucracy? Anthony H. Birch noticed that there is the 'tradition of anonymity' in British bureaucracy.[144] This modesty is based on its formidable efficiency. In contrast, there seemed to be the permanent 'tradition of self-aggrandisement' in Japanese bureaucracy which is based on its tightly concealed inefficiency. They try to control everything, without surrendering any powers, while constantly keeping their deficiencies intact, even when challenged by somebody cleverer in the private sector. Every major Japanese newspaper reports who's who in the high ranks of bureaucracy as soon as changes are announced in the ministries.

Furthermore, if you carefully analyse the situation, they have the best salaries and pension packages in Japanese society. The executives of some top Japanese companies might be able to receive a bigger package than a so-called career bureaucrat, but government officials can hop around the public corporations after 'retirement' with privileged packages. In this process, after just two or three years' service, they are entitled to receive a neat sum of a 'retirement grant' for the second time carrying an exceptionally low tax rate. One official repeated this process three times in a row before he actually retired. One of the main reasons for constantly including so many public corporations inside the Japanese government was actually for this appalling purpose.

The problem is, quite against the principle of capitalism, that the system does not encourage individual freedom and prosperity in society. For instance, young key bureaucrats rely on state benefits for everything including state-furnished accommodation. Consequently, in a rising property market, bureaucrats might be comparatively poorer but in a declining property market, they are richer. One may conclude from this that in order to save and push up Japanese real estate value or to get out of chronic deflation, you first need to abolish this practice in Japanese bureaucracy!

At the beginning of post-war Japan, there was no concept of 'public' or 'people as a whole' until the Americans introduced the concept. In Japanese, 'public', which is literally *Kou*, could mean bureaucracy, government, state or imperial court. On the other hand, the new word like 'public servant' *Koumuin*, was rarely applied. Or like 'civil service' was completely ignored! The Japanese media, without thinking of its consequences, frequently use the old word of *Kan-ryo* instead. When the Japanese express 'government and private sector', they usually say the word *Kan-Min* that is literally 'arch-bureaucrats and private sector'. In this environment, the Japanese subconsciously overlap the meaning of 'public', 'government', 'civil service', 'state', 'administration' and its affiliated businesses as only one entity, 'arch-bureaucracy' – *Kan* or *Kan-ryo*.

With such a mentality, everything was possible in this bizarre relationship in the modern political scene, between the automatically 'qualified' arch-bureaucrats and the instantly 'disqualified' people who were quite willing to let the state powers handle all issues. The bad news is that, by continuing this easy way of politics, the people have to practically provide a blank cheque to the arch-bureaucracy from their bank accounts.

To make politics even more obscure, old practices were gradually restored. In addition to using the Gregorian calendar, the government decided to use the old Chinese-style name for an era – *Gengo* – suddenly again in 1979 i.e. the Showa 54th year under the Ohira administration, and people had to adopt this old-fashioned way of counting again. Japan became the only country, even in East Asia, that decided to continue with this ancient Chinese custom as Mao Zedong had abolished it completely in China itself.

All the peculiar legal structures in Japan had to be endorsed by untrained administrators with insufficient knowledge and experience because, in practice, professional lawyers had no independence under this political ideology. There is no comprehensive law institution for legal professions, the equivalent of Britain's Law Society or Inns of Court. In Japan, all those are divided in various sub-organizations so that they can barely function as an independent legal body or take the leadership in society. In addition, the Japanese arch-bureaucracy deemed not only that drafting a law or ordinance was their responsibility, but as a rule, its interpretations were also kept under their exclusive discretional power.

'To behave rationally is the cause of a dispute but an emotion cannot be controlled. Life is indeed difficult.' – wrote a popular novelist, Soseki Natsume, almost a hundred years ago. It is clear, however, that Japanese society as a whole prefers to be emotional, if there is a choice. Completely different to life in the West, most Japanese end their lives without ever seeing a lawyer. There was even propaganda that one should avoid contractual relationships in Japan's 'harmonious' society. The people were told the myth of Prince Shotoku in the seventh century whose favourite saying was, 'Compromise is the best.' It should have meant that there was no need for unnecessary power struggles to protest his fragile position but the 'official' interpretation of his remark was that people can live without any legal protection by leaving everything under state control that will exercise power on behalf of the entire 'family'. Some lawyers struggle in vain to counter this nonsense.

What has happened in Japan is that ordinary Japanese who are not protected by contract or legal systems are the target for abuse by company racketeering or organized crime who do have the necessary legal knowledge. There is no credible system by which legal experts can provide help to victims, or to punish the perpetrators severely and quickly. This dreadful uncompromising situation leaves the Japanese service industries little room to grow in this non-transparent market. It is difficult to envisage how western democracy could survive if their lawyers and other legal professionals suddenly vanished one day, but that is the real situation in Japan. And of course, the solid rule of law in the West protects its society from the emergence of such an arch-bureaucratic system.

THE 'LIBERTY' OF THE PRESS

Why then does the Japanese media keep silent on this issue? Unfortunately, the western idea of the liberty of the press never ever existed in Japan. From a modern political viewpoint, what is particularly disappointing about the current Japanese press is their lack of desire for their own freedom or the sense of a profound mission to protect modern journalism for the benefit of Civil or Social Liberty as once defined by John Stuart Mill. He convincingly argued, 'The struggle between Liberty and Authority is the most conspicuous feature in the portions of history…' 'By Liberty, was meant protection against the tyranny of the political rulers' because 'the power itself is illegitimate.' He envisaged that nothing is more dangerous systematically than an irrational state power in politics. And he forewarned us all, 'The whole strength and value, then, of human judgement, depending on the one property, that it can be set right when it is wrong, reliance can be placed on it only when the means of setting it right are kept constantly at hand.'[145]

The role of the modern press, however, is ignored on Japan's native soil. In Japan, no respected newspaper and magazine has ever specialised in politics or ever existed, that covers global political and economic issues for its readers. Historically, there was only one quality paper published in this category in Japan and that was *Jiji-Shimpo,* founded by an exceptional Meiji liberal, Yukichi Fukuzawa, in order to criticise the government.[146] It failed to progress soon after his death in 1901 and lost all prestige.

There are three large newspaper companies in Japan: *Yomiuri*,

Asahi and *Mainichi* which started business as types of tabloid papers covering social, entertainment and criminal incidents, then gradually extended their coverage into the area of politics. In post-war Japan, Yomiuri under the leadership of Matsutaro Shoriki, an ex-police officer, seized the opportunity to expand aggressively and overtook Asahi to become the largest press group in Japan. In addition, there are newspapers which concentrated more on economic and industrial coverage, such as *Nikkei* and *Sankei*. The big newspapers together with the two news agencies of *Kyodo* and *Jiji* make up the whole of the major media in Japan.

Most influential newspapers are not publicly listed in Japan. All previous attempts from other Japanese entrepreneurs or any foreign interests that tried to enter the market have failed. Once they have joined directly from universities, journalists are trained exactly like most other Japanese company employees, moving gradually up a bureaucratic ladder. As a rule, newspapers do not hire established professional reporters from the job market place. The newly employed go first to a small rural office to be trained to write up criminal reports or are trained to write about economic matters. After a few years, they will be called back to their head office to take on a more specialized subject.

Whatever route they follow, most of these crucially positioned reporters are bound by Japan's notorious press club agreements and run the risk of being barred from issuing a press release. No Japanese intellectuals criticise the reality of this old deplorable state information- controlling system or see it as a serious political issue. But luckily, we have William De Lange who made critical remarks on the doubtful nature of Japanese press freedom, '…in spite of the repeated attempts to break its hegemony over the most important political news, the Japanese press club, epitomized by the Cabinet Press Club, has remained firmly at the centre of newsgathering. Moreover, due to the binding club agreements, the reporters attached to the Japanese press clubs have become virtual hostages to those whom they are supposed to scrutinize. It is this aspect of the Japanese press club that seriously threatens its members' liberty of reporting.'¹⁴⁷ I could not agree with him more.

How were these matters strictly controlled in pre-war Japan? Again, we need to ask a foreign expert on this 'sensitive' subject. As Ben-Ami Shillony investigated the issue, there were 'the Newspaper Ordinance of 1875, the Publication Law of 1893, the Newspaper Laws of 1885 and 1909, the Military Secrets Protection Law of 1899, and the Peace Preservation Law [PPL] of 1925.' The PPL was revised to offer the sanction of a death penalty in 1928. Since the outbreak of the Chinese War, it was decided that 'all items concerning national economy and foreign relations were designated as state secrets that could not be published without the prior consent of the authorities' in 1937.¹⁴⁸

And it became impossible for a Japanese journalist to report his views freely without risking his life. Yet the arch-bureaucrats in post-war Japan decided that this sacred 'tradition' of the press club was to continue. Incidentally, the Japanese journalist association rejected (or was forced to reject) a suggestion from the European Union in 2005 to change those old practices saying, it is 'a good Japanese tradition'.

Despite all of the problems, we must acknowledge that Japan has occasionally had heroic journalists who have dared to risk their jobs. However, a trend has developed in the last twenty years or so whereby it seems that these brilliant and critical reporters have been eliminated from influential posts and replaced by run-of-the-mill correspondents who are content with the status quo.

As far as television reportage goes, the same major newspaper groups own most of the broadcasting companies with the exception of the public company, *NHK* (*Nihon Hoso Kyokai*), which is the equivalent of the BBC. They carry extremely limited documentaries about politics, historical analysis, foreign reportage and serious political coverage in cooperation with academics and specialists. No popular news channel concentrates on world politics. A Japanese journalist once bitterly described this clearly appalling situation of the modern media in Japan as 'a total idiotisation of the nation' – '*Kokumin no Sou-Hakuchika*'. Despite all these restrictions and poor programmes, however, crude facts had to be revealed on air as depression and social problems deepened. But these reports could never produce any results or start a justified media campaign in this stagnant political environment.

The dictum of 'Pen is mightier than Sword' is not applicable in Japan where the sword, whether it was in or out of the scabbard, constantly silenced the pen. The challenge and opportunity which the spirit of Japanese journalism is facing today are immense and quite overwhelming. The industry as a whole is definitely not ready to undertake a crucial mission to help Japan and, at the highest level, has a philosophy of failure.

OPINION LEADERS AS PROPAGANDISTS

Does Japan have no freedom of speech? It is true that unlike some other East Asian countries, the Japanese do at least have freedom to express their views in public. This was a complete change from the pre-war period. But if you carefully observed this freedom in detail, one would notice that there was a similar kind of situation, which was once criticised by the US trade negotiators during the 1980s as a 'structural impediment' that blocked US exports to Japan despite there being no identifiable regulations to ban various imports from America. The publishing 'business' was based on its own specific political needs, which were quite invisible to Westerners' observations.

Two major established monthly magazines for political affairs, *Bungei Shunjyu* with its affiliates and *Chuo Koron*, were regarded as opinion leaders and dominated the market since the pre-war period. *Chuo Koron* was originally funded by a Buddhist sect and once deemed as 'liberal'. Compared to current world competitors, however, both desperately lacked a global perspective and took a 'strictly domestic' approach in their arguments. They had neither a branch office nor a network abroad, and thus closed their eyes and ears to the constantly changing global political and economic movements.

Part Three – Japan in Crisis

In fact, the name of 'Bungei Shunjyu' actually means 'Literary Criticism' in Japanese, so political analysis took second place behind reviewing novels, which consist of a sizable chunk of text in this most prestigious literary magazine. Again, this old 'trivial' and flimsy 'intellectual' structure has never gone out of fashion in post-war Japan. Despite the depth of an unprecedented political, economic and social crisis, the world of Japanese publications is quietly muted and keeps up an optimistic mood of 'business as usual'.

In complete contrast to western opinion leaders, Japanese writers on current affairs merely take quotations from other books. They tend, therefore, to be dogmatic and often abuse intellectual property and copyright but the 'advantage' is that when several publishers copy a bestseller they become propaganda 'machines'.

Among the top Japanese opinion leaders, I would first introduce Hajime Karatsu's *The Potential Power of the Japanese Economy* as a perfect example of understanding how the publishing business works in Japan. Firstly, the book sticks to the 'Japan is the best' principle relentlessly criticising anything foreign. He asserted, 'When the Japanese or a Japanese corporation's identity is lost, it is clear that the country will experience its downfall. This is indisputable if we just look back at the history of Rome and Carthage.' Instead of comparisons with those ancient western empires, why could he not use more familiar, relevant and sensible examples about the collapse of the Japanese Empire?

The second important thing is to block any serious analysis. Karatsu repeatedly concluded that adopting the newest technology was the key for Japanese economic recovery. By saying that this alone will be a solution, he refused to analyse Japan's politics, the financial mess, the unfair distribution system or other urgent and pressing social issues.

Thirdly, he doesn't forget to express his scepticism about democratic values in a subtle manner, '...if we do something bad (under the Japanese standard), they say it is against democracy. In addition, there could be a criticism of our controlled society. But public opinions are ephemeral. If our new model is successful, society will accept it.' This is actually, a typical expression of old Japanese power politics: '*Kateba Kangun*' 'If one could win, one would be the emperor's army (But if you lose, you would become a bandit's army).' With these opinion leaders, the problem is, even if a policy was unsuccessful, society has to accept it anyway.

As a finale, commentators always paint a rosy picture of the desperate outlook by ignoring the harsh reality of Japanese political gridlocks, 'It is unarguable that Japan has been successful with its economy.'[149] Thus earning maximum 'brownie' points from editors, editorial board members, critics, media and all the unseen powers watching his political correctness.

Another popular author was Kenichi Omae who had an impeccable academic and business career in Japan and the United States. One would expect that he might be the one to criticise Japan from his extended background, experience and pragmatism. Indeed, he launched his slogan of *Heisei Ishin* – The *Heisei* Era's Reform – which was regarded in Japan as a radical reform just after the burst of the Japanese bubble. Frankly, however, *The Omae Report* was a disappointing work to readers who expected something groundbreaking from Japan's top 'reformer'. It is hard to believe that there will be any new form of either democracy or capitalism in Japan, even if his 'reforms' were all successfully applied.

In his criticism, he adamantly believed, 'If the numbers of Members of the House of Representatives (MHR) were half of their current membership, Japanese politics would be enormously improved.' There was no convincing explanation why this should be so. 'Then, their sense of the responsibility would change,' he said. Alternatively, 'They will have no time to work at other matters and would concentrate fully on the issues of state.' It is not a convincing argument that Japan's problems are solely related to the number of its politicians. He may be talking about the US Senate in comparison that has 100 members under the US presidential system in which the president enjoys executive power. The British House of Commons has a larger number of Members of Parliament in order to form a parliamentary body identical to Japanese constitutional requirements. Or how about the even larger French National Assembly?

Part Three – Japan in Crisis

The main agenda of his 'reform' ended up as a sort of federal system that would divide a new Japan into eleven provinces from the current historical divisions of the smaller forty-seven prefecture base.[150] Despite these 'radical' reforms, he said he was optimistic about Japan's financial problems in his later report. If so, why was his rethink radical policy necessary in the first place? More worryingly, this shortsighted policy was randomly accepted by many Japanese politicians, bureaucrats and business leaders despite the danger that this was only a superficial remedy that did not tackle the real issues and wasted limited time.

A bestselling writer and propagandist, Keitaro Hasegawa, was also a very popular analyst of international affairs despite his purely domestic background. In one of his hundreds of popular books, *The Reviving Japanese Economy under Uni-polar Control*, he assured the readers that US-originated IT would save the Japanese economy – another example of the same old tactics. By completely ignoring the reality in Japan, he continued as if his task was just to tell the Japanese, 'Don't worry, just keep going,' or, 'No problem. Carry on, mates!'[151]

In Japan, some editors seem to use their influence on an author, including which direction his writing should take, especially on expressing biased views on foreign subjects. One rare academic who contributed to an actual political argument, Terumasa Nakanishi, 'confessed' that his book *The History of the Decline and Fall of the British Empire* was written following a suggestion from an editor of a monthly magazine.[152] Well, in my view, he simply did not criticise the problem deeply enough!

Foreign authors cannot penetrate into the Japanese market, as they are entirely out of the loop of these Japanese editing criteria. There are two recognisable groups among them. One is a sort of Japanologist who has studied the language and has specialized in Japanese affairs or even worked on the ground, but often covers only a very limited area. The other is an expert on politics, law or economics, who can see Japan from the outside with a wider perspective but still needs to rely on secondary-sourced information and often hopelessly lacks adequate local knowledge and research capability.

On the Theory of Chinese Ideology

Both seem to have their limits. As an example, by writing *Stock Market Capitalism: Welfare Capitalism – Japan and Germany versus the Anglo-Saxon*, Ronald Dore was hailed by the Japanese media and this book was immediately translated into Japanese. In contrasting Anglo-American versus German-Japanese, however, he drew a false parallel.[153] Post-war Germany, after all, is a functioning democracy, and therefore there is no essential political or economic similarity, as he tried to argue in this book. Understandably, if you make your lifetime work a study of Japanese matters, foreign specialists cannot afford to upset their Japanese hosts or organizations that are guided by a highly sensitive arch-bureaucracy – unless they are ready to commit career suicide after a spectacular shot of 'fireworks'.

As an example in the latter group of western authors, I would name Brian Reading's early warning, *Japan – The Coming Collapse*, published in 1992, which was completely ignored by Japanese publishers. As a foreign expert, he boldly criticised the Japanese problems, 'The Japanese political system, in its present form, cannot possibly implement a radical reform programme. Japan is not a democracy and never has been, on the contrary, it is a country run by and for powerful vested interests, masquerading behind the formal trappings of democratic institutions…'[154] His work did not, however, convince the perceived view in Britain today, which could be loosely defined as just random criticism, or frankly, just shooting in the dark.

In these situations, we cannot expect a solution to evolve from Japanese public opinion circles.

'FAIR-MINDED' BUSINESS LEADERS?

In a country like the US that claims 'America's business is business', their business leaders have a lot to say and actually act as a political pressure group, with some of them even joining the government to form its economic policy. The business leaders in the East, however, were until recently reticent despite their growing influence.

Part Three – Japan in Crisis

After the miraculous rise of the Japanese economy in the 1960s driven by its export industries, there was a notable growth in traditional manufacturing businesses such as steel and electricity providers while banks took the important role of providing a back-up system for the growing economy. Japanese bureaucratic control on big business was extended in the 1970s after the 'oil shock' and the petroleum price hike in 1973. The sudden surge of inflationary pressure had to be eased by a high volume of governmental financial injections under the Fukuda administration. It was the first visible sign of an unbalanced economic policy which set up a trend for fiscal indulgence and subsequent deterioration.

The Japanese export industry as a whole was still smaller than domestic 'essential industries', the *Kikan Sagyo,* as defined by the bureaucrats. In the 1980s, export industries such as automobile and electronics grew fast as their production bases gradually shifted to the US and other overseas locations to avoid trade disputes and so these businesses became more global market-oriented and transparent in nature. Early in the 1990s, they surpassed the 'old' industries in terms of their profitability and numbers of worldwide employees.

Gradually, the executives of these new industries took over the important business leaders' posts as well. Meanwhile, the shareholding structure of Japanese companies and the scope of business for Japanese companies dramatically changed as the influence of the global financial markets grew at a rapid pace. In particular, when Japan's bubble burst, a general feeling appeared in society that, after all, Japanese bureaucratic control was a failure. In this new environment, some began to hope for the possibility that successful business leaders would exercise their political influence on politicians to save the Japanese economy.

But there were a few notable differences, which hindered this kind of positive movement. Firstly, Japan's problem ran much deeper than the cyclical mismanagement of boom and bust. In other words, its malaise came from more fundamental political reasons which were wholly embedded in Japanese business culture, compared to the situation in the US free markets. Secondly, the US business infrastructure enjoyed economic independence and legal protection which was hard to obtain or simply did not exist in Japan. Thirdly, due to this business environment, most of the Japanese export and services industry still had to rely on the 'direction' of arch-bureaucracy in the vital Japanese domestic market. Over the years, therefore, 'Free trade' for overseas markets was advocated, but at the same time, 'Protectionist' measures based on the old structures for the domestic market meant that in reality, this concept was constantly compromised.

As soon as the arch-bureaucracy detected the growth of new rising economic and corporate powers, it tried to contain these various political influences inside the old system, by exercising its same old 'eternal' power. Furthermore, the arch-bureaucracy actually took a posture of supporting the private sector in an extraordinary way which completely ignored market principles. Some top business leaders even requested the government make such a move without incurring any shame or criticism in Japan. One of these examples was the unilateral US dollar buying operation to keep the yen's exchange rates low without any international coordination. As the result of this operation, the Japanese government ended up holding 70 trillion yen equivalent to US$650 billion by the end of 2003. By early 2005, however, this policy was given up (at least temporarily!) due to the staggering exchange rate losses accumulated by the subsequent appreciation of the yen.

In contrast, David Vogel, who examined the basis of US corporate behaviour predicated on the free market, shows that the pattern of anti-state interference is visible throughout American society, 'The distrust of the state that characterizes the consciousness of the American bourgeoisie is built into the structure of American capitalism; it is as much a characteristic of the American political order…' He concluded, 'The attitude of American businessmen toward government cannot be fully explained with reference to the relatively passive and limited role of the state in American industrial development; it is also critically linked to the legitimacy of democratic traditions in America.'[155] But in the case of Japan, we need to apply the principle of arch-bureaucracy.

When Toyota's Tadashi Okuda was appointed to be the chairman of *Keidanren* – The Federation of the Japanese Economic Groups (FJEG), however, the organization's political stance suddenly became presentable on the back of a strong business trend in exports. During his tenure, a booklet for a new vision on the Japanese political economy was produced. In this proposal, they emphasised the importance of private sectors and individualism for the first time.[156]

The major point of failure for continuing in this direction was that the FJEG had no independent research capability, for instance, compared to its British counterpart, the CBI which holds hard data and information. Given the state of existing real politics, it would be naïve to believe it is possible to create a meaningfully effective organ independently, that is without any interference from arch-bureaucracy.

We would all agree that successful companies are made not by government initiatives but by company managers adopting sensible ideas. But success depends upon, at least, fair market practices, good business infrastructure and free competition. Above all, we cannot ignore the fact that Japan is clearly lacking the necessary political philosophy for this business environment defined as capitalism. Without this guidance, we need to assume that the social influences of Japanese business leaders – even the existence of an open-minded leader such as Chairman Okuda – would be politically negligible.

AN UNDERGROUND WORLD IN DAYLIGHT

There is another notable element in Japanese society which hinders the development of a democracy although it is rather unofficial. The underground world run by *Yakuza* – the organised crime syndicates – maintains a special status in Japanese society, the scale of which is in no way matched by other industrialised nations in the West.

The Japanese police agency announced in January 2004 that despite the continuing countrywide recession, the organized crime rate increased over eight consecutive years. The combined big three organizations had around six thousand members and associate members and this represented 70.2 per cent of the entire underground world. This monopolization rate was 24.8 per cent in 1985. The total number of criminals was 85,800, showing a five hundred member increase on a year-on-year basis. The police also reported that right-wing political activities substantially increased during this period.

The main reason for this abnormality is clear. Again, in those societies under the system of Chinese ideology, there is no proper legal infrastructure in place to control criminal activities or to govern fair business relationships. For instance, a type of crime that is regularly reported in Japan, such as forging a legal registered document to steal property without the owner's will or knowledge, seldom occurs in the West. Modern legal practice and a severe penalty system make this kind of crime unthinkable as a way of profitable business. Many of Japan's legal experts or business executives who were sent to the US or Europe would have known about Japan's problematic legal infrastructure but once back home they were powerless to change it. There is no political will to protect the economy.

Some Japanese experts suggested that the authorities give implicit consent to Japanese Yakuza and do not press too hard on them as long as they behave 'properly' in post-war Japan. This might be an overstated view but certainly, Japan does not emulate one of the new trends of the twenty-first century, that is by employing special police forces, as in Italy, where, hidden by balaclavas, they storm Mafia bosses' secret hideouts. The Japanese mafia, despite continuously committing crimes, are not anonymous as in other countries. They have their own headquarters at a known established address and their activities are often reported on as a sort of 'celebrity' event by various soft entertainment magazines.

During the last decades, Japan seemed to be firmly included in the 'territory' of the Korean and Chinese crime rings, the latter known as the world's largest illegal syndicate. In this situation, the Japanese police that had once boasted its record as arguably the best in the world, became one of the most ineffective police organizations, relying on old techniques which neglected forensic investigations. Fraud, felony and organised crimes have increased rapidly in the longest on-going depression in Japan.

But a far more serious and disturbing problem arising from criminal activity is of a political nature. In Japan, some criminal gangs were disguised as political right-wingers, as if by doing so, they could get some sympathy from the police. In pre-war Japan and Germany, there were violent incidents carried out by these political terrorists that crippled the democratic movements of both countries. In 2004, the German police raided the headquarters of neo-Nazi groups and showed their determination to tackle this kind of dangerous political movement. Unfortunately, things have evolved differently in Japan.

Almost unnoticed by global media, in October 2002, Koki Ishii, MHR of the Democratic Party of Japan, was butchered in front of his house. He, as an exceptional Japanese politician, was well known for his tenacious investigations into the dark sides of Japanese parliamentary politics. So far, nine victims made up of politicians and ex-senior bureaucrats including the head of the National Police Agency (but excluding lawyers and journalists) have been attacked since the Japanese bubble burst. The credibility of Japanese politics and the judicial system was put at stake by those acts of terrorism with their secret agenda. No political assassin behind those actual killings has ever been caught in Japan. But the resolve to prevent a similar crime threatening the existence of Japanese democracy and capitalism was not forthcoming from Japanese political circles.[157] In this situation, nobody can deny that someday Japan could return to the pre-war period of constant political assassinations even if someone decides to reform its rotten politics.

Ernest Satow, a British diplomat who lived in Japan just before and after the Meiji Restoration, encountered many of those bloody killings. From his abundant experience, he intuitively detected that they neither came from the bloodthirsty character of the samurais nor as just simple crime, but from political motives. He observed, 'It was impossible not to hate the assassin, but looking at the matter from a Japanese point of view, I confess that I could not help regretting that a man who was evidently of such heroic mould, should have been misguided enough to believe that his country could be helped by such means.'[158]

The Japanese attitude of compromise toward illegal crime organizations, therefore, is not just a crime issue for society but it is seriously hampering the development of Japan's prosperity and security. Peter Hill rightly queried, '... the question must be asked whether the authorities are serious in their professed aim of Yakuza eradication. For a comprehensive anti-Yakuza drive, the introduction of the *Botaihou* (Anti-gangster organisations act) would need to be accompanied by significantly increased use of the existing criminal law.' He noticed the existence of 'usual suspects', 'The influence of foreign pressure and the reaction to repeated political scandals as catalysts in creation of this law suggest that a certain degree of symbolism may be involved.'[159] And a deeper problem is that Yakuza was certainly not the only organisational entity responsible for serious political crimes.

THE OPPOSITION AND THE ANTI-AMERICAN WRANGLE

Largely influenced by the 'people's democracy' in East Asia, the Japan Socialist Party (JSP) enjoyed themselves as a sort of pure permanent opposition group supported by trade unions in the Japanese parliament, without any solidarity with the business community, and because of this, ex-bureaucrat politicians like Eisaku Sato refused to join the opposition camp despite their solicitations. The growing anti-American sentiment of the JSP was hard to sell in the midst of the Cold War. At that time, Japanese bureaucrats only joined the Liberal Democratic Party as it provided a perfect political environment for their initiatives and paved the way for the LDP's long reign.

A major reshaping of this long-established political balance arrived in the midst of the Japanese bubble. It happened first in the Upper

Part Three – Japan in Crisis

House (Term: six years) or *Sangi-in* – the House of Councillors – in the 1989 election as the voters gave a majority to the JSP while the Liberal Democratic Party (LDP) retained their position in the House of Representatives. In the process of passing a bill in Japan, if the Upper House rejected it, the Lower House have to pass it a second time by a majority of two-thirds or more for a bill to go through.

In seizing an opportunity that arose from the disarrayed opposition camps, Ichiro Ozawa dropped out from the largest Takeshita sect – *Keisei-kai* – of the LDP, forming the Shinsei (Rebirth) Party in opposition, to control parliament and avoid a breakdown in politics. He promoted a coalition for the Hosokawa administration that successfully replaced the LDP's forty-five-year reign in 1993.

After the long dominance of the LDP, a partial single constituency system was finally introduced in the midst of internal and international criticism of Japanese politics but it was linked to a newly invented scheme of proportional representation for each political party that could act as a 'parachute' for important candidates who had lost their seats in a single constituency. The world's most peculiar election method had to be worked out as a compromise between the political parties and faced fierce resistance from all sides.

Soon after a stilted meeting between Morihiro Hosokawa and Bill Clinton at the White House, however, the short-lived government ended as struggles inside the coalition intensified. What Ichiro Ozawa and his groups tried was a political power-game in a disguised two-party system that was just an extension of the same old LDP politics: secretive, manipulative and money-driven, a dangerous 'battlefield' which he dominated as master.

Again, there seemed to be no foundation for a proper opposition party with public support which would stand for the benefit of the Japanese people by starting a different political course for the common good and a national goal. He changed the name of his political party to *Shinshin* (New Progress) Party and then to *Jiyu* (Liberal) Party as if it was his own personal plaything. Talking about the necessity for an anti-LDP movement, he joined the LDP as part of the coalition the next day. He acted as if his real role was actually to destroy the Japanese opposition movement, or in more crude Japanese terms, to control this rather 'unnecessary' political creature.

In the 2003 general election, Ichiro Ozawa joined as Number Two of the Democratic Party of Japan (DPJ) under Naoto Kan and stood against Junichiro Koizumi's LDP. The DPJ gained forty seats and its members made up 177 of the 480 seats – which was surprising since they had not put up a candidate for all the constituencies. Like the opposition in Spain during its 2004 election, Naoto Kan repeated in this campaign that his opposition party, if elected, would be likely to say 'No' to the United States on major diplomatic issues, such as sending peacekeeping troops to Iraq. Junichiro Koizumi attacked him on this point. He simply countered that America would accept Japan's 'democratic' decisions (whatever they might be!). Analysing the views of the major 'bosses' of the DPJ, a veteran watcher of Japanese politics, Kichiya Kobayashi, predicted in 2000 the possibility of a future fundamental change to the post-war US-Japan relationship under their leadership of 'a naked lust for power'.[160]

In contrast, South Korea announced it would send over three thousand combat units to Iraq. After criticising the war in Iraq, France and Germany did not send any troops to Iraq but they participated in the joint military operations to Afghanistan. The Spanish government withdrew its commitment to Iraq and sent its military forces under NATO to Afghanistan while the Japanese kept silent on any contribution.

Compared with those countries, what the Japanese politicians were proposing was tantamount to a full denial of western diplomatic efforts for global security. A third of the opposition at the time actually consisted of the residues of left-wing populists who had originated from ex-JSP extremists and acted as a 'permanent' opposition and denounced any sort of Japanese military commitment. In this regard, it is important to realise that the anti-war movement in Japan did not come from modern diplomatic arguments as seen in European politics. Rather, this pretext originated in the return of the old Japanese isolationism in the archipelago driven by its traditional political ideology.

Against general Japanese public opinion, the Koizumi administration successfully managed to send Japanese troops to Iraq. In an escalating phase of the war on terror, his policy failed to impress Japan's western allies whose deployment was increasing. Nobody said either in Japan or indeed in the rest of the world that it was humiliating that the Japanese army had to ask another country's military force to provide security protection for Japan's peacekeeping operations, instead of doing it by themselves, as every other country, and even their own ancestors, had done, thereby demonstrating their political independence.[161] No prime minister of course could ever change this kind of general political 'consensus' in Japan. On this fragile power base, which existed as a dominating factor in political decision making, it was a tactical necessity to assume a reformist posture, but it would be a strategic failure to carry out any kind of serious reform.

In this political environment, the opposition DPJ, although lacking a viable strategy, was elected with 311 seats to lead the country in a different direction in the August 2009 general election, but it failed to attain the two-thirds (320 seats) majority in the House of Representatives. As things get much tougher, a political compromise similar to the pre-war Grand Coalition of all parties – *Taisei-Yokusan-Kai* – will have to be brought in at some stage, as increasingly vulnerable politicians need to cooperate on the important issues such as a change to a new constitution. In other words, the 'evaporation' of political parties, the virtual death of parliament and the full restoration of arch-bureaucracy as a prelude for the ending, seem to be lying in wait in a different form at the next corner.

The crucial fact is that there is no opposition to arch-bureaucracy itself in Japan despite all noisy claims and feigned movements against it. In Japanese politics, arch-bureaucracy never requires the sovereign people's consent to govern and it can rely on 'legitimate' executive power, which is under their strict control and out of reach of ordinary people.

On the Theory of Chinese Ideology

ERODED SOVEREIGNTY

In 1945, facing the ruin in Europe, the US and Britain wanted the war in the Pacific theatre to end as soon as possible, where Japan stood alone. To most Japanese leaders it was apparent that, after the surrender of Germany, the defeat of Japan was only a matter of time. Rational thought was eventually infiltrating to the Japanese political scene.

In the summer of the same year, the Allied powers met at Potsdam to discuss Japan and warned the Japanese government to surrender unconditionally (26 July). Meanwhile, the newly elected US president, Harry Truman, informed the British and the Russians that the US had successfully produced a new type of weapon just a day before the conference.

Japan ignored this virtual ultimatum threatening a thermo-nuclear attack in the form of Prime Minister Kantaro Suzuki's statement. The Japanese government could not act decisively as the military and other fanatics insisted on final battles on the Japanese mainland even though the navy was losing the war by 'waves' of mass suicidal attacks in front of the fully modernised naval power of the United States. Finally, the world's first atomic weapon was launched on Hiroshima (6 August) and then the second on Nagasaki (9 August). As agreed by the US and Britain, Soviet Russia declared war on Japan (8 August) and the Red Army swiftly advanced into Manchuria, then to southern Sakhalin (11 August). The situation for Japan was rapidly deteriorating.

Suddenly, the Soviet communists' occupation of eastern Japan struck as a nightmare scenario in the minds of Japanese leaders, and simultaneously, they feared another possible atomic-bomb attack on Tokyo by the US bombers. Leon Sigal focused on this historical moment, when on the next day (9 August) the Japanese government used Swiss and Swedish intermediaries to notify the Allies of its willingness to accept the Potsdam terms, but on one condition: 'with the understanding that the said declaration does not comprise any demand which prejudices the prerogative of His

Part Three – Japan in Crisis

Majesty as a Sovereign Ruler.'[162] This was the last point the Japanese arch-bureaucracy wanted to negotiate with the Allies. People were still listening to announcements from the Imperial headquarters – *Dai Honei Happyo* – which began with naval march music, and according to this illusory propaganda machine, Japan was winning the war all the way right up to those final moments.

After half of a century, the Japanese economy derailed again. The bigger problem, however, was that with its secretive techniques and gift of camouflage, it was difficult to know how this gigantic entity had actually expanded. James Babb argued as staggering, citing the Civil Watch website, that there were 7,146 special corporations just after the Japanese bubble.[163] He seemed to be prematurely astonished. The government announced that the total number of public corporations – *Koeki-Hojin* – increased to around 25,000 by mid-2009. And 1,531 among those received funds or contracts from the ministries 'during 2006 to 2007'. There were 9,900 employees 'descended' from the ministries. In addition, there were other forms of *Hojin* – public corporate entity – businesses in Japan, which were still intact at the time.

More than hundred years ago, Fukuzawa knew that the degree of the coming new challenges facing Japan were far greater than people imagined. He explained this challenge once as 'facing a raging torrent that could sweep you away' and asked Japan to hold on. He argued that Japan should act together with the West for Eastern Asian affairs, as there was no other choice. Japan should 'reject *in mind* (the way of) the old "bad friends" (Qing China and Yi Korea) in the East'. (16/03/1885 – Jiji-Shimpo) In other words, he was aware of the impossibility of dealing with modern diplomatic life on the basis of Chinese ideology.

His suggestion was simplified as the publicly well-known slogan of '*Datsu-A Nyu-Ou*' with four Chinese characters. Literally, these words can be most appropriately translated as 'Leave the Chinese ideology and accept Western political philosophy.' The early Meiji government moved successfully on the course he chose. But his warning was soon to be forgotten.

On the Theory of Chinese Ideology

Against his advice, the military-led Japanese government went in the opposite direction by meddling in East Asian politics and directly negotiating with the 'bad friends' without any consideration for the interests of Japan's western allies and a global concept of freedom. This political process was explained by the arch-bureaucracy with the counterslogan of '*Wa-Kon Yoo-Sai*'. Literally, that meant 'Japanese spirit and Western technology'. In order to clarify what was actually said, however, we would need to extend the number of the Chinese characters from four to six – 'Japanese spirit, Chinese ideology (or political system) and Western technology'. This is written in Japanese, '*Wa-Kon Chu-Sei Yoo-Sai*'.

There was also a wrong emphasis as the Japanese spirit survived even when the Chinese political system was introduced. Even if Japan had accepted a western political philosophy and system, therefore, the nation's spirit would remain, as is the case in Europe. For instance, Germany could have this slogan, 'The German spirit, the western political system and western technology'. Despite people who are trying to create a European spirit, 'British spirit' or 'French spirit' is still alive and well in Europe. How can a man forget his own identity? Even a drastic injection of British politics including colonisation and the English language failed to produce the same spirit in the United States. China is now following the path of Japan with the idea of 'The Chinese spirit, the Chinese political system and western technology'.

Based on this mentality, instead of introducing western political philosophy, the Japanese have kept what they call Eastern thought, *Toyo Shiso,* that originated with the Chinese classics. Eiichi Shibusawa, an early business leader in pre-war Japan, once boasted his capitalistic backbone was Confucianism despite the fact that all his successful businesses originated in the western world.

In the current political environment, a modern constitution means nothing to the Japanese people who are still living with their rights and duties eroded as before. Takeshi Umehara, a leading Japanese academic, claimed, 'To study (humanities or social science) is an unlimited pleasure.' In Japan, it was definitely not studied as the 'pursuit of truth' as Georg Hegel and others aspired to in the West. The lack of understanding about democracy among the Japanese people is rooted in their educational and academic system where social and historical facts are constantly ignored. But for how long would Japan's sovereign rulers afford these pleasure-seeking intellectuals free rein?

THE 'ASSAULT' OF THE 'LAND STANDARD'

At least, we all know how and when the Meiji Empire, or the first Japanese modern state, began to crumble. In this context, the fatal advance was made in September 1931 when the staff officers of the Japanese Kwangtung Army – *Kantogun* – blasted the railway near Mukden, falsely accusing the innocent Chinese for the attack, and occupied Chinese Manchuria. The background to this Japanese military initiative was that the South Manchurian Railway, Japan's principal asset in Manchuria, was losing ground to China's own expanding railway network.[164]

When this grave security failure was exposed, however, it was an alarming warning to Japan that their reputation for maintaining the principles of international law and order – which the Japanese Empire had carefully observed in order to expand as the most credible western ally in East Asia up to that point – was in jeopardy. Under normal circumstances, what the Japanese government reaction should have been was to rectify the situation in a sensible way both for the sake of keeping military discipline and from the viewpoint of international cooperation. Instead, dysfunctional Japanese military leaders approved this dangerous plot without thinking about the serious consequences of such an illicit act. How about Japanese politicians? After the assassination of Prime Minister Osachi Hamaguchi in November 1930, Japanese politicians were virtually powerless in the face of the prevailing militaristic fanaticism, as we have reviewed in Part One.

By this period, Japanese domestic politics had almost completely denounced western social and political values and ignored the West's prosperity and power which had been shaken by the Great Depression. And what Japan finally got from this elated madness was a strange form of 'hyper-elitism' based on the distorted old concepts working within the 'modern' administration. As a decision-making system, it was even worse than in Japan's own feudal past where the equivalent of a lieutenant colonel without proper authority could ever start a war on behalf of the entire nation in the name of the emperor without even seeking approval first. They insisted that they had the prerogative of the supreme command of Japan in Manchuria! The Japanese government and army horribly indulged these psychopathic elites who had been taught only to fight since the age of thirteen without receiving a proper general education.

According to Kikuo Nakamura, a learned expert on pre-war Japanese political history at Keio University, in complete contrast to their British and American counterparts, the Japanese Army College after the First World War allocated its 'elitist' of the elites to Operations, then the second lot to Logistics, and the lowest grade to Intelligence. Not only did the Japanese military belittle Intelligence but also these elevated officers in Operations were given excessive powers to disregard Intelligence findings. This was the cause of Japan's appalling military failure.

To make matters worse, no one in Japan could stand up and say, 'it is fundamentally wrong' without risking his or somebody's life in this rigid system. Because of this inflexible and emotional 'atmosphere' they rejected all the international criticism for their invasion of Manchuria, and Japan walked out of the League of Nations after the Japanese representative, Yosuke Matsuoka, made a disgraceful speech in 1933. Using Karl Marx's famous simile, this was the second 'farce' which cemented the first 'tragedy' in Japanese history. And in carrying out this horribly damaging diplomatic move, Japan had no thought of any modern state strategy. It was as if Japan has decided to go back to its former policy of seclusion under the Tokugawa Shogunate, only this time with new weaponry and an extended territory.

Part Three – Japan in Crisis

As war with Hitler's Germany was declared, the British public asked a well-respected politician, Winston Churchill, to lead the nation in its time of crisis. Under the double standards of Japanese politics, even though the third Konoe administration was 'trying' to reach a peace deal with the United States, Hideki Tojo, a little-known lieutenant general who had always insisted on a policy of dogmatic military aggression on the Chinese continent, was promoted to be a general and then prime minister 'to avoid' the coming unwinnable war.

When the United States demanded the Japanese withdrawal from China, it was impossible to agree to because nobody else but General Tojo could implement such a policy. This would mean admitting all his and his colleagues' previous guilt in advocating the ill-conceived undeclared war in China, thereby embarrassing and endangering his faction and its supporters. Thus, an opportunity to change course was substituted by a fervent rejection of the idea without paying any political consideration to the US suggestions. And in making this most dreadful blunder on behalf of the Empire of Japan, Tojo had no regrets – he did it, not for his own personal interests (and absolutely not for his country), but for the objectives of its 'supreme' factionalism.

A similar sort of peculiar political mindset and behaviour has never diminished in post-war Japan. This time, almost completely unnoticed by global media, Japanese arch-bureaucrats made a new irrational advance under a different political initiative soon after the Japanese economy took off. The ministries of Construction, Finance and Interior mutually agreed and launched their own untested economic policy spurred on by their own secret political needs. As before, the issue was never discussed in a serious manner in public, and as usual, neither the press nor opinion leaders could oppose their fanatical ideas. Like the sudden advance into Manchuria, it abruptly emerged as a reality before the eyes of the Japanese people. Furthermore, once it was launched, nobody in Japanese politics could stand up and protest at this 'sacred' advance. In both cases, Japan tried to apply faulty political and economic logic without any national solution in mind.

This new decision was the extraordinary Japanese system of a 'Land Standard' based on the Land Price – *Jika* – an index for real estate values all over the country which was approved by parliament as the Land Price Announcement Act in 1969. Afterwards this economic policy became part of Japan's 'unshakeable' tradition and nobody in Japan put a stop to it. With his impeccable rhetoric, Kiyohiko Nishimura explained the political situation around this newly-created myth, 'It is impossible to condemn that all the "myths" are absurd, as there is a background, which produces such a "myth", and movements in people's minds, which believe in "myth", and finally, the social system to upkeep a "myth". The Myth of Land is no exception.'[165]

The reality of this political 'myth' which emerged in Japan, was the decision to protect landowners' interests to such a degree that the economic balance of property prices was destroyed. By accepting this myth, the Japanese government emerged as the only central government in the world to fix the country's land value, by controlling the peculiar valuation methods and the business of valuers regardless of the building above the land, different geographical differences and other distinctions, keeping without any economic foundation this dogmatic annual index.

Despite this, the Japanese public started to believe in this arbitrary method created by a state decision with unknown objectives, as every major Japanese newspaper started to solemnly announce on their front pages the price of this year's 'sacred' land value without even a single drop of criticism. And all members of the Japanese financial industry 'religiously' followed this index by using the artificial land value as collateral without a proper credit analysis for the security of their loans. As a consequence of this politically predetermined calculation, the market mechanism of demand and supply was ignored – even as a concept. In addition, as a final blow to the economy, the government created various taxes based on this arbitrary land value.

Pain was not felt initially, as most of these values were deliberately set at a much lower price level than the actual market price. The problem, as identified in the Japanese Land Agency's 'White Paper on Land' lay in the fact that between 1955 and 1989, the Land Price Index in Japan's six major cities increased 128-fold, compared to the market-guided two-fold increase on the wholesale price index over the same period calculated by the Bank of Japan. A large-scale credit boom based on this artificial land value was created to inflate the Japanese economy. Japanese society as a whole pushed up these speculative land prices to their maximum extent.

When major Japanese city banks were suddenly announced as the biggest global banking institutions in terms of total asset value in the late 1980s, bankers in New York were stunned and puzzled. Nobody knew that the source of these new assets came from the inflated value of land in Japan based on extraordinary, illogical ideas. Some even seriously believed that the 'victory' of Japanese capitalism was imminent. Then, this immense bubble burst, dealing a devastating blow to the Japanese banks.

As in the past, the Japanese government decided to continue with the system even though the cause of this horrible financial blunder was now publicly exposed. Foreign critics unfortunately failed to identify this distorted 'Japanese' phenomenon. But some Japanese experts took a risk and criticised it. I also published an article on this specific issue and its consequences for Japan's economic system in the *Financial Business Review*, which was once the bastion of criticism on the Japanese economy read by most bankers, economists, businessmen and bureaucrats.[166] But nobody tried publicly to either agree or disagree, just as in the 1930s, when no one wanted to discuss the 'Manchurian invasion'.

Unless this myth of a distorted 'Land Standard' is abolished, Japan's deflationary stagnation and its inherited risks will not be eliminated. The 'blood' in the form of a limitlessly increasing public debt is still leaking from this horrendous political venture of incompetent 'capitalists' and is the modern equivalent of spreading an undeclared war in the vast Chinese continent and beyond by old disqualified 'imperialists'.

II – THE ORIGIN OF THE DEFLATIONARY SPIRAL

THE BUBBLE THAT FAILED TO BE DEFINED

On 29 December 1989, the Tokyo stock market recorded its peak of ¥38,915.87. This was the final day of the Japanese business year just before the New Year Holiday season. As usual, there was a repetition of triple hand clappings and high spirits equivalent to western cheers, and smiling female employees were wearing colourful *kimono* to mark this special occasion. Everybody was thinking ahead to their own relaxed festive plans and no one believed that this was going to be the last day of post-war Japan's longest and tumultuous boom.

The New Year started with an awkward opening and continued jitters in the market. After a 'dead cat' rebound, the average stock price continued to decline, and dipped below ¥20,000 by October; thus, the equivalent value of 270 trillion yen was wiped off the Tokyo stock market.

We must pay an attention to a situation peculiar to Japan. Of course, Japan was not the first country to experience the burst of a financial bubble. In economic history, there was the 'Black Tulip' bubble in the Netherlands in 1637, the 'South Sea' bubble in England in 1720 and many others. Indeed all successful economies have had to go through this process but those incidents never rocked their fundamental economic systems or political structures.

Why was it so different this time in Japan? A notable distinction common to these historical cases was that the causes of the bubble were properly analysed by economists so that the specific problem was solved 'mechanically' to make sure that it would never arise again, at least in similar form, and these bubbles caused by human ignorance and greed were properly repented of. The seriousness of the Japanese bubble was that none of the politicians in power, government advisors or experts have defined the cause of Japan's bubble, as if it remained a political taboo. In Japan, therefore, avarice and insanity are still rife as the defect is still alive and well inside its economic system.

The current 'sub-prime securitisation' bubble described by some, or even 'derivative casino' bubble defined by others, is claimed by many as the biggest economic downturn since the Great Depression and should touch the boundary of politics. No doubt, the world's politicians, economists, professionals and academics will investigate the issue vigorously in order to restructure the global financial economy. In doing so, perhaps we first need to know the origin of the Japanese bubble if we assume the global economy intends to be either really 'global' or interdependent. Secondly, because historically the Japanese deflationary process began the crash and then spread all over the world. But naming this process as an 'asset' bubble, as many western financial experts did at the time, is obviously not good enough.

In his bestselling and most quoted book on this issue in Japan, *A Complex Depression*, Giichi Miyazaki tried to depict what exactly happened during this Japanese bubble and its process as it burst. He concluded, 'With the opening of the global financial market, Japan accepted the Bank of International Settlement's (BIS) regulation. I presume that this change made the Japanese style credit crunch inevitable while decreasing the money supply. This forced the process of negative growth on the actual GDP.'[167] But then, one is tempted to ask, why did other countries that accepted BIS regulations not experience the same systemic risk?

Naming the interrelated movements of an economic process often creates a cumbersome judgement. But this Japanese process of bubble and burst had an irregular but distinctive characteristic like the old speculation which once happened in Holland. While you might have not known this before (until you read this book, of course!), it was a specific 'Land Standard' bubble exactly like the Dutch 'Black Tulip' scandal.

After the late 1980s, the Japanese economic policy relied entirely on its export trade and the government was under huge pressure from the US government to reduce its massive trade surplus with the United States. *Naijyu Kakudai* – stronger growth for domestic demand – became an important aspiration for Japan. By rejecting reforms in its consumer markets, the Japanese government focused on bank lending to stimulate domestic demand. The fact was that the Japanese policymakers not only refused to open their domestic market to the Americans but they also stopped its growth for fellow Japanese entrepreneurs by failing to establish a modern business infrastructure. After an implicit nod from the Ministry of Finance (MOF) who controlled the banking business in Japan, All Japan Inc moved in one direction like a big stampede of cattle in Kansas City.

In 1987, the total value of residential land in the Japanese archipelago was calculated as amounting to 1.8 trillion yen which is 4.3-fold (as per ¥130/$1) more than that of the US, which in terms of land volume is twenty-five times bigger than Japan, according to a Japanese Land Agency report. But who could have possibly calculated such a figure accurately?

Furthermore, the Japanese Economic Planning Agency boastingly announced that at the end of 1987, compared to the previous year, the value of the total land in Japan increased to 248 trillion yen, as if Japan had became suddenly rich without doing any hard work. This figure was equivalent to 74 per cent of Japan's total GDP of ¥335 trillion in the same year.

The aggressive expansion of Japanese bank lending based on this artificial land value was then crushed by falling share prices. New trading techniques like short selling in the futures market approved by the MOF earlier also played a significant role in this fall. The pattern of expansion based wholly on a myth first became defensive, and then it caused panic in the opposite direction. The expansion was made on the assumption of a constant capital gain but suddenly contraction and capital loss now appeared in everyone's mind.

Real estate price started to tumble after Japanese banks announced controls on the total volume of loans – *Soryo Kisei* – in April 1990, as they obviously could not go further in their abnormal lending. A building site in the Minato district in Tokyo, which peaked at 77 million yen per tsubo (or 3.3 m2), was now sold at 28 million yen per tsubo at the end of 1991. This was a fall of 64 per cent.[168] The stock market still remained above the 20,000 yen level. But eight months later, it finally dipped to 14,309.

Nobody wanted to calculate any longer how much Japan's total land value was compared to that of the United States! The Japanese realised that the myth of land was, after all, not the truth. In the nearby airport location of Makuhari in Chiba prefecture, many deserted building sites indicated that planned developments had to be abandoned due to lack of demand. People now also understood that one could create a significant supply by building a lot of space in skyscrapers on a relatively small land area.

What this extraordinary process of Japan's bubble and burst should have exposed to the public was Japan's systematic lack of economic, banking, legal, tax, accounting, and property infrastructures, and above all, its failed politics. In this financial crisis, some banks like Long-Term Credit Bank or Nippon Credit Bank did collapse as if market forces were functioning; but Japan's old business model was still intact even after this unprecedented economic disaster.

AN IDEOLOGICAL PROBLEM INSIDE ITS ECONOMY

Shigeto Tsuru, one of the more influential Japanese economists, wrote in his book on Land Price, 'The problem of Land Price (in Japan) is horribly complicated and multi-dimensional. If a layman tries to explain it, he would be easily caught out by a specialized expert.'[169] But why did he have to be so sensitive about such a straightforward issue? With such a stance, his explanation was disappointing as he failed to mention the economic principle that property prices like all other investments should be based on returns in the market where specialised experts could play little or no role. There seemed to be an irreconcilable ideological split in his arguments.

How did other Japanese economists view this tremendous crisis? While no one could provide an economic policy package because of this political deadlock in Japan, some preferred to simplify the issue by stressing the previous economic and financial policy of a policymaker or politician, making them a scapegoat responsible for the failure of the Japanese economy. Two of the most preferred victims to target were Yasushi Mieno, the Bank of Japan governor during the boom era who raised interest rates rapidly during the process of the bursting bubble and Yuu Hayami, the next governor, who resisted various political demands on central banking policies including the lowering of the interest rate.

In their study *Misapprehensions of the Structural Reform Theory*, Akira Noguchi and Hidetomi Tanaka cited Paul Krugman's comment, 'The Japanese monetary policy was like a driver who ran over a man and said "sorry" but then ran over him again by going into reverse.' They criticized the fall as if only the failure on monetary policy was the cause of Japan's disastrous economic failure.[170] Under this analogy, Yasushi Mieno was responsible for the first accident and Yuu Hayami for the second one.

Japan's central bank governors were not put under pressure to explain the status of the economy, economic policies and public finance matters in front of politicians in various committees and take personal responsibility like they usually do in the United States. More fundamentally, it was doubtful if Japan was equipped with a similar financial market management system, or that a central banker had the necessary capability as an economist or the political flexibility to establish a new scheme on their own initiative based on sound economic assessments.

Since 1995, the abnormal status of a less than one per cent

interest rate has continued in Japan. This world record itself is a clear indication of this unusual economic problem and it is proof that interest rates alone cannot solve this economic crisis.

A solution will have to involve a radical change to the effectiveness of the Japanese central banking structure, but this task cannot be independently performed without taking into account the other serious political barriers on Japan's economic scene. A worrying fact is that Japanese economic failure is perhaps not made due to the fault of accidental drivers – but rather by a greater number of careless suicidal people who timidly refuse to join their own country's reform movement despite the revelation of obvious problems and despite the mortal dangers ahead.

Another preferred target of Japanese economists was the former prime minister, Ryutaro Hashimoto, who had tried to reduce the government deficit in 1997 by cutting the injection of state funds. He is remembered in Japan as the last prime minister whose political agenda included budgetary discipline. By doing so, he lost his political career like an unlucky matador who had to unexpectedly confront the most powerful, aggressive and monstrous raging bull in the world. But his critics could not provide the right solution either on growing public debt.

Kazuhide Uekusa criticised the failure of the Hashimoto administration's economic policy in his book, *Japan's Final Settlement*. He argued, 'Implementing the economic policy, the Hashimoto Administration focused on reducing the government deficit as the top priority toward the two problems facing him between the stabilization of economic growth and budgetary discipline... The right policy would have been to put priority on economic growth and tackling the budgetary discipline as a medium term target.' It sounded perfect.

The following Obuchi administration increased its financial injection to the then unprecedented level of 30 trillion yen (US$300 billion). By that time, the total stimulus package which had been injected under the LDP administrations for eight consecutive times reached 100 trillion yen (US$1 trillion). Uekusa analysed it, 'Among the stimulus package of 23.9 trillion yen declared in November 1998, *Mamizu,* Fresh Water [He defined this as an 'effective portion for GDP increment' of the stimulus package] is 15 trillion yen.' How could he balance the budget in the medium to long term? On this point, he delved further into the debate, 'The government budget should be cut first. A reduction of 5 or 10 per cent should be targeted'. Indeed! Was it possible, however, to attain this kind of reform in the current reality of Japanese politics, which he uncompromisingly criticised as 'bureaucratic sovereignty'?[171] Or perhaps, did a large portion of the 8 trillion yen of investment for public works disappear by purchasing the land required at an artificially high price which reduced the effects of *Mamizu*?

Another type of Japanese economist is those who use economic arguments fitted to suit political convenience. In *The Truths of the Japanese Economy,* Masaru Yoshitomi explained that 'The American S&L (savings and loan) problems in the 1980s, the major banking crisis in Sweden during the 1990s and the problems in today's Japan, basically all appeared as the result of the financial and property (market) cycle although Japan's was the biggest.' According to him, Japan's real estate bubble was no different from those that had developed in other parts of the modern world. But Japan is different, he insisted, '…The people who are sustaining the foundation of Japanese society could make it better, compared to those who are managing the country in the West.'[172]

Some economists gave out serious warnings but their voices did not reach the public domain. In his book, *Is the Japanese Economy Sitting and Waiting for an Eventual Death?*, Hiroshi Kato argued the failure of the Japanese public debt policy and the alarming reality of its scale.[173] As an experienced government policy expert, he depicted the deteriorating situation of the state-run Japanese economy – a very rare occurrence in Japan. But without any tangible solutions offered, Japan seemed to be doing nothing but continue the crisis, sitting and waiting for eventual death!

A successful novelist and ex-Economic Planning Agency chief, Taichi Sakaiya invented a new Japanese word for 'Revolution' just as

Sakuzo Yoshino invented a new word for 'Democracy' almost ninety years before without any substance. The intention of both seemed to be the same, to avoid 'Democracy' and 'Revolutionary change'.

Naoki Tanaka was another big shot in the Japanese media whose name always came to the top of the list of economic commentators. In *A Prelude to Japan's Rebirth*, he insisted that the Japanese economy's long stagnation finally ended in 2005. Many experts had already argued about this untenable stance but he had never done so until then. As a solution, he provided the Japanese readers with a one-line comment that the country needed 'a smaller government and an increase in private sector business.'[174]

Nobody would disagree on this. But is this really all that he needs to say as Japan's top economist in this crisis? He put several catchy words such as 'individualism' or 'Emperor's bureaucrats' in his explanation just like a smart chef uses expensive spices on his cuisine. But we can see neither beef nor sashimi on his empty plate.

Again, a common excuse for these attitudes by Japanese economists would be, while they were hopelessly wrong in their economic views, they were absolutely right in their political behaviour. That was why they were regarded as first-class economists in this non-capitalistic country.

BANKING BUREAUCRACY – WELCH VS. MIYAZAWA

One of the major problems for Japanese banks is that they are rarely private enterprises. Japan had no banking expertise like that in the West which had been accumulated over a long historical process since the era of the Renaissance and the Medici. In Europe, it was born out of international trade from the very beginning and it was always a vital core business. On the other hand, the banking industry never evolved naturally in Japan. Historically, it was also the structurally weakest part for Japan's single model of Chinese ideology competing from an isolated island. As an example, pre-modern Japan was always a gold and silver exporting country to China.

Throughout history, there was a notable political resolve not to open up this mainly 'domestic' industry exclusively controlled by bureaucracy, to play a supporting role for the Japanese industrialization rather than facing a global 'unimaginably' enormous commercial experience. Consequently, nobody from Japan went to Europe or the United States to learn about this critically important industry in a serious manner, like the Baltimore merchant, George Peabody, did by sailing to London in 1835.[175]

In post-war Japan, the banking industry did not materially change from its pre-war bureaucratic structure which included the regional banks. Norio Tamaki explained this situation in his very well-observed analysis when the American fund of GARIOA/EROA provided help to the Japanese after the war: '…Dodge insisted that the institution projected should be, despite being owned by the government, independent.' Kiichi Miyazawa, a future prime minister who then acted as interpreter openly recalled this issue, 'We originally had an idea of setting up "an Export Import Finance Bank". But Mr Dodge, I have yet been unable to understand why, strongly objected to the term "bank" being used…That was why we drafted a plan for the "Export Finance Corporation".' The unmentionable problem with this American advice was, 'Nobody knows how, in Japan, this kind of bank could be independent from the government, as Dodge strongly insisted.'

To meet further industrial demand, another government bank, the Development Bank, was created which under American guidance was 'prohibited from issuing debentures'. And the bank 'was warned not to compete with city banks'. As soon as the Allied powers' occupation ended in 1952, however, the Japan Export Finance Bank Act was amended to change its function as The Japan Export Import Finance Bank. The conditions of the Japan Development Bank were revised, 'so that the Bank would be allowed to issue debentures together with conducting business guarantees, floating foreign loans and borrowing foreign currency and government money.'[176] The arch-bureaucracy have ever since freely established additional state banks and banking entities.

Japanese private bankers had to live with this shrunken market with its constant control and intervention from public financial 'guidance'. Due to these origins and market environments created by a 'growing' public-sector banking business, Japanese banks are yet to evolve as private enterprises. The so-called 'main' banks constitute the core of *Zaibatsu,* conglomerate business groups assisted by the *Sogoshosha,* general traders.[177]

Under their bureaucratic positions, Japanese banks gave preferential treatment to their own groups or specially related companies, although in a competitive banking finance market, aggressive and successful companies should make use of all links. This banking practice was often criticised as the cause of bad debt problems as they tended to lend excessively in good times and consequently, to lose more by tightening lending in bad times.

Above all, banking is fundamentally a bureaucratic organization in two ways. Firstly, various bureaucracies regulated private banks with absolute control including meticulous formality checks, although real supervision on their business was ineffective and weak. The Japanese version of the Financial Services Agency – *Kinyu-cho* – was established at the same time as the Japanese 'Big Bang' but as a governmental department with a minister. Furthermore, the MOF constantly tried to appoint ex-bureaucrats to the various banks' boards. This was regarded as normal in Japan as the business itself was not market-oriented but politically structured. As a young man Kiichi Miyazawa was confused by US opinions, because the Japanese banks were run with completely different motives and philosophies.

Secondly, Japanese bank executives had no freedom on the selection and appointment of their team employees, especially at a higher level as they were not chosen on merit. In reality, therefore, professional management was thus 'structurally' discouraged. This practice was 'encouraged' by Japanese bureaucracy which means that no Japanese CEO of the mega-banks can change matters as they would like to.

As a contrast to such a management policy, a legendary magnate, Jack Welch remembered his experience in the US. A year after he joined General Electric, he was frustrated to receive a 'standard' pay increase with his colleagues despite his exceptional commitment to the company. He had almost decided to quit the job but his boss's boss, a young executive, Reuben Gutoff, invited him and his wife to dinner and promised him, 'to get a bigger raise and, more important, vowed to keep the bureaucracy of the company out of his way.' He recalled the occasion, 'I was surprised to learn that he shared my frustration with the bureaucracy'.[178]

This happened quite a while ago in 1961. Even in the twenty-first century, imagining this kind of story in Japan's financial world would be utterly impossible. In Japan, the personnel department of Tokyo headquarters decide the matter by checking the data on all employees on a shifting basis. This is virtually a secret arrangement where you have almost no control on who will be your subordinates. Like a tired old army, bank managers have to accept reinforcements from the 'newly enlisted'. On the other hand, even under this arrangement, nepotism can be worked out behind closed doors.

What would have been the case if Jack Welch were Japanese? To put it simply he would have stood no chance. He would be accused of chasing his own self-interests instead of the company's and being uncooperative with his colleagues! More importantly, the Japanese 'Mr Gutoff' however capable he was, would never dream of such power in Japan Inc. How could he explain this kind of 'preferential treatment' to his arch-bureaucratic board? With its strict pecking order, he could not exercise such a 'personal' judgement as a well-respected arch-bureaucrat... Consequently, there was neither a leader like Jack Welch nor an excellent company like GE in Japan.

Power, in this case management power, was split throughout the organization in the Japanese way. The Japanese banks never hire a proven executive with extraordinary expertise for a challenging job. Nor would they quickly promote someone to an executive post no matter how capable. A crude 'jealousy' operates, which actually comes from the lack of a rational philosophy and this, together with the existence of trade unions, could actually rock the company itself. In this scenario, success in banking or any company largely depends on the economic cycle rather than an individual's capability!

In this political structure, the concept of seeing an employee in banking as someone with the highest standard of expertise, experience and judgement, was yet to be established in Japan. There was a shocking incident which confirmed the difficult challenge facing Japanese bankers. In early 2003, Financial Services Minister Heizo Takenaka asked the mega-banks to submit a business plan after the public injection of funds. To restructure the banking business, one of the points he brought up was that the bank lending policy and loans should be based on cash-flow projections. It seemed that this 'technical term' was mentioned for the first time in Japan. The banking leaders' protest was frank, extraordinary and amazing. One of the CEOs finally made their point by saying, 'Are you trying to change the game's rule from football to rugby?'

Motoshige Ito analysed 'the (Japanese) bank lending versus GDP ratio' since 1970 and pointed out that this ratio almost hit 100 per cent in the bubble era. He concluded that Japanese banks have still an over-lending situation in 2003 at the level of 80 per cent of this ratio. This ratio was about 60 per cent before the bubble, therefore, he believed that Japanese banks still need to control the overall volume of their loans.[179] It stood at 438.4 trillion yen as at the end of 2008 while Japanese exporting companies' dependency on corporate bonds increased steadily. And of course, as a further headache to Japanese bankers, all of Japan's gigantic public banks and financial entities were not included in these statistics.

A QUICKSAND OF DETERIORATION

Somebody named the political and economic situation in Japan after the 'Land Standard' bubble as *Ushinawareta*, the 'lost' decade. This was meant to be a harsh criticism. But after the collapse of the land standard economy, it was not quite true that the Japanese arch-bureaucracy did not do anything about it or just sit back. Thanks to their initiatives, the situation afterwards rapidly deteriorated by enlarging public-sector business which crashed even further, together with the already shrunken private-sector markets.

The prospect for Japan's finances after 1990 also worsened due to such constant policy failures and mismanagements. For instance, when an ill-conceived indirect tax was introduced for the first time under the Takeshita administration in 1989, the new issuance of the government bond was still comparatively modest at 6.6 trillion yen. A sum of around 30 trillion became quite normal by 2005. And as a 'static stone' also gathered moss, it hit over the 40 trillion level mark by 2010 and greatly exceeded total tax revenue. Just to remind you, this is equivalent to only the base interest rate of 3.3 per cent on the most optimistic public debt estimate of 1,200 trillion. Why is Japan trapped in this bottomless swamp?

Even on political issues, understanding is clouded, for instance, a renowned expert on Japanese modern wars, Tetsuo Furuya, questions the country's history, 'If somebody asked you about the Nippo-Chinese War, it would be not easy for us Japanese, to give a clear answer of what kind of war it was after all.' He pointed out the difficulty in identifying its causes: 'A few years after the Manchurian invasion broke out, the Rokokyo (Lugouqiao) incident followed. Then the war spread to Shanghai and Japan was drawn into the quicksand of a total war with China. Even for those who understood this process, it would still be difficult to have a clear image as to why all these things had to happen then.' As he concluded, even if this continental war with China had continued on its own without Japan entering into the Second World War arena, Japan would have been defeated by a China that managed a successful tie-up with the Allied powers.[180]

As we saw earlier, the Japanese arch-bureaucracy neglected global values completely all the way up to the final ultimatum and they never looked back. In this strictly controlled 'battle mode', as facts were established, it was getting more difficult to confront society's deeply hidden political defects. By the late 1930s, it was simply impossible for a Japanese individual, whichever sector he belonged to, to criticise public failure without risking capital punishment.

In Japanese 'capitalism', where fair rules were deliberately ignored, only a cheater and liar could benefit from the system, as illegal or inequitable conduct could not be dealt with. In Japan's arch-bureaucratic society, those who do not pay their debts are treated very differently from those in a western system. Japan's legal system has insufficient judicial functions to enforce the law like quick court decisions, bailiffs or other punishments to keep up the sanction of legal authority.

In this political soil, only arch-bureaucracy was there to act on 'salvaging' operations by further destroying legal and economic principles. In the growing economic difficulties, the Private Sector City Development Promotion Scheme (PSCDPS), *Minkan Toshi Kaihatsu Suishin Kiko,* was launched which extended the 'established' irrational economic policy. This public financed company bought real estate from troubled companies on the condition that these debt-suffering companies would buy it back at a higher price than the purchased price with interest and costs within ten years.

In 2002, another bureaucratic organization called the Industry Resuscitation Scheme (IRS), *Sangyo Saisei Kiko,* was created with a similar objective to pretend that genuine efforts were underway – without attempting to tackle the main issue of Japan's problematic and outdated political and economic system. In 2005, IRS budgeted ten trillion yen (US$86 billion) to keep the failed system ongoing.

Kyodo News Agency reported (14/08/03) that PSCDPS and IRS were in dispute on who would bear the loss of PSCDPS's loans, which were unpaid by the original debtor company in Kumamoto prefecture. As a result of government policy of putting taxpayers' monies into this bus company without a convincing reason, public funds of around 7.5 billion yen were lost. Yet, the arch-bureaucracy could legally carry out this sort of 'mysterious' manoeuvre as if it was paid with their own pocket money without any public scrutiny.

Peter Tasker, a British investment banker in Tokyo, warned, with his sound economic sense, of the importance of taking action without delay by citing the example of a 'death of a frog' in a pot of slowly, slowly, boiling water where the temperature is gradually rising, whereas if the frog jumped out immediately it would be saved even if the initial water was hot.[181] In Japan's hyper-state complex, however, the image of the outside world is different. Tasker's imagery was perhaps based on the green fields in Britain where you could start a new life with proper business infrastructure. Unfortunately, for the Japanese their foundations resembled a red magma sea under an active volcano, living under such stringent arch-bureaucratic controls and prejudices and lacking another social beacon. If a false move could only mean instant 'death', most would prefer a slower one.

All these military arch-bureaucrats spoke about their operational achievements and sounded plausible when they were expanding deeply into the Chinese continent or over the Pacific and Indian Oceans. But once they put aside any sound political principles, only a fanatic could control the situation. In this political environment, reform became categorically impossible. Only a man who could claim 'black' as 'white' or 'problem' as 'no problem' could survive in this Chinese ideological leadership whereby all his remaining colleagues with a conscience were removed and not allowed to speak up about society's worsening future.

If a certain factional business could not survive, arch-bureaucracy was ready to build excessive roads, gigantic bridges, transport and industrial infrastructures or real estate developments with public funds. Despite temporary modern technological feats, public debts were accumulating dangerously with these indulgent investments. Not only did these hyper-artificial plans cause the failures of the projects themselves, as experienced in many rural cities in Japan, many of the regional business environments and the long-term prospects for small businesses – an essential element of capitalism as taxpayers – were destroyed by this short-term spending spree. And who would pay the maintenance or repair costs for these architectural extravaganzas?

We need to acknowledge the appalling events taking place in Japan, rather than keeping them hidden, simply because it is crystal clear that either this 'war' or the process of implosion, cannot be continued, and therefore, somehow in the end, it has to be stopped before it reaches the point of catastrophe.

On the Theory of Chinese Ideology

THE 'BIG BANG' WITHOUT THE INFRASTRUCTURE

During this deteriorating period for the Japanese economy, the government launched its version of the 'Big Bang' in 1996, copying the global financial expansion in Britain. Margaret Thatcher once explained the intention of the original 'Big Bang': 'the Stock Exchange made a commitment to dismantle long-standing restrictions on trading and the process was begun that led to the Financial Services Act (1986) and the "Big Bang" in October of that year. These reforms allowed the City to adopt to the highly competitive international markets in which it now operated and was crucial to its continued success.'[182]

In Japan, this swiftly executed 'Big Bang' became a lengthy negotiating process, which inevitably ended up as a failure. While Prime Minister Hashimoto was right to decide on this direction, Japan had no competent social and business infrastructure to support it nor the expertise of the City of London. Above all, there was neither determination nor consensus among the Japanese public to back this global move to build up a new system with the necessary reforms. Ryutaro Hashimoto's proposal was received as a negative signal by all the determined protectionists with existing interests who were further enriched by global trading wealth, but still living in a strictly indigenous economic environment. Consequently, it only appeared to again exemplify what the prime minister's power meant in Japan.

The stock exchange itself was the product of compromise between Japan's central and regional political interests. Apart from Tokyo, there was another stock exchange in Osaka, which was considered sleazy and prone to scandal with its lack of transparency, and others in Nagoya, Fukuoka and Sapporo. The MOF and others sent their own people to the executive posts 'to control' them. In Japan, once such an interest group is formed, it becomes impossible to abolish because it is protected by attached factional political interests. Why did they not simply merge these operations under the supervision of one national stock exchange in Tokyo, as every other country decided to do?

Part Three – Japan in Crisis

At least, then there would have been a common goal for a national asset policy, although, no doubt, in reality, it would still have hit the 'wall' of arch-bureaucracy and fall, as soon as it was proposed. So the Japanese 'Big Bang' ended up only as the deregulation of fees on buying and selling shares as the rate became completely free by October 1999, although the authorities pretended as if something important was done.

The prime minister said at the time that Japan required a revolutionary change like the Meiji Restoration. But where were those reforms? Even in America, a kind of optimism prevailed that the Japanese economy would soon re-emerge like a 'come back kid' even the influential Brookings Institute in Washington DC expressed a similar view. But current Japanese politicians look more like the *ancien regime* of the Tokugawa Shogunate unable to reform in this time of huge change and hanging on to the rapidly shrinking assets from the past.

At the time of the Meiji Restoration, Japan had nothing except an extraordinary politician. Toshimichi Okubo (1830-78), who emerged from a relatively modest background, was picked out for an unprecedented promotion by merit to the top administrative post of the Satsuma clan at the age of thirty-two by his lord, Hisamitsu Shimazu.

He showed his brilliant political ability and leadership during the negotiations with the British during the Satsuma-British war in 1863, which occurred as the result of the killing of a British national who bumped into a Satsuma procession while horse riding near Yokohama (known as the *Namamugi* incident). The British demanded punishment of the murderers and compensation from both the Shogunate government and the fiefdom of Satsuma. The government agreed but Satsuma refused, as the killing was 'legal' under the samurai code.

The British immediately dispatched seven naval ships equipped with new Armstrong guns to Satsuma's capital, Kagoshima, to settle the case. Satsuma was determined to counter them and built up the forts on the bay side of the city to Sakura-jima Island with old top-quality canons. The British wanted to negotiate first by revealing their visibly superior war machine, but soon realised that it was impossible to reach an agreement.

Satsuma knew that the entire country was watching what they were going to do in this threatening situation. A reputation for cowardice was the only thing Satsuma wanted to avoid. After having been mocked by his colleagues as being 'petrified with fear' – *Koshi-wo nukashita* – (literally, it means 'his hip fell off') as he slipped on a wet roof while watching the British fleet entering the harbour,[183] Okubo ordered the gunners to shoot first after the British seizure of the Satsuma's new steamships. It was a rainy, windy and day of high seas and it was difficult for the British to fix a gun standard on the pitching and rolling ships.

The British fleet destroyed all the batteries of Satsuma, the port and industrial area of the city, and won the war. However, they suffered heavier damages than the Satsuma side in terms of death tolls and casualties, although none of the British vessels were sunk. Okubo negotiated a peace with the British by liaising with the Shogunate government that now promised to pay compensation. After this battle, they appreciated each other's strength and Satsuma became a British ally. Afterwards, Okubo ruled Japanese modern politics and established its foundations, until his life was suddenly ended at the age of forty-eight by the sword of an assassin just as he was about to start on newly planned reforms in 1878.

There was a strong sense of *noblesse oblige* among the leaders of the early Meiji government as articulated by one of Okubo's colleagues, Takayoshi Kido, who sighed in his poem, 'How can we save thirty million people?' During Okubo's leadership, modern Japan was launched on a new historical dimension. Okubo dwarfed his contemporaries, and they, including his colleagues who were still deeply immersed in the old style of politics, could not grasp his advanced ideas.

In particular, after Okubo's long trip to US and Europe from 1871 to 1873, he was rapidly overturning the straitjacket of Chinese ideology. In the Meiji Restoration, Japan revamped its old political system with cultural and religious reforms which radically changed society. Nobody but Okubo himself knew that it was not good enough. Suguru Sasaki rightly reiterated that Okubo's reform was '...the only reform in Japanese modern history, which was done regardless of party political, personal or organizational interests.'[184]

To put it more precisely, Okubo was reforming Japan based on modern political reason without the old factional interests. Toshimichi Okubo was a rare example of Japanese statesmanship and Japan was luckily to have this colossal political figure in power during the successful Meiji Restoration. After his death, some of his best and most radical reforms were thrown into confusion and reactionary movements arose that sealed Japan's long-term decline.

Why, at this time, can the Japanese not change? It is true that there are no Japanese politicians of Okubo's calibre. But the current crisis is also much more serious and challenging for the Japanese than previous ones. Japan has to do more, not less. The economic prosperity attained by post-war Japan was significantly larger and so were the ensuing problems.

And the Japanese could not see the subtle changes of social revolution, as changes do not always appear like a black iron ship with new and accurate cannons visible to the naked eye. Japan should have understood that the West's political system had eventually defeated them in the Second World War. New forms of combined social science and technology were to change the world economy on a global scale, but because of their invisibility on impact, they were also vulnerable to dismissive propaganda.

Soon after 1967 when the first new cash dispenser in the world was installed at a bank branch in Enfield, London, banking was to emerge as a complete global business. The British 'Big Bang' was brought in line with this phenomenal change just as the Japanese 'Big Bang' should have been. In this revolution, the British were proactive but the Japanese were reactive.

The failure of the Japanese 'Big Bang' visibly exposed the weakness of the country's fundamental business infrastructure. In fact, Japan's problem started as a financial crisis because it was the most sophisticated part of its capitalism although the business sector could be equally vulnerable and troublesome. But as the crisis started here, it must be ended here. Without this financial business reform, Japan can never come out of the on-going deflationary economy. Japan should have faced this challenge instead of running away. Many countries adapted themselves to change and it is simply inconceivable that only the Japanese have no such capacity. All Japanese need to dedicate themselves to the direction of the required political change, not by using the same old ideology, but by adopting a modern social science approach to meet this new challenge.

THE MINISTRY OF 'IRRELEVANT' FINANCE

As we observe this massive irresponsible state complex topped by a prime minister with nominal power, we need to focus on the mighty Ministry of Finance as one of the major 'perpetrators' responsible for the grave negligence which may be the cause of this extraordinary Japanese financial meltdown. Broken concepts appeared most strikingly apparent in this elitist organisation.

As a modern bureaucratic organisation, the Ministry failed, with its equally outdated politicians, to perform the daily financial needs of the newly born democratic state of Japan. Perhaps, the most damaging act conducted by the MOF was that as the key governmental department on public finance, it failed to promote a fair accounting standard, sound economic principles and administrative transparency over all state organisations. But this does not exonerate the conduct of the other ministries or numerous entities in this hidden economic, or rather uneconomic, venture.

Let us be clear first, the MOF – in Japanese, *Okura-sho* (the same word since the eighth century!) or since 2000 renamed as *Zaimu-sho*, which sounds more like 'Treasury' in English – was not an equivalent of the Treasury in either the US or UK. If you scrutinised the way it operated, it could be described more appropriately as an 'independent financial state' inside the state of Japan. In essence, it served its official constitutional function, but simultaneously, had its own iron rules as an arch-bureaucratic clan.

In addition to its historically tightly-guarded budgetary adjustment role, the MOF controlled an entire financial business via its Financial Investment Fund (dubbed as the 'second budget' by the Japanese press), instead of delegating such a role to the private business sector through market mechanisms. As of 2005, the fund's handling of this accumulated lump sum of around 333 trillion yen (US$3 trillion) was still under wraps and no one knew how much it has actually lost on its investment. It only reconfirms again an established precedent in Japanese modern politics that the superiority and 'prestige' of the arch-bureaucracy could not be broken even with these repeated seriously fundamental failures.

Not only did the MOF have irregular powers in its bureaucracy but it also had evident influence on other government organs and functions, such as the Bank of Japan, the Financial Services Agency, Japanese banks (and various state banks/financial corporations), local governments and stock exchanges. All those were regarded as its 'sphere', in which it played an influential leading role. With its financial capacity, no other government organ, including the cabinet or parliament had such a wide range of functions in executing economic policies in Japan. But it is wrong to imagine a western-style rock solid powerful organization here.

In the case of Britain, actual financial policies are attributable to the successive Chancellors of the Exchequer and a growing independence for the Bank of England with a newly established Banking Commission. If matters were getting very serious, the prime minister would also get involved as the First Lord of the Treasury. Politicians and professional economic experts, including the governor of the Bank of England, or the bureaucrats in the Treasury move together in one political direction. Simon James described the principle of this relationship, 'Britain is governed by the creative friction generated by putting amateur ministers in charge of professional civil servants.' And this 'parachuted ministers, largely unversed in administration or departmental subject matter, yet given ultimate command and responsibility...'[185]

In the case of the United States, the President, his economic advisors and the Secretary of the Treasury have the key role, together with an independent Federal Reserve Bank , for banking policies and the Securities and Exchange Commission for regulatory measures, which have to be constantly checked by Congress. In each case, the existence of a modern impartial bureaucracy that analyses the subject while staying away from making a political decision – leaving it to the elected politicians who take responsibility for any drastic policy package – becomes a prerequisite condition for the creation of a new course for the nation. Again, the existence of the free market, a transparent and fair management standard, and the rule of law are essential to implement such policies effectively and to run the national economy for all citizens.

In the current traditional Japanese political system, real power does not belong to any of the organs of the government's appointed elected authority but only to the ministries' inside bureaucrats. From this position matters become even more confusing, as the power of the ministry is further divided among the inner departments, different sections or even its subsidiary public corporations. With this weakened power structure, sometimes a holder of special interests outside the government can manipulate specific issues by influencing politics. On the other hand, nobody can control overall Japanese financial policy due to the existence of this power 'vacuum'. Hence, you cannot name the person responsible for each specific policy in Japan.

How could they manage this kind of relationship, say, on taxation matters? In the early days of post-war Japan, a tax mission headed by Carl Shoup in 1949 came from the United States with the task of reorganizing the old Japanese tax system as a whole, two years before the signing of the San Francisco peace treaty which marked the actual time limit for US intervention.

This mission had a significant value for Japanese capitalism but the Japanese failed to grasp its importance. Hiromitsu Ishii captured this critical moment in his study, 'Thus, the entire tax system was fully reconstructed, producing epoch-making change. However, the ideal tax system achieved by the initiative of US influence was of temporary duration: many taxes were abolished or modified soon after enactment.' As he showed, the taxation process under the Japanese and western or US systems differed completely.

The existence of the Tax Advisory Commission (TAC) is peculiar to Japan. And there was not only one but two – one for the government, and one for the inner party politics of the LDP. The members of the government TAC 'are selected from a variety of people, including academics, tax experts, tax lawyers, journalists, former government officials of each ministry, representatives of big and small business, labour union leaders, and so on'. And they were not influential in any case. Why was this kind of process required? Ishii further explained, 'Without them, the government would encounter obstacles in having any tax proposals implemented, chiefly because it is difficult to obtain public support for tax changes. The LDP's own tax committee finally intervened politically.'[186]

But a more problematic issue about this irregular mechanism is if someone unknown, even outside the government, influenced this nameless LDP tax committee and could virtually control Japanese tax policy without any responsibility. At this point, power could actually vanish from state control and remain quite hidden. And more importantly, nobody in the administration could make a fundamental change to Japanese taxes. In other words, even when the ship is colliding, the captain cannot touch the fixed radar (set by someone unknown).

Reflecting the worsening implosion in progress, the era of once-experienced career bureaucrats in ministries moving on to become influential politicians serving as finance minister or prime minister, people such as Hayato Ikeda, Takeo Fukuda, Masahiro Ohira, Kiichi Miyazawa and many others, seems to be over. Recent tendencies confirm rather that a complete layman with a sharp mind who was willing to take nominal responsibility for the on-going unprecedented financial mess would be the first choice. They would need to accept further massive political and financial indulgences without any conscience or sensible thoughts. To use a Japanese expression, the challenge was to appoint someone reckless enough to go on with a mentality of 'eating all poisons together with the plate' – *Doku kurawaba Sara made*. Alas!

THE MECHANISM OF THE ZERO INTEREST RATE

When the Argentine economy went into free fall in 2001, many Japanese economists and experts quickly pointed out that the situations in the two countries were completely different. There was no net foreign debt in Japan thanks to its export industry and the US and Europe were continuing importers with their solid consumer markets. The Japanese argued that mounting debt was a domestic matter that could be solved whatever the amount might increase to. Under this newly invented 'myth' of unlimited public debt, they insisted that accumulating government debt should not be worried about as it simultaneously created assets on the balance sheet, ignoring the variant market value, interest rates and the burden to the future generations.

When the US government was once heavily indebted in 1990s, the Japanese press criticised the Americans every day. But during the eight years of the Clinton administration, the United States came back as a financially strong and sound state showing the inherent resilience of its powerful democracy. Japan's problem was that this kind of political discipline and financial reform could not be expected even after its debt level far surpassed America's red line and its interest rate hit rock bottom. But how did such an unusual mechanism of an almost zero interest rate evolve in a capitalist state of the East? Why did the interest rate not rise rapidly after a massive issue of Japanese government bonds as a conventional economist would have expected?

Japan's public debt exceeded well over a 100 per cent of GDP. If a steady increment of GDP could not be expected, to raise interest rates became a dangerous scenario with the risk of an uncontrollable decrease in market value, which would then have to be added back as higher interest costs to a further enlarging public debt, until this cycle came to a dead end.

Another extraordinary and irrational idea by the arch-bureaucrats was implemented. To minimise the constantly increasing cost of Japanese government bonds, Japan's zero/quasi-zero interest rate had to be kept for political reasons, ignoring all the inherent economic risks attached. In attaining this prime political objective, an extraordinary uneconomic measure had to be launched. The arch-bureaucracy 'asked' every Japanese public and quasi-public bank (that is all private sector banks as well!) and financial institutions to buy back these bonds from the market. Thereby, the function of interest rates in the market, once described by Keynes as a 'balancing factor', was completely lost in Japan's financial economy.

Since the 'patient' is insisting it is not sick, it is difficult for a 'doctor' to write a prescription. But we still could see symptoms as the result of this ill-conceived policy. The principal indicator is GDP in nominal yen figures. This was in a long stagnating trend after it hit a peak of slightly more than 520 trillion yen during the 1990s. This figure had increased as a blip by 2006 with the rapidly growing diversion of exports to China and then took a hammering after the last quarter of 2008 as the repercussions of the Lehman shock arrived on Japanese shores. In sharp contrast to the US and major European economies, the size of the Japanese economy of around 500 trillion yen, or even less, has been constantly stagnant for the last twenty years, even without considering the 'aggressive' inflationary element in the global economy during the same period. In 2010, it dipped to around 480 trillion yen as Japan was severely hit further by the global credit crunch, while the figures in US dollars could change upwards most of the time due to the appreciation in the yen exchange rate. Given the extreme level of the fiscal injection, it is most unlikely that Japan can significantly reverse this downward trend anytime soon.

The vital issue was not short-term growth as Japan could produce a positive growth during some quarters, even in this prolonged stagnation, by a massive financial injection. In this 'growth' period, the danger was that this distortion of the system would be amplified in the form of extravagantly indulged public debts, irrational funding and bank loans to zombie corporate entities, which constantly upset the market mechanism.

Japan's total costs (including the issuance) of government bonds in 2004 was 36.6 trillion yen, which was equivalent to 44.6 per cent of the government budget. The total debt of the state excluding regional governments was 729 trillion as of June 2004, and it was close to 150 per cent of GDP. No accounting firm would dare to audit these figures. So neither did the government's auditing office. The MOF official disclosed the previous estimate of 774 trillion yen was wrong and the correct figure was 1,093 trillion yen as of end 2005, if short-term bonds were included. This was revealed in front of the Upper House committee members and stunned everybody – at least for a while. But how could one be sure it was the final figure after such constantly dubious behaviour?

The danger was that the increasing ratio on those debt figures was far exceeding the nominal growth rate (including a negative one) of its GDP in yen since the burst of the Japanese bubble as no fundamental reform was made. This situation where a tired old man is almost crushed by a young huge Sumo wrestler who is constantly gaining weight is the actual picture of Japanese public finance that has always postponed taking decisive action.

Historically, since the era of the medieval Kamakura Shogunate, a special decree to offset all public debt as a one-off declaration during the severe depression named as *Tokusei-rei* – the benevolent administration act – had to be issued to save the upper class debtors but it could never stop the process of implosion. Does the government think about something like this happening again in Japan? As in the past, it would never be effective. This time, it would be horrific due to global implications. On the other hand, whether the government declares it or not, there could be a situation where it becomes impossible to find someone generous enough to buy these unlimitedly over-issued government promissory papers at a nominal interest rate. But how can the IMF or anybody else provide a loan to such a dreadfully irresponsible government and political system of such an enormous size?

It should be remembered, however, among the Japanese politicians who seemed to be living on the moon, there was at least one politician who was honest in Japanese post-war politics. The former finance and prime minister who was largely regarded as a credible economic expert, Kiichi Miyazawa once let his guard slip in public with his 'confession' that 'Japan is almost bankrupt'. This was in 2000 just before he was replaced. But of course, Japan's financial debt is astronomical today, comparing to that modest level in 2000, and further worsening of the debt-ratio is anticipated from the same old political rot spreading into economic policies. When will one of his successors be ready to remove the word 'almost'?

GLOBAL CAPITALISM IN DANGER

Asia is one of the three pillars of global capitalism for expansion. Every day the market movements start from Asia due to the existence of the date line. This real-time news then relays to London in Europe, afterwards to New York in the American continent. Tokyo together with Hong Kong, Sydney, Shanghai and others in the Asia Pacific is currently quoted between these two principal capitals of the global financial market.

On the other hand, the recent major expansion of global capitalism began with the defeat of Soviet-style communism in Europe. With this historical turning point, European capitalism expanded vigorously to the east. The European Union was enlarged and the old 'enemy' Russia with its new capitalistic-flavour joined this monumental change for this vast area. This sudden reformation will probably take sometime to consolidate, in particular in the Russian Federation and troublespots in the countries between the EU and Russia such as Belarus, Ukraine and the Caucasus. But the trend of this new expansion seems irreversible with strengthening democratic movements despite the recent economic hiccups in Western Europe. The option of staying outside this economic development would be utterly bleak and isolate a nation.

It seems rather a long time ago that Japan emerged as a rising modern economy with a strong yen, which took on the role of a regional currency. And this development pattern was gradually extended to the whole of Asia, reaching 24 per cent of the world's GDP by 2008, second only to the EU as a critical economic mass. With discouraging prospects in Tokyo, however, a 'policy of disengagement' by the West began as many global banking and financial institutions for various reasons left the Japanese capital to conduct their regional business in a better location such as Singapore. In the tightening of indigenous regulatory measures, Tokyo further lost its attractiveness. Above all, any global financial centre must prosper with the foundation of a long-term sound economy as a prerequisite condition.

East Asia, as the industrial core of Asia, remained unique even in this rapidly changing situation. Firstly, it was established as a modern economic centre as the only outside region which could master western science and technologies quickly with full-scale equal efficiency. Secondly, its size is not negligible in terms of its historical assets, growth rate and population. Thirdly, geopolitically, East Asia forms a strategic crossroad preventing Europe and North America being sandwiched by the other growing western world of Russia and Australasia.

From this aspect, it would be a fatal political error for the West to 'segregate' the industrialised East leaving their old political and economic management intact. It is obvious, therefore, that to maintain only the traditional Atlantic relationship will not be sufficient for today's new challenges, as many Western leaders are perhaps already aware. And it is further apparent that the modernisation of Asia could not be completed without the inclusion of the region's two principal centres, China and Japan.

Japan has always claimed to the outside world that it is run on capitalist ideals while trying to hide the crucial information about its secretive politics. This policy is approaching its limits, as the crack is day by day becoming irreparable. And the West will observe a more serious politico-economic stalemate in Japan in the future. The country's 'Big Bang' has ended up with an economic disaster rather than prosperity because of this self-invented new separatism.

This was indeed a defeat of the limited materialism of Japan, which was once brilliantly depicted by Ryunosuke Akutagawa in his novel, 'Potato gruel', *Imogayu*. The old story of a low-grade bureaucrat known only by his court rank, *Goi* or the fifth grade. Goi's dream was that someday he could eat as much as he wanted of his most favourite potato gruel rather than only enjoying just a small quantity of it once a year at the New Year's dinner at the court. One day, however, he was unexpectedly 'forced' into a situation where his secretly admired potato gruel was served in abundance in front of him by his rich, capricious and new aristocratic acquaintance. (Or Lord West, perhaps?)

As soon as he started to eat it, however, he lost his appetite together with his dream. It seems that, like Goi, a hardworking exporting Japan has lost sight of its national objective as soon as it became rich enough to satisfy their material thirst. Thereafter, a constantly misbalanced economy was put in place as if Japan's political aim was deliberately to keep this hungry spirit ongoing in society.

China has successfully developed as the new leading economic power and its status in the world continues to grow. But if the main engine of Japan failed, could the region or global capitalism move further? An even bigger potential threat is that the current booming Chinese economy is most likely to follow the Japanese path of implosion. The US and Europe are the richest nations in terms of consumers. But they are not so limitlessly abundant that both governments could ignore this constant growth of goods and funds imported from the combined force of the world's second and third largest 'closed' economies, together with the various imbalances created by it, as has appeared in the recent economic turmoil.

Facing this quantitative expansion at full tilt, the reality is that what is at stake for the West would be not just a third of this entire global business that used to be represented by Asia and the Pacific region which still is, in real terms, the last frontier in its global expansion. As the showcase of capitalistic expansion, the stake here would actually be 100 per cent for the future of global capitalism, as every CEO agrees.

The imbalance in the world economy is the basis of failure in the last global long-term economic cycle. For the previous global shock of the Great Depression, H. Clark Johnson skilfully depicted a historical summary of deflation on the two factors in his *Gold, France, and the Great Depression, 1919-1932*.[187] The problem was indeed 'the result of human errors in the area of economic policy'.[188] Above all, the political failure of adjusting to a new global economic trend has to be recognised. The obstacles of previous political decisions emerged as the result of the First World War where the reparation burden for Germany was too excessive. In this paradigm, precisely, 'self-exploiting' Japan was struggling to compete with the other powers.[189]

In post-Second World War politics, this old error was duly rectified in Europe. The current problem in global capitalism, however, is that, like Germany in the pre-war period, the foundation of Japanese capitalism is not firmly built on its political structure, despite the fact that post-war Japan was allowed to join the global economic 'club'. And today, somewhat 'self-exploiting' China is trailing behind, somewhere outside of this system, by taking up a sort of pre-war position comparative to Japan's status.

In solving this problem, attention must be shifted from the benefits of global capitalism to the function of global capitalism in the region, which has to be shared by all the Asian states as part of the global economy. For further expansion, new global capitalism requires the spread of a functioning global standard and fair business rules, and the West should not flinch from this unprecedented historical challenge. Leaving the Japanese or Chinese standards as they are means the benefits of global capitalism can neither penetrate to the largest chunk of people in these nations nor stop implosion happening in both countries and beyond.

III - AN IMPOSSIBLE REFORM

THE MANDATE GIVEN

After decades of failing politics in Japan, people's anticipation of political reform was rising. Finally, an emerging political consensus gave Junichiro Koizumi, the newly elected Japanese prime minister, the mandate to rule with a support rating of a most unusual 80 per cent in 2001. He launched his 'reformist' campaign against the head of the biggest faction and ex-prime minister, Ryutaro Hashimoto and won this party election.

Originally, he 'inherited' his constituency in Yokosuka from his father, Junya Koizumi, who moved there from Kagoshima prefecture and later served as defence minister. Thus, he deemed himself as from *Satsuma* descent, blue-blooded in Japanese 'modern' factional politics. His grandfather, third generation of the Koizumi family, was also a local politician. The city is the home port for the US 7th Fleet and the Japanese Naval Defence Force, and therefore it hosts a large foreign population, creating a very different atmosphere from other parts of Japan.

When Junichiro Koizumi was suddenly recalled from his studies in London to stand for his first election following his father's unexpected death, he failed to secure the seat, being just short of a few percentage of the votes due to his lack of experience and popularity. To get the seat back, he had to serve as a private secretary to one of the most influential contemporary politicians, Takeo Fukuda, MHR of the LDP from Gunma prefecture who had solid experience in the bureaucracy as the top official of the MOF. In actual terms, this meant that he joined the prime Fukuda faction of the LDP. This was subsequently run by his 'senior' MHR from Ishikawa prefecture, Yoshiro Mori, at the time of his premier election.

Important changes had emerged by this time and Japanese politics was losing momentum as the economic situation continuously worsened. Many Japanese banks were asking foreign and domestic financial institutions for help. The percentage of foreign ownership among many of the manufacturing exporters was dramatically raised. At the time, it was estimated that there was a three trillion yen (US$27 billion) allocation of global investment funds for Japanese equity. In the circumstances, Japan could no longer entirely ignore world opinion on its long overdue reform.

In this climate, people began to realise Koizumi's 'radical' reform was a last hope and something different from the ideas of other insulated Japanese politicians. One of his unusual ministerial appointments was Makiko Tanaka from Niigata prefecture to the post of foreign minister, a job previously regarded as a key post for the experienced 'old guard'. She was the daughter of an influential former prime minister, Kakuei Tanaka, and well known for her witty remarks.

The flamboyant new foreign minister soon clashed with key bureaucrats in the ministry who were determined to stop her 'excessive' advance into inner ministerial matters. The rather shadowy MHR of the LDP, Muneo Suzuki, supported a counter political move against her from his constituency in northern Hokkaido, where he was constantly trying to intervene and control, without any proper authority, Nippo-Russian diplomacy, in particular, on the issue of the former four Japanese northern islands in dispute.

But she had her own views on this diplomatic policy. Her father as prime minister had once visited Leonid Brezhnev in Moscow and made progress on the issue in 1973, overcoming previous Soviet rejections to even acknowledge the existence of the problem. The Soviet Union's most powerful general secretary after Stalin acknowledged to Kakuei Tanaka that there was an issue of four (not two) islands between the two nations by replying to his query on this point, 'Ya znayu.' – 'I know'.[190]

Apart from this dispute, she had another problem. Chinese leaders regarded her as the true successor to her father who had opened post-war diplomatic relationships with China as a 'friend'. The people closely watching China suspected that this – *pengyou* – relationship might have some disadvantages as well, as the Chinese would in the future expect a contribution from their 'friend' in exchange for a given favour. In contrast, her less enthusiastic attitude to US diplomacy was exposed when Makiko Tanaka turned down without a proper explanation the request for a courtesy visit of Richard Armitage, American Deputy Secretary of State responsible for Asian affairs.

Because of this row in the Ministry of Foreign Affairs, the prime minister had to eventually dismiss his most popular foreign minister. His popularity dived at once after this incident. Despite this embarrassment, the Koizumi administration's diplomacy seemed to be working well with western allies as, soon after 9/11, Prime Minister Koizumi flew to New York and pledged in English, Japan's firm support for the United States in the war against terrorism. He also visited the British prime minister in London and the French president in Paris on the same trip, fostering a cordial relationship with western leaders.

The Japanese voters were attracted to him on hearing that he denounced Japanese sectarian politics. Despite this official commitment to change Japanese 'political custom', he took full advantage of the old factional benefits with other key posts in the Koizumi administration, while establishing a strong link with Mikio Aoki from a rival faction, a master of the old politics who controlled the Upper House. The tactics of a fresh prime minister were after all nothing new.

He appointed Masajuro Shiokawa, his old pal from Osaka, to finance minister and Yasuo Fukuda, the son of his former boss, to cabinet secretary, both from his 'former' Mori faction. He further picked from his old faction, Shinzo Abe, a young prince of a Japanese political family, to be the deputy cabinet secretary who accompanied him on his overseas trips. The latter both later served as prime ministers. Furthermore, the prime minister appointed Taku Yamazaki, his closest ally running his own small faction, to be the secretary general of the LDP.

Shortly afterwards, he moved the postal services from the ministry to a government corporation, declaring he would reform it in due course. But it became soon apparent that he was not bold enough to preside over a radical change to current Japanese politics. His tactics for what was supposed to be a revolutionary reform, which even the Japanese press started to criticise as a 'throw away all' – *Marunage* – method, was to appoint an 'experts' committee under bureaucratic influence, to find a compromise between the government and LDP's policymakers, rather than deciding on a new course with fresh and different ideas for Japan. The same old disappointment... but could another Japanese politician have done any better?

In retrospect, therefore, the purpose of Junichiro Koizumi's reforms were not the success of his reforms itself. His task was rather to try everything using conventional methods and show to the Japanese public, by failing spectacularly, as he did, the limit of old politics to those who innocently believed they might still be workable. Whether the people liked it or not, the fact was that Japan's traditional politics were the cause of this on-going disaster. Without overthrowing these precepts there would be no reform in Japan. In this sense, he was just representing the Japanese people's illusion that an 'easy-quick reform' could be carried out while watching TV at home. He proved that such a reform was impossible, perhaps paving the way for serious reforms in the future.

THE YASUKUNI SHRINE AND CHINESE ANGER

Before the LDP election, Junichiro Koizumi pledged to the surviving families of the war dead which existed as a strong political lobby that, if elected, he would visit the Yasukuni Shrine on 15 August every year. This was the day the Second World War, or as it is better known in Japan, the Pacific War, officially ended in Japan.

Part Three – Japan in Crisis

The Yasukuni Shrine was built with state funds to enshrine Japan's fallen soldiers in pre-war Japan. In 1978, the Shrine accepted the enshrinement of former A-grade war criminals. This 'religious' move mystified many as the Shinto shrine that was built only for the war dead now suddenly embraced military leaders (who had not died in the war), plus politicians and diplomats.

Why did it have to be modified in such a manner after so many years of silence? Was it because a priest woke up one morning and decided to do it? It was not clear if a Japanese politician or somebody else was involved in this decision when the press investigated. Many Japanese politicians, including the prime minister, insisted that this was an issue of religious freedom. From a strict Japanese ideological viewpoint, there was nothing wrong in 'honouring' those people who had taken on themselves the responsibility for the war 'on their behalf' like sacrificial lambs at the Tokyo International Tribunal.

Only it was not consistent with the new constitution. Article 20 of the Japanese constitution stated, 'No religious organization shall receive any privileges from the State, nor exercise any political authority. No person shall be compelled to take part in any religious act, celebration, rite or practice. The State and its organs shall refrain from religious education or any other religious activity.' The Allied powers were worried about the revival of state Shintoism as it seemed to have played a significant role in Japanese wartime fury.

Yasuhiro Nakasone, who took the post of premier roughly in parallel with Ronald Reagan and Margaret Thatcher, also visited the shrine in 1985. But in the face of Chinese and Korean protests, he stopped the practice. He was nicknamed by the Japanese media as *Kazami-dori* – a weathercock – because of his political flexibility. While his stance was much more extreme than Junichiro Koizumi, he survived with his own small sect by forming a coalition with the larger influential factions of the LDP.

Since then, however, the enlarging right wing of the LDP insisted on repeating this ritual and the prime minister did not deny this faction of the party as it would strengthen his power base. Not knowing fully how China and South Korea would respond, Koizumi insisted he could 'persuade' China and South Korea in accepting his stance, as he had been successful on a similar occasion regarding domestic policy.

However, his sneaky attempts to revise the historical practice unleashed serious anger in those nations that had suffered harshly under Japanese wartime atrocities and oppression. As the Chinese press expressed its indignation, Chinese counter-action first appeared as a ban on the leaders' visits to each other and then refused to invite the Japanese prime minister to China. In this situation, he avoided going to the shrine on 15 August but went there instead on 13 August.

In addition, there were other political elements in the Koizumi administration which the Chinese government did not like. Above all, the new government was curtailing its government loans to China. This was partially due to Japan's own financial problem. But criticism was mounting in Japan caused by the growing reality of the prosperous Chinese economy and its hidden defence expenditure, which started to appear as an attempt for aggressive territorial expansion in the region. The Chinese government quickly decided to play hardball with Japan.

South Korea had also objected concerning the sensitive issue of visiting the shrine but they exercised a more measured diplomatic approach – at least initially. But this attitude gradually intensified because of hardening of public opinion in South Korea, overlapped by a rekindled territorial dispute with Japan and the weakening power of President Roh Moo-hyun. All was multiplied by the stronger Chinese reactions on this issue, and all was further inflamed by a clumsy explanation from the Japanese prime minister. Meanwhile, Japanese insistence looked more difficult to sustain and isolated, especially after the German Chancellor, Gerhard Schroeder, expressed an outright apology over Nazism in Poland on his official visit in 2004.

Meetings in a third country with the Chinese president or premier were not helpful either, as the issue of Yasukuni always had to be discussed first with no abating of sentiment on either side. Under this diplomatic aggravation, China escalated its stance by not holding any face-to-face meetings with the Japanese leader even in a third country. Sino-Japanese diplomacy cooled although the future of their relationship was emerging as important as ever in the region.

In this peculiar situation, Japan, which had contributed so much to China's industrial development with large-scale investments, could not see the head of the Chinese government to discuss an all-important political agenda for the two nations. Japan had provided ODA (Official Development Assistance) of around US$11.8 billion every year directly to China since 1980, which amounted to Y3.3 trillions (US$31.4 billion) by 2004 together with separate government loans of similar amounts and accepted some 77,000 students from China as of 2004, which represented two-thirds of all foreign students in the country.

Facing those intensifying Chinese objections, the best thing Japan's 'most powerful' prime minister could do was to try another dodgy attempt to visit the shrine with a lower profile. But the Chinese were again furious. The move took place on 1 January 2004. The newly invented pretext was that he went there as part of the New Year Japanese custom of visiting a shrine. But why Yasukuni? Being fully aware of Japanese customs, China and South Korea again vigorously protested.

On 5 January, Junichiro Koizumi also paid homage with four cabinet ministers to the Ise Shrine, which was the principal Shinto shrine in Japan. *Asahi Shimbun* reported (06/01/04) what he said on this visit, 'I feel something like inspiration here. Isn't it wonderful? I like the atmosphere here that is different from the other shrines. I feel great. For this year, I wish a calm and peaceful year.' The press continued, 'The first prime minister who worshiped at the Shrine was Ichiro Hatoyama in 1955. When Nobusuke Kishi did it, the ministers followed. Hayato Ikeda never visited there. Since 1965, Eisaku Sato did it with his ministers. This became an official event afterwards. Masayoshi Ohira, a Christian, and Tomiichi Murayama, ex-Socialist chief, were no exception.'

After the Osaka High Court ruled that his Yasukuni visit was unconstitutional, the prime minister changed the nature of his worship at the shrine, declaring it a private matter on his return in

On the Theory of Chinese Ideology

October 2005. He no longer signed himself as prime minister in the visitor's registration book. In fact, he did not sign at all and wore a normal business suit instead of his previous formal wear. He did not even enter the main shrine. He went there merely in a manner any Japanese individual might have done, by throwing a coin and praying. What a difference from Remembrance Day in Britain! But even this self-degrading and 'legally' adjusted action failed to appease the Chinese and Koreans.

There were lessons to be learned for the future of Japan from this incident. Firstly, the responsibility for the dreadful invasion, agony and other sufferings in East Asian history cannot be eliminated even after more than sixty years of peace and prosperity. If the Japanese try to revive state Shintoism, ignoring previous experience, Japan will be isolated exactly as before. Secondly, Japan's global success depends on keeping essential diplomatic relationships in East Asia. It is, therefore, very dangerous to make any diplomatic moves on such a fragile basis of explanations vis-à-vis China and South Korea. Thirdly, as the issue is so vital for those nations, it should not be left open to the random decisions of a politician or at the discretion of unknown bureaucrats or religious leaders but should be decided by a clearly defined national policy and goal.

A final blow to Mr Koizumi's reputation, which came as a relief to the Japanese people, was revealed in July 2006 by *Nihon Keizai Shimbun*, in the most sensational scoop ever made by the Japanese press, reporting of a 'Tomita memo' in the form of a letter dictated by Emperor Hirohito to his chamberlain in 1988. The emperor clearly expressed his displeasure on the enshrinement of the A-grade war criminals in 1978 and explained this as the reason why he had ever since stopped visiting the shrine. Furthermore, it was confirmed in this letter that the person who had asked for the enshrinement was actually the ex-Ministry of Health and Welfare. (Again!) The newspaper and reporter received no honour for their brilliant detective work but were afterwards harassed by a petrol bomb.

On the other hand, the Japanese people, or indeed the world, have to be cautious as this case has demonstrated that Japan's new political leaders could be far more 'extreme' than even the most ever-criticised wartime Japanese emperor. Emperor Hirohito was the only Japanese who had actually experienced what the Japanese supreme power meant by living with deep remorse throughout this turbulent period. More alarmingly, this stance emanated from such a nice bloke – always smiling, fully-educated, fun-loving and cultured, the Junichiro Koizumi who was relied on in the US to be a top western sympathiser in Japanese political circles.

Knowing the ex-emperor's view had been published just a few weeks earlier, the prime minister paid his final official visit to the shrine as 'promised' again in formal wear, before leaving his office on 15 August 2006, the day the repentant emperor announced the end of the war fought under his name to the Japanese people. In sensing an immense 'dark force' behind his move, the Australian government and some lawmakers in the United States for the first time started to condemn the conduct of the Japanese Prime Minister.

SURPRISE VISIT TO PYONGYANG

In contrast to his slow progress on the reform agenda, Junichiro Koizumi made a bold initiative on the diplomatic front with his surprise visit to Pyongyang to see its mysterious leader, Kim Jong-il. The opposition party criticised the prime minister for having this kind of meeting with a rogue state leader. But the fact was that North Korea had approached the Japanese government via diplomatic channels to say that they would be at last ready to admit to the scandalous abduction of Japanese nationals. Previously, the North Koreans had vehemently denied this but their position was changing.

As a background, it was Japan or, more precisely, North Korean immigrants living in Japan, who supported a good part of North Korea's economy by sending hard currency and goods to the world's last remaining isolated state. Under Japanese financial boom and bust, the bank owned by North Korean immigrants had also fallen into bad debt problems. North Korea seemed to do everything it could, including the forgery of US dollar bills, to obtain economic benefit out of this financial squeeze. A prospect of a normal relationship with Japan appeared again as an attractive option in their growing economic predicament. Meanwhile, US intelligence warned the Japanese government that Japanese exported parts were being used for North Korea's weapon programmes including its ballistic missiles.

Knowing the difficulty about the negotiations, Prime Minister Koizumi was cautious not to let the talks be interpreted as a compromise with this controversial and unpredictable militaristic state. It was planned as a day visit that would concentrate on the issue of kidnapping; that was Japan's aim but North Korea's objective was diplomatic normalisation plus arranging an eventual financial package. Just before this encounter, however, the US government supplied the Japanese prime minister with the shocking information that North Korea had secretly restarted their own atomic weapon programme.

The meeting was cordial but no smiling faces were seen on either sides. Kim Jong-il was very different in his manner from the previous occasion when he met Kim Dae-jung, the president of South Korea, when he was relaxed and expressed his hospitality with confidence. He was rather tense and gloomy in front of the Japanese leader, as if he knew he had to eat humble pie while apologising for embarrassing past brutality.

In a ponderous conversation, Kim Jong-il admitted to the Japanese delegation that North Korea was responsible for this dreadful conduct. He disclosed the sensational fact that five Japanese abductees were still alive and detained in his country. He showed his remorse for this incident. But he insisted that it was not carried out by his orders and his government had already punished the illicit acts of their subordinates. This announcement was greeted in Japan with grave shock and anger but with a sense of achievement after decades of North Korea's denials.

The once-diminished approval rate for the Koizumi administration soared after this visit to 60 per cent, offsetting the reaction to the snail-creeping pace of his 'reform'. The opposition were in tatters as the

Japanese media criticised the left wing of the DPJ including its leader, Naoto Kan, as once being a sympathiser of North Korea and for not addressing such appalling behaviour. The diplomacy and the human tragedies seemed to have suddenly changed to a domestic political game, as the Japanese hostages were allowed to come back home in a dramatic encounter.

For North Korea, the Koizumi-Kim summit produced neither the expected economic benefits nor political normalisation with Japan as the relationship between the two countries plummeted after North Korea's official admission of its nuclear research for its weapon programme. It became obvious that Kim Jong-il had not manipulated this entire event from the viewpoint of gaining a positive future diplomatic relationship but from outdated tactics of seeking a short-term economic benefit. The new Japanese diplomatic initiative toward North Korea only revealed the difficulty of dealing with this peculiar state and any long-term solution had to include the US and China.

But the idea that North Korea might shoot a ballistic missile with a nuclear warhead at Japan changed the scope of the Japanese conventional defence argument. The stronger the 'North wind' blew ensured that Japan had to tighten its 'coat' of defence. A leading Japanese strategist, Hisahiko Okazaki argued, '…especially regarding the new naval and airforces, the American and Japanese combined force in the region will be absolutely prevailing among others…The sole answer for these questions will be to strengthen the US-Japanese Alliance.'[191]

Indeed, even before the threat of North Korea and the continued Chinese military build-up, Japan had gradually adopted its new defence strategy to increase its budget on defence spending for its own military forces, especially for the hardware of naval and air forces to protect its supply line from the Persian Gulf defined as the 'Sea Lane'. The US government initiated the policy that Japan shares the cost of its own defence since the 1980s. In addition, Japan had to equip a TMD (Theatre Missile Defence) system under the possible threat of attack from North Korea. To build this advanced systematic military force is an expensive exercise. Japan also has to bear the partial cost of the US forces based in Japan and in the Pacific. With its declining financial power and further confusions in Japanese politics, however, overall Japanese defence capability was actually declining to a dangerous level in contrast to the newly-advanced Chinese military deployment in the region.

MANIFESTOS FOR DELAY AND NO DECISIONS

The Japanese media was busy covering the general election in 2003, as competition for the manifestos between the LDP and the DPJ intensified. According to the press, it was the first time in Japanese politics that this British-style method of a public declaration of policy before the ballot was introduced and it was seen as a positive move forward for Japan's two-party system. The convincing nature of this story became more plausible, as it was reported widely in Japan; even the *Financial Times* in London insisted so in its editorial. However, some Japanese reporters were critical at the time, claiming that despite the increased size of these documents that these new 'manifestos' were lacking a real policy direction and were nothing different from the old public pledges – *Koyaku* – expressed with a few slogans not clear objectives with a vision, but rather were trying to attract voters with a hidden political agenda.

The reality was that the Japanese political parties took notice of the growing anxiety of voters at the election and came up with the idea of new 'manifestos' together with some of the British practice of creating a 'shadow cabinet'. But there was neither a tangible strategy in the manifestos nor a serious working ethic attached to them, and as such, these could hardly be a first step for Japanese democracy. For central government reform, the LDP had only two main plans: the privatisation of the Road Corporation and Postal Services. And the DPJ had none.

The DPJ hastily revealed the appointment of a few popular figures from outside the party at the last minute to become key 'shadow cabinet' members. Under the Japanese constitution, less than half of the cabinet ministers could be non-MPs. They chose the former novelist and the governor of Nagano prefecture, Yasuo Tanaka, to deal with regional governmental 'reform'. Another 'inspiration' to work as shadow finance minister was Eisuke Sakakibara, an ex-MOF official, who was once nicknamed by some in international economic circles as 'Mr Yen'. These appointments were immediately withdrawn after the failed election result was announced. 'Sorry, your bet has been lost, now please go away.' The people must have despised the nature of the party's shallow behaviour at the heart of this contest which claimed to be 'Japan's historically important' election.

Addressing a British audience, Prime Minister Koizumi explained to *The Times* on 30 May 2003, 'When I took office two years ago, I stated that I needed to ask people to put up with zero growth for two or three years.' He sounded like George Osborne. 'We shall continue to push ahead with structural reforms, leaving to the private sector what the private sector does best.' But his comments did not materialise in the LDP manifesto which did not mention the matter of zero growth for two to three years or structural reforms.

On the other hand, to go forward with his reform plan, the prime minister, under his own direct supervision, established the Economic Finance Consultative Conference with a minister responsible for all economic matters including Heizo Takenaka, the alleged mighty 'economic tsar'. After January 2002, the medium-term economic and financial prospects were titled 'Reform and Prospect', *Kaikaku to Tenbo,* and this was revised every year during his tenure.

In the 2004 version, for basic revenue and expenditure, the so-called 'primary balance' was targeted to become positive by the early 2010s. This phrase was heard for the first time by the Japanese public. In a press interview, as Economic and Financial Policies Minister and also Financial Services Minister, Takenaka emphasized the importance of a positive primary balance and boasted of the recent improvements in Japan's financial status. According to the press report, there was a pointed question from a reporter on this issue. 'Regarding the recent primary balance improvement as you mentioned, here we are talking about 500-600 billion yen and the actual deficit is now 19 trillion yen. How could you attain your goal to increase the revenue from this in a time span of ten years?' The 'mighty' minister murmured. Unfortunately, we can testify today that the journalist's commonsense was proven to be correct.

Another carefully considered question asked by the media was, 'Under this financial situation, I think the importance of the deregulation of various businesses would be vital. But I heard that the bureaucracy is resisting this move. How can you overcome it?' The 'economic tsar' replied, 'I am not the minister responsible for that. I hope the minister responsible would act properly with this difficult situation.' The chairman of the conference for the General Deregulations, Yoshihiko Miyauchi, Orix Group chief executive, whose appointment by the prime minister was presented to the public as an extraordinary event, later confessed to the press in a moment of stress, that he was utterly disappointed after the results of his discussions led by the bureaucrats.

But the real problem existed in the aims of the political factions which overshadowed the entire Japanese political movement, recklessly seeking power in order to survive, or to expand their old secured interests while disregarding the new common goal for the nation. There was no meaningful political debate in this political quagmire where none of the ministers had any real power. And of course, a further dreadful reality was that the Japanese people had to endorse this system by elections without expressing any effective criticisms or analysis.

THE ROAD CORPORATION FIASCO

Despite all the deferments of major political reforms, there was at least one attempt at a confrontation so people could assess how actual reforms could happen in Japan. And it was plain for everybody to see how Japan's 'most powerful' prime minister was completely humiliated by what he named as the 'resisting powers' inside the LDP on the issue of the heavily deficit financed, Road Corporation, which was criticised for lavishly building road networks all over Japan without public scrutiny.

When Prime Minister Koizumi appointed the members of the Road Corporation Privatisation Committee by calling them the 'Seven Samurais' in 2002, voters were excited to hear the news. At last, they all thought, a 'super-politician' was ready to tackle this previously 'prohibited' issue in Japan. The members announced were: 1) Takashi Imai, the ex-president of Nippon Steel, who also acted as the chairman, 2) Hideo Nakamura of Musashi Institute of Technologies, 3) Kazuaki Tanaka of Takushoku University, 4) Masashi Matsuda, chairman JR East Japan, 5) Eiko Ohya, journalist, 6) Naoki Inose, writer and 7) Hiroko Kawamoto, McKinsey & Company.

Afterwards, the outline of the committee members' discussions was openly reported and it seemed they were moving forward in a positive direction, and more importantly, the public were 'allowed' to see the talks in progress. During the course of the debates, Takashi Imai and Hideo Nakamura, took an opposing view from the others as the committee was trying to finalise the report. In failing to achieve a consensus, the committee took a ballot and approved a final draft to allocate all the toll income to pay the existing debt and not to allocate it to new construction projects. The chairman resigned in frustration and he and Nakamura decided not to attend the committee meetings any more. In this situation, people's expectation grew as they watched the committee hammering out a new reform.

In parallel with these discussions, the status of the Road Corporation's management was revealed by an internal leak of information about its operations. The public were astonished to find out that this gigantic public corporation had neither a proper balance sheet nor consolidating accounts with its subsidiaries.

Then, suddenly in a dramatic squabble over his likely dismissal, the governor – *Sosai* – (A Japanese title only used for the head of a major public corporate entity. It sounds certainly more 'powerful' than CEO!) of the Road Corporation, Haruho Fujii, tried to change his 'superior's mind' by indicating the involvement of a 'dark force' behind this issue. This was conveyed during his 'off the record' private face-to-face meeting with Nobuaki Ishihara, the newly appointed Land and Transportation Minister, which lasted more than three hours.

But an unperturbed Ishihara, a son of the charismatic and powerful Tokyo governor, Shintaro Ishihara, disclosed this troubling part of the conversation on a TV chat show following day. All the media were thrown into an uproar in guessing who those politicians were or what exactly they did, quite an unusual topic from their ordinary news coverage. Most alleged the 'Road Tribe'– *Douro-Zoku* – in Japan were influential politicians in the LDP who although they could not be party leaders, controlled party politics behind the scenes with shadowy deals.

Governor Fujii subsequently 'readjusted' this story, however, to say that what he meant was politicians who were closest to the prime minister but his bluff failed to produce his intended result. The matter was finally decided by the prime minister not to pursue this specific issue as it would open up a Pandora's box. In threatening again to go to court about his dismissal, he finally backed down. Haruho Fujii retreated from public life, perhaps also from his 'dark force', by publicly disclosing his 'illicit' conduct and contact.

But the people of Japan were now aware of the existence of the huge political powers of the interest groups behind the Road Corporation. In this case, he showed his determined resistance against reform or any intervention to protect the interests of the established factional 'business' which had carefully conceived 'legal' protection, and perhaps, also with strong political back-up in complete disregard of the common good.

Meanwhile, the new government's decision to rely on these independent members to analyse the situation and come up with a proposal seemed to have born fruit. No matter that their proposal was inadequate, Prime Minister Koizumi would certainly have been given credit for what he achieved in attempting a new transparency in Japanese politics.

But here the real Japanese politics began. This final draft was frozen for almost a year as if the politicians and the bureaucracy waited for the right timing for the 'assault'. Then in December 2003, after the Koizumi administration secured its second term with a comfortable majority, the LDP and the government decided to completely change this final draft.

As soon as they saw the government plan at the end of December, 'Three Samurais' arranged a press conference both to resign and to attack it, 'This is just an adaptation of the old Financial Investment.' They argued that the principal structure of government insistence on bank loans for new construction works using the toll income was faulty. 'Under the plan, the construction of new uneconomical roads could not be stopped and the financial position of the corporation would never be improved.' It was exactly the plan that the bureaucracy, or more precisely, the 'tribe' of politicians wanted to retain their disguising old power under the new phrase of a 'drastic review'.

Naoki Inose, who, all the way, remained supportive together with Eiko Ohya, of the bill, wrote about his 'successful' inconclusive result: 'The Ministry of Land and Transportation wanted to put some superficial improvements on the four corporations but I defended my bottom line to divide the Corporation into three...and to secure the lower toll charge.'[192]

This political fiasco simply reconfirmed that any politicians in Japan had to kowtow to the factional balance of power. In this context, the end of Junichiro Koizumi would have come when Yoshiro Mori, his faction chief, deserted him despite his strong support from the people. Under factional politics, the dignity of an individual has no place to shine. Senior (or *Senpai*) Mori gauged the timing and acted on this 'signal' for a policy from an arch-bureaucratic consensus to push this already failed political system to another plausible breathing space. As this episode shows, the 'most powerful' Japanese prime minister's reform ended as an impossible dream.

THE FARCE OF THE POSTAL CORPORATION 'REFORM'

During his political career, Junichiro Koizumi took two posts as cabinet minister before he became the prime minister. First as the Minister of Health and Welfare, he was deemed as average. Then, as the Minister of Posts and Telecommunications, he made his career as a renowned maverick in Japanese politics by clashing with the powerful inner bureaucracy. Unlike the other LDP politicians, he stood up to criticise the ministry's established policies and launched his own view on the privatisation of all its functions.

It was a risky gamble to take this stance as many LDP politicians were firmly locked in with various ministry-related interests, while it was also regarded as the main 'tribal' business area of his major rival, the former *Tanaka* faction. Even the opposition were reluctant to get involved in an argument with this huge governmental business of Japan's largest bank and life insurance company which employed more than 280,000 people all over Japan as of 2004. By launching this 'reform', however, Junichiro Koizumi apparently 'sailed' on a different course from the LDP mainstream. Somehow, it paid off as the 'wind' of public opinion suddenly changed in his favour.

In particular, after his faction's leader and the short-lived administration of Yoshiro Mori collapsed because of constant and intolerable gaffes made in front of the media, Koizumi emerged as the only credible candidate in the LDP. He not only stood up for Japan's reform programme, and more importantly, could win the general election – without him no candidate had even discussed the topic.

In this sudden change of environment, the new prime minister declared he would pursue the privatisation of the Postal Services as his main political agenda and the final goal of his political career. Backed by public opinion, Prime Minister Koizumi gradually shaped his 'grand design' for the eventual privatisation despite the existence of a huge 'opposition force' in his own party. But a surprise came on his announcement of the privatisation that the entire process would only end by 2017, with a possibility of changing its progress before then.

Part Three – Japan in Crisis

Having heard the details, many of the LDP politicians supported this 'reform' despite their earlier negative criticism and strong rejection. It was not because they were suddenly woken up by Koizumi's warning, but because they found it rather acceptable. Exactly, as in the case of the Road Corporation, this 'reform' was watered down in two ways. Firstly, old Japanese politics kept control by leaving the current corporate structure intact. And secondly, the arch-bureaucracy would still retain the 'vital' part of the principal functions of the Postal Corporation businesses leaving it unchanged even after privatisation. In this new plan, there was no clear strategy or business model for this new corporate entity as to how the largest saving bank, insurance company and postal services in Japan's market economy would function except to continue their current operations with a nominal change even after 2017.

Without giving equal status to all small businesses and changing its old employment practices, there could hardly be justifiable large-scale redundancies in Japan. It was a custom in the City of London with its free labour market when somebody was leaving a job, that he would buy a drink or two for his former colleagues in a farewell party at the pub. With new prospects and challenges in mind, jokes and smiling faces would be seen everywhere. Quitting a job in the closed labour market of Japan was too serious to celebrate in such a manner. Everybody knows that the past employee would be unlikely to enjoy better prospects once he left his supposed 'lifetime' employment by which his reputation was likely to be reduced, and his 'talent' would mean little in the next 'worse-off' arch-bureaucratic hierarchy.

There is another serious issue for Japanese financial business. Under a 'compromising' society, both the creditor's and debtor's rights are not properly protected in Japan. In the law of the jungle where various factional powers are allowed to dominate, it is impossible to expand in a dignified manner with seller and buyer treated as equal participants. Japan could learn a lot from a country like Britain. In fact, William Shakespeare, having thought about all the important things in life, once depicted the prime importance of supreme mercy in the interpretation of law in *The Merchant of Venice*. Mercy had to be balanced by law as Portia, disguised as a Doctor of Laws, told the court:

> It must not be. There is no power in Venice
> Can alter a decree established.
> 'Twill be recorded for a precedent,
> And many an error by the same example
> Will rush into the state. It cannot be.[193]

Thus, a lawless Japan and its factional 'mercies' end up with salvaging disasters and taxpayers' misery as a global economic tragedy unfolds. The Postal Corporation reform was bogged down by the policy of covering up, which would lead the nation to continued proliferations of public sector business into the private sector. But this was the recipe for state bankruptcy which avoided cutting few people's jobs, ignoring the job prospects of many other forgotten people.

The 'reform' of the Postal Corporation could not shift the old entrenched methods of its gigantic and opaque business. The bill created after negotiations with LDP interests was to divide the three businesses of the Corporation into four entities: –1) a saving bank, 2) an insurance company, 3) a postal service company, 4) the counter service company in 2007. Is there any reason for this irregular split? This irrational scheme was simply designed to preserve the existing business entity.

Then, the newly elected DJP administration in October 2009 scrapped the plan to go 'back to the past' as their first major parliamentary act. We must conclude, therefore, that the entire process of this Japanese 'reform' was just another piece of a state-funded political farce, which stunned domestic and foreign audiences to silence.

PART THREE – JAPAN IN CRISIS

THE 'MAIN CASTLE' INTACT

Japanese public sector reform is long overdue. To discuss the details of such an overall reform, however, first requires an analysis of the facts of the failed arch-bureaucratic-driven politics in this gigantic business complex. Above all, we need to inject adequate accounting transparency to first assess the scale of the problems. But at the same time, most Japanese journalists, economists, researchers and academics or conscientious politicians are all aware that there is an insurmountable, and sometimes dangerous, 'political barrier' to launching such an investigation in Japan.

Apart from 'ministerial business' via public corporations, many of these which are today classified as private companies such as Japan's leading oil exploitation industry, electric power or public transport companies, should be included in this category judging from their structure, degree of control and immense loss-making history. There were also nine state banks in Japan at the time of the Koizumu reform.

In March 2005, the wearied prime minister suddenly asked his lieutenant, Heizo Takenaka, to deal with public sector banking reform. Then he announced that all the current public banks with assets above 90 trillion yen (US$82 billion) would be privatised by 2013. Nobody including the press reporters seemed to understand what this 'expeditious reform' meant exactly. Judging from the annual injection levels from government funds, it was doubtful that all these banks were running at a profitable level. But how to solve the deficit of the public sector banks was never publicly discussed before deciding to set a course for this 'rational' remodelling.

No Japanese economists even seemed to know of the existence of the problem. However, there was one exception – Hiroshi Kato estimated in 2000 that this hidden level of bad debt at public sector level, including public corporations, was around 120 trillion yen (US$1.2 trillion).[194] It was roughly two times larger than the cash injection to the private banking sector even at that date. This must have reached colossal proportions by 2005.

There was a public bank called the Public Enterprise Financial Coffers for Governmental Enterprise – *Koei-Kigyo-Kinyu-Koko* – which was virtually unknown to the public, as even the press rarely reported on its activities. The bank business was expanding and its volume of government debentures was well above half of the notorious Road Corporation according to the MOF figure. In December 2005, the government council suddenly announced that this bank would be abolished – *haishi*. They used rather strong words like the sound of *Taiko* drums. Then, it was subsequently 'reconsidered' that the bank would survive under the authority of regional governments. Nobody seemed to know what this actually signified in terms of its activities, funding and operations.

However, the objective for these frequently made public sector 'reforms' was that they had to show the Japanese people that the government sector had done everything possible to minimise planned indirect tax increases. But this Japanese tax plan has been constantly delayed for decades due to its obvious negative impact on the consumer economy and public unpopularity. The rate of indirect tax is much lower in Japan compared with EU countries. But the Japanese consumer tax method was rather 'toxic' as it includes essential foodstuffs. This was totally different from VAT in Europe, which is highly rated, but also capped, carries exemptions and is refundable. Again, tax accountants or lawyers are not 'allowed' to argue about these things in Japan.

During this crisis, the degree of independence in Japanese banks significantly decreased, as they became entities too fragile for the economy. Under the Financial Function Resuscitation Act of 1998, the bureaucratic 'leadership' and public fund would eventually 'save' all the Japanese private sector banks. In other words, all the loss-making banks could become state or quasi-state banks if the situation worsened further. It was obvious, unless people could establish the principle of efficiency into Japanese bureaucracy, the banking sector as a whole could not be salvaged. But who could ever accomplish it in Japan?

The prime minister depicted the Postal Services Corporation as the 'Main castle' in 2005. But in reality, it seemed that the arch-bureaucracy saw it as a 'fortress' to protect the other loss-making 'main castles' of ministries, public banks and various state financial entities, and keeping their own 'sacred' rights to create further such entities with disastrous financial consequences. As revealed by Koizumi's 'reform' attempts, there were no arm's length contractual relationships between the government and these political entities existing under their dubious accounting principles and appalling 'legal' practices.

Is that all? No, not yet. There is yet another serious widespread problem in the background. If you visited Tokyo recently you might have noticed a shiny Notre Dame de Paris-shaped skyscraper in the Western-Shinjuku district which is owned by the Tokyo regional government or the *Sankei* newspaper report (12/12/03) that the regional assembly in Kyoto had sent a letter to the central government to be cautious with regard to the dispatch of the Japanese self-defence force to Iraq.

Like this eye-catching building or these extraordinary arguments by highly paid and pensioned local politicians and its bureaucracy were indicating, their problems were also becoming desperate. Regional services are highly overlapped by prefecture and city level systems despite the fact that Japan has no federal system. What is required here is a Thatcher-style thorough political reform at regional levels. But in Japan, things have moved exactly in the opposite direction in the last decades, as an enormous amount of public and commercial investment work was injected into the regions, in complete disregard of economic principles, pushing most of the major regional governments' debt up to an alarming level; albeit this was often done through initiatives from central government. None of these heavily in debt regional governments have been successful in countering these worsening trends, and time is ticking for another financial 'blast' elsewhere.

On the Theory of Chinese Ideology

CONFLICTS AMONGST CHINESE IDEOLOGICAL STATES

With an irreparable crack in Japanese capitalism on one side, a new situation was emerging on the other side of the region. The integration of the growing Chinese economy to the global economy provided hope for the future of East Asia although it appeared as a sharp contrast to what was happening in North Korea. Adjusting to this fast-expanding capitalistic trend including its global environmental obligations in its own political space, however, would not be an easy task for China, even as it became a more confident industrial power. Despite the rapidly expanding size of its national economy, because of its large population, China's per capita income was still a modest US$4,382 as of 2010, according to IMF calculations. In the imbalance between the state and the individual level of wealth, some might already see the root of instability in its political structure.

On the other hand, North Korea, which had already imploded, was experiencing the old political cycle where by losing its economic independence, it waited for a major political change. Parallel to this reality, Japan also entered into a chaotic political stage. What we need to understand is that, no matter what incredible things took place politically, it was quite normal within the political perspective of Chinese ideology.

In order to catch up with the rest of the industrial world, China always focused on the newest technologies using its state research capabilities. But with a growing private sector in the economy, the remodelling of Chinese society should have given an impetus to somewhat 'undesirable' democratic development. The challenge for improving Chinese social and business structures in accommodating these changes is now becoming vitally important, as ignoring this will hurt its future. In reality, however, the second ill-advised battle of an East Asiatic power against market forces is almost certain to be fought, changing the venue from Japan, as Chinese arch-bureaucracy must cling onto its power.

Part Three – Japan in Crisis

A worrying signal was China's determination to spend a larger portion of its economic proceeds to build up a sophisticated military power base with a huge secret budget and unidentified political aim. The newly developed Chinese nuclear submarines with improved long-range SLBM (submarine-launched ballistic missile) capability will soon affect the US or even European defence systems. Meanwhile, the US 7th Fleet and the Japanese navy are expected to encounter unprecedented pressure by the two planned Chinese aircraft carriers which are to be commissioned in the not too distant future, and a fleet of new type of destroyers, which are already starting to appear near Japanese waters. With this future in prospect, the shape of the Pacific military balance is now about to change fundamentally.

Diplomatic tensions are frequently due to differences in political values. East Asia is far behind Europe in terms of economic and further political integration. For example in the nineteenth century Britain and France, for the first time in history, stopped fighting each other over today's area of Belgium through diplomatic negotiations. But unlike Europe, there are still no mutually agreed boundaries in East Asia and territorial disputes existed between almost all the countries.

China is trying to exploit oil resources in the disputed area of the East China Sea and South China Sea, having unilaterally claimed its right to all waters the other side of the coastal states, including Japan. South Korea abruptly demanded that the internationally recognised name of 'Sea of Japan' should be changed to 'Eastern Sea' to force Japan to accept its self-defined sea line. On the other hand, the South Koreans were furious with the claims of a prominent Chinese scholar in 2005 that the old Korean state of Koguryo in the northern peninsula could actually be defined as a Chinese state, which raised suspicion among the Koreans of a possible Chinese military intervention in case of an 'emergency' scenario in the North. The conflicts amongst Chinese ideological states were fluid and unpredictable and constantly affected by changing power balances in domestic politics.

But perhaps we need to pay attention to one point here. The new reality for all the East Asian export economies is that they are all relying on the US and European consumer markets as the final destination for their exports. In this situation, it is not only militarily but also economically cataclysmic to even contemplate any aggression against the deployed forces of the United States in the region. From this power structure and mutual relationship, we should realize that Western diplomacy could produce a significant breakthrough in East Asia, perhaps more than anywhere else in the world.

Contrary to its aggressive diplomatic expansion in Europe, the new capitalistic Russia has a very different position in the region. Its relationship with Japan was one of restraint, despite Russia's cultural and artistic popularity in Japan. This not only comes from the issue of wartime experience or a pending peace treaty. Actually, any problem exists largely on the Japanese side. In contrast to the attitude of Germany, most Japanese have failed to understand the rapid changes in Russia and keep an old prevailing prejudice of regarding Russia as a non-European state.[195] Exactly as experienced at the end of the Second World War, the West will eventually require the active participation of this major western power on the ground as a partner in a different form to engage fully with the East Asian states.

While the East Asian regimes are thriving under the old ideology, as they have no other option, it is expected that their positive diplomatic relationship with the West could lose momentum due to this basic politico-intellectual hiatus. The reality is, therefore, that East Asia will never attain political stability under this divisive old political ideology. Without a doubt, the region remains today as one of the world's last and largest frontiers for global democracy to expand into.

JAPAN AS THE CORNERSTONE OF GLOBAL DEMOCRACY

Great advances in technology have always historically affected politics. When travel around the world took more than eighty days, a large-scale war tended to be the exclusive affair of a great state although its scale was limited. To manage an effective force at a remote distance was simply too expensive and the methods used were difficult for ordinary people to access. Nowadays, even an insurgent force can attack the world's superpowers from a secret hideout seven thousand miles away where a missile can fly in a few hours and a satellite can take detailed and exact pictures.

With today's remarkably advanced technology, global capitalism has grown rapidly just as people took to air travel leaving slow carriages behind – now even the other side of the globe is readily accessible. In this changing social environment, many professions are interlinked to the worldwide movements of a combined market, with its unprecedented multiplied force to expand their own businesses under the benefits of this enlarged economy.

At the same time, fears have arisen about climate change causing global environmental disasters by these uncontrolled developments, excessive production and waste, as these benefits carry unwanted and potential risks of an equally massive calamitous mismanagement downturn. The world community recognised the need for various measures to solve these negative movements by regulating greenhouse gas emissions and the development and maintenance of nuclear power plants as vital issues for global security.

Newly intensified dangers coming out of the accumulated global political risks from activities of national states have now been clearly recognised, and therefore, the idea of global democracy should today move up the agenda even in East Asia. Simply put, if we maintain the old protective attitude of national sovereignty, the world will soon break up. Obviously, the undemocratic regime of Japan is not as visible as one ruled by an eccentric dictator but the effect of non-democracy is the same. Japan must first identify the concealed political mechanism it works by.

A warning has to be given for both sides on this issue. With successive victories and quasi-monopolisation of the ultimate weapons, the West enjoyed a sort of complacency on their recent successful expansion. As history tells us, however, the evolution of technological progress never stops and the pattern of human conduct itself does not change despite scientific progress although we can be slightly better educated and disciplined. In order to assess future political needs, perhaps, it is time for all of us to reflect on the meaning of global, or rather western, expansion, which will be discussed next in Part Four.

Simultaneously, there was a solid expansion of universal values to all the corners of the world. In the real world, however, human political decisions arrive rather unpredictably, sometimes emotionally and often out of reach for ordinary people. And even the advantages of the advanced West in the process of required political judgements is always only comparative and not an absolute one. Yet, as a harsh reality, it is obvious that today's enlarged global economy cannot be further expanded without an equally extended democratic adjustment for establishing this principle on a global scale.

This new situation means if a country's politics were wrong and fundamentally against common global values, national sovereignty would be put under scrutiny by the global community. Thus, Slobodan Milosevic was removed from Yugoslavia by force. The West and the UN have so far demonstrated their right to intervene further in Albania, Macedonia, Kosovo, Cambodia, East Timor, Sierra Leone, Ivory Coast, Liberia, Sudan, Congo, Afghanistan, Iraq and Libya in order that these regions can remain in the economic scheme for global security.

On the other hand, people are now reasonably convinced that economic growth is closely attached to political freedoms. The 2002 United Nations Human Development Report insisted, 'Since 1980, 81 countries have taken "significant" steps towards democracy, with 33 military regimes replaced by civilian governments. Of the world's nearly 200 countries, 140 now hold multi-party elections. That may not make them fully democratic, but 82 of them are, and those are home to 57 per cent of the world's population.' Despite the said progress, the degree of each functioning democracy among these nations varies to a huge extent.

But what should happen with these invisible or hidden problems in East Asia? As Jean Grugel rightly argued, despite a stunning temporary economic success, the important issue remains,

'Democratization does not constitute a complete rupture with the past. Democratizing states cannot be understood outside of their histories, contexts and capacities. This means that the introductions of elections and the writing of new constitutions do not, in themselves, challenge non-democratic state cultures and practices. Nor do they necessarily transform power relations within society.'[196] This element should be taken into consideration particularly when you think about East Asian countries that have enjoyed their own political system backed by a solid recognisable historical prosperity long before the new trend of global democracy began.

As the actual situations in East Asian 'capitalism' would indicate, democracy with full disclosure and transparency should be required first for the state sector to solve the other problems in society. The world cannot move forward without East Asia. But it is now unlikely that these outdated political systems hiding under their double standards will accept global and universal social values as a matter of principle for the sake of their own democracy and developments.

If we put it more philosophically, by using a dialectic approach of 'thesis' as East Asiatic politics and 'anti-thesis' as western capitalism based on democracy, the 'synthesis' as 'the East Asian democracy' will not evolve automatically in the current passive mode. In other words, the political base may naturally alter with economic progress, but for a new political decision, the nations still require endorsement by human agreement or acceptance (by force) as before.

Francis Fukuyama applied a comparison of liberal democracy versus Maoism to assess the Chinese past and future. He argued, 'The current leadership of China seems to understand that it cannot turn the clock back on economic reform, and China will have to open up to the international economy. This has discouraged any return to a Maoist foreign policy, despite the attempt to revive aspects of Maoism domestically.'[197] But the difficulty for his scenario is that Maoism has to be replaced by a much broader and deeper Chinese ideology in this assumption, therefore, neither 'bureaucracy' nor 'nationalism' is 'a specifically modern phenomenon' in East Asia as we have earlier argued.

With a coming turning point in mind, however, it is perhaps time for the West to tackle the problem of their ultimate 'antagonists' in East Asia. Frankly, it would be an utter illusion to believe that the world could attain something meaningful in leaving these two most undemocratic, yet decisively influential, states of China and Japan as they are today. But where to begin? Despite similar fundamental functions, progress on East Asiatic democracy and capitalism varies. If a change has to be made, it has to reach to China, Korea and Japan, and eventually to all of East Asia.

With this strategic aspect, the 'thrust' has to be focused on Japan, the most advanced and problematic economy, yet the easiest to tackle in terms of political structure. In this sense, we need to realise that today's Japan is emerging as the cornerstone for global democracy. The West must establish a principle to prove to everybody in the world that it could be planted in East Asia or elsewhere. For only a democratic Japan in a strong partnership with the US, British Commonwealth, Europe and Russia can influence China and Korea to form a political union in solving the various issues in the region. And the prosperous future of East Asia and the entire world can only begin with this successful political restructuring.

PART FOUR
THE CHANGE

SUN YAT-SEN AND THE POLITICAL BASE OF MODERN CHINA

China's old dynastical regime finally fell in 1912. But the reality was that the new leader, Sun Yat-sen, soon had to yield the acting presidency of the new republic to Yuan Shikai, a northern warlord, in response to the threat of the remnant Qing forces still under his command. Despite the joy for a newly born emancipated form of Chinese politics on the streets, a turbulent era for China was set to continue.

Sun Yat-sen's political life was also hanging in the balance, as he went into self-imposed exile to Japan. In struggling with threatening Japanese demands for their own five major rights in China including taking over the German rights and interests in Shandong province against his government, however, Yuan unexpectedly passed away in despair in 1916, after trying to hold onto his status as the emperor of the Empire of China – *Zhonghua* – which in fact lasted less than three months. The outrageous Japanese move united all the opposition against him and the Chinese republican movement was sustained in this most difficult time by this Japanese 'counter revolutionary' aggression.

In the stormy days of this first Chinese revolution, it must be remembered that Sun Yat-sen actually played the role of 'founder' in defining Chinese modern polity both for Chinese 'republicans' and for Chinese 'communists'. This is the reason why many parks are called after him – Zhong Shang (his pseudonym in Mandarin) Parks – and are still flourishing on both sides of the Taiwan Strait. More importantly, by naming his revolution as the first, the second revolution by Chinese communists was never outside his own definition of the 'modern' political core of China at this critical moment.

While the power balance in Europe was readjusted as one result of the First World War, the Chinese revolution of Sun Yat-sen was suddenly accelerated by an incident called the 'May Fourth movement', led by young intellectuals and students which influenced public opinion all over the country. This was a most rare window of opportunity for Chinese freedom of speech which appeared in a sudden political vacuum, fuelled by a sense of fury, just after the Great War where the Allied powers, including Japan, emphatically rejected all Chinese demands as an independent state at the peace conference in Paris.[198]

The centre of this movement was at Beijing University where influential thinkers from the communist Li Dazhao to the liberal Hu Shih emerged. In seizing this opportunity, Sun Yat-sen adopted the name of the Chinese Nationalist Party (KMT) for his political movement in 1919. The Chinese Communist Party (CCP) was formed soon afterwards. Then, in 1923, Sun Yat-sen took a pragmatic decision via a KMT-CCP alliance to accept the seniority of Soviet Russia and the help of the newly established Comintern, which lasted until Chiang Kai-shek's anti-communist *coup d'etat* in 1927. In 1924, the KMT selected the central committee members and its candidates including Mao Zedong and other CCP members who joined the KMT on an individual basis at the first party conference in Guangzhou. Sun Yat-sen's realistic policy seemed to be evolving, but in the following year, he died, leaving his uncompleted revolution behind.

Faced with the visibly weakening status of Chinese nations since their defeat in the Sino-Japanese war, Sun had wanted China to be modernised as soon as possible with modern railway links and a new commercial and industrial infrastructure. But at the same time, he did not want China to be destabilised, perhaps, reflecting his own fragile position in Chinese politics. Despite the fall of the old dynasty system, the most traditional and authoritative elements at the centre of East Asiatic society and politics, were regarded as 'too

Part Four – The Change

fundamental' to abolish.

In his famous *Three Principles of the People*, he raised this issue and made his position very clear: 'Let us take the clan system as our small foundation and work at building up the nation upon this.' How could he use China's old legacy for its modern revolution? 'Suppose China has four hundred clans: it would be just as if we were working with four hundred individual people. We would make use of the original organization that each family name already has, and, in the name of the clan, begin to rally the people together, then in the provinces, and finally throughout the country, until each family name has become a large united group, and with such a union we need not fear outside adversaries or our inability to revive the state.'

At the same time, he was aware of criticisms for this policy but he insisted, 'this idea of "reverencing ancestors and being kind to the clan" has been embedded for millennium in the Chinese mind'. He also confessed the difficulty in deviating from this principle '… if anything was said about the possible extinction of his clan, he would be in terror lest the ancestral continuity of blood and food be broken, and he would give his life to resist that.'[199]

When Sun launched this principle for the new China, he had no other option. Put simply, he would not be elected as the new Chinese leader if he had thought any other way about it. On the other hand, it had always been a given that traditional Chinese political power would directly continue into the age of modern politics. As we reviewed earlier, Mao and his colleagues in the CCP survived under his iron rule, which was in fact, the old Chinese principle of 'revolution'. And Mao Zedong also accepted the 'modern' version of the Chinese political core as defined by Sun Yat-sen rather than confronting it; as he too knew, there was no other possible method that would succeed in delivering his essential political objectives.

Could Sun Yat-sen or Mao Zedong, however, have imagined the subsequent vigorous modernisation that happened in China? By 2005, Shanghai had emerged as the biggest city in East Asia with *c.*15 million people in the midst of shining skyscrapers and loud pop music. In 1988, when I first paid a visit there, Pudong was just a plain field! The world became fully accessible for all those Chinese people with a will and means as for all Americans. In this situation, the agrarian economy, arch-bureaucracy and finally, die-hard Chinese communism itself became obsolete as a reality, as every Chinese can see from his or her own experience today. Yet, as a historical fact, those amazing things happened in an extremely short time period, due to the global economic environment and new technological prowess. More importantly, this process would have been beyond the political imagination of those two great 'founders' of the modern Chinese nation.

The majority of Chinese people who started to work in cities faced daily survival options in living urban lives and encountered a quite different style of commitment from the old Chinese country ways. Unlike the traditional landscape, various goods, monetary assets, services and management are invisible and notional. Transparency and law binding contracts have to be the key for inter-related business communities where the people would be annoyed if others do not respect these principles. China must reform its politics. But where were those Chinese know-alls now? Confucius told them, of course, nothing about it. There was nothing equivalent in China as the philosopher Hu Shih convincingly concluded. Elsewhere in East Asia? This time, Japan could not provide any of the required modern social science for China to follow, except by showing its own disastrous example. Suddenly, it became clear that to survive outside this new and real global philosophy was no longer possible – even for proud Chinese people.

THE RESURGENCE OF SHINTOISM

Like in Scotland, Hogmanay or New Year's Day is the biggest celebration of the year in Japan. Surprisingly, 'Auld Lang Syne' is also sung. But strictly only before midnight. In the Japanese version, the words are made up of phrases from Chinese historical tales and this is deemed the song for farewell in Japan.

Part Four – The Change

After that time, the celebration becomes very different from a scene in Scotland where probably party music and toasts with glasses of whisky would continue till the early hours. While Japan also has a good single malt locally made in the authentic Scottish way, New Year turns into a religious event that is solemn and quiet. Many people go to nearby Shinto shrines to pray for the coming New Year. The main public transport will run all night to help the circulation of traffic. A large shrine will receive over a million visitors on this day. These are the holidays where everyone is a churchgoer. It is difficult indeed for foreigners to understand Japan if they have not experienced this special event.

It is absolutely right, therefore, what Gentaro Matsumura believed – that to understand Shinto is to understand Japan. He wrote about it eloquently, 'In the beginning, five gods appeared in succession in the heavens and seven generations of gods and goddesses followed. The first two generations were gods, while the succeeding five generations were couples... The last generation was the couple Izanagi and Izanami, who gave birth to the islands of Japan. Then followed Ama-terasu-o-mi-Kami (the Heaven-Shining Great Deity or the Sun Goddess) and her brother Susano-o.'

This is the world of human gods, as he explained, 'This is mythology and not a scientific narrative.' He also carefully paid attention to a major function of this 'religious' concept that human gods were created constantly in Shinto, '...real persons were enshrined after death... shrines are a kind of monument to particular persons, and their souls are thought to dwell at each shrine as a god or goddess.'

Why do the Japanese prime ministers go to the Ise Shrine every year? Matsumura had also provided an answer for us all, 'The Sun Goddess is now enshrined in the Ise shrine... The object of this shrine is the mirror which was given to Ninigi-no-Mikoto by the Sun Goddess when he descended from heaven. It is written in the *Kojiki* that she told him to look into this mirror whenever he wanted to see her. In the third century, replicas of these three divine objects were made to symbolize the emperor's sovereignty, and the original mirror was installed in the Ise Shrine...'[200]

Shinto is the religion of ritual, as he astutely pointed out. 'Shinto has no founder, no inspired scriptures and no moral code' – something like a void exists in its centre. No doubt, the formalism of Japanese bureaucracy originated in these religious rituals subordinated by Shintoism. 'Shintoists' and all other politicised or Shintocised religions in Japan, no matter what the content might be, must strictly follow the formal ritual as an expression of conformity to this supreme political ideology.

But I disagree with him on one point. Shinto had a founder. In other words, it was the Japanese ruling class who were equipped with modern iron technology, Chinese characters and many other clever ideas to enrich the islands inspired by this 'religious' power. The author of this religion was, therefore, strictly speaking, the ancient state of Japan and its arch-bureaucracy who wanted to remain anonymous. Without this political power, Shinto and the other (Shintocised) Japanese religions could never have survived in the heart of the Japanese people. From these peculiar origins, there was no need for religious principles except finally to protect the state.

Compared to the native Japanese, the new rulers with their strong continental links possessed tremendous information and knowledge about all of the eastern and western worlds. The conception of the Sun God was a creation of the ancient western states before the idea emerged in Japan in the eighth century. With this new East Asiatic concept, they claimed to be the founders of Japan. Afterwards, the native population were ready to be conquered by this powerful state. New politics were forged for this political necessity, whereby the subjugated population were integrated under a single political ideology in Japan's newly born state.

Due to this mechanism, religious freedom was rejected from the beginning as a matter of principle by this political ideology. In modern times, it became illegal and carried harsh penalties to even criticise the state 'religion' and the political role of the emperor who was claimed to be the descendant of these mythic gods. There were strict rules banning the freedom of speech.

Under the pre-war Meiji constitution, the emperor was stipulated as 'divine and inviolable' (Article 3). Effectively, this allowed a form of politics where Japanese arch-bureaucracy was protected by state Shintoism and all other subordinate political organs became 'divine and inviolable' with their biased judicial powers functioning inside the state. Thus, universal religious freedom continued to erode in the 'modern' Japanese state and to be 'banned' politically in society.

This old Japanese nationalism with all its political deficiencies collapsed because of its extreme mechanism *per se* that had created a 'sacred' state power which allowed no conceptional mistakes. It was finally defeated by western liberalism, a new concept born out of aggressive competition, where mistakes are constantly made but it is a sufficiently flexible concept to put matters right.

Reticence is a respectful virtue in Shintoism. Each individual's silence meant consent to this old historical political principle and all the new political decisions based on it. For most Japanese, it is too sensitive an issue to speak freely about. But everybody knew that there was huge political power behind the gigantic Shinto shrines and old Japanese Buddhist temples, or the mixture of both, which could instantly change your position in society, if you dared to object to this 'sacred' political argument camouflaged as religion – however degrading it was to accept it.

Japanese arch-bureaucracy, which cannot be scrutinised because of this religious conscience, played its decisive role in the previous cycle, as it was the only means for the Japanese to direct the nation under Chinese ideology. In this politico-religious reality, people had no alternative but to follow state arch-bureaucracy. In successfully silencing all possible criticism in society, this immense uncontrollable power that derailed the nation in paralysing democratic politics, again, had to be revived in post-war Japan. Since then, despite all the economic failures and miseries in Japan, this political ideology disguised as religion is firmly protected by the state arch-bureaucracy and shows no sign of abating.

On the Theory of Chinese Ideology

A SENSE OF CRISIS

Compared with China or Japan where a degree of cultural isolation and their political power base is relatively stronger, the political progress of smaller East Asian states, namely Taiwan and South Korea, had a noticeably different evolution. Traditional Chinese ideology was maintained in those countries too, but the difference was that a period of political difficulty for both nations was experienced when the people felt a sense of crisis. The war in China between the Kuomintang and communists and the Korean War both had the aspects of a civil war in China and Korea respectively.

In each case, increasing western influence over indigenous politics and religious beliefs appeared. As the Chinese communists advanced to all corners of China, there were clashes between Christians and communists trying to control all religious movements under the Bureau of Religious Affairs. The Kuomintang and many Christians fled to Taiwan at this time. The notable fact was that Chiang Kai-shek had a completely different view on religion from his antagonists.

He expressed his view on this issue to the missionary publication, *Maryknoll* magazine, in January 1959, 'Those most aware of the true nature of Communism are Catholics and the opposition of the Catholic Church is on moral and not political grounds. The Catholic churches realize the pertinency of conflict between atheism and belief in God.' He was then asked, 'Asian Communists accuse Christianity of being a Western religion. Would you answer this charge as an Asian and a Christian?' He replied emphatically, 'Those who say such a thing have no understanding of Christianity. Christianity is a religion that knows no geographical distinction between East and West. It is the same for all men.'[201]

Having been protected by US naval power, Christians in Taiwan enjoyed freedom under Chiang Kai-shek and the total number soon reached to almost 5 per cent of the total population in Taiwan under American influence. Confucianism was still predominant there but in post-war Taiwan, visible changes have been made to the politics of this island nation. Furthermore, while this could be one of the most difficult statistics to interpret, China has 111 million Christians and ranks as the world's third largest Christian (inhabited) state after the United States and Brazil as of 2005.[202]

For South Korea, the crisis period arrived during the Korean War when the country was almost destroyed by North Korean invaders. The South Korean people lost everything and fled to the southeastern edge of the peninsula in their search for freedom. There was a real sense of the crisis among those Korean people who had to desert their homes for their survival. When the US-led 'Big Push' began to the North, American aid arrived and many Christian volunteers helped the shattered people.

Today it is difficult to find a city without a church in South Korea. It emerged as the biggest Christian nation in East Asia with over 25 per cent of the entire population embracing the faith. David Chung who studied the history of the Korean Christian movement concluded, 'The historical and social environments were most favourable. And the churches successfully met the need of the society, religiously and culturally, by providing new but well-tested systems, institutions, organizations, as well as effective methods and good leadership. And we believe that the miracle was thus wrought.'[203] While the Koreans as a whole made such solid progress or not still remains to be seen in the changing political environment in the Korean peninsula, but we must admit that its religious freedom was certainly part of the background for recent positive democratic movements in South Korea.

In the late sixteenth century Japan, as we briefly saw, experienced a similar sense of crisis and a contingent political reaction. After the seizure of power in Central Japan, Oda Nobunaga (1534-82), as the protector of Christianity in Japan, faced immense difficulty in Japanese politics despite his extraordinary ability in expanding the Japanese economy with many previously unthinkable reforms and technological innovations. Nobunaga was a unique Japanese hero who acted for the unification of Japan in an era of divided warlord states (1467-1582) while all others were only concerned with preserving their own territory and power. In this most dynamic moment in Japanese history, he also emerged as the sole Japanese leader who ever tried to change its old political core.

By allowing the Jesuit missionaries' request to return to the state capital of Kyoto for religious activities in 1569, Nobunaga directly confronted the will of the imperial court and the traditional Japanese establishment's view on religion with its strict political interpretation. The edict of Emperor Ohgimachi declared foreign priests were forbidden from entering into Kyoto. But the most powerful leader of the samurais 'disobeyed' him.[204]

Yet Nobunaga still required the issue of traditional imperial court ranks by the emperor to help rule his constantly growing army. Notably, two of his camp's prominent generals, in particular, Toyotomi Hideyoshi (1536-98) and Tokugawa Ieyasu (1542-1616), had more established political views than Nobunaga and as his power and territory grew, so did those of his subordinates.

Despite his victories against some warlords around Kyoto, rebellious armed-Buddhists from various sects seemed active elsewhere. It was another form of insurrection from local samurais and peasant groups who refused to submit to Nobunaga's law and order. The largest Jodo-Shin (or *Ikko*) sect headed by Kennyo of the *Ishiyama-Hongan* Temple (-*ji*) controlled the Ikko rebellions from Japan's richest independent territory and the ports near today's Osaka which monopolised the most lucrative maritime trading links of Central Japan and beyond. After three years of unpleasant negotiations with 'insolent' Nobunaga who was determined to snatch their vital coastal links over Lake Biwa, and after his opponents' secret plots failed to trap him, they finally declared a full-scale war against him in 1570, by opening fire on his army and fighting and expanding aggressively in their 'territory'.

Ikko monks taught the believers to die for *Gokuraku Jyodo* – the Paradise of Perfect Bliss – and many warlords put them in the forefront of attacks. The Ikko rebels fought ferociously; they were the most tenacious revolts that Nobunaga had ever encountered, he suffered heavy losses, and his policy of *Tenka-Fubu* – Military Order all over Japan – had to be vigorously enhanced. The old privileged wealth of all the Japanese Buddhists over their domains was now seriously at risk in the face of Nobunaga's new powerful revolutionary force.

At first, it appeared as at Nagashima/far northern Mie that the Buddhist rebels had greater numbers (and a better quality fighting force as well) of matchlock battalions than Nobunaga.[205] By this time, access to guns and cannons emerged as the decisive factor on the battlefield of Japan. Only those who could afford this expensive ordnance could survive the wars. It also meant, therefore, that these armed Buddhists had actually controlled Japanese politics and economy before Nobunaga. Nobunaga's strengths were his flexibility and ability to overcome failure and enjoy future successes. With his unconventional and audacious plans and well-considered diplomatic tactics, he launched many forceful attacks against his adversaries, carefully gathering the necessary intelligence, appointing capable generals on merit to command his army, which was formed with respect to a totally new concept of equality, and by constant introductions of advanced weaponry on land and at sea.

Despite various difficulties, therefore, he was making solid progress against his formidable opponents. Out of the three major armed-Buddhists, in 1571, he burned down the Enryaku Temple in Kyoto outright, the focus of the traditional powers that had allied with his fatal enemies, Asakura Yoshikage of Echizen/Fukui and Asai Nagamasa of northern Omi/Shiga. Nobunaga finally took Osaka in 1580 after eleven years of siege and bloody battles throughout Central Japan. He completed the task of land surveying the manors of the ancient temples in Yamato/Nara as part of the process of depriving them of their privileges and only the Shingon-sect of *Koya-san* in Kii/Wakayama, defended by mountains and a formidable spy network, held out against his offensives. Three of his prominent generals betrayed him during these 'religious' wars but with resolution, he removed them.[206]

In pursuit of the remnants of the Ikko rebellion in Echizen, Ettsuchu/Toyama and Noto, Kaga/both Ishikawa, Nobunaga's core army was defeated by the northern 'Dragon' warlord, Uesugi Kenshin

(1543–1578) based in Echigo/Niigata, at the Battle of Tedorigawa in 1577. But the damage was limited and Kenshin unexpectedly died early in the following year. As Uesugi's 'empire' was crumbling, the major threat on the eastern front suddenly disappeared to Nobunaga's advantage. His northern district army soon took most of Kenshin's extended territories in the west. But he did not rush to combat, assessing the changing situation in the east carefully.

In 1582, his eastern district armies together with their 'allies' swiftly invaded Shinano/Nagano, Kai/Yamanashi, Suruga/Central Shizuoka, and importantly, Kozuke/Gunma plus small areas from each of Musashi/Saitama and Tokyo and Shimotsuke/Tochigi, in the Kanto area. Nobunaga took all those remaining Takeda Katsuyori's feudal states whose main force he had destroyed at the famous matchlock-based Battle of Nagashino in 1575 (notably depicted in Kurosawa's film). Actually, there were a lot of similarities with the Battle of Naseby, which was fought seventy years later by the Parliamentarian New Model Army in England.

At last the major hostilities ceased on the eastern front. In the Japanese court ranks, a prerequisite condition of being a 'Shogun' meant, holding the Kanto plains. Nobunaga secured it (but only on *de facto* basis) by appointing his confidant, Takigawa Kazumasa, to be his Governor General of the Eastern Districts – Kanto Kanrei – based in Umayabashi Castle (today's Maebashi City) in Kozuke. Almost all eastern warlords including the Hojyos, the strongest amongst them, accepted his rule.

Meanwhile, Christian faith was spreading amongst the people of Japan, with a possibility of massive conversions even in the most secluded island, Shikoku. In this situation, Nobunaga's confrontation with the imperial court escalated. The tension was climbing to a dangerous level as many more churches were opened in Kyoto and its vicinities – *Kinai* – and, what was previously unthinkable, many Japanese, including the nobility, became Christian.

Yet the only option for Nobunaga was to control his 'own' emperor by his power as he had done earlier with the Ashikaga Shogunate, weakening and finally demolishing its status in 1573. But the court nobles – *Kugyo* – and all remaining anti-Nobunaga forces rejected his proposal for Emperor Ohgimachi's early retirement. In a landmark decision, Nobunaga rescinded his tenure of all the imperial court ranks in 1578, relying solely on the systematic progress of his formidable military capability. Soon, he was executing imperial administrative decisions because of this power. For instance, Ieyasu received the state of Suruga directly (but soon the imperial endorsement followed) from him.

Although Nobunaga supported Christianity, he did not himself convert. (But his brother did.) A Jesuit missionary and translator, Luis Frois always admired Nobunaga and his respectful attitudes towards the Christian missionaries in Japan. But he criticised him rather harshly when Nobunaga built a strange temple in which to worship himself named as *Soken-ji* – the Temple overseeing all temples – adjacent to the magnificent castle overlooking Lake Biwa in his capital of Japan, Azuchi.[207]

At the same time, Nobunaga approved all the Jesuit's pleas to build a cathedral (1579) and Central Japan's principal abbey and seminary (1580) right in the city centre of Azuchi and showed his earnest support for the entire construction project including its extension. (According to Frois, the extension of the abbey which was still under construction, before it was destroyed after Nobunaga's death, was a three-storey building in an Euro-Japanese architectural style with a spectacular exterior. Nobunaga allowed no one except the Christian religious houses to use the same roof tiles as he did on his castle.)

What Nobunaga, the sole supreme power of Japanese western rationalism on an enormous scale, encountered in this era would still be valid to many of the Japanese who would be unconsciously following him on the same path. For this reason, Japan is still haunted by 'Nobunaga syndrome'. His tragedy was equally Japan's tragedy.

The alleged assassin and one of his most capable, quickly-promoted and trusted generals, Akechi Mitsuhide (1528-82) also acted as his advisor for imperial court affairs from his adjacent feudal domain of Sakamoto in Omi and Tamba/northern Kyoto. Mitsuhide was aware of the dangerous political situation around Nobunaga, in particular the problems arising from his religious reformation, and he might have been also conscious of his own delicate position being involved in such a hypersensitive negotiation between two implacable sides.

When he received the master's order to join the western front, he could have been perplexed about his eventual destination. From his observation, the at one time 'sluggish' Hideyoshi was recently making brilliant progress with two consecutive decisive victories against the once-mighty Mori camp (which once claimed twelve feudal states) in western Honshu.

After Nobunaga crushed Mori's 'invincible' navy with his new iron-clad ships armoured with cannons and secured the command of the inland sea in 1578, then came the fall of their ally in Osaka. And since the warlords in Kyushu were all getting ready to obey Nobunaga, the Moris negotiated a peace with him allowing them to retain only five of their territories. Hideyoshi and the Moris signed the peace agreement on 4 June (that is two days after Nobunaga's unexpected death) before Hideyoshi's withdrawal from Takamatsu Castle in Bittsuchu/Okayama. Exactly when Hideyoshi and the Moris were informed of his assassination in Kyoto is unknown (likely to be 3 and 4 June respectively). As an actual example, Shibata Katsuie, the commander of Nobunaga's Northern District Army, was completely unaware of his master's death when he attacked and took Uozu Castle (in Ettsuchu/Toyama) on 3 June while the people in Azuchi already knew of it by midday on 2 June.

By this time, the Moris had realised that it was impossible to resist Nobunaga's unparalleled military might and knowing the situation full well, the imperial court made a supreme offer of any one of the three highest official ranks including Shogun for him to choose in May 1582. Nobunaga turned it down. Indeed, he no longer required any help from the imperial court. In hindsight, however, this might have been a diplomatic *faux pas* which alienated all his supporters in and around the imperial court.

Only Mitsuhide's contact, Chosogabe Motochika of Tosa/Kochi, once epitomised by Nobunaga as 'a bat in the island of no birds', stood up as one of the desperate rebels in refusing the order to contain

PART FOUR – THE CHANGE

his expanded territory to one-and-a-half feudal states instead of all four in Shikoku. Nobunaga directed his Shikoku expedition army to assemble and the bridgehead was secured without much resistance in Sanuki/Kagawa and Northern Awa/Tokushima. His unification of Japan was completed in practical terms.

With this prospect in mind, Mitsuhide took a chance to take power, or more likely, he succumbed or was trapped in joining the plot of liquidating Nobunaga in Kyoto. Like all other Nobunaga's enemies who had wished to assassinate him before, Mitsuhide had insufficient intelligence on Nobunaga's movements and what security measures were in place in the national capital which was under his control.[208]

So who were the real culprits? Numerous Japanese historians and novelists are still busy guessing who actually killed Nobunaga behind the scenes when he was staying at Honno-ji, the *Hokke* – Saddharma-pundarika (in Sanskrit) – sect's temple, in its annexed residence which had been constructed by his order two years before the revolt.

Apart from Mitsuhide's mysterious conduct, there is another angle to this argument of 'Who killed Nobunaga?' from the viewpoint of Chinese ideology. Even if Mitsuhide had failed to eliminate Nobunaga, there would have been another way. In other words, Japanese politics itself had to evict Nobunaga in this way. That is why all the serious reformers who have tried to enter the 'sacred' political area have met the same fate in Japan. In other words, whoever attempts to fill this supreme hollow centre by force, rightly or wrongly, had automatically to be countered by the superior old-established power of arch-bureaucracy. Thus, with the death of Nobunaga, Japan's earliest modernisation attempt ended. And afterwards, Chinese ideology was revived and became even stronger with this precedent of 'success' in Japan.

From the present political viewpoint, it is important to understand that in order to support Christianity in Taiwan and South Korea, focus now has to be given to the possibility of the revitalisation of Christianity in Japan. Even though it looks most unlikely on the surface.

Arthur Lea once saw a significant impediment to the acceptance of Christianity in Japan, 'Perhaps the greatest obstacle to the Japanese reception of Christianity is embodied in the phrase, *Kokutai ni awanai*, by which it is meant that Christianity does not amalgamate with the spirit of Japanese nationalism, it is impossible to obtain a satisfactory reply. We cannot doubt, however, that the meaning of the statement is that Christianity relegates to the region of mythology the story of the origin of Japan and the descent of the imperial line from the gods. Christianity will eventually subvert the type of loyalty now seriously inculcated throughout the length and the breath of Japan.' Despite this discouraging observation in 1905, he concluded firmly, 'The greatest battle of foreign missions in modern times must henceforth be fought out in Japan. For the first time in history, a nation educated according to naturalistic principles is asked to accept Christianity with its doctrine of the supernatural. Victory for Christianity in Japan will mean victory throughout the East.'[209]

While Japan seems merely to be a negligible nation in the world today, deeply submerged into an endless economic implosion, his prediction is still politically justifiable. Unless Japan is Christianised (or de-Sino-politicised), progress in Taiwan and South Korea will not be stabilised. East Asia as a whole, therefore, cannot move with the rest of the world if it keeps its double standards, as China has now joined the Japanese marching path at full speed. To dissuade China from its currently set 'ancient course', one of the most vivid and convincing examples would be nothing but the resurgence of Japanese capitalism.

THE LAND OF HUMAN GODS

Thomas Hobbes wrote *Leviathan* in 1651. New philosophy was required to control the rapidly expanding British Empire. In his book, he attempted to develop a comprehensive theory on ideal government that was called a 'Christian Commonwealth'. He emphasised the importance of the use of reason for political matters:

'The use and end of reason, is not the finding of the sum, and truth of one, or a few consequences, remote from the first definitions, and settled significations of names; but to begin at these; and proceed from one consequence to another.'[210] He tried to define the existence of this political side of Christianity, and by doing it, he started a new philosophical age in Europe.

A little later in Holland, Benedict de Spinoza realised the essential point for all social science in his *A Theologico-Political Treatise*: '… Christ was sent to teach not only the Jews but the whole human race, and therefore it was not enough that His mind should be accommodated to the opinion of the Jews alone, but also to the opinion and fundamental teaching common to the whole human race – in other words, to an idea universal and true.' Yet he denied the absolute superiority of Christianity as a religion in the human world: '…if a man is absolutely ignorant of the Scriptures, and none the less has right opinions and a true plan of life, he is absolutely blessed and truly possesses in himself the spirit of Christ.'[211] Both men voiced their new philosophies a century before Georg Hegel and others in Germany elaborated further at a different level.

As the influence of Christianity is thus visible over European political philosophy as a whole, concurrently, state control over Japanese religious concepts and social science is also quite recognisable. Two features of the Japanese doctrine were myths or opaqueness and the existence of irrational 'human gods' who also exercise power. From this 'religious' reality under the politics of Chinese ideology, in both the pre-war and post-war period, there was no basic set of guidelines in Japanese society to respect truth, or rather to criticise dubious facts, at the centre of state power, and to differentiate logically between what was good or bad in society.

The myth itself might be innocent but it had a dreadful effect on real politics in the changing realities in Japan. This monstrous power hiding under the most opaque government in the world kept all 'slave' gods behind the scenes for their political convenience. In actual Japanese society, a thousand human gods were still being created, not only by arch-bureaucracy, such as the 'god of tax' but also by the misguided people, such as the 'god of pachinko', not knowing what it meant.[212]

In Japanese companies, there often can be one of these 'human gods' wielding inexplicable power. All the subordinates knew that past failures could not be mentioned as long as he sat there as a 'god'. The Japanese press never censure these 'human gods' in the political field unless they decide mutually to dump him by exposing some scandal of an indefensible nature, which 'unfortunately' leaked out from the 'iron protection wall' of the Japanese press club. Until then, these protectors of freedom are obsequiously willing to act as propaganda agents for these disguised 'gods', not because of what they are saying, but because of what power they could exercise over them.

The shocking case of the well-known novelist, Yukio Mishima, who entered into a Self-Defence Force barracks and committed suicide in the old Japanese way with his colleagues in 1970, would be one example of this process of 'sanctification' of irrational behaviour. And if you denounced him, you could not be a leading Japanese 'intellectual'. Behaving completely irrationally, he actually became one of the 'gods' by 'successfully' putting himself in the heart of the Japanese 'religious' mindset like the legendary ancient Kusunoki Masashige who purportedly said – 'I wish I had seven lives and death to serve the emperor,' *Shichi Sho Hou Koku*. A bigger problem, however, was that these 'exposed' human gods, including the Japanese emperor, never ruled Japan. The real ruler was power itself, and those powerful human gods with a more devilish side would be hiding in the darkness controlling the world of those identifiable human gods.

When the Japanese go to a Shinto shrine or Buddhist temple, people are expected to follow a certain formality but then there is no rule or responsibility arising from that relationship in society. 'Do not think,' is the message given there, or emptiness – *kuu* – in more loquacious Japanese Buddhism. Whatever idea one has or whatever a person is doing is insignificant and irrelevant. In other words, right or wrong is not the issue for Japanese politicised religions, and this is exactly what is required for politics. The only 'sin' in Shinto or

Part Four – The Change

Japanese Buddhism is just not to participate in their rituals or not to show one's total obedience to established authority.

The political scope of Shintoism and its subordinate Japanese Buddhism is, therefore, broad and unpredictable just as the behaviour of the Japanese either at state or individual level is. Like economic reality, the effects of power, whatever it was, ultimately control this central unfilled part of political thought, which changes through experiencing either joy or life's struggles, and sometime it could appear as a shocking outburst in the face of an unexpected ordeal. An American anthropologist, Ruth Benedict, encountered these human characteristics in her research on Japan and its culture in an intensive study financed by the pre-war US government.

'Both the sword and the chrysanthemum are part of the picture.' she recorded. 'The Japanese are, to the highest degree, both aggressive and unaggressive, both militaristic and aesthetic, both insolent and polite, rigid and adaptable, submissive and resentful of being pushed around, loyal and treacherous, brave and timid, conservative and hospitable to new ways.'[213] I must emphasise, however, what she recorded here about the Japanese in her remarkable observation was extrinsic in nature despite the fact that what she said is still valid today under the current political system. Perhaps, 'both superbly successful and disgracefully powerless with their economy' would be the phrase, which she might like to add today!

Certainly, the Japanese as a nation have to overcome this crucial political defect as a modern state. In his autobiography, Yukichi Fukuzawa wrote only a short paragraph about the future of Japan. In fact, this is the only place where he discusses the future, as he recalled his experiences and memories of the past in this narrative. He dreamed, 'What I would like to do in the rest of my life is three things. (First) To improve gradually men's and women's elegance in Japan to the level of our substantial civilization. (Second) To soften the minds of people, either by supporting the philosophy of Buddha or *Christianity*. (Third) To invest in studying the profound theory of visible and invisible sciences.'[214]

To understand these phrases, we need perhaps to give attention to the following points in his book. Firstly, Buddha's philosophy – *Buppo* – based on freedom from avarice, love (by not killing) and devotion has a universal religious similarity. Secondly, he clearly questioned the theological significance of Shintoism and that of Japanese-Buddhism in the early part by saying, 'Since I was a child, I was never afraid of gods – *Kami-sama* – or praised Buddha – *Hotoke-sama*.' Thirdly, before uttering his wish, he touched on this sensitive issue saying, 'I would like to leave the matters of diplomacy and constitutional politics to the politicians…' It was a fundamental ideological argument for Japan put forward by this exceptional Japanese modern thinker on the importance of Christianity and religious freedom for Japan.

THE ROMAN EMPIRE AND CHRISTIANITY

In order to affirm the formation of western political thought, it is useful to look back to turning points in history. It actually started with no religious motive when Emperor Caracalla gave Roman citizenship to all his subjects in 212 to enhance the empire. The move, however, created *de facto* freedom of religion in Rome. It served as a catalyst for the subsequent penetration of Christians to the heights of the Roman political hierarchy and meritocracy.

Then, why did Constantine the Great promote Christianity as the first Emperor of the Romans in 313? No doubt, his decision was the most important one made by any man on earth if we think of the subsequent changes to Europe and the world. Michael Grant frankly expressed his surprise at the extraordinary event, 'Then came the conversion of Constantine the Great to Christianity, and his gradual conversion of the Empire to the same faith. These events were astonishing because the Christians were still a minority, and not a very influential one at that.'[215]

It seems that the greatest emperor made three important political achievements in his life. Firstly, he adopted Christianity. Secondly, he restored political stability in the empire in the wake of a massive

Part Four – The Change

flow of barbarian invaders throughout its territories. Thirdly, he dropped the long-established defence systems of Rome and applied a new strategy. It may be that, to solve the latter two problems, he took his first decision.

In a turbulent epoch-making change, Constantine had to unite the Roman people with his perceived Christian political ideology. It was the moment that a philosophy, which was conceived to inject righteous discipline into an individual life, was now conjoined with the efficiency of a state. One of the poetic stories of this moment was that before a critical battle in 312 against his joint emperor, Maxentius at Milvian Bridge near Rome, he saw a vision of the cross superimposed upon the sun, bearing the words 'by this conquer'. Constantine's decisive victory in this battle resulted in the edict of Milan in the following year that recognised Christianity as one of the religions legally permitted within the Empire.

But what was the religious background of Rome at the time that affected his decision? In considering the political implications of Roman religion, J.H.W.G. Liebeschuetz recognized the merits of the ancient auguries and public divination in Rome, '...to ensure that the proper procedure was observed, and that the signs indicated divine approval...in fact it provided a mechanism for tracing the temper of the gods in much the same way as radar traces the dangerous obstructions which lie in wait for shipping. It also provided a discipline, a discipline for politicians.' He also pointed out the link between the Roman myth of Apollo and Christianity, 'To the outsider it would seem that the sun had a privileged place even in Christianity. He could read that Jesus had risen from the dead on Easter Sunday, that is, a day consecrated to the sun. The weekly Sunday service too would seem to be honouring the day of the sun. During worship, Christians faced east, the direction of the rising sun...The one reason most commonly given was that the movements of the sun provided a visible model of the supreme truth of theology.'[216]

Then, what was the background of this fundamental change to Roman politics? At first, it started with the barbarian invasions into Roman territory. Peter Wells explained the situation and its problem,

'In the frontier zone in temperate Europe, textual sources describe attacks on the *limes* boundary and incursions across the border by a group called the Alamanni, first mentioned in AD 231...in the years 259 and 260 the Alamanni attacked with such force that they effectively destroyed the imperial boundary, causing Rome to give up the Agri Decumates (roughly what is now the southwest German state of Baden-Württemberg) and to re-create the earlier imperial border along the upper Rhine and upper Danube Rivers.'[217] The new and aggressive power of the barbarians was bound to change the basic nature of the Roman Empire.

The biggest change in Roman grand strategy came with Constantine the Great because of the constant pressure on the northern frontier. Arthur Ferrill claimed, '...Constantine organized a large mobile field army (probably 100,000 or more), stationed centrally, by withdrawing units from the frontiers, leaving them in a weakened condition.' He further displayed his insight on this issue, '...Mommsen and virtually all modern analysts since his time have ventured to overturn the judgement of antiquity and of Gibbon. According to them the strategy of preclusive security along firm frontiers was no longer valid... Protection of the Empire in the trying times of the fourth and fifth centuries required a new grand strategy relying on a central mobile army and a system of defence-in-depth.'[218]

The old strategy became untenable because of the constantly increasing force of the northern barbarians who were steadily joining the empire. Constantine was forced to undertake this defence system in order to avoid a strategic defeat. However strong it was, the defended line's weakness was, once it was passed by the enemy, it became irrelevant like the Maginot line in the twentieth century. Moreover, Constantine was positive about the advantage of the assimilation of Germanic barbarian tribes to his new empire rather than excluding them. He saw that there was a future in living together and recognized that the greatest threats to the security of his Empire came from these Germanic tribes and other barbarians. With this menace in mind, the chief location for conflict was Gaul (today's France), originally a Celtic land but a most Romanised country, then being constantly invaded by waves of Germanic tribes. When Constantine was attached to Gaul as the joint emperor, he was aware of this evolution and the opportunities of a potential political role for other barbarians. Constantine knew that only Christianity could cover all the divided nations in his 'virtual' Grand Empire, in particular, to unite the strong new West and traditional East where the New Testament was first written by the end of the second century; while the Old Testament was translated in Alexandria (then a Greek city) from the third to second century BC.[219] Christianity with its universal values was the only religion that could perform this role.

Constantine was born in the southern Balkan peninsula (Naissus/Nis) where Greek influences were predominant, as a son of the joint Roman emperor, Constantius. While, since 306, he had spent most of his days in the western empire, as successor after his father's death in York, it seemed that his respect for the Greek world, its history and culture remained firmly in his mind during the period of his leadership.

In 324, Constantine's dream was realised after he defeated Licinius, the emperor of the eastern empire, which confirmed his status as sole Roman ruler. As the founder of Christian political ideology, he presided over the church's first council at Nicaea (Asia Minor) in 325. Elspeth Davies explained this historical event, 'Although this was part of the Empire, Greeks were very much in the majority, and only four or five came from the Latin West. The Council appears to have achieved the unanimity demanded by Constantine, since 218 of 220 bishops signed their acceptance of the creed it formulated.'[220]

Only Constantine's broad view of the Roman world with its spiritual attachment to Hellenism and its rich intellectual heritage made this great enterprise of uniting West and East possible. The profound political expertise of the man should be noted, as he became the most important religious leader at Nicaea where orthodox theology and the divinity of the Trinity – God the Father, God the Son and the Holy Spirit – was adopted. It is amazing as he lived earlier than Augustinus. On the other hand, he firmly condemned the Arian theology as heretical as it denied the complete divinity of Jesus, and furthermore, he insisted on allowing freedom of religion within the empire.

With this vision and all the resources of the new empire, Constantine moved his residential capital to Byzantium on the strait of the Bosporus, a strategic point for the empire's maritime economy and trade since Greek days, redeveloping the city and renaming it as Constantinople. By Constantine's decision, history suddenly shifted like a huge tree cut down by an axe, from ancient to modern in its political nature.

In reality, it did not mean that all the inhabitants practised Christian-led idealism immediately; however, it could prevent the state and subsequent successors reverting to power politics with only a human dimension, which had even destroyed the glorious Greek empire. The new ideology became a driving force for emancipating people from the world of old politicised religions or anarchy. The origin of European politics was thus created and its expansion was now about to unfold even to those still unconquered by Rome.

Expansion was driven by not only the power of the state but also by the spirit of individuals. Perfectly united and yet thoroughly diversified – this was the new political order for the subsequent ecumenical movements that have, since then, affected all the rest of world. The political entity first conceived by Constantine survived not because of his number of subjects or the lands in Rome which became the biggest or most powerful empire like the ancient Chinese empire, but because this political concept was more competitive than that of other parts of the old world. It was the birth of a truly global and universal political concept.

EUROPEAN EXPANSION

This new expansion begun by Constantine advanced further into the whole of Europe. In northern Europe, people believed in Odin or Woden, the god of war. The ferocious Vikings conquered many of the major cities and countries including Britain and Russia during the first millennium and created a new and undeniably influential political base all over Europe, but they could not subjugate a Christian state by force; but instead adopted the faith. In retrospect, every current European land had its own traditional gods and myths but no god or other political principles could be sustained against this vital movement.

The Franks, Germanic tribes, entered into northern Gaul and finally put an end to Roman rule in 486. But this end was also the beginning of a further expansion. The early Merovingian king, Clovis, who was only twenty, became a power to be reckoned with when he mounted his first attack on the Thuringians in the same year. Peter Lasko briefly explained the significance of his move, 'thus beginning the process of making himself ruler of all Germans.'[221] In 496, he further conquered the Alamanni and defeated the Visigoths at Tours.

He formed an alliance with Burgundy, the most influential kingdom in the Rhone valley, by marrying the princess, Clotilda, a niece of the king of Burgundy and converting to Christian faith in Rheims. The traditional French version of events relate that Clotilda, who was an ideally pious French lady, persuaded the king to convert.[222] The alliance with Burgundy was vital for Clovis to join battle against the Visigoths and the Ostrogoths – which both subscribed to the Arian heresy at that time. He, as the honorary consul, also maintained a strong relationship with the Eastern Roman Empire. Again, the political aspects of his conversion were sound.

Russell Chamberlin depicted the event from a pragmatic standpoint, 'He had one objective, and one only: to push out from those cold, flat lands and marshes of the north down towards the rich lands of the south, to the valleys of the Seine and the Loire and even the fabled lands beyond, Provence, the lush daughter of Rome.'[223] Clovis expanded the rich inheritance of Rome to the newly combined Gallo-Roman worlds with his ancestral northern Germanic culture also playing a major role. The different pattern of European expansion compared to that of the ancient empires is quite visible here. It was not by conquering others as slaves, but by ensuring the participation of others while their combined economic markets expanded.

A threat to this extended Europe arrived in 732 as the Umayyad Arabs decided to advance towards the Frankish lands. But a Carolingian king, Charles, the illegitimate son of Pepin of Herstal, was ready to counter-attack and finally defeated them at Poitiers. He was nicknamed Martel 'the Hammer', as he halted this seemingly unbeatable advance of an Islamic invading force.

The foundation and prosperity of the Umayyad Caliphate in Spain alarmed even the Carolingian kings who had no naval power to counter them. Only the old Roman provinces in Italy and the Eastern (or Byzantine) Empire had kept their naval forces. The need for naval defence motivated Charlemagne to invade Barcelona and Italy. He expanded the Frankish empire with new laws and a new monetary policy. He even thought about fighting at sea against the Arabs when he ordered the construction of a fleet in 813.[224] The Viking ships, which combined 'lightness with strength and flexibility by using excellent craftsmanship and carefully selected timber' were remarkable exceptions in the region.[225]

The latest comers from the east which formed a European national state were the Bulgarians and Hungarians. An important development, under the initiative of the Eastern Empire, was the movement of Bulgaria who emigrated to the old Roman province of Thracia from the conflux area of the Volga (near today's Kazan in Russia) by the seventh century. They were keen to co-operate with the Slavs who had already settled there.

Hristo Hristov summarised the reasons for this extraordinary historical event. First, it was necessary to unite the nation, '… the adaptation of Christianity as the official religion of the Bulgarian state was not due to its slow infiltration among its subjects, but was rather necessitated by supreme state considerations…The well-understood state interests demanded that this state of affairs be done away with by introducing a single common religion as a means of reaffirming the state power and uniting the subjects based on a predominant common ideology.' Second, there was a diplomatic necessity, 'The adoption of Christianity was also necessitated by foreign-policy considerations. Bulgaria was flanked by two powerful Christian empires that treated her as a "barbarian" state.'[226] In fact, this consideration was applied by many other European nations in the past. Christianity spread gradually with this accumulation of astute political decisions by various nations.

The Romans built the magnificent cathedral of St Sophia – Holy Wisdom – over looking the Bosporus in the capital city of Constantinople/Istanbul. A Viking trade outpost of Kievan Rus, the origin of Russia and Ukraine, embraced Christianity where St Sophia emerged again as the principal church on the hill looking down the Dnepr River that could virtually connect the Baltic Sea with the Black Sea. It was made after Vladimir became prince in *c.* 988. He suddenly left his eclectic pagan faith and embraced Christianity. His father, Sviatoslav, when pressed to convert, is said to have replied, 'But my druzhina (guard) will laugh at me!'[227]

Russians needed Christianity to consolidate and to expand. In competition with Kiev, later, the principal church which was named as *Uspensky Sabor* – Assumption Cathedral – moved to Vladimir, the first capital city in the north founded by Andrey Bogolyubsky in 1169, which Arnold Toynbee described as Russia's 'Kamakura'.

But the somewhat slow and divided eastern European states of the Russian principalities were suddenly awoken by a historic wonder or terror from the East, the Mongol invasion. Only Prince Aleksandr Nevsky's Novgorod remained independent by defeating Swedes (1240) and Germans (1242) on their behalf and for its own benefit. In this struggle, the Great Principality of Moscow finally emerged and moved toward the direction of the invaders' incoming route to expand eastward (and westward as well), with the Tsar wielding absolute power as the successor to the Roman Empire. To conquer the vast eastern land to ensue their security, Russians reformed their political system from a European kingdom into a Eurasian empire. The expansion began by absorbing the required innovations in science and art from the West, and integrating the people living in all the lands of the former conqueror and beyond.

This aggressive expansion had to be constantly balanced with a rational form of politics. Peter the Great took the drastic decision to move the state's capital to a completely newly planned European-style city at the mouth of the Neva River, to be known as St Petersburg, the gateway to the Baltic Sea and Western Europe, after his decisive victory against the strong northern European power of Sweden at Poltava. While Peter the Great succeeded in this vital western expansion using the first Russian navy, he was severely beaten by the Ottoman Empire in the south. But his dream and established policy were later proven to be right as Catherine the Great, together with her trusted military commander Grigory Potemkin, went on to defeat the Turks, and Russian territory and naval power finally reached to the Black Sea.

In central Europe, Moravia played a political game between the western and the eastern churches. Facing indifference from the Roman authorities, its first church was built with the support of Byzantine missionaries. But in 885, having seen the 'menace' of not participating, western missionaries replaced it. The first Bohemian to become bishop of Prague was Slavnik Adalbert (Wojciech in Polish) who later became the founding bishop in Gniezno, Poland.[228]

From the eleventh century, the Moorish Iberian Peninsula under the Caliphate of Cordoba became the most advanced place for learning and research in the world as the Islamic community revived all the Greek classics and ancient sciences from the east which had been long neglected by medieval Western Europe, together with their own developed maritime technology. As the process of the *Reconquista* movement began and was completed in the Iberian Peninsula, this precious knowledge fell into the hands of the Spanish and Portuguese, just like German advanced rocket technology was transferred to the United States and Soviet Russia after the Second World War.

With this advanced science and technology, Spain and Portugal emerged as the first successful colonial states leading the Great Age of Navigation. Their first global empires were established with its colonies linking America and Asia. In the Germanic world, the

Part Four – The Change

Austrian-Habsburg's influence grew as the European link for this newly created wealth. The shipping technologies were transferred all over Europe's largest empire under Charles V, from Spain to its most adaptable colony, the Netherlands, and then on to England.

As soon as Martin Luther started the Reformation movement, the two new maritime states of the Netherlands and England were determined to join the Protestants' camp to serve their own interests. Full-scale western expansion was about to unfold as a political battle between the old empires tried to keep a monopoly on a stunning economic global fortune with the new aggressive states eager to catch up. Ultimately, revolutionary changes to global politics forced this break-up. The medieval concept of a single Europe was fractured and a real competition began to squabble over modern national powers.

On the continent, for a state like the Netherlands, however, war with a strong land power like Spain was a costly exercise. Niall Ferguson explained, 'Around ninety per cent of the budget of the Dutch Republic in the seventeenth century went to pay for the Eighty Years War with Spain, the Anglo-Dutch Wars and the Nine Years War.'[229] Finally, England emerged as the winner in this competition as an efficient island state that could concentrate on the naval power race.

The British Empire emerged with its accumulated maritime wealth as the largest ever in geographical and economical terms. As J.M. Roberts noted, 'The English, unlike the Spanish and Portuguese, transplanted whole communities – men, women and children – who set to work as farmers. Like the colonies of the ancient Greek cities…'[230] And unlike the Greeks, the English could rely on all the other available European human resources in their colonies due to the existence of Christianity.

The British population was soon moving to the New World after the industrial revolution as the base of its global economy expanded. Between 1861 and 1900, 7.5 million people left the British Isles, over one million to Australia and New Zealand, some 800,000 to Canada, and a few hundred thousand to South Africa. The overseas settlement of the 'surplus' population was of vital importance for

British imperial expansion at the time. Some thought that the United Kingdom could not support a population above 40 million without a grave risk of civil war and internal chaos.[231]

With this new expansion, the global economy began to be shaped with the participation of the discoveries of the New World and enhanced by constant and massive emigration from the heartlands of Europe to all corners of the extended empires. Eric Hobsbawm analysed these trends and concluded, 'For the historians the great boom of 1850s marks the foundation of a global industrial economy and a single history.'

Its momentum accelerated – 'the British exports to Turkey and Middle East rose from 3.5 million pounds in 1848 to a peak of almost 16 million in 1870; to Asia from 7 million to 41 million (1872); to Central and South America from 6 million to 25 million (1872); to India from around 5 millions to 24 millions (1875); to Australasia from 1.5 millions to almost 20 millions (1875).'[232] And this unprecedented economic expansion was to change the shape of the entire world as the British developed the most sophisticated form of global politics while leading this important movement.

AMERICAN GROWTH

'There is no science more dependent on facts than political economy. Indeed, the art of collecting, arranging, and drawing conclusions from them constitutes almost the whole of the science.' It was not Marx who said this but the 'ultimate survivor' of French revolutionary politics. To the Americans, he must be remembered as the man who swiftly sold the vast French Louisiana colony, 'igniting' all the subsequent US movements to the Pacific and beyond.

Talleyrand argued that the independence of the United States was 'far from being of disadvantage to England, has benefited her in many respects.' This idea came from his careful observations: 'America consumes annually more than three million sterling of English merchandise. Fifteen years ago, she did not consume half that quantity...This fact, inscribed in the registers of the Custom-House, cannot be disputed.'[233] The Atlantic relationship earlier described by this political genius grew even more extensive, as various export-import businesses and services from and to the US increased, in which America's economic power strengthened compared to the nations of a slower, more traditional, divided and often more troublesome, continental Europe.

Carl Degler focused on this vital element of historical American politics and its principles: 'The failure of America to inherit a feudal aristocracy carried implications for the future, which transcended the mere matter of land tenure...it meant that wealth, rather than family or tradition, would be the primary determinant of social stratification.' For this objective, America applied more flexibility to its social structure to grow, with people's expanded participation and mobility transforming the society itself to a multi-racial community. America, however, inherited many things from England as well – above all, the basic management of economy and the rule of law or the 'principle' of 'as business expanded, so did the lawyers'.[234]

With this concentration on its economy, America emerged as the champion of democracy and capitalism. As if to offset this materialistic foundation, various churches of Christianity were introduced which constituted its political base. Despite its many religious backgrounds, people never fought a religious war in America. In fact, the idea of religious freedom was deeply ingrained in all American society and formed the basis of all other freedoms in the United States, and it created one of the strengths of America as a nation.

On this basis, various forms of investments and human resources were constantly injected from Europe. Industrialised America became a decisive political player in determining even European matters; by the time the First World War started capitalistic and democratic Britain was backed by the young industrial power of the United States whose participation in decision-making in this relationship was also increasing, and finally came to be equal, or sometimes even surpass, the 'mother country' during the Second World War.

By this time, it was clear that only the Atlantic relationship, or the combined power of America and Europe, could solve some of the serious issues in the world as the United States further developed its own inventions and power base.

Despite its historical background as a late starter, however, Americans were never content to see themselves as second-class Europeans. America invented its own heritage and expanded this concept while always keeping itself open to other parts of the world with their own traditions. The secularity of an advanced America attracted many capable people who fled from all sorts of places and persecutions and the land of freedom became a new home for them. Inevitably a different political culture was born, which was a powerful hybrid. With this growing popular power, America soon took the important role of criticising Europe. America, as the most advanced industrialised state, started influencing European politics.

One of the insightful observations emphasised by William Brock about the major movement of American politics was regarding Benjamin Franklin's view on revolution: 'Rebellion' [perhaps with the event of 1745 in mind] was an unjustifiable attack upon legitimate authority; a 'revolution' [certainly 1688 in mind] was justifiable action against authority that had forfeited its claim to legitimacy. Rebellion repudiated rightful allegiance; revolution derived its authority from allegiance to a higher law. If cynics might say that a revolution was, then, nothing but a successful rebellion, the jibe misfired among men brought up to believe in God's Providence; defeat was evidence of divine displeasure, success bore witness to God's blessing.'[235] It explained perfectly the meaning of American independence and the essence of its political principles. With this determination, America successfully participated in the wars in Europe and in the Pacific as the final victor. But America lost or could not win wars such as Vietnam which were fought without this conviction or when this principle was blurred.

What then can be the role of America in East Asia? East Asia's various problems from China, Korea to Japan all originated from the same root but the type of predicament these nations face varies.

PART FOUR – THE CHANGE

There seems to be no single solution for all the ailing regimes, but it is necessary to focus on one main issue held in common by all these states for the good of America's vital Pacific relationship, which may grow even bigger than its current Atlantic relationships. In this process, as once Britain and Europe did for America, America must convey its own modern principles in full to East Asia, without flinching from facing up to their old and dubious traditions.

The universal value of the American political tradition, which was partially introduced in Japan, is now facing a new menace and the challenge remains to overcome the country's indigenous full-blown political ideology, which was not fully eliminated last time around. Both the causes of East Asiatic failure and its potential success for the future could be learned from American history and its modern principles, which show that although the birth of the US is the most recent, it has still become one of the world's greatest powers. Unlike the Americans, the Japanese and Chinese expanded their businesses without the firm commitment of their people to establish similar sound political and economic principles in their society. This should be the key to the progress of every nation as no nation, not only China and Japan, or even America and Europe, can survive without these universal principles.

Despite amazing news coming in, such as that the market value of Exxon has been taken over by PetroChina, the long-stretched manoeuvrability of the new Chinese or Japanese technological success stories under their double standards will soon be reaching its limits. This inevitable social process once described by Anthony Eden as 'nauseating hypocrisy' is already rife in Japan. Facing this realty, the last thing America would want to do is to disguise the situation.

America needs to prepare for this unparalleled showdown in world politics arising from the current immense economic power shift by tying up with the people in East Asia. In fact, the entire western 'force' has to be assembled as it is bound to be the biggest challenge for Western civilization and for its *raison d'etre*. While the date is still unknown, 'D-Day' will certainly come, as the ultimate collapse of East Asian expansion without principle will become inevitable everywhere in the region and beyond. Above all, if we all understand this political mechanism correctly, there should be no need for another war in East Asia.

MISUNDERSTANDING OF MAX WEBER

Among western experts, Max Weber wrote two stimulating books on this specific subject early in the twentieth century. One of these is *Confucianism and Taoism*, in which he tried to depict the Chinese political and social system. This book must have been fascinating to his contemporary audiences, and generally speaking, formed the basis of the current western political view on Chinese ancient polity, as Weber explained the principal structures of Chinese civilization such as 'The Charismatic and Political Position of the Emperor', 'Confucius', 'The Examination System' and 'Kinship Group Organization' and so on. But the fatal crack in his argument is that he believed, that the 'Literati Class' ran China.

On this issue, he insisted, 'For the last twelve hundred years in China social rank has been determined not so much by property, but far more by qualification for office as confirmed by education, and in particular by success in examinations. More exclusively than any other country, in a more exclusive fashion even than in Europe during the Humanist period or ultimately even more than in Germany. China has made literary education the yardstick of social appraisal.'[236] This was, however, merely a repeated Chinese cliché for consumption to the outside world to disguise its true militaristic colours.

Consequently, Weber failed to discuss the real entity of the Chinese political core, above all, about the origin of its militarism, and was drawn into arguments on Confucianism or Taoism that never existed as the supreme authority, and so he missed the true entity of Chinese power behind his observations. He put this ancillary issue without reservation as the equivalent centre of Chinese polity, by replacing and comparing those Chinese 'religious' arguments with his concept of the importance of Christianity in western society.

Likewise, in Weber's other work, *The Protestant Ethic and the Spirit of Capitalism*, he made some controversial remarks that were thoroughly criticised by Anthony Giddens. As major points of doubts on the validity of Weber's arguments, Giddens introduced criticism from other philosophers such as Lujo Brentano. And he agreed with Weber's critics, 'Weber's characterisation of Protestantism was faulty. Critiques here have been directed to Weber's treatment of the Reformation, to his interpretation of the Puritan sects in general, and to Calvinism in particular. It has been held that Weber was mistaken in supposing that Luther introduced a concept of "calling" which differed from anything previously available in scriptural exegesis...'[237] As far as Weber's theme of Protestantism is concerned, Giddens' argument seems to be rather convincing.

To understand the difference between these two ideas more clearly, however, perhaps one needs to take a closer look at the historical environment surrounding these two scholars than to explore the differences in the philosophical arguments. A typical Anglican would be immediately aware of Weber's mistakes simply on the basis that their theology is not very different from Catholicism, after all. But Protestantism played a political and historical role in Germany, and it was deemed to be completely incompatible with Catholicism for hundreds of years, regardless of how it differed in substance.

Above all, a German, not a Frenchman or Englishman, launched the Reformation, and in fact, led this important global historical evolution. Jean Calvin was only eight years old and still living in a town in Picardie when Martin Luther nailed down his ninety-five theses to a church door in Wittenberg in 1517. Henry VIII broke up with the papal authority in England some fifteen years after this incident.

It is also important to understand that Germany was the last country which fought a 'Holy War' in Europe. The crusades began when an ambassador for the Byzantine Emperor Alexius I abruptly asked Pope Urban II for help against the advancing Selujuk Turks in

March 1095. The first crusade was an exceptional success although continuing ones were disasters.

In northern Europe, after the Swedes started a crusade in Finland, their advance was gradually shifted by the German military order of the Sword Brothers by the early thirteenth century, together with Denmark, towards various heathen people living on the Baltic shores. Then, came Duke Conrad of Masovia under the era of a 'fragmented Poland' who had to ask for help from Conrad von Landsberg, a commander of the Teutonic Knights, when his subjects were attacked and carried off into slavery traders by pagan Baltic invaders – the Prussians.[238]

Having successfully destroyed the enemy, the Teutonic Knights decided to stay on this fertile land of black soil to cultivate it and to keep its military order for further expansion towards the northeast, absorbing the former territory of the Sword Brothers (roughly today's Estonia and Latvia) who were earlier unexpectedly defeated by another Baltic pagan power, the Lithuanians. Their main headquarters were relocated from Venice to Marienburg/Malbork as they intensified their aggression over other pagans and the Teutonic Knights were soon to emerge as the largest German feudality by taking over additional territory and developing their capital city of Koenigsberg/Kaliningrad.

But 'the Lithuanians, the next likely target for subjugation by the Order, pre-emptively adopted Christianity', when their Grand Duke Vladyslav Jogaila (Wladyslaw II Jagiello) married the successor to the Polish throne, Jadwiga, in 1385.[239] Both the Lithuanians, experienced colonisers, who had taken on the western Russian principalities from the control of the Golden Horde, and the Poles knew that this was the only way to avoid their downfall, and above all, to secure their own independence. The Order, however, did not stop their aggression, despite losing their religious justification.

While this Polish-Lithuanian aspiration for a commonwealth *–rzeczpospolita –* that once reached to the Black Sea also courted disaster by being placed at the centre of territory threatened by an aggressive Sweden (or Swedes-Finns), a powerful Germany and a gigantic Russia, it first enjoyed a brilliant success with a decisive victory at Tannenberg against the Teutonic Knights in 1410. The German military were to remember this defeat as their greatest humiliation ever experienced for centuries to come.[240]

More importantly, it completely broke the trajectory of the Knights' expansion over the Baltic region. While the Spanish crusaders' mission in Europe ended when the previously unassailable hilltop fortress of Alhambra in Granada finally fell to their hands in 1492, German endurance was to continue as soon Prussian estates were incorporated into the Polish crown under the subsequent tremendous growth of Poland-Lithuania.

This pattern of confrontation revived when the power balance of Europe changed as the inflow of wealth from the Americas began to affect the fundamental shape of the European economy. Clearly, the commercially minded Germans benefited more than the agrarian Poles in this new economic environment which was to lead to a new world order ultimately divided by Catholics, Protestants and Orthodoxies, where even Catholic Spain had a religious invention of its own.[241] Sensing a fresh opportunity, the last Teutonic Grand Master, Albrecht von Brandenburg-Ansbach of Hohenzollern, converted to Protestantism in 1525 to strengthen his new Duchy of Prussia and dissolved the Teutonic Order, under Polish feudal supremacy, by linking it to the Reformation movement in Germany.[242]

On the other hand, Poland threatened the Russian Orthodox throne through its intervention on the 'False Dmitrii' affair when a pretender masqueraded as the son of Ivan the Terrible. Historic antagonism became irreparable as the Poles regained Smolensk, the hub of the Russian far west, or of the Polish imperial far east, and the Polish army occupied Moscow from 1610 to 1612. Eventually, Poland emerged as the loser in this triple confrontation, as Sweden ransacked the Polish heartland, before Russia took away all their booty in the following century. In this struggle, what the Russians were afraid of was Polish influence in the east and Poland's hope of uniting the two nations against the advancing Turks in Europe, which would jeopardise its larger aim of controlling the vital Eurasian hegemony.

The changes brought by western European expansion to the outside world began to influence politics – as seen in the central and eastern European states. Martin Brecht's intensive study revealed the actual situation surrounding the great reformer of his age. Luther's career started when Staupitz picked him as his successor for the Wittenberg Bible professorship. He noted how Luther's confidence grew, as he 'emphasized his doctor's title when insisting on his authority and competence to teach before his ecclesiastical superiors such as Archbishop Albrecht of Mainz, Cardinal Cajetan, or even the pope.' Moreover, German political circles supported Luther and the process of the Reformation.[243] With his *Kühnheit* or boldness Luther was convinced of his new ideas that to strengthen people's understanding of Christianity he should translate the Bible into German and sing hymns in German or in other vernaculars – a practice later accepted by the Catholic Church. The age was ready for Luther and his new movement.

From this historical turning point, Gerhard Benecke analysed the vital issues and background of the religious wars, 'Between 1550 and 1620 many German territories were adjusted to harder terms of trade, higher inflation, increased population and greater underemployment,' and 'From 1620s war brought guaranteed price ready markets and new opportunities for industry and manufacture.'[244] Under this new economic environment, the Germans regenerated their eastern economic enterprise in Prussia. Just as Protestant England engaged in a war against Catholic Spain, Protestant Germany was gradually moving eastwards to the ailing state of Catholic Poland and its links with Russian Orthodoxy. Something had to be done to unite this great but divided nation.

Max Weber was nothing else if not a German, still showing a nationalistic flavour for its eastern expansion. He was attracted to the Pan-German League (Alldeutscher Verband), formed in 1890 and he proclaimed in his inaugural lecture in Freiburg that if Germany did not begin imperial expansion, the unification of 1871 was merely a 'prank'.[245] But the fact was that even Bismarck's Germany was predominantly Roman Catholic, represented by 52 per cent of the

German Confederation in 1855.[246]

Despite his misunderstandings on Protestantism, however, it is still important to pay attention to the value of Weber's argument, noticing that the word 'Protestantism' has disappeared here. Weber elaborated his thoughts, '…In order that a manner of life so well adapted to the peculiarities of capitalism could be selected at all, i.e. should come to dominate others, it had to originate somewhere, and not in isolated individuals alone, but as a way of life common to a whole group of men.'[247] He asserted that this process of economic selection and the emergence of a dominant power come from 'a reflection or superstructure of the economic situation'.

In fact, what he argued was 'rational jurisprudence of Roman law and of the Western law' and 'A structure like the canon law is known to the West'. On this basis, perhaps Sophia Fredica Augusta agreed to convert from Protestant to Russian Orthodox to become the future Catherine the Great, following a request from King Frederick of Prussia.[249] From the theologico-political aspect, it was not a matter of the principles set by Constantine but further differences on the interpretations of them.

Weber emphasised the importance of ethos for business organization. But it was also visible in what he called '*traditionalistische*' economy, which he described as 'The form of organization was in every respect capitalistic; the entrepreneur's activity was of a purely business character; the use of capital, turned over in the business, was indispensable; and finally, the objective aspect of the economic process, the bookkeeping, was rational.'[250]

Again, Weber's comments were apparently directed to western civilization as a whole and not to the limited world of Protestantism. There are no convincing differences or forms of discontinuation between the two forms of his divided economy, either '*traditionalistische*' or '*kapitalistische*' as both pursue a rationale in the end. Or perhaps his technical term, *Berufserfüllung* or 'professional fulfilment', existed long before the religious reforms in Germany. For instance, when Columbus discovered America, the state evolved from the same and only ethos. Without it, perhaps the first Catholic-led global expansion could not have been launched.

Exactly as with Weber's earlier conceptional mistake on China, therefore, we should forget about his comments on Protestantism. But we can never ignore the basis of his assertion. Above all, the foundation of western expansion was based on rational activities and Christianity played an indispensable role as the supreme authority acting at the political heart of each state, influencing all the political, social and economic movements. In other words, capitalism or democracy without rational judgement cannot be capitalism or democracy. And, of course, another point Weber made relied on his intuitive knowledge that none of these ethical criteria could be found in Chinese society and politics, nor in Japan.

NO VALID SOCIAL SCIENCE

Nowadays, political values are tremendously diversified in the world. But to identify a solution for the mounting political and economic difficulties, we all require a rational social science such as political science (unfortunately, this may include everything!), economics, sociology, jurisprudence, and importantly, history as case studies for all those, the value of which must be universal. On this basis, there are no differences between social and physical sciences.

As one fatal defect under Chinese ideological politics, however, leaders were selected without any consideration to their defined merits on solving social problems. In reality, not only does this fundamental flaw exist, but in an intensified political struggle concerning a declining economic cycle, the worst sort of man who belongs to a major faction or its sub-groups is given the power to rule. And the vital issues that occur in all these entangled developments could all converge into one plain fact. They all reject the benefits of the progress of human social sciences in their politics, although the intensity of this might vary.

Indeed, this becomes purely a matter of the level of social science in the end. It is important to reiterate, however, that the West did not achieve its rational standards because of its matured sciences or the natural progress made in its own social science. Nor has it equipped itself because of its racial or intellectual superiority. Progress came from the principles of Christianity and the western nations established laws and rules based on this fair spiritual tradition in their own society where the value of intellect is appreciated.

Here we may enter into confusing territory, as some may say that the Japanese economy and its technology have been very successful, at least once or twice. But even today, major technical inventions still come mainly from the US and Europe. Japan actually participated in these western technological links with its own inventions, which should be universal in nature. In other words, Japan could not survive without these global links like any other country.

The same thing is taking place in the world of social science but without any real participation from the East. Many western professionals often found in Tokyo that the Japanese government was sometimes hostile to practical economics or western contractual law. But then one notices, it is not only the law or economics, which were insufficient in Japan. The list is endless – you can ask about history, journalism, broadcasting, political philosophy, accounting, banking, archaeology, criminology, property valuation, law, parliamentary procedures, corporate management or electricity company management in particular. Then, we suddenly realise that Japan lacks, in fact, all the important functioning modern social sciences.

For explanation purpose, it would be easier to understand if one conceives a treble ball. (see over) We call, for example, the smallest core centre as I-Ideology, A-Art for the middle part, and finally, S-Science/Technology at the outer portion. Social Science belongs to A. By keeping I, or fragmented irrational parts of Chinese ideology as power movements here, one, or Japan in this case, could still develop S – rational science and technologies as long as S keeps its beneficial contacts with the outer rational world.

This is what Japan has been doing in the last hundred years with occasional interruptions. If this contact is to be cut off as appeared

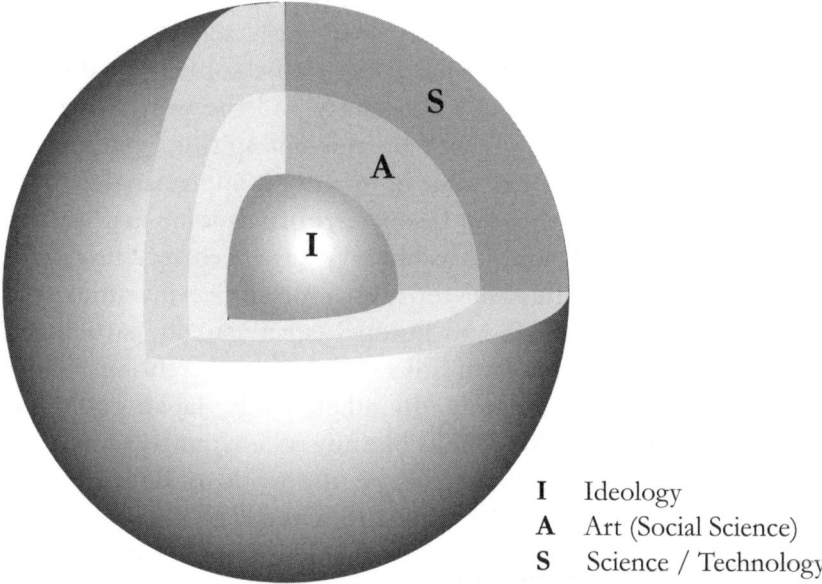

I   Ideology
A   Art (Social Science)
S   Science / Technology

in the seventeenth to nineteenth centuries or in the 1930s, its S becomes quickly degraded and obsolete. The point is, by keeping I, or fragments of irrational behaviour here, Japan could not develop its own A part. This is because, unlike part S, part A is more sensitive or directly attached to part I, which appears as political authority. And part I would eventually influence the final decisions of A activities, which require equal, or more consequential, powers of human judgement as a fundamental function. For correct political decisions, therefore, a rational A is indispensable.

    The absolute critical role of Christianity is recognised here as a vital influence on social science. To survive and be sustained, the usual evolutionary pattern for nations under Christian ideology would evolve from the inner core to outer A and then to S elements naturally. But Japan's case requires a movement in the opposite direction from the outer S element to inner core I in order to activate the A function, which would be artificial in this case. The problem of this pattern is that the often-irrational political core –

I, with its biased factional criterion could reject this movement as soon as it identified it as an element of the outer or alien 'aggressive' movement. In this reality, the normal process would not function, unless there was another force/pressure such as fresh creativity and resilience at the launch of a new administration or a strong diplomatic control applied as in the early stages of both the Meiji and Showa, governments from Britain and America respectively.

To show the superiority of rational politics versus irrational politics, it would be easier to use a simpler model here: see below. The applied assumptions are as follows:

We presume there are two states, one named as the White State and the other called the Red State. And each state has four members named A, B, C & D. A further assumption here is that in each state, only A, B and C have one *Manju* (The Japanese teacake) each as the necessary resources. D has nothing.

In this situation, Power=X and Technical Expertise=Y for each individual are equal. All numbers are constant. Therefore, the national strengths of White State and Red State are equal as 4XY at this stage.

Let us compare this with a dynamic model of the situation, say, three days later.

We further assume an evolved situation here that no one can survive unless he eats at least a half of a Manju within two days and

	day 1	day 4	strength
White State	ABCD 4	ABCD 4	4XY
Red State	ABCD 4	ABC 3	3XY

X = power
Y = technical expertise

the next supply or output of Manju will be made only three days later. In a rational model of the White State, ABC could solve this crisis by each slicing one fourth or thereabouts of their Manju and giving it to D. But in the Red State's irrational model no similar action could be taken as some insist on eating it all and refuse to change their habits. As the result of this irrational political decision, D will die out.

The superiority of rational politics in the White State is confirmed when the White State (4XY) and Red State (3XY) perform a power game on Day 4. Despite the fact that the Red State had equal technical expertise and power, making rational judgements or decisions on the right policy was not forthcoming because of political reasons. In the real world, such competitions in different forms are happening at all levels and areas, including power and expertise covering all the functions of society and individual achievements.

In seventeenth-century Japan, a Confucianist, a completely irrational leading scholar under the early Tokugawa Shogunate, Hayashi Razan, dismissed the growing trend of Christianity in Japan as unacceptable because, 'Christians treat people equally regardless of whether they belong to the lower or the upper class and preach the virtue of the single matrimonial relationship to confuse a stupid woman.'[250] Despite disastrously failing to understand family values, which are the key to social functions, he showed absolute political correctness from the Chinese ideological viewpoint. He demonstrated his total obedience to the supreme power without considering any rationale, logic or sympathy. And this attitude and action created the standard of indigenous social science in Japanese politics, although many did not agree with such monstrous views in Japan.

One major difference about Christianity compared with East Asiatic religions was that it was accepted by the free will of people who lived in various provinces in one of the largest empires on earth without any state influence – at least for around three centuries. For instance, Buddhism was born initially in Buddha's (*c.* 566-486 BC) homeland in northern India and stayed there as a local religion for a long time until the mightiest autocratic ruler, Emperor Asoka (reigned: *c.* 268-232BC), was attracted to its religious principles – *Dharma* – as he faced the decision to perpetrate genocide to annex the province of Kalinga/ Orissa. And it was the matchless power of his first Indian empire that spread Buddhism to the rulers of neighbouring nations which then disseminated to all the population in East Asia.

We tend to forget today that the great Indian civilization with its innovative iron technology, science and extended commercial economy actually represented the western (or Aryan as 'promoters' of the iron technology) world to eyes of easterners at this particular time. Aryan documents were known as the oldest existing, the *Rig-Veda* – hymns and praises – during the twentieth century, that is before the Hittite clay tablets were excavated or Mycenaean Greek was deciphered. And only the Indians used zero in mathematics. To import the superior ideas of this advanced civilization was of paramount importance for many sensible political leaders in East Asia.

In the subsequent 'Indianisation' process, the important canons of Buddhism like *Sutta-nipata* – Buddha's teaching – were never translated in full to Japanese.[251] The Chinese leaders invented *Mahayana* or Great Vehicle Buddhism based on the scriptures translated and created (undoubtedly with the help of at least an anonymous Chinese) in Chinese by Kumarajiva, a monk of Indian descent, in the fourth century. Subsequently, Xuanzhuang, a Chinese monk, went to India to study the Sanskrit texts in the seventh century. Again, the ancient Koreans and Japanese imported this sinicised, that is politicised, Buddhism under the rule of supreme Chinese ideology.

Buddhism was indispensable as an educational system for Japan to establish vital links with the more advanced Chinese civilization. But it was allowed to be practised under strict subjugation to Shintoism where various politicisations on its religious principles were inevitably made. The Tokugawa Shogunate did not hesitate to ask all the Buddhist temples to force the Japanese people to obey supreme Chinese ideology by issuing a religious certificate – *Terauke Shomon* – that he or she belonged to their temple in order not to be executed in the war against Christianity. Neither real Buddhists nor other religious believers could resist this forceful conversion in the island state. By demeaning the Buddha's teachings and religious freedoms, Japanese Buddhism was completely detached from Buddha's original ideas.

Kiyoshi Inoue, an outstanding Japanese historian, expounded that the religious value of Japanese Buddhism was finally degraded to 'the lowest grade of magic charm words for the protection of state power'. He concluded the political meaning of this entire process, 'was not a progress but stagnation, and nothing for the ancient Japanese to be proud of except its splendid artistic value'. Yet he assessed the real value of this important moment in Japanese history, 'What the ancient Japanese should be really proud of was their spirit of enterprise for studying an advanced civilization at all costs for the survival of Japan.'[252]

Universal principle seems to be the original US drafter's aspiration for the Japanese constitution as the word 'universal' is used two times in its preamble. First, it was stated, 'This is a **universal** principle of mankind upon which the Constitution is founded.' The second one was emphasised as the key word in conclusion, 'We believe that no nation is responsible to itself alone, but that laws of political morality are **universal**; and that obedience to such laws is incumbent upon all nations who would sustain their own sovereignty and justify their sovereign relationship with other nations.' Not surprisingly, these sentences have been completely deleted in the new Japanese constitution draft prepared by the LDP in late 2005. (What could be the purpose for carrying out such a wholesale change?)

WHEN JAPAN HAS THE PRESIDENCY?

'First of all, I would like to confirm the system of our country. This government will change our history fundamentally and curtail the role of government to be one as small as possible. The all-traditional old administrative functions will be abolished and our governmental organizations will concentrate only on regulating the business…For financial business, only the central bank and financial committee as an independent organization will control…'

the President explained.[253] This was a dream scenario for Japanese reform depicted by Yoshiki Hidaka. Similarly, the possibility of a directly elected prime minister was argued for from time to time in Japan.

With all its attractiveness, however, this idea for a Japanese presidential system or similar quick solution has overlooked one major problem. The mishaps of Japan did not originally start from a situation where Japan had no proper constitution or adequate political tools at official levels. Despite many Japanese failing to understand its real value, the new post-war Japanese constitution provided by the Allied powers was an effective modern political tool. But because of the country's dysfunctioning Chinese ideology, the arch-bureaucracy would continue to sit there, forever! This stimulating argument, therefore, looks rather like social science fiction as it could not happen without first demolishing the invalid old system, which is still firmly in charge of running the country.

In this political environment, all the former Japanese leaders (if you remember one of them!) or other globally unknown politicians are retaining their highly regarded arch-bureaucratic status, even as Japan is deeply submerged under a world-record governmental debt. Nobody did anything wrong in Japanese 'democracy' as all the Japanese press would undoubtedly agree! As if Japan was a country, being run by a proper consensus of the Japanese people whose symbol was the emperor of Japan. There seemed nothing in between this implausible myth and horrible reality. Could the East Asiatic idea of a permanent political 'elite' corps, totally disconnected from the people, be sustainable, even if the modern concept of responsible government completely disappeared?

From a completely different angle, of course, it is of no use trying to find out who is responsible in Japanese politics. It was, from the beginning, a system open to neglect which could ignore responsibility by avoiding unified political power.

Mark Ramseyer and Frances Rosenbluth questioned the situation, 'Pre-war bureaucrats were never autonomous. They suffered in fact from a multiplicity of overseers, and were unable to play off those overseers against one another. The conventional wisdom – that bureaucrats made the important policy decisions because politicians could not easily fire them and because they drafted most of the laws – is based, we argue, on the wrong kinds of evidence.'[254] They tried to depict Japanese life in both conceptual and empirical terms by applying the western idea of 'bureaucracy' in their minds and thereby failing to understand the real seat of Japanese power, the existence of arch-bureaucracy, based on the utterly different political criterion of the East. In this old system, one would need to include 'oligarchs' and 'political parties' as a part of it, as all of them belong to this legitimate organ under the Japanese emperor. It is here again that all sense of responsibility disappeared.

Kenneth Ruoff argued about the change of the Japanese emperor's status, 'On 1 January 1946, the Imperial Household Ministry issued an imperial rescript in which the emperor denied his divinity, "The ties between Us and Our People have always stood upon mutual trust and affection. They do not depend upon mere legends and myths. They are not predicated on the false conception that the Emperor is divine and that the Japanese people are superior to other races and fated to rule the world." '[255] This political denial made in post-war Japan was apparently insufficient.

The process also underlined a sensitive issue for the Japanese people. Herbert Bix noticed Japanese anger regarding wartime responsibility when Emperor Hirohito visited Kyoto University on 12 November 1951, as students with a huge placard saluted him, 'Because you once were a god, those who studied here before us died on your battlefield. Please, never again be a god; never again have us cry out "Listen! The voices of the sea! (*Kike wadatsumi no koe)*." '[256] But was the war really the fault of the Japanese emperor?

As once occurred during the 1930s, the current rock solid, old arch-bureaucracy is again vigorously on the march, derailing Japan's economy even by creating re-emerging global depression. But there is one difference today. Past problems happened because nobody, including the Japanese in the 1930s or 1940s, could understand the mechanism of this old Japanese political ideology, not to mention the total ban on this kind of study in pre-war Japan.

In 1935, however, there was at least a hard-working individual in England who warned us with his unparalleled political scientific analysis, '**We must ask why** Japan never gave birth to an independent civilization, corresponding to the Japanese environment, but eventually found vacant, and annexed, by the continental, non-maritime Far Eastern civilization.'[257] Toynbee's thesis on Global Politics needed to be answered as he insisted at the time – but he was so advanced from the rest of the world. The war became inevitable. To envisage an explanation of this mechanism, we had to wait for the progress of social science in general, including the advanced study of Japanese and Chinese history, which finally arrived as a positive side of the Japanese bubble.

The latest tragedy occurred as if unnoticed, not by human misjudgement but by the historical environment surrounding the East Asiatic power. As Toynbee successfully summed it up, the answer is contained in these events under the Japanese double standard while disguised as a modern maritime nation, which were repeated again in post-war Japan. Above all, the role of this irresponsible old political system is about to be finished, simply because nobody inside or outside of Japan, including the Japanese emperor or the Chinese Communist Party, can afford it any longer.

IMPLICATIONS FOR CHINESE POLITICS

The bloodshed at the Tiananmen – *Heavenly Peace Gate* – Square is remembered as the day the People's Liberation Army shot at their fellow non-violent Chinese demonstrators. It was a grave tragedy. Or like the pro-Tibetan independence movement in 2008, it could be connected to threatening protests from less numerous tribes who reside in China's border area with its vast mountains and desert regions. After all, to clamp down was the only option available to Chinese leaders because all these aggressive demonstrations could bring down the rule of Chinese communists. But a bigger headache for the Chinese government is that a similar confrontation could be repeated again.

We need to first understand, however, that the Chinese communist regime is not a democracy but it is not evil either. It emerged perhaps as a necessary transitional polity for modern Chinese democracy. Facing global accusations, the Chinese government, even today, does not want to acknowledge that this brutal incident ever took place in its capital and tries to eliminate the event from the record. They knew as modern politicians, that it was indefensible.

From the Chinese ideological viewpoint, it was not surprising. Stability was of prime importance for any regime of this large and hugely populated state. With this greater systemic risk in mind, their reaction to protest had to be vicious as a warning to the public that this kind of action would never be tolerated. A similar philosophy is quite plain in Chinese criminal law cases. Again, if the 'rebels', either good or bad in nature, had interpreted the compromising measures as weak, China could enter into uncontrollable chaos where all sorts of outlaws could join in with this prematurely released 'revolution'.

Even by the poorer human rights standards of communism in Europe, however, such an approach was not politically acceptable. In fact, it was a fatal blow to Mikhail Gorbachev in the Russian reform movement to have been associated with Chinese 'hardliners' during his official visit to Beijing. He had to face severe criticism from the opposition leader, Boris Yeltsin, on his lukewarm response to this matter.

Michael Dobbs highlighted this fundamental political dilemma, 'The bloodshed in Tiananmen Square…had crystallized the options facing Gorbachev. In the phrase of one of his Communist Party aides, he now stood at "a political and moral crossroads." His revolution from above had become a revolution from below. He could permit the revolution to continue, in the knowledge that reformers like himself would ultimately be swept away, or he could use force to stop the revolution in its tracks. That would mean abandoning the hope of radical reform for another generation.'[258] He was about to leave Russian politics.

Part Four – The Change

Under the fall of communism, the degree of Russian political control was shrinking rapidly. In December 1991, the formation of a new Commonwealth of Independent States was finally witnessed. President Gorbachev argued, 'In 1954 Crimea ended up as part of Ukraine…And if one goes back to 1923, when Donbass and Kharkov joined Ukraine?... If everyone begins to separate off, then tomorrow the fourteen million Russian speakers in Ukraine will find themselves living in another state.' A Ukrainian journalist reminded him that '90 per cent of the fourteen million "Russian speakers" in Ukraine voted for Ukraine independence.'[259]

What was the fundamental strength of European communism? On this issue, David Satter elaborated his view, 'The ideology was powerful because it offered an alternative to the agnosticism of the twentieth-century modernity… Perhaps more important, the ideology imparted a sense of purpose. Soviet citizens were understood as taking part in a great historical enterprise, the building of communism, and the effect of this delusion was to give meaning to what often were bleak and directionless lives.'[260] This was particularly important for a country like Russia, diverse in all possible ways and yet which must be controlled by a cohesive power in this virtual empire where the two elements often failed to balance.

In East Asia, while its experiences were very similar to Europe's at the beginning, the 'exit' was totally different. And it should be dissimilar. Mao Zedong and Kim Il-sung wrote and discussed communism publicising their opinions, which were not always reasonable but negative criticism against them was banned in those countries and will not emerge on the surface until regime change actually happens; until then they are protected by a cult of practical 'divination' by the arch-bureaucracy for political leadership.

Concerning the danger of bureaucracy in modern communist states, even Marx himself could not have foreseen the problems. Maurice Meisner analysed this, 'Marx, and Marxists generally, gravely underestimated the threat that bureaucracy might pose in the wake of a socialist revolution in the economically and socially backward lands where they have in fact occurred in the twentieth century...Less than five years after the Russian Revolution, Lenin pondered the reasons why the new Soviet order had so quickly become so bureaucratic and so oppressive.'[261] The problem was multiplied in an arch-bureaucratic East Asia as it was cemented to its old indestructible political system.

Another important point that needs to be mentioned was that there was a similarity between Marx's new materialism and traditional materialism under Chinese ideology despite the fundamental difference of their power structures. While the Russian Marxists only ignored the existing religions (in fact, only very few prominent churches were destroyed), the Chinese ideologists subordinated religion exactly as the old dynasties did.

The Chinese communists set up various people's representative organs and claimed themselves as a modern state of the people – but only as a formality. In reality, the Chinese arch-bureaucracy equipped with new science and technology skills will continue to confront all the moves against their state power by using every political and social means at their disposal against the people. Above all, an effective and democratic legal system will never emerge in China as long as this 'eternal' control stays effective in rejecting rational social science. This is the ultimate reason why Marxism, once declared dead in the West, can still survive in the East.

With this old political style, 'modern' China has entered the competitive global political stage as a capitalistic nation without any preparations or strategy in mind, exactly as the grossly misbehaved 'modern' Japan did and is shamelessly repeating its failure today for the second time. It will not be sufficient for a third Chinese revolution just to see the fall of the Chinese communist regime. This type of traditional 'revolution', where only another arch-bureaucratic regime could emerge with a Japan-like superficial form of capitalism, would be inconceivable – just imagine the chaotic bursting process of the current Chinese expansion and its eventual bubble and its impact on over 1.3 billion people. A multi-party system would be also required for China; however, unlike Soviet Russia, this should not be the final goal for its reform.

For the future of East Asian cooperation, therefore, it is categorically impossible to promote new and modern political ideas based on Chinese ideology. Unless the reform reaches to that level, the implosion will never be contained. Everybody needs to face this crucial fact in East Asia. It does not matter if one is 'communist', 'socialist', 'capitalist', 'republican', 'nationalist', 'liberal' or 'democrat' as none of those modern political ideas can be sustained as long as the old political core remains intact.

DISINTEGRATED STATE POWER

It started with Russia's refusal to withdraw its troops from Manchuria, having entered there to pacify the Boxer Rebellion in 1900. Japan was suddenly thrown into the fray as one of the global imperial powers. Jutaro Komura, the foreign minister, was asked to submit a proposal for countering this Russian move to the senior advisors' council of the Japanese government in December 1901. He insisted that, as diplomatic approaches only had a limited effect, it was necessary for Japan to tie up with Britain in order for both to prepare for a coming war with Russia and to show Japan's determination to keep long-term peace in the region.[262]

On the other hand, Britain had a good reason to support Japan in the event of possible military conflicts against Russia in the Far East. It perhaps originated in the painful memory of the experience of the Crimean War with its horrendous costs of fighting with the Russian army on their chosen battlefields. Trevor Royle observed even twenty-nine years after the war, 'at the time of the Congress of Berlin...there was universal relief and a feeling, in Britain at least, that no one wanted a repetition of the experience of the Crimean War.'[263] We could presume that this sentiment remained even after a further seventeen years when the Anglo-Japanese Alliance was signed.

This Russo-Japanese War, however, was most peculiar in its nature. Indeed, although Japan won the war, the Japanese public never understood the real power balance behind this military encounter due to domestic propaganda and British diplomatic reticence. The fact was that even the most ailing advance of the Russian Empire remained unbeatable by the Japanese but, with the British Empire's help, it was achievable.

The Alliance with Britain meant Japan's entry into the world of western diplomacy. Britain advised the Japanese leaders to create its modern army as a Satsuma-Choshu combined force that replaced the old Tokugawa Shogunate, and to form the Meiji government. But it was Germany who assisted Japan in the practice of modern warfare by sending one of its finest training strategists, Major Klemens Meckel, to the Japanese Military College for three years to give instruction on general military science and field operations.[264] The British, German, French and Americans brought new military technologies and techniques including machine-guns, heavy artillery, shells and fortifications that pushed up Japanese strength – a prerequisite for this first large-scale modern war in East Asia.

The leading Japanese strategist, General Gentaro Kodama, was selected on merit, with Meckel's endorsement, effectively without any political intervention. The combined factions of Satsuma and Choshu knew that they needed to appoint the best general available who was capable of accepting this critical role. Kodama supervised major operations as Chief of Staff under the Commander in Chief of the Manchurian Expedition Army, Field Marshal Iwao Oyama of the Satsuma faction. The Third Army under General Maresuke Nogi of the Choshu faction fought a bloody battle against the modern fortifications of Port Arthur/*Ryojun*/Luda which was protected by machine-guns and barbed wire, and the remaining Russian Pacific Fleet in the harbour was finally annihilated by Japanese fortress guns carried up a 203-metre-hill to shoot at them.

But the Japanese army was completely exhausted by its huge sacrifice, despite a lesser loss (70,000 men) than their Russian counterparts (90,000 men) at Mukden/*Hoten*/Shenyang, the last major field battle fought in this war. It was by no means a decisive victory as the Russian army still stood firm at the front. The next possible target, Harbin, was almost 400 kilometres to the northeast and Vladivostok was even further away although it was also accessible by sea. Logistically, it was significantly risky and costly for the Japanese to advance further to the Russian capital, which was more than 6,000 kilometres to the north-west!

Britain's seemingly unlimited help as an Allied power was also vital for the battle of the Tsushima strait. All the major battleships of the Japanese Combined Fleet were new British models with highly improved gun power. The war indemnity that China had paid to Japan after the Sino-Japanese War enabled Japan to purchase these battleships. At the time, Japanese shipyards could not build armoured ships larger than destroyers while the Russian Baltic shipyard was able to deliver five battleships prior to this naval encounter.[265] The key Japanese naval commanders had been trained abroad. Heihachiro Togo stayed almost eight years in Britain working on British ships under British supervision. His 'right hand man', leader of operations, Saneyuki Akiyama studied operation strategy and tactics directly from a legendary American naval strategist, Captain A.T. Mahon in the United States.

Above all, the strategy used by Admiral Nelson at Trafalgar almost a century before was still largely applicable in this sea battle, just before the age of Dreadnought. Nelsonian tactics such as the elements of surprise and boldly taking initial risks for a subsequent advantage could be adopted again. In this battle, Togo took a 'T' crossing, instead of the '+' crossing of Nelson's sailing fleet, by turning to the left in front of the Russian fleet advancing in a row, taking into consideration the engine power of the ships and their range of fire. Having decided to stand up on the upper deck like the iconic admiral, Togo signalled to the entire fleet, 'The fate of the Empire depends upon the outcome of this battle. Let everyone do his utmost.' In this almost identical phrase to the British original, 'duty' was replaced by 'utmost', in order to appeal more to Japanese sailors.

Admiral Rozhestvensky had less than five minutes to hammer the exposed Togo's flank. The Russian shells hit the Japanese flagship

Mikasa repeatedly but this new Vickers-armoured model sustained the attack and the lining-up Japanese fleet finally opened fire at *Suvorov*, the Russian flagship.[266] The main Russian Baltic Fleet (renamed as the Second Pacific Fleet) was smashed one by one in confusion by Japanese accurate gun and torpedo shots, a tribute their constant training of the last six months while their enemy were travelling around half of the globe before this decisive sea battle. Of thirty-eight ships sent out from the Baltic, only four ships, one cruiser and two destroyers and one transport, were able to return to Vladivostok.[267]

Despite this brilliant naval victory against Russia, Japanese war-finances had exceeded the planned budget and its calculated limits. The original budget of 500 million yen was about double the cost spent on the Sino-Japanese War and had to be repeatedly revised, as the scope of war was extended and it finally reached around the two billion yen mark. As Japan had no capacity for this level of huge expenditure, 78 per cent of the required fund had to be financed abroad with British and American help including a 800 million yen debenture subscribed in London and in New York.[268]

In this critical situation, the US President, Theodore Roosevelt, agreed to intervene and offered a peace treaty. At Portsmouth, New Hampshire, Japan negotiated a final compromise with the Russians. Firstly, Russia agreed that Korea became a Japanese protectorate. Secondly, Japan took over various Russian interests mainly on railways in southern Manchuria and gained the right to post troops to guard it. Thirdly, the Tsarist government ceded Southern Sakhalin to Japan but the Japanese did not receive any war indemnity from Russia. As we saw earlier, Japan could not consolidate any further on their spectacular success and the status gained by this victory.

Equally, despite the similarity of the wartime atrocities committed by Germany and Japan in the Second World War, it is important to see a notable structural difference between the two countries. In a drifting diplomacy, most of the Japanese military leaders who took a political role knew that Japan would definitely lose the war against the United States at the time the conflict began. No western leader would have decided to go to war on such a basis.

Why did the Japanese act like this? Because most Japanese realised, with their own political instincts, that their expansion into China's borders was reaching its limits, and there was no other way forward but to destroy their distorted and uncontrollable politics. A chance of reform to change the course of rigid Japanese factional politics, let alone the on-going horrible economic implosion, was impossible in their inherent 'political destiny'.

The Germans never perceived the war in this way. Vladimir Lenin had noticed as the first foreign expert the fundamental changes in German capitalism after its so-called Second Industrial Revolution (with electricity) since the national state was constructed by Prussian power in 1871. Germany, once divided into around four hundred political units, now emerged as the latest Superpower in Europe. In his influential book, *Imperialism,* Lenin analysed the German industrial powers such as AEG, which were globally comparable only to their counterparts in the United States. The communist leader could not hide his admiration for Germany and the trend of its new financial economy. He quoted Schultze-Gaevernitz, 'Imperialism, i.e. the highest stage of capitalism is the eve of the proletarian social revolution.'[269] It was a year after the Weimar Republic had been inaugurated when Lenin made his prediction.

Despite setbacks, Germany's industrial power grew and accelerated its pace under Nazi Germany. Peter Pulzer noted, 'From 1934 onwards Schacht…combined the Ministry of the Economy with the presidency of the Reichsbank, thereby becoming the economic architect of the Third Reich. His ingenuity was concentrated on foreign trade: exchange controls, export subsidies, and bilateral trade agreements with supplier countries, based on exchange rates tailored to each individual case.'[270]

The long-time German dream of a united *Großdeutscheland* was finally realised by the Austrian-born Adolf Hitler as *Anschluss* – the annexation of Austria – in March 1938. This change to the power balance alarmed Britain, but having been exhausted in the First World War, France was more cautious on the prospect of a possible war against Hitler at the time of the subsequent German invasions to Sudetenland in September, and to Czechoslovakia in March 1939, which were in clear breach of Hitler's previous insistence to unite all 'Germans'.

Nazi Germany's illicit expansion seemed set to continue, and it was unstoppable by diplomacy alone. Finally, France and Britain were convinced to act together to protect Poland in case of a further German invasion. Losing Poland would mean the deprivation of all that had been fought for in the Great War. Churchill was also convinced that it was 'quite impossible for Germany to denude the Eastern front' and whether Russia occupied Poland as 'allies' or as 'the enemy', the difference in fact was 'not however so great as might seem'.[271] Hitler ordered the invasion of Poland by *Blitzkrieg* with dive-bombers and mechanized divisions in September 1939, hoping Britain and France would not intervene if he achieved a quick victory under the non-aggression 'alliance' with a 'fearsome' Soviet Union, which was hastily signed just before the invasion. But this time, the Allied powers were ready to join the war against Hitler's optimistic delusions.

In the following year, an encircled Paris fell as Mussolini's Italy 'enthusiastically' joined the victorious advance. The Germans were intoxicated with glory on hearing the unbelievable news from Compiegne that Germany had managed to sign their dictated armistice with France in the same train where France had forced them to sign in November 1918 – this took place as the *Wehrmacht* marched into the Champs-Elysees.

The British Empire stood alone. But as Hermann Goering's false promise to quickly secure British airspace had to be soon broken, Hitler was secretly disappointed. German (or any) bombers were still vulnerable to the speedy fighter attacks which Britain launched with various innovations in terms of machines and systems. The German leaders of this no-longer-valid flawed military plan of confronting Europe's two strongest imperial powers on both fronts had only one alternative. Either to raise the stakes with the invasion of Britain, or to first crush Russia to enrich Germany with 'its immense territorial space' – *yeyo nyeobyatniye prostranstva* (as described by Pushkin). Finally, Hitler recognised the hard choice he had to make.

The attack on the Soviet Union began in June 1941. The German forces that thrust into Russia 'consisted of 153 divisions, 3.05 million men, together with more than half-a-million allied troops from Finland to Rumania. With 3,550 tanks (as well as 600,000 horses) and over 2,770 aircraft this was the most powerful force ever assembled in European military history up to that time.'[272] Manfred Zeidler analysed his objectives, 'Hitler was bent on making Germany the unchallenged continental power by cutting out the Soviet Union both politically and militarily, while at the same time continuing to make use of her economic resources. But this latter aim was now no longer to be pursued via normal forms of international trade, but rather by means of a colonial system of exploitation under the auspices of the "Wirtschaftorganization Ost"'.[273]

Facing this formidable foe from the west, Russia had only one option, to revive its traditional defence of avoiding a decisive battle and retreat deeply into the ultimate fortification lines of Leningrad, Moscow and Stalingrad. A quick withdrawal or to do nothing, however, was not an option. The strategy originally invented by Peter the Great teaches an unforgettable lesson to cocksure invaders before any decisive encounter. Mikhail Kutuzov sacrificed Smolensk and Moscow, but this time, it was Kiev and others turn to suffer. Meanwhile, the British-Soviet Agreement for joint action was signed a month after the invasion. The first aid to the Soviet Union came in the form of a credit of £10 million pounds provided in the following month.[274] Soon American economic aid also flowed into Russia, which amounted to 5.6 per cent of Soviet net material product between 1942 and 1945.[275] Even in Stalingrad, Singer sewing machines were sent to manufacture uniforms to keep Russian soldiers warm.

The words 'total war' or *totaler Krieg* was first proclaimed by Goebbels in a speech in Berlin on 18 February 1943, eighteen days after the capitulation of Marshal Paulus at Stalingrad.[276] When he said this, he really meant it. And the words was even more appropriate to Soviet Union who lost some twenty-five million lives in the war. The scale of destruction became intolerable for all sides.

The Second World War appeared as a new type of war for air powers. The Germans took the initiative and the most advanced ballistic missile system was in their sole possession. Despite immense losses incurred by bombing crews, the British and Americans systematically and constantly improved their destruction deliverability on a massive scale with new generations of heavy bombers and finally, long-range fighter P-51s to protect themselves.

The first raid by twenty RAF bombers to Berlin on 26 August 1940 delivered twenty-two tons of explosive. By 3 December 1943, the RAF dropped 8,656 tons at its seventeenth assault on the German capital in five raids with a total of 2,166 bombers.[277] Bombings were getting more accurate and powerful all the time. German wartime industrial capacity and the people's morale were gradually hampered by these ferocious day and night air attacks.

After the consecutive successes of the initial German victorious advances, Hitler was accustomed to intervene in the military decision-making among his generals, while in Soviet Russia, a gifted commander, Zhukov, could draw up all major defence plans at the front after the Red Army's initial chaotic defeats. Stalin made a 'furious' purge of generals who seemed to 'share' the responsibility for the appalling Soviet defeats. But the suspicious dictator was also flexible enough to admit his mistakes, and picked the one who constantly impressed him with his military advice. This different command structure in those two totalitarian states never changed up to the ultimate German defeat at the Battle of Kursk.

Robin Cross assessed, 'A *Materialschlacht* – clash of machines – had been sought at Kursk in the full knowledge that the attacking forces were inferior to the enemy and that there were insufficient reserves to exploit any success to the hilt.'[278] The Russians continued to out-manoeuvre the Germans by luring the enemy there with clearer objectives and better intelligence.

The information from a captured sapper of the German 6th Infantry Division revealed the exact time of the planned German assault on the northern front at 0230 hours of 5 July 1943. Having been informed of the imminent danger, Zhukov took immediate action to counter at 0220. The overwhelming Russian heavy artillery and inventive rocket weapons opened fire targeted at the German artillery position. It resulted in dreadful confusion among German soldiers as many men, ammunitions and guns were randomly hit. The mood of the battle changed completely. The German force invading from the north into a heavily fortified and mined area soon halted its advance.

The Allied landing on Sicily, just five days later, killed any optimistic hopes for sufficient reinforcements to the German assaulting force in Russia. In this largest tank battle ever fought in history, the advancing Army Group South commander, Field Marshal Erich von Manstein, had no choice but to take his chance with the strongest ever German assault force assembled under his command. He could not foresee, however, the degree of the Red Army's preparations and readiness to sacrifice all as testified in this decisive battle.

The German advance had to stop soon after von Manstein's powerful machines successfully penetrated as planned deep into the Kursk salient, crushing fierce Soviet defences. But Zhukov had a hidden reserve force there. It soon became apparent that the Germans could not break the Soviet attack formation, as more tanks and infantries equipped with anti-tank guns were constantly called for the counter-offensive into this deadly battlefield near Prokhorovka. Russia lost more men and tanks but sustained its air superiority. Even today, some Russians have not stopped criticising the commander for the huge losses suffered. But the defeat at Kursk was insurmountable to the Germans, just like the victory of Cannae was insuperable to the Carthaginians.

It was a war of attrition and industrial power. The Russian mills, oilfields and factories spread over the Urals, Caucasus and Volga regions were running at full speed and were immune from German air raids in preparing for this moment. As Soviet artilleries started to bombard Berlin with 1,236,000 shells for the final assault, the remaining German forces in the city fought tenaciously until they were finally conquered by the two subsequent superpowers.

Both Nazism and Bolshevism, therefore, were political forms of trying to forcibly integrate the power of their nations at a maximum level. The responsibility was clear in both cases. Adolf Hitler and the Nazi leadership acted with their immense state powers and used their commanding capability, and took all responsibility for war.

In the Second World War, many Japanese soldiers died on the various fronts by refusing to surrender due to the policy of their own military rule. But no such political determination as shown on the European front was executed by the top cadre of Japanese military power since the beginning of the war to its end. We can observe a rather different scene in Japanese East Asiatic operations from the Chinese continent to Burma where those in the Japanese headquarters ran away first, leaving the defence of Rangoon to newly recruited civilians.[279] The fierce battles in the Pacific islands had to be fought with suicide attacks to cause maximum damage on the US without any hope for victory.

Disregarding completely what was then occurring in Europe, the empire of Japan failed to establish a coherent command for its air campaigns due to a fierce rivalry between its army and navy. Instead, the world's largest battleships, desperately outdated as an assault force, the twin models of *Yamato* and *Musashi*, were developed only to satisfy the 'pride' of its once glorious naval faction, or sub-sect of that faction.

Japan struggled a great deal but in a different way. In contrast to the situation in the Third Reich, the lack of modern unified state power was the cause of the spectacular downfall of the Meiji Empire. The Japanese expansion to Manchuria was an economic disaster, contrary to what was generally believed in the West. Japan annexed only Korea and southern Sakhalin in addition to Taiwan, and Manchuria was never ceded to Japan, which meant that political control remained in Chinese hands; but despite this, the Japanese government agreed to invest a massive sum there, even larger than the combined figures for helping Korea and Taiwan.[280]

This misguided Japanese investment, however, benefited agrarian Manchuria in transforming it as a better place economically as its population doubled from seventeen million in 1908 to thirty-four million in 1930.[281] Then, the Japanese suddenly realised that larger Chinese political powers were also growing locally to a menacing level. As the myth of a 'dreamland' was advocated, 'Manchurian factions' of the Japanese arch-bureaucracy created a military policy based on an irrational illusion that Japan could compete with both Russia and America. The Japanese economy further imploded under this colossal economic mismanagement as Japan rejected vital cooperation with the international community.

The US government had finally realised the hopeless situation in Japan and saw the likely invasion of Japan into South French Indochina, now under the command of Vichy France, effectively as Japan's first war move. This time, the US and Britain were ready to stop the Japanese advance with a possible military confrontation and warned them accordingly. One thing was certain. The Japanese 'factional' military ambition would have never given up at this point. The airfield and port of Saigon/Ho Chin Minh City were indispensable for its further planned advances to South East Asia.

In this fatal implosion, the Japanese government knew that the expected oil embargo from the United States, which was subsequently declared in July 1941, was tantamount to the declaration of war but nobody in Japan dared to halt the country's military expansion into South French Indochina.[282] The majority of people never actually planned or proactively joined in the war aggression in Japan, but everybody, without exception, participated in it reactively, and therefore, unlike the German people, there was no Japanese unity for even a single protest to stop this folly.[283]

The fact was that Germany had aimed for victory in this war. But it can be concluded that the Japanese just fought for better terms of surrender so they could preserve their old political system and to start a new economic cycle! In other words, a global policy was never the issue for Japan. One might say that Japan was not even defeated in this self-determined war objective.

The political situation of post-war Japan was, therefore, somewhat similar to that of Germany after the First World War when it could not deny its outdated *Ostpolitik*. Critically, Japanese democracy, like that of the Weimar Republic, was established without the people's firm commitment. Hence, it would have to face possibly another fatal collapse and humiliation.

ON THE ROAD WE WERE BEFORE

Similarly, the argument, not only voiced by the Japanese but also by many foreigners who say this when they live in Tokyo, that Japan is not a capitalistic state but a socialist state is false because even a socialist state requires united state power, which in reality Japanese modern politics has so far failed to produce. For this peculiarity in Japanese politics, Jean-Marie Bouissou, a French Japanologist, pointed out that between the balance of new democracy and wartime responsibility, post-war 'Japan was defined neither as a monarchy nor a republic. It is just Nihon-koku, "le pays du Japon".'[284] Or in English, just Japan as its passport states. His frank views have touched on this unresolved issue for all Japanese to consider: whether their political system belongs to any modern concept of a state at all.

Under this 'transcended' situation, the old arch-bureaucracy is still in the driving seat in Japan. On this political basis, the relationship between foreign affairs and domestic policy in the modern state is constantly blurred. It could be better explained perhaps in the French words, *politique extérieure* and *intérieure*, showing the direction of the efforts of the state clearly. Furthermore, *politique intérieure* under the Japanese double standard is functioning, based totally on local factional power. On the other hand, Japan has no proper *politique extérieure* in a sense that all domestic policies follow a higher political lead and its radiating national objectives within its boundary to/from the outside world. And if we apply the concept of modern politics here, there is absolutely no vector for Japan's *politique extérieure* to come from the will of the Japanese people or the emperor as *autorité suprême*. Even wars were entered into purely on this continuation of factional politics with materialistic objectives.[285]

From this aspect, one remarkable characteristic of the old Chinese agricultural expansion was that it was actually carried out as an extension of domestic factional politics. In this mode, the function of foreign policy could sometimes be made solely by power movements derived from factional conflicts. In the end, it was all about the Chinese, or more strictly speaking, the Chinese 'supreme' factional powers that took control of Chinese state politics, which other nations, believing they had equal rights (like all other smaller factions in China!), were supposed to respect. In this logic, there was no equal relationship between the states in East Asia, as each sectarian power had a predetermined rank of inequality in accordance with Chinese or Japanese domestic politics. This was the reason that, in modern times, when external and superior interference or difficulties came, East Asians tried to hide their heads like a turtle withdrawing into its shell, into their own world of 'absolute' factional politics by creating double standards.

In post-war Europe, historical Franco-German arch-rivalry was finally reconciled and converted to a cordial relationship for the future of Europe. To achieve this goal a diplomatic consensus between the two first had to be established for both modern nations to agree upon so that they could act together in changing domestic political barriers. But how could this kind of diplomatic consensus be established in East Asia, when there is no visible objective in each other's foreign policy?

The Nippo-Chinese undeclared war was a tragedy. The museum for the massacre in Nanjing vividly exhibited what atrocities the Japanese army committed in 1937. All the Japanese who have shamelessly claimed that nothing like that happened should go there and see the many appalling exhibits, including a copy of old Japanese newspapers. But we should not perhaps neglect to see also an East Asiatic element here. For instance, Mitsuo Arai, ex-staff sergeant of the Japanese Imperial army, who fought around Shanghai and the Nanjing area in China and later in Singapore, recorded the difference between the 'false surrender' tactic frequently used by the Chinese and a proper surrender with a white flag by the British army, which he saw for the first time in Singapore.[286]

The report of Lieutenant General Nakajima at the museum stated his fear at the time of the Chinese surrender and the fall of Nanjing castle. He noted that many Chinese soldiers came out with weapons and expressed his concern for the difficulties of the Japanese army in disarming the outnumbered Chinese soldiers who 'temporarily lost their will to fight'. It might be partially out of this panic against potential danger on the part of the Japanese invading army which ignited this disgraceful wave of massacres, which went beyond any rational explanation.

The empire of Japan expanded with fluctuating domestic factional politics all the way to its downfall. During the Russo-Japanese War, the Japanese army as a sub-unit of the government respected international laws in time of war, especially the treatment for prisoners of war, when a stronger state power and leadership then controlled its domestic politics at an early stage of its economic cycle and included a vibrant alliance with Britain. At the time of the Japanese invasion of China and afterwards, however, the status of Japanese domestic politics and economy was at its lowest ebb in a state of implosion, and this negatively affected the behaviour of Japanese soldiers. As a result, it came out as a completely different and shameful army.

Again facing an endless deflationary spiral, old ideologists are still determined to continue with the same politics on all fronts even by changing the entity into private sector business. No economic policy can be effective within this political stalemate where you cannot find any modern concepts or the necessary power to correct these failed ideas in any of the principal corners of Japanese society.

The practice of buying a house as an investment – either as a social concept or as a macroeconomic factor – does not exist in Japan, together with the concept of individual consumers and entrepreneurs. Put simply, the arch-bureaucratic society has never promoted these elements as vital for the economy but tried to scupper them ideologically as soon as they detected any major movements towards them. John Maynard Keynes emphasised, 'Given the social and political environment and the national characteristics which determine the propensity to consume, the well-being of a progressive state essentially depends...on the sufficiency of such inducements (to new investment)' – but Japanese economists could never grasp the principle of capitalism, or they were forced to ignore it. At the same time, they could not see the meaning of his reiterated remark, 'Consumption – to repeat the obvious – is the sole end and object of all economic activity.'[287] The old politics destroyed actually (successfully, in their terms!) all of these important economic factors in Japanese society for the expansion of their own state money-grabbing businesses.

But do they not feel guilty in committing those acts of larceny? Naoki Komuro, a brilliant Japanese political commentator, explained why this deplorable mechanism in which 'public goods' could be always regarded as 'goods belonging to nobody' under the traditional concept of a 'pre-capitalistic' Japan. Since 'the concept of "public" does not exist as a reality' in Japan, 'the actual control is deemed as absolute proprietorship'.[288] With this **Absolute Principle of No Responsibility**, the 'modern' Japanese arch-bureaucrats are expanding every day their own 'eternal' factional business as Japan faces constant embarrassment everywhere by their disastrously and miserably failed politics.

ONLY ALTERNATIVE TO ABYSMAL BREAKDOWN

We have argued that this peculiar East Asiatic political system, which had, in the past, convinced many Japanese and Chinese as being intrinsic or arising naturally in their blood, and therefore could never be altered, was not the truth. Any product of human artificial expertise, like all the other political structures in the world, could be either revised in its progress or abolished by its failure to adopt modern technology and social sciences.

On the Theory of Chinese Ideology

The conclusion of this analysis urges that to solve the current political impasse and overcome the process of implosion under its traditional political ideology, all Korean, Chinese and Japanese should pay attention to the importance of Christianity that has provided a foundation for a universal political philosophy and social science. The passive policy of defending the status quo by double standards, which effectively ignored all those political sciences, would be no longer tenable. Like all the rest of the world, East Asians also require constant reform to make its democracy function, proper economic management, and above all, a unified political power in order to uphold rational politics and avoid economic downfall.

In a larger historical picture, following Christian ideological expansions in the Mediterranean and European world in the first millennium, and the Greater European expansion to America, Africa, Australasia and Northern Eurasia that took place in the second millennium, future moves in East Asia will be repeated in the third millennium.

Facing this change, every westerner would first require recognition of the fact that Christianity should be opened to all corners of the world, beyond geographical, racial and cultural boundaries, to assist change in East Asia. We, of course, are not talking about a religious state of any kind here. Rather, only that this global movement could produce an effective political tool to nullify fraudulent human politics with its auxiliary religions, which is firmly locked inside the centre of an obsolete Eastern state structure.

Let us assume an 'X-day' when the majority of Japanese people are convinced of the serious political defects of their current political system which has completely lost its way with visibly cataclysmic results so that finally, the people want at all costs to change their lives and reverse the course of this abysmal breakdown. Are there any measures applicable to this political requirement?

Only one exit exists. In the Japanese system, the only way to change its political core instantly, without risking any political instability, would be that the Japanese emperor, as the symbol of the Japanese people and its traditions, will become a Christian using his individual right to do so and the freedom of religion which is protected by the current Japanese constitution. And he also emphatically resigns from his political role as the head of the Shinto-Japanese Buddhism political complex currently controlled by state arch-bureaucracy. In other words, to abandon Chinese ideology on behalf of the Japanese people, who are powerless under the old rules, in order to stop disguising the horrible reality of the on-going implosion of Japanese double standards. By establishing a principle between the state symbol and the people, the Japanese emperor could also protect his individual rights and freedoms.

Until this process succeeds, arch-bureaucracy as a whole will turn down any moves, good or bad, against the old political core, and Japan's eventual clash with the West will become inevitable. By removing its legitimacy, however, just as an electric machine can be cut off from its generator, the old arch-bureaucratic movements will stop functioning. Thereafter, rationalism and individualism can gradually saturate all the segments of Japanese society. By making this essential change to the political core, radical reform will be given legitimacy for the first time in Japan. As the old arch-bureaucracy loses its political privileges, the centre of hollow state power will now be filled with political rationale, which will generate unified Japanese power, together with individual freedom.

Only Japan has this specific political mechanism in East Asia. But as an example a successful Japanese model will show the Chinese and Korean people the way forward or how to achieve their own path to fresh and vital modern politics together with a reform movement. All over East Asia, the current tenacious refusal for change would be expected to turn afterwards into a most enthusiastic acceptance for this revolution.

East Asians have nothing to be ashamed of. Nobody on earth existed whose ancestor was not a barbarian or militarist. N.J. Higham focused on this recognisable historical fact and the meaning of the Norman Conquest that once brought the political *Death of Anglo-Saxon England* in 1066, and built the foundations of Britain's modern political core.[289] Thereafter, Britain moved on a different political path, which is still visible today, while other Celts, Romans, Scandinavians and Anglo-Saxons were brought in to play a vital role in this successful political evolution, and perhaps all other subsequent immigrants played the same role.

This influential global power has finally reached East Asia. It is rather belated but there is an advantage in that the Japanese should be able to embrace all the advances of Christian theology arrived at since the days of Constantine. All the pure state Shintoists must follow the emperor's decision as a ritual obligation on their part by accepting Christianity. Then this could extend to the major Japanese-Buddhist sects. If there were people who still inclined to Shintoism or Buddhism, as some may still insist on, then all religions supported by people should be allowed fully fledged religious freedom, just like all other religions in Japan, as stipulated in the constitution.

For this coming religious transformation, the Anglican Church should provide a model for Japan to follow while the Japanese would have to make their own decision in order not to alienate the religious traditionalists in this rationalisation process, keeping continuity with its political past. Above all, the modern Japanese Church has to assume its role by extending fraternity to all Christians and other religions all over the world. The Japanese emperor and his family could extend Japan's solidarity with all the people's representatives in the world including the royal families in Europe.

To look at it from a different perspective, Shinto has to be emancipated from being a subjugated religion under the arch-bureaucracy of the state to change to a universal religion which presides over the state of the people, by the people, and for the people, as defined by Abraham Lincoln. All righteous minds that have previously existed and that still exist in Japan under Shinto or Japanese-Buddhism shall be respected.

This change will create a visible difference obvious to all the Japanese, signalling that the entire 'fleet' is moving to a new direction. No other alteration will be required; in particular, the Japanese islanders' unique culture of hard-working discipline, a passion for detail, and the culture of saving energy and materials should stay in Japan forever. The new political core will influence the corporate behaviour of Japanese companies completely, especially in the financial institutions to stop the current implosion. Any real reforms will have to wait for this fundamental political shift. To signify their entry into modern politics, Japan could be renamed as 'The State of Japan' or 'L'État du Japon', simply by changing the translation of '*Nihon Koku*'.

How could actual political reform then begin in Japan? The purpose of this political reform must be to create an effective political system of competitive selections based on merit in the heart of state politics for the protection of private businesses. Japan needs to use all its capable human resources in every part of society.

For this purpose, the Japanese parliament first needs to pass a Declaration of Imminent National Bankruptcy – *Kokka Hasan Fukahika Sengen*. It would be important for all Japanese parliamentarians to declare their repentance for this colossally negative position in order to make clear the issue of responsibility. In exchange, they all should be pardoned for their previous misconduct and misbehaviour. Any incumbent prime minister then asks for the creation of a National Emergency Council (NEC) which is a public commission completely independent of the current political scheme but will function in parallel with the existing political system which will be put into passive mode.

By injecting the spirit of democracy into the current constitution, the NEC will decide, in the form of a Great Charter, necessary reforms with a concentration on fundamental political functions of government such as a new national identity, political parties, parliamentary procedure, administrations, civil service, electoral system, rule of law, freedom of the press and the principal objectives of Japan's new politics. The members of the NEC will be appointed from Japanese nationals purely on merit, but if Japan lacks the specific expertise to identify and achieve necessary reforms, the chairman of the NEC could ask for help from Britain, the United States or the European Union – whoever could provide appropriate assistance. The role of the NEC is to produce fair principles for Japanese political reforms to make sure the people's political choices will be possible and effective and that a democratic Japanese government will function with a proper responsibility.

Under this new political system, the first election will be fought between the two newly established major political parties and others in forming the first truly democratic administration and its opposition to start real reform. The entire process including new parliamentary elections should be completed, say, within nine to twelve months.

Japan has entered – and China is entering – into the last phase of its old historical cycle where opportunity and danger co-exist. Let us hope that human rationale could prevail in this final crucible over Chinese ideology.

Notes

1. Hu, *The Chinese Renaissance*, p. 2
2. According to T'ang Leang Li, the Nanjing oligarchs accused him of having 'overstepped the limit of scholarly discussion and indulged in meaningless quibbling', Hu and Lin, *China's Own Critics*, vii
3. Aristotle, *Politics*, p. 54
4. Thurow, *Japan's Economic Recovery*, pp. 82-83, p. 98
5. van Wolferen, *The Enigma of Japanese Power*, p. 18
6. Johnson, *Japan: Who Governs?*, p. 41, p. 323
7. Unknown to most westerners, the level of Chinese History Studies in Japan is maintained at a world top standard in particular, at Kyoto University. As an advantage for Japanese scholars, we Japanese all learn classic Chinese – *Kanbun* – as part of the Japanese language – *Kokugo* – in high school.
8. Gernet, *A History of Chinese Civilization*, p. 253
9. Tanigawa, *The Formation of Global Empire*, p. 6, p. 219
10. Jin and Liu, *Prosperity and Crisis*, pp. 94-95
11. Elvin, *The Pattern of the Chinese Past*, p. 285, p. 289, p. 292, p. 309, p. 317
12. Roxburgh, *The Second Russian Revolution*, p. 5
13. Wang, *The Chineseness of China*, p. 263
14. The Zhou had a military force based on centurions like the Romans. Military divisions based on decimal units seemed to

appear as part of the nomadic element in Asia. See Kaizuka, *The Ancient States in China*, pp. 207-208

15   Huntington, 'The Clash of Civilizations?', p 25
16   Toynbee, *A Study of History, Volume I*, p. 89
17   Confucius, *The Analects*, p. 99
18   Other Chinese Five Canons not mentioned here are: 4) *Shujing* – the Scripture of Documents, 5) *Chunqiu* – the Chronicle of Lu
19   Fairbank, *The Chinese World Order*, pp. 4-11
20   Kajiwara, *The History of Korea*, p. 36
21   Miyazaki, *The Classic Examination System for Bureaucrats in Feudal China*, p. 15
22   Saneto, *Letter Reform in China*, p. 247
23   See Parkinson, *Parkinson's Law*, pp. 16-23
24   Miyazaki, *opus cit.*, pp. 180-184
25   Church, *Revolution and Red Tape*, p. 72, p. 296
26   Bielenstein, *The Bureaucracy of Han Times*, p. 156
27   Harries-Jenkins, *Bureaucracy in Great Britain*, p. 82
28   Mitchell, *Control without Bureaucracy*, p. 5
29   Mano, *The History of Central Asia*, pp. 103-105. Before the ninth century, various people of Aryan descent i.e. Indo-European language speakers (such as Hittites, Greeks, Europeans, Iranians and Indians), used to live in southern Central Asia. As the remnants of aggressive outward expansions in early ages, they rarely formed states in the farming areas of the southern oases with rivers and water irrigation systems compared to other mainly steppe and desert areas occupied by nomadic tribes in the north. In this particular environment, the old Turkish (such as Uygurish) and then Mongolian writing systems were both originally born under the influence of the Sogudian language which was spoken among their oases trading union, which spread from Samarkand to the East. It belongs to the Iranian section of the proto-Indo-European group, *ibid.*, pp. 48-50, pp. 87-91
30   Confucius, *opus cit.*, p. 33
31   Menges and Naumann, *Language and Literature – Japanese and*

NOTES

the Other Altaic Languages. The languages classified as Altaic language are Turkic, Mongolic, Tungusic, Korean and Japanese. In other words, all the nations that once constituted the Sino-barbaric synthesis in East Asia. Some extend the link to Uralic languages such as Finnish and Hungarian.

32 The other Chinese dynasties which could be classified as of Sino-barbaric synthesis are: Western Jin (265-317), The Sixteen Kingdoms of the Five Barbarians (317-439), Northern Wei (439-543), Western Wei (543-557), Northern Zhou (557-581) and Sui.
33 See Ueda, *The World of Wo*, p. 173, p. 190. A picture of a large ship, advanced iron armour, gold and silver accessories indicating a strong link with the continent, were found as the personal belongings in a burial for the first time in this era.
34 Kito, *The Yamato Imperial Court and East Asia*, p. 118, pp. 129-140
35 Kim, *The East Asian Region*, p. 87
36 The first Japanese victory against the Chinese army was made by Konishi Yukinaga, a Christian general, at the Battle of Pyongyang Castle in July 1592. He also saved this ill-advised campaign from a total disaster with his diplomatic skills.
37 Takeda, Miyajima and Mabuchi, *Korea*, pp. 128-129, pp. 159-160
38 Egami, *The States of Horse-Riding People*, pp. 144-145
39 Toynbee, *A Study of History – Abridgement*, p. 59
40 Sakamoto, Ienaga, Inoue and Ono, *The Chronicle of Japan, Volume I*, p. 315
41 It started with Manyo Gana used in Manyo Shu – The Poetry of Ten Thousand Leaves –, which was the first Japanese national literary achievement in the eighth century. See Inoue, *The History of Japan, Volume I*, p. 81-82 & p. 115
42 Huang, *China*, p. 141
43 Koyasu, *Motoori Norinaga*, p. 177
44 Akutagawa, *The Smile of Gods*, pp. 97-98
45 Peyrefitte, *The Collision of Two Civilisations*, p. 199

46 Cremer, *Macao*, p. 10
47 Yano, *The Opium War and Hong Kong*, pp. 208-242
48 Nish, 'Japan in Britain's View of the International System, 1919-37', pp. 27-28
49 Hamashita, *The International Opportunities for the Modern China*, p. 40
50 Miyazaki, *Yandi of Sui*, p. 27
51 Undoubtedly, the loss of one of its best air forces was most discouraging to the Japanese army on the ground. The Soviet military claimed that Japan lost 660 airplanes from May to September. 204 airplanes among those were shot down during the Japanese air campaign, which had to be launched prematurely from 20 to 30 August due to the initiative of the earlier Soviet offensive. Shishkin, *The Battle Actions of the Red Army at Khalkhin Gol River in 1939*, p. 84
52 In trying to be cleverer, the Japanese arch-bureaucrats were completely outmanoeuvred by Stalin from the beginning to the end of the war to the extent that they even tried to ask him to mediate a peace with the Allies.
53 Several books mentioned this story but I heard it from Professor Nakamura directly who clarified all my queries about the Japanese wartime movements. I remember when he referred to it in his study where four of us students used to attend his weekly seminar. He said wryly, 'He predicted it right, didn't he?' This was sometime in 1972, one of post-war Japan's best periods.
54 Zhukov, *Vospominaniya i Razmyshlyenya*, p. 190
55 Tokuyama, *Japan that Can't Confront 'Human-Evils'*, pp. 177-178
56 Owen Haley, *Authority without Power*, pp. 13-14
57 Peyrefitte, *opus cit.*, p. 506
58 Sejima, *The Reality of the Great East Asian War*, p. 16
59 Karl von Clausewitz, a Prussian officer in Napoleonic Europe, wrote *Vom Kriege* in 1833. During the Suez crisis in 1956 and the Cuban missile crisis in 1962, however, it appeared that his thesis of conventional strategy was no longer applicable. In these

nuclear confrontations, political objectives were lost first on one side and then on both sides respectively.

60 Cotterell, *East Asia*, p. 197, pp. 211-212
61 Nomura, *Mao Zedong*, p. 94
62 Saich, *China: Politics and Government*, p. 141
63 Medvedev, *China and the Super Powers*, pp. 32-33, p. 39
64 Schwartz, *Chinese Communism and the Rise of Mao*, p. 43. He quoted this phrase from Trotsky's book, *Problems of the Chinese Revolutions* published in New York in 1932.
65 Saich, *Governance and Politics of China*, p. 33
66 Yabuki, *The Chinese Economy*, p. 18
67 Han, *The Biography of Deng Xiaoping*, pp. 5-11
68 *Ibid.*, pp. 158-161
69 Nelson and Kuzes, *Radical Reform in Yeltsin's Russia*, p. 3
70 Hua, Zhang and Luo, *China: From Revolution to Reform*, p. 65
71 Patten, *East and West*, p. 11
72 Fewsmith, *The Politics of China*, p. 512
73 Chang, *Jiang Zemin and Zhu Ronji*, p. 154
74 Faust and Kornberg, *China in World Politics*, p. 159
75 Wang, *A Bureaucratic Paradise of China*, p. 154
76 Jing, *Factionalism in Chinese Communist Politics*, p. 417
77 Chao, *Moving China – Leaping Japan*, p. 19, p. 91
78 Cooper, *Taiwan in Troubled Times*, Preface
79 Galli, *Taiwan R.O.C.*, p. 49
80 Ho, *Economic Development of Taiwan*, pp. 300-301
81 Gold, *Taiwan Miracle*, p. 110
82 Wakabayashi, *Taiwan*, p. 188
83 Liu, *The Asian Financial Crisis and After*, p. 18
84 Ferdinand, *Hong Kong in Transition*, pp. 55-56
85 Miners, *The Government and Politics of Hong Kong*, p. 85
86 Thatcher, *Downing Street Years*, p. 494
87 Wurtzburg, *Raffles of the Eastern Isles*, p. 606
88 Baker, *Crossroads*, p. 281
89 Tanigawa, *The Success of Singapore*, pp. 18-19
90 Yoshioka, *India and Britain*, p. 119

NOTES

91 Goh, *The Practice of Economic Growth*, Preface by Toshio Watanabe, xv
92 Tremewan, *The Political Economy of Social Control in Singapore*, p. 39
93 Nagazumi, *The History of South East Asia*, p. 88
94 The sultan of Malacca had a force fifteen times larger than that of the Portuguese in this conflict. Chinese help was, therefore, indispensable for the Portuguese victory. *Ibid.*, p. 100
95 Takagi, *Hakka*, pp. 82-90
96 Nagazumi, *opus cit.*, p. 113
97 Hiizumi, *The Connection of Chinese Merchants*, p. 70
98 The new national language, Bahasa Indonesia, was introduced on a common basis with the Malay language after the Second World War.
99 Tsurumi, *Poverty in Asia*, pp. 30-50
100 Yu, *The Overseas Chinese*, pp. 19-21
101 Wi, *Christ and Caesar in Modern Korea*, pp. 54-55
102 Yamamoto, *Takashi Hara*, pp. 19-20
103 Takashi Davide Hara (1856-1921) from Morioka, Iwate Pref., studied French under French missionaries in northern Japan before entering the government's law school. He lived in Paris, as a secretary at the Japanese legation, from 1885 to 1889.
104 Donaldson, *America at War Since 1945*, p. 13
105 In complete contrast to the Japanese, Korean leaders drafted their constitutions on their own initiative by studying the US and French systems, albeit from a poorer political experience, to create the backbone of Korean democracy.
106 Lovel, 'The Military and Politics in Post-war Korea', p. 181
107 Watanabe, *South Korea – A Venture Capitalism*, pp. 62-64
108 Cheong, *The Politics of Anti-Japanese Sentiment in Korea*, p. 1
109 Chi, *The History of the South Korean Presidents*, p. 209
110 Graham, *Reforming Korea's Industrial Conglomerates*, p. 101, pp. 111-112
111 Saxer, *From Transition to Power Alternation*, p. 199
112 Medvedev, *opus cit.*, p. 22

NOTES

113 Komuro, *The Fall of South Korea*, pp. 84-85
114 Dvorchak, *Battle for Korea*, p. 7
115 Khrushchev, *Khrushchev Remembers*, pp. 395-396
116 George, *The Chinese Communist Army in Action*, p. 26
117 Wainstock, *Truman, MacArthur, and the Korean War*, pp. 100-101
118 Attlee, *As It Happened*, p. 232
119 Garthoff, *Assessing the Adversary*, p. 6
120 Lowe, *The Korean War*, p. 91
121 Ilpyong, *Communist Politics in North Korea*, p. 1
122 See Suzuki, *North Korea*, pp. 109-110
123 Kim, *Kim Il-sung's works*, p. 354
124 Zhebin, *The Splendour and Poverty of Kim's Empire*, p. 61, pp. 69-70
125 Zagoria, 'Soviet Policy Toward North Korea', p. 180
126 Kuroda, *Fin de siecle in the Korean Peninsula*, pp. 13-14
127 Sigal, *Disarming Strangers*, p. 23
128 Manning, 'United States-North Korean Relations', p. 76. The non-binding letter dated 20 October pledged that 'in the event that this reactor project is not completed for reasons beyond the control of the DPRK (Democratic People's Republic of Korea), I will use the full powers of my office to provide, to the extent necessary, such a project from the United States, subject to the approval of Congress.'
129 Scalapino, 'Korea–The Options and Perimeters', p. 17
130 Lu, *The Real Story of Ah Q*, p. 155
131 The image that most Japanese bore swords in the old days is not accurate. Contrary to the US idea of gun possession, Toyotomi Hideyoshi decided the course of military control in Japan in 1588 by declaring the decree of *Katana-gari* – Hunting for swords – that the exclusive possession of lethal weapons should be by the ruling Samurai class only, which was roughly about 5 per cent of the population.
132 Thucydides, *History of the Peloponnesian War*, p. 145, p. 147
133 Dower, *Embracing Defeat*, pp. 354-355

134 Fukui, *Japan and the World*, p. 128
135 Kanda, *Occupation and Democracy*, p. 290
136 'L'ENA face au cap de la soixantaine', *Le Monde*, 16-17/10/2005
137 Neary, *The State and Politics in Japan*, p. 42
138 Tsuda, *The Japanese Philosophical attitude*, pp. 24-25
139 Large, *Emperor Hirohito and Showa Japan*, p. 3. He quoted this from Charles D. Sheldon, 'Scapegoat or Instigator of Japanese aggression?' Inoue Kiyoshi's Case Against the Emperor', *Modern Asian Studies*, 1978
140 Kanda, *opus cit.*, pp. 132-134
141 Nakamura, *The Japanese Monarchy*, pp. 84-85
142 Antoni, *Der Himmlische Herrscher und Sein Staat*, pp. 58-59
143 Dower, *Japan in War and Peace*, p. 237
144 Birch, *The British System of Government*, p. 133
145 Mill, *On Liberty*, p. 5, p. 21, p. 25
146 Yukichi Fukuzawa (1834-1901), a liberal political thinker in modern Japan, made three trips to the West. First, he set off as an official translator (he studied English and Dutch) for the Japanese delegations to the United States from January to May 1860. The second voyage was from January to December 1862 when he visited via Cairo, France, Britain, the Netherlands, Germany, Russia and Portugal. The last journey was again to the United States from January to June 1867. He asserted the importance of independence and self-respect – *Dokuritsu Jison* – as the foundation of democracy.
147 De Lange, *A History of Japanese Journalism*, p. 192
148 Shillony, *Politics and Culture in Wartime Japan*, p. 93
149 Karatsu, *The Potential Power of the Japanese Economy*, pp. 258-259
150 Omae, *The Omae Report*, pp. 158-162, pp. 176-178
151 Hasegawa, *The Recovery of the Japanese Economy under Monopolar Dominance*, pp. 46-47, pp. 67-71, p. 133
152 Nakanishi, *The History of the Decline and Fall of the British Empire*, p. 332
153 See Dore, *Stock Market Capitalism: Welfare Capitalism*, inset

Notes

154 Reading, *Japan – The Coming Collapse*, p. 230
155 Vogel, *Kindred Strangers*, p. 29, p. 40, pp. 43-44
156 NKDR, *Seeking for a Japan with Vitality and Charm*, pp. 55-99
157 Other prominent politicians attacked in the last twenty years: Kiichi Miyazawa who was injured at a hotel meeting room when he was competing for the premiership with Yasuhiro Nakasone. Koichi Kato's house was set on fire when he opposed Juniichiro Koizumi's visit to the Yasukuni Shrine. In 2007, Kazunaga Ito, Mayor of Nagasaki, was shot dead by an unknown gunman during his election campaign. Blackmail incidents suffered by politicians were also frequently reported in the press.
158 Satow, *A Diplomat in Japan*, pp. 59-60, pp. 139-140
159 Hill, *The Japanese Mafia*, p. 176
160 Kobayashi, *First-Class Leaders and Second-Class Bosses*, p. 46, p. 99
161 In addition to a small contingent air and naval force, Japan sent ground troops and armed vehicles of around six hundred men and women for the first time to the war zone in Iraq. Under the three-month rotation system, some 5,500 Japanese army (self-defence force) peacekeepers in total participated in this mission. After a two-and-half year peacekeeping assignment, their withdrawal was completed by July 2006. The ground troops of the Netherlands, UK and Australia were responsible consecutively for the security of Japanese peacekeeping activities.
162 Sigal, *Fighting to a Finish*, p. 2 Emperor Hirohito, of course, signed and sealed the acceptance of the surrender terms on the Potsdam declaration of 26 July 1945 in full.
163 Babb, *Business and Politics in Japan*, pp. 72-74
164 For the detailed analysis on this subject, see Matsusaka, *The Making of Japanese Manchuria, 1904-1932*, pp. 363-377
165 Nishimura, *The Way to Value Land Price in Japan*, p. 10
166 Kosuge, ' The Conditions for Regenerating Property Investment', pp. 66-69
167 Miyazaki, *A Complex Depression*, p. 256, p. 262
168 Hiramoto, *The Story of the Waterfront District*, p. 148

Notes

169 Tsuru, *Thinking of Land Price*, p. 3
170 Noguchi and Tanaka, *Misapprehensions of the Structural Reform Theory*, p. 171
171 Uekusa, *Japan's Final Settlement*, p. 80, p. 92, pp. 192-216, p. 238
172 Yoshitomi, *The Truth of the Japanese Economy*, p. 174, p. 382
173 Kato, *Is the Japanese Economy Sitting and Waiting for an Eventual Death?*, pp. 150-158
174 Tanaka, *A Prelude to Japan's Rebirth*, pp. 213-218
175 Chernow, *House of Morgan*, p. 3
176 Tamaki, *Japanese Banking*, pp. 199-200
177 After various mergers, Mitsubishi UFJ, Mitsui Sumitomo and Mizuho are the three major banking institutions in Japan as of January 2011. At the general traders' level, it further spreads to Mitsubishi, Mitsui, Sumitomo, Itochu and Marubeni. And almost all big companies in Japan could be classified as belonging to one of these groups, or to state bureaucracy, no matter if the actual relationship seems to be weak and negligible. In addition, there are many smaller regional banking networks, which are outside this trend of mergers.
178 Welch, *Jack*, pp. 23-24
179 Ito, 'Excessive Debt behind Risona', *Nihon Keizai Shimbun*, 02/06/2003
180 See Furuya, *The Nippo-Chinese War*, p. 1 & pp. 204–208
181 Tasker, *Will Japan be Ready in Time for the Coming Second Golden Age of Capitalism?*, pp. 18-19; also see Kerr, *Dogs and Demons – The Fall of Modern Japan*, p. 370
182 Thatcher, *opus cit.*, pp. 311-312
183 Mori, *Toshimichi Okubo*, p. 60
184 Sasaki, *Toshimichi Okubo and the Meiji Restoration*, p. 210
185 James, *British Cabinet Government*, p. 16
186 Ishi, *The Japanese Tax System*, p. 4, pp. 12-15
187 See Clark Johnson, *Gold, France, and the Great Depression*, pp. 178-182
188 Hall and Ferguson, *The Great Depression*, p. 2

NOTES

189 Rothermund, *The Global Impact of the Great Depression*, p. 118
190 Togo, *The Inside Story of the Negotiations on the Northern Territory*, p. 93
191 Okazaki, *Diplomatic Strategy*, pp. 94-95
192 Inose, *The Power of the Road*, p. 469
193 Shakespeare, *The Merchant of Venice*, pp. 139-140
194 Kato, *opus cit.*, p. 151
195 Hakamada, *Putin's Russia*, pp. 144-148
196 Grugel, *Democratization*, pp. 90-91
197 Fukuyama, *The End of History and the Last Man*, p. 266, pp. 278-284
198 Only Soviet Russia was ready to abandon the various unequal rights in Manchuria owned by the Tsarist Russia in 1919. Ono, *The Road to People's China*, p. 116. But at the same time, Soviet Russia was still a 'sword of Damocles' to China, as the People's Republic of Mongolia was proclaimed with the Comintern's help (under Stalin's leadership) and overthrew its long established Chinese rule in 1924.
199 Sun, *The Three Principles of the Peoples*, pp. 24-25
200 Matsumura, *The Emperor's Islands*, pp. 11-17
201 Tong, *Christianity in Taiwan*, p. 219
202 See 'Weltmacht Religion', Spiegel Special (Nr. 9/2006), pp. 62-69. The figures were cited from Gordon-Conwell Theological Institute.
203 Chung, *Syncretism*, p. 179
204 The first Japanese ruler who officially acknowledged the right of Christian religious activities in Japan was the thirteenth Shogun of the Muromachi Shogunate, Ashikaga Yoshiteru, aided by a Buddhist (Hokke-shu) monk, Eigen-an, in 1560. This act subsequently caused a significant controversy in the Japanese political and religious scene. Later Yoshiteru was attacked and killed at his palace by his subordinate warlords, Matsunaga Hisahide as their head, in 1565. According to Frois, Hisahide was most influential in obtaining a decree from the imperial court for banning Christianity in Kyoto.

NOTES

205 The strongest of those Buddhist gun-battalions were from Negoro Temple and Saika in Kii/Wakayama. They quickly bought matchlock technology from Tanegashima and improved it while Nobunaga subsequently controlled the other gun-manufacturing locations, Sakai in Izumi/Osaka and Kunitomo in Omi/Shiga. The richest free commercial port of Sakai (also his main naval port since 1575) under Nobunaga's administrative control became, at that time, Japan's second largest city in terms of population, surpassed only by Kyoto. Its biggest trading item was gunpowder (or saltpetre), for which Japan then relied on imports from Portugal – since 1580, Philip II of Spain had taken the throne of Portugal. (Meanwhile, the first Dutch ship – De *Liefde* or the *Love*! – arrived, or rather was cast away, on the coast of Japan in 1600 and opened the trading relationship between Japan and the Netherlands; also with England as on board there was an Englishman, William Adams, who later became naturalised as a Japanese citizen taking the name Miura Anjin, the first and only ever Western samurai.)

Nobunaga invaded Saika/Wakayama-city with a massive army of around 100,000 and signed a peace treaty with its seven leaders in 1577. But it was by no means an outright victory. Taniguchi, *The Details of All Oda Nobunaga's Battles*, pp. 156-159

206 They were (the related Buddhist sects in the incidents): Matsunaga Hisahide (Hokke-shu/Hongan-ji) in 1577, Araki Murashige (Koya-san/Hongan-ji) in 1579 and Sakuma Nobumori (Hongan-ji/Koya-san) in 1580. As soon as Hongan-ji's power and influence were reduced, Koya-san seemed to take over in the camps of armed Japanese Buddhists. Nobunaga launched the war against Koya-san in October 1581 after subjugating Iga/western Mie, and by cleaving their eastern territory.

207 See Frois, *Historia de Japan*, pp. 20-27, pp. 132-138 in the Japanese translation. Dominicans and Franciscans also joined the Japanese mission at this time.

NOTES

208 Mitsuhide's brigade is estimated as 13,000. Nobunaga's eldest son and his appointed successor, Oda Nobutada, was also killed in this *coup d'etat* executed sometime in the early morning of 2 June 1582. Nobutada was already a battle-hardened warlord as the Commander in Chief of the Eastern District Army with his inherited feudal states of Owari/western Aichi and Mino/southern Gifu, and he had further expanded his power east to the former Takeda's territory. In the Japanese historical measurement of power (as an indication of mobilization), he had around 120 *mangoku* and Mitsuhide had around 30 *mangoku* (1 mangoku is 10,000 seki and 1 seki is 0.18 kilo of rice). The most strange story of this alleged rebellion was that there was at least few hours' difference between the estimated times of the attack on Nobunaga and on Nobutada respectively although the distance between the two crime scenes is only a ten-minute walk.

Nobunaga's trusted head of the Kyoto administration/police was Murai Sadakatsu. In addition, Nobunaga usually kept a special guard troops – *Umamawari-shu* or the Horse Guards – of at least 700 ready-to-die samurais by him. He was to join the western and Shikoku district armies to lead a final campaign by himself (most likely from Sakai) departing from Kyoto on 4 June. Some of his battalions could be in the vicinity. It would never have been such an easy opportunity for Mitsuhide to take power and to kill his two living targets of Nobunaga and Nobutada when they were moving separately in a vast area, from twenty kms away. Actually, Nobutada was supposed to be visiting Sakai with Tokugawa Ieyasu on that day but he seemed to change his mind or somebody advised (definitely not Nobunaga) him to stay in Kyoto.

Originally, the imperial court had solicited this visit of Nobunaga to Kyoto. Konoe Sakihisa then headed the Imperial aristocracy. A few authors claimed (sources: diaries of courtiers) that the two men had an argumentative meeting about the selection of traditional Japanese calendars on 1 June, although the general atmosphere was cordial over a ceremonial tea event at Honno-ji. Quite unusually, Ota Gyuichi (1527-1610), the official historian of Nobunaga and usually a very reliable source, completely omitted a description of what happened on this day. (In Europe, the Gregorian calendar had been introduced in February that same year, and Spain/Portugal immediately adopted this new and advanced calculation. It might be the case that Nobunaga had known about this western calendar as well. No one, however, recorded if this matter was discussed at the meeting or not.) The shrewd noble occupied the two highest ranked posts, firstly as the former chief advisor to the emperor – *Kanpaku* – also as the premier – *Dajyo Daijin* –, and had actively led a secretive anti-Nobunaga campaign (which of course, Nobunaga knew about but he continued to see merit in using him as a main 'conduit' to the imperial court). Despite the damage suffered by the falls of many warlords and armed Japanese Buddhists, Konoe Sakihisa would never allow the imperial court to 'vanish' because of Nobunaga's revolution. He was later accused of allowing the rebels' gun-battalions to enter his mansion to shoot at Nobutada who was fighting bravely with his guards at the next-door Nijyo Palace from the rooftops. Sakihisa left the capital after this massacre for his retirement.

209 Ion, *The Cross and the Rising Sun*, pp. 118-124
210 Hobbes, *Leviathan*, p. 29
211 Spinoza, *A Theologico-Politico Treatise*, p. 64, p. 79
212 *Pachinko*, a sort of slot machine, is the only indoor gambling legally allowed in Japan. The business has been expanding during this depression to the main streets of major cities adding to a sleazy atmosphere.
213 Benedict, *The Chrysanthemum and the Sword*, p. 2
214 Fukuzawa, *The Autobiography of Yukichi Fukuzawa*, p. 317
215 Grant, *The Fall of the Roman Empire*, pp. 155-156
216 Liebeschuetz, *Continuity and Change in Roman Religion*, pp. 7-8, pp. 282-283
217 Wells, *The Barbarians Speak*, pp. 259-262

Notes

218 Ferrill, *The Fall of the Roman Empire*, pp. 43-45
219 Kodama, *The History of West Asia*, pp. 48-49, p. 88
220 Davies, *The Years of the Barbarians*, pp. 29-33
221 Lasko, *The Kingdom of the Franks*, pp. 33-34
222 Tours, *The History of Franks*, pp. 142-143
223 Chamberlin, *Charlemagne*, p. 8
224 Pirenne, *Mahomet et Charlemagne*, p. 13, p. 121, p. 133
225 Roesdahl, *The Vikings*, p. 84
226 Hristov, *A History of Bulgaria*, p. 33
227 Hosking, *Russia and Russians*, p. 37, p. 615
228 Kantor, *The Origins of Christianity in Bohemia*, p. 11
229 Ferguson, *The Cash Nexus*, p. 44
230 Roberts, *History of Europe*, pp. 324-325
231 Robbins, *The Eclipse of A Great Power*, p. 22
232 Hobsbawm, *The Age of Capital*, p. 66, p. 88
233 Talleyrand, *Memoirs* (excerpt in English), pp. 3-5
234 Degler, *Out of Our Past*, p. 5, p. 43
235 Brock, *The Evolution of American Democracy*, p. 22
236 Weber, *Confucianism and Taoism*, pp. 8-37
237 Giddens, *The Protestant Ethic and the Spirit of Capitalism*, Introduction xxiii
238 Urban, *The Teutonic Knights*, pp. 51-52
239 Friedrich, *The Other Prussia*, p. 20
240 Almost five hundred years later, the German army, overjoyed by a victory at 'Tannenberg' (so named to wipe-out the past!) in the First World War exploited a gap between two Russian divisions in 1914. As a national hero, Paul von Hindenburg was promoted to field marshal and chief of the general staff, and more importantly, later to be president of the Weimar Republic, and then to accept the new chancellor, Adolf Hitler.
241 Spain relied on the cult of St James (*Santiago*), which would not meet the Catholic unanimity, to launch their reconquest. See Perez, *Histoire de l'Espagne*, p. 54
242 Haffner, *The Rise and Fall of Prussia*, pp. 14-15
243 Brecht, *Martin Luther*, pp. 126-127, p. 389

NOTES

244 Benecke, *Germany in the Thirty Years War*, pp. 2-4
245 Kitchen, *Germany*, p. 13
246 Taylor, *The Course of German History*, p. 110
247 Weber, *The Protestant Ethic and the Spirit of Capitalism*, pp. 53-55
248 Troyat, *Catherine the Great*, p. 11
249 Weber, *opus cit.*, p. 67
250 Inoue, *opus cit.*, Volume I, p. 252
251 Nakamura, *Suttanipata*, pp. 433-434, p. 438
252 Inoue, *opus cit.*, pp. 85-86. He quoted Kumazawa Banzan, a thinker in the Edo era, who made a straightforward remark on this incident: 'By joining the persecution against Christians, unrighteousness without principle of (the Japanese) Buddhists was exposed, and thereby the real value of Buddha's philosophy was lost.' *ibid.*, p.282. Kumazawa was absolutely right but it did not start with this conduct, it had been like this from the beginning, as Professor Inoue explained.

For the origin of the confusion of Japanese Buddhism's link to Shintoism, we must look at Saicho and Kukai – monks who had both studied in China funded by the state – who launched their teachings on the Japanese ruling class based on Esoteric Buddhism which prevailed in early ninth century China, as a sort of 'paramilitary' function to the supreme Shinto 'militarism'. Two original establishments – i.e. Enryaku-ji (805 by Saicho) and Koya-san (816 by Kukai) were only made under the full protection of the powerful Emperor Kanmu, the founder of the imperial court in his new capital Kyoto in 794, and his son, Emperor Saga respectively.

According to *Shoku-Nihon-gi, More Periods of Japan* and *Nihon-Koki, Periods of Later Japan*, Emperor Kanmu had strong contacts with Greater Korea (namely Silla and *Pohai*, the country founded by an ex-Koguryon occupying the current area of northern North Korea, southern Chinese Manchuria/Liaoning-Jilin-Heilongjiang and Russian Primorskiy Kray between 698-926) which was quite unusual for a Japanese emperor.

Later Honen (Shinran as his successor) and Nichiren – both these and other major 'new sect founders' studied in Saicho's traditional Enryaku Temple/ *Tendai-sect* in Kyoto's *Hiei-zan*, which existed as the 'gateway to Japanese Buddhist honours'. By simplifying the teaching, both created the magical charm words of *Nenbutsu* and *Daimoku* respectively, making a massive impact on popular Japanese Buddhism in the thirteenth century.

This entire movement of Emperor Kanmu toward the transfer of the imperial capital during the first ten years to the adjacent strategic location of Nagaoka-kyo/Muko and then to Kyoto was motivated by his 'revolution' against the old establishment in Nara – in particular, the most powerful Fujiwara clan with its traditional family temple of Kofuku-ji who controlled the feudal state of Yamato/Nara until the arrival of Nobunaga. The Japanese aristocracy who were attached so closely to state power, including the Konoe and other so-called five *Sekkan-ke* – Regent and Imperial Advisor Houses – all existed at the heart of the arch-bureaucracy based on this parasitical and die-hard kinship network of the Fujiwara clan who over many years consistently allied themselves with those of the imperial blood and other leading establishment families.

Why did the Fujiwara, Kanmu and other nationalistic Japanese supremacists compromise themselves with their adherence to Chinese Buddhism? The Chinese language, like Latin in Europe, was a prerequisite for diplomatic and official communications in East Asia. And no Japanese ruler before Nobunaga could ignore the fact. Many Japanese-Buddhist monks played an important role as they acted as drafters and/or advisors for writing these official documents for political leaders. No Japanese monks actually went to India to study teaching in Sanskrit or in Pali. Nor did Japanese monks tried to translate classic Chinese texts into ordinary Japanese until Japanese scholars did so in the twentieth century following academic progress in Europe. It was all about Chinese civilisation.

253 Hidaka, *When Japan Has the Presidency?*, p. 335
254 Ramseyer & Rosenbluth, *The Policy of Oligarchy*, p. 73, p. 166
255 Ruoff, *The People's Emperor*, p. 204
256 Bix, *Hirohito and the Making of Modern Japan*, p. 644. The words related to the most popular wartime song of 'Going over the sea' (*Umi yukaba*) to praise the sacrificial deaths to the emperor.
257 Toynbee, *opus cit.*, p. 260
258 Dobbs, *Down With Big Brother*, p. 263
259 Dunlop, *The Rise of Russia and the Fall of the Soviet Empire*, p. 36
260 Satter, *Age of Delirium*, p. 416
261 Meisner, *Mao's China*, p. 260
262 An idea for the Anglo-Japanese Alliance was raised first as a German diplomatic initiative in London for the Anglo-German-Japanese Alliance. Furuya, *The Nippo-Russian War*, pp. 37-41.
263 Royle, *Crimea*, p. 489
264 The German government was serious in selecting the capable Major Meckel for this special assignment in Japan. Helmuth von Moltke (the elder), a renowned Prussian chief of the general staff, was directly involved in this decision. This factor was significant for subsequent political developments in Japan, in particular, the army's sentiment towards Germany. German was regarded as the elite's foreign language in Japanese army cadet schools where many influential officers including Hideki Tojo learned it.
265 Westwood, *Russia Against Japan, 1904-1905*, pp. 33-34
266 Pleshakov, *The Tsar's Last Armada*, p. 261, pp. 269-270
267 Furuya, *opus cit.*, p. 176
268 *Ibid.*, pp. 87-88
269 Lenin, *Imperialism*, p. 69, pp. 131-132
270 Pulzer, *Germany, 1870-1945*, p. 145
271 Gilbert, *The Churchill War Papers*, p. 147
272 Bullock, *Hitler and Stalin*, p. 790
273 Zeidler, 'German-Soviet Economic Relations during the Hitler-Stalin Pact', p. 111

274 Rzheshevsky, *War and Diplomacy*, p. 4
275 Ferguson, *opus cit.*, p. 401
276 Kitchen, *Nazi Germany at War*, p. 303
277 Zentner, *Der Bombenkrieg*, pp. 190-191
278 Cross, *The Battle of Kursk*, pp. 233-234
279 Tamura, *On the Escape from Burma*, pp. 117-124, p. 247
280 Matsuoka, 'Economic Co-operation of Japan and China in Manchuria and Mongolia', p. 12
281 Jones, *Manchuria since 1931*, p. 4
282 The United States banned exports of all necessary war materials, except oil and iron scraps, to Japan under the Shepherd Law, made to deter a possible Japanese advance to North French Indochina, after the surrender of France in June 1940. At first, President Roosevelt insisted on including also oil and iron scraps but he was later persuaded by the State Department to drop this due to its serious effect – equal to a declaration of war on Japan by leaving it without oil resources. After the Japanese military advanced to North French Indochina, the Americans banned the export of iron scraps to Japan. By this time, 'oil' remained the only item for the next US sanction against Japan. (Sejima, *opus cit.*, p. 126)

The Japanese leaders knew, therefore, that a US oil embargo was the most likely outcome of their new military move to South French Indochina (July 1941) and this would mean war against the Allied powers. The reason for this new move to South French Indochina, the Japanese government insisted, was because the oil purchase negotiation with the Netherlands had broken down. In fact, despite the fact that an oil deal could have been secured, Japan broke off the talks after a military geographical survey (needed for the future Japanese invasion) was completed at the oil fields in Dutch Indonesia. (Inoue, *opus cit.*, Volume III, pp. 199-200)

Normally, serious diplomatic decisions should have been discussed at the Supreme Council in the emperor's presence – *Gozenkaigi*. But the Imperial Headquarters-Government

Liaison Conference decided to seek official approval by way of a memorandum to the Throne – *Jyososaika*, which was a lesser form of approval process in writing due to the difference of opinions among the members. Even the navy who were pressing hard for this occupation was divided. (Sejima, *opus cit.*, pp. 151–152)

283 Prior to this move, Fumimaro Konoe, representing the aristocracy, politicians, bureaucracy and special-interest holders including big businesses, gave sanction to a virtual war by 'the essential points for dealing with the current changing world's situation' – *Sekai Jyosei no Suii ni tomonau Jikyoku Shori Yoko*, which was implemented as the first act under his second administration in July 1940. It was then agreed: 1) To enhance the wartime economic system, 2) To strengthen the Tripartite Axis, 3) To sign the nonaggression pact with Soviet Union while developing an 'invincible military force against them', 4) 'To deal with positively' in order to include the colonies of Britain, France, Dutch and Portugal in South East Asia into 'the new (Japanese) order of East Asia', 5) To apply a resolute determination to oust 'forceful interventions from the United States', 6) To execute the operations and to blockade thoroughly in order to complete the conquest of China, 7) To raise the spirit of National Structure – *Kokutai* - and to establish a 'new political system to amalgamate the nations'. (See Inoue, *opus cit.*, pp. 198-199.) Even in Japan's drifting politics, somebody had to decide one way or other. And the only reason he came to power at this particular moment was that, although he was a man with no relevant merit, he could convince the Japanese by his pedigree (the head of Japanese aristocracy and close relative to the emperor) which perfectly matched their political ideology.

But even if he was, as an individual, the most capable politician in the world, the one who was fully capable of modern political reform and diplomacy, could he have persuaded various Japanese militants and others to seek peace with the West? Definitely not. No one had such powers in

Japan! By this time, Japan's political system had completely imploded in real terms. Japan's downfall became inevitable under the last cycle of this inherited ideology, but this time together with a new reality of unprecedented military power, which no other Japanese was able to stand up to the hopeless and rotten political structure. The choice in front of him, therefore, was either to wait until Japan miserably collapsed in chaos or to destroy it altogether with better goals through his own initiative (by using the power of Chinese ideology). Prince Konoe acknowledged his own responsibility by committing suicide after Japan's surrender.

284 Bouissou, *Le Japon depuis 1945*, p. 10
285 De Gaulle, *Memoires d'espoir*, p. 13 According to Charles de Gaulle's idealistic viewpoint, the reason for France going to war since Merovingian times was only when this supreme authority was at stake.
286 Arai, *Records on the Singaporian Front*, p. 190
287 Keynes, *The General Theory of Employment, Interest and Money*, pp. 61-63, p. 104, p. 335
288 Komuro, *The Principles of Capitalism*, pp. 87-90
289 Higham, *The Death of Anglo-Saxon England*, Introduction

Bibliography
In order of the Notes and Text

1. Hu Shih, *The Chinese Renaissance* – The Haskell Lectures, The University of Chicago Press, 1934
2. Hu Shih and Lin Yu-tang, *China's Own Critics* – A Selection of Essays, China United Press, 1931
3. Aristotle, *The Politics*, Translated by T.A. Sinclair, Revised and represented by Trevor J. Saunders, Penguin Books, 1992
4. Lester C. Thurow, *Nihon wa kanarazu Fukkatsu-suru – Japan's Economic Recovery*, Translated into Japanese by Yoichi Yamaoka and Yuko Hirose, TBS Britannica, 1998
5. Karel van Wolferen, *The Enigma of Japanese Power*, Macmillan, 1989
6. Chalmers Johnson, *Japan: Who Governs? – The Rise of the Developmental State*, W.W. Norton, 1995
7. Jacques Gernet, *A History of Chinese Civilization*, Translated by J.R. Foster from *Le Monde chinois*, Cambridge University Press, 1982
8. Michio Tanigawa, *Sekai-Teikoku no Keisei – The Formation of Global Empire*, Kodansha, 1977
9. Jin Guantao and Liu Qingfeng, *Chugoku-Shakai no Cho-Antei-Shisutemu – Prosperity and Crisis – About the Ultra-Stable Structure of Chinese Feudal Society*, Translated into Japanese by Masahiro Wakabayashi and Yujiro Murata, Kenbun Shuppan, 1987 from *Zai-lishide biaoxiang beihou – Dui Zhongguode fenjian shehui chao-wending jiegoude tansuo*, Sichuan Renmin Chubanshe, 1983

Bibliography

10 Mark Elvin, *The Pattern of the Chinese Past*, Stanford University Press, 1973
11 Angus Roxburgh, *The Second Russian Revolution*, BBC Books, 1991
12 Wang Gungwu, *The Chineseness of China*, Oxford University Press, 1991
13 Shigeki Kaizuka, *Chugoku no Kodai-Kokka – The Ancient States in China*, Chuo Koronsha, 1984
14 Samuel P. Huntington, 'The Clash of Civilizations?', *Foreign Affairs*, 1994
15 Arnold J. Toynbee, *A Study of History*, Oxford University Press, 1935 & *A Study of History (Abridgement)*, Oxford University Press, 1946
16 Eiji Mano, *Chuo Azia no Rekishi – The History of Central Asia*, Kodansha, 1977
17 Confucius, *Lunyu – The Analects*, Translated by D.C. Lau, The Chinese University Press, Hong Kong, 1992
18 John K. Fairbank, *The Chinese World Order*, Harvard University Press, 1968
19 Hideki Kajiwara, *Chosen-Shi – The History of Korea*, Kodansha, 1977
20 Ichisada Miyazaki, *Kakyo – The Classic Examination System for Bureaucrats in Feudal China*, Chuo Koronsha, 1963
21 Keishu Saneto, *Chugoku no Moji Kaikaku* – Letter Reform in China, Kurofune Shuppan, 1958
22 Ichisada Miyazaki, *Chugoku Shi – The History of China*, Parts I & II, Iwanami Shoten, 1977
23 C. Northcote Parkinson, *Parkinson's Law*, Penguin Books, 1965
24 Clive H. Church, *Revolution and Red Tape – The French Ministerial Bureaucracy 1770-1850*, Oxford University Press, 1981
25 Hans Bielenstein, *The Bureaucracy of Han Times*, Cambridge University Press, 1980
26 Gwyn Harries-Jenkins, 'Bureaucracy in Great Britain' in *Bureaucracy as a Social Problem*, Edited by: W. Boyd Littrell, Gideon Sjorberg and Louis A. Zurcher, Jai Press, 1983
27 David Mitchell, *Control without Bureaucracy*, McGraw-Hill, 1979
28 Edited by Karl H. Menges and Nelly Naumann, *Language and Literature – Japanese and the Other Altaic Languages*, Harrassowitz Verlag, 1999
29 Masaaki Ueda, *Wakoku no Sekai – The World of Wo*, Kodansha, 1976
30 Kyoaki Kito, *Yamoto Chotei to Higashi Azia – The Yamato Imperial*

Bibliography

Court and East Asia, Yoshikawa-Kobunkan, 1994

31 JaHyun Kim Haboush, 'The Confucianization of Korean Society', *The East Asian Region*, Edited by Gilbert Rozman, Princeton University Press, 1993
32 Sachio Takeda, Hiroshi Miyajima and Sadanori Mabuchi, *Chosen – Korea*, Asahi Shimbunsha, 1993
33 Namio Egami, *Kiba Minzoku Kokka – The States of Horse-Riding People*, Chuo Koronsha, 1991
34 *Nihon Shoki – the Chronicles of Japan*, Edited by Taro Sakamoto, Saburo Ienaga, Mitsusada Inoue and Susumu Ono, Iwanami Shoten, 2002
35 Kiyoshi Inoue, *Nihon no Rekishi – The History of Japan* – Volume I-III, Iwanami-Shoten, 1991
36 Ray Huang, *China – A Macro History*, M.E. Sharpe, 1990
37 Nobukuni Koyasu, *Motoori Norinaga*, Iwanami Shoten, 1992
38 Ryunosuke Akutagawa, '*Kamigami no Bisho*'–The Smile of Gods – in *Hokyonin no Shi – The Death of a Believer*, Shinchosha, 1995
39 Alain Peyrefitte, *The Collision of Two Civilizations – The British Expedition to China 1792-4*, Translated by Jon Rothschild from *L'Empire Immobile ou Le choc des Mondes*, Harper Collins, 1993
40 B.V. Pires, 'Origins and Early History of Macau' in, *Macau – City of Commerce and Culture*, Edited by R.D. Cremer, API Press, 1991
41 Jinichi Yano, *Ahen Senso to Honkon – The Opium War and Hong Kong*, Chuo Koronsha, 1990
42 Ian Nish, 'Japan in Britain's View of the International System, 1919-37', *Anglo-Japanese Alienation 1919-1952* (Edited by Ian Nish), Cambridge University Press, 1982
43 Takeshi Hamashita, *Kindai Chugoku no Kokusaiteki Keiki – Choko Boeki Shisutemu to Kindai Azia – The International Opportunities for the Modern China – Tributary Trade System and the Modern Asia*, Tokyo University Press, 1990
44 Ichisada Miyazaki, *Zui no Yodai – Yandi of Sui*, Chuo Koronsha, 1987
45 G.K. Zhukov, *Vospominaniya i Razmyshleniya*, Izdatelystvo, Agentstva pechati Novosti, Moskva, 1990. English translation, *Reminiscences and Reflections*, Progress Publishers, 1985
46 C. H. Shishkin, *Boyeviye dyeystviya Krasnoy Armii u reki Khalkhin-Gol v 1939 godu*, 1946, *The Battle Actions of the Red Army at Khalkhin-Gol*

River in 1939, 1946 & Konstantin M. Simonov, *Dalyeko na Vostokye: Khalkhin Golyskiye Zapici, Far to East: Khalkhin-Gol Notes*, 1969, Translated in Japanese by Katsuhiko Tanaka, *Nomonhan no Tatakai*, Iwanami Shoten, 2006

47 Jiro Tokuyama, *'Ningen Aku' ni amai Nihon – Japan That Can't Confront 'Human Evils'*, Reitaku University Press, 2000

48 John Owen Haley, *Authority without Power – Law and the Japanese Paradox*, Oxford University Press, 1991

49 Ryuzo Sejima, *Dai-Toa Senso no Jitsuso – The Reality of the Great East Asian War*, PHP Kenkyujo, 1998

50 Arthur Cotterell, *East Asia – From Chinese Predominance to the Rise of the Pacific Rim*, John Murray, 1993

51 Koichi Nomura, *Mou Takuto – Mao Zedong*, Kodansha, 1978

52 Tony Saich, *China: Politics and Government*, Macmillan, 1981

53 Han Shanbi, *To Shohei Den – The Biography of Deng Xiaoping*, Edited and Translated into Japanese by Kiyoshi Ito from *Deng Xiaoping Pingchuan*, Chuo Koronsha, 1988

54 Roy Medvedev, *China and the Super Powers*, Translated by Harold Shukman, Basil Blackwell, 1986

55 Benjamin Schwartz, *Chinese Communism and the Rise of Mao*, Harvard University Press, 1979

56 Susumu Yabuki, *Chugoku no Keizai – The Chinese Economy*, Sososha, 1992

57 Tony Saich, *Governance and Politics of China*, Palgrave, 2001

58 Lynn D Nelson and Irina Y. Kuzes, *Radical Reform in Yeltsin's Russia*, M.E. Sharpe, 1995

59 Sheng Hua, Xuejun Zhang and Xiaopeng Luo, *China: From Revolution to Reform*, Macmillan, 1993

60 Chris Patten, *East and West*, Macmillan, 1998

61 Joseph Fewsmith, 'Reaction, resurgence, and succession: Chinese politics since Tiananmen', *The Politics of China* – Second Edition, Edited by Roderick MacFarquhar, Cambridge University Press, 1997

62 Chang Kai, Jiang Zemin and Zhu Ronji, *Ko Takumin to Shu Youki*, translated in Japanese by Mo Bangfu, Kawaide Shobo Shinsha, 1993

63 John R. Faust and Judith F. Kornberg, *China in World Politics*, Lynne Rienner, 1995

Bibliography

64 Wang Hui, *Chugoku Kanryo Tengoku – A Bureaucratic Paradise of China*, Translated in Japanese by Daizaburo Hashimoto, Iwanami Shoten, 1994 from *Zhong-guo-de 'Guan-chang-bing'*, Zhongguo Funu Chubanshe, 1989
65 Jing Huang, *Factionalism in Chinese Communist Politics*, Cambridge University Press, 2000
66 Chao Wendou, *ugoku Chugoku tobu Nihon – Moving China – Leaping Japan*, Kodansha, 1991
67 John F. Cooper, *Taiwan in Troubled Times*, World Scientific, 2002
68 Anton Galli, *Taiwan R.O.C.: un defi chinois au monde: de la puissance commerciale au centre de technologie*, Weltforum Verlag, 1988
69 Samuel P.S. Ho, *Economic Development of Taiwan, 1860-1970*, Yale University Press, 1978
70 Thomas B. Gold, *State and Society in the Taiwan Miracle*, M.E. Sharpe, 1986
71 Masahiro Wakabayashi, *Taiwan – Democratization in a Divided Country*, Tokyo University Press, 1992
72 Liu Pak-wai, *The Asian Financial Crisis and After – Problems and Challenges for the Hong Kong Economy*, Hong Kong Institute of Asia-Pacific Studies/ The Chinese University of Hong Kong, 1998
73 Peter Ferdinand, 'Hong Kong and the currency board system – A model for a globalizing world?', Edited by Robert Ash, Peter Ferdinand, Brian Hook and Robin Porter, *Hong Kong In Transition*, Routledge Curzon, 2003
74 Norman Miners, *The Government and Politics of Hong Kong*, Oxford University Press, 1981
75 Margaret Thatcher, *The Downing Street Years*, Harper Collins, 1993
76 C.E. Wurtzburg, *Raffles of the Eastern Isles*, Oxford University Press, 1954
77 Jim Baker, *Crossroads – A political history of Malaysia Singapore*, Times Books International, 1999
78 Shinichiro Tanizawa, *Shingaporu no Seikou – The Success of Singapore*, Simul Press, 1981
79 Akihiko Yoshioka, *Indo to Igirisu – India and Britain*, Iwanami Shoten, 1975
80 Goh Keng Swee, *Singaporu no Keizai-Hatten o kataru – The Practice

of Economic Growth, Translated into Japanese by Toshio Watanabe, Hiroshi Takahashi and Shigeo Arai, Imura Bunka Jigyosha, 1983
81   Christopher Tremewan, *The Political Economy of Social Control in Singapore*, Macmillan, 1994
82   Akira Nagazumi, *Tonan Azia no Rekishi – The History of South East Asia*, Kodansha, 1977
83   Keizo Takagi, *Hakka*, Kodansha, 1991
84   Yoshiyuki Tsurumi, *Azia wa naze mazushii-noka, Poverty in Asia*, Asahi Shimbunsha, 1982
85   Katsuo Hiizumi, *Kakyo Konekushion, The Connection of Chinese Merchants*, Shinchosha, 1993
86   Chukun Yu, *Kakyo – The Overseas Chinese*, Kodansha, 1990
87   Wi Jo Kang, *Christ and Caesar in Modern Korea – History of Christianity and Politics*, State University of New York Press, 1998
88   Shiro Yamamoto, *Hara Takashi – Seito Seiji no Akebono – Takashi Hara – The Dawn of Party Politics*, Shimizu Shoin, 1984
89   Gary A. Donaldson, *America At War Since 1945*, Paraeger, 1997
90   John P. Lovel, 'The Military and Politics in Post-war Korea', Edited by Edward Reynolds Wright, *Korean Politics in Transition*, University of Washington Press, Seattle and London, 1975
91   Toshio Watanabe, *Kankoku – South Korea – A Venture Capitalism*, Kodansha, 1986
92   Sing-hwa Cheong, *The Politics of Anti-Japanese Sentiment in Korea: Japanese-South Korean relations under American occupation, 1945-1952*, Greenwood press, 1991
93   Chi Tong-wook, *Kankoku Daitoryo Retsuden, The History of the South Korean Presidents*, Chuo Koron Shinsha, 2002
94   Edward M. Graham, *Reforming Korea's Industrial Conglomerates*, Institute for International Economics, 2003
95   Carl J. Saxer, *From Transition to Power Alternation – Democracy in South Korea, 1987-1997*, Routledge, 2002
96   Naoki Komuro, *Kankoku no Hokai – The Fall of South Korea*, Kobunsha, 1988
97   Robert J. Dvorchak, *Battle for Korea – A History of the Korean Conflict*, Combined Publishing, 2000
98   Nikita Khrushchev, *Khrushchev Remembers*, Translated and Edited by

Strobe Talbott, Penguin Books, 1971
99   Alexander L. George, *The Chinese Communist Army in Action*, Columbia University Press, 1967
100 Dennis D. Wainstock, *Truman, MacArthur and the Korean War*, Greenwood Press, 1999
101 C.R. Attlee, *As It Happened*, Odhams Press, 1956
102 Raymond L. Garthoff, *Assessing the Adversary – Estimates by the Eisenhower Administration of Soviet Intentions and Capabilities*, The Brookings Institution, 1991
103 Peter Lowe, *The Korean War*, Macmillan, 2000
104 Kim, Ilpyong J, *Communist Politics in North Korea*, Praeger, 1975
105 Masayuki Suzuki, *North Korea – Resonance of Socialism and Tradition*, Tokyo University Press, 1992
106 Kim Il-sung, *Kin Nissei Chosakushu – Kim Il-sung's works* Part 1, Translated into Japanese by the North Korean Commission in Japan, Miraisha, 1970
107 Aleksandr Zhebin, *Watashi ga mita Kin Oucho – The Splendour and Poverty of Kim's Empire*, Translated into Japanese by Kanichi Kawai from 'Blesk i Nishcheta Imperii Kimov', Bungei Shunjyu, 1992
108 Donald S. Zagoria, 'Soviet Policy toward North Korea', *North Korea in a Regional and Global Context*, Edited by Robert A. Scalapino and Hongkoo Lee, University of California, 1986
109 Katsuhiro Kuroda, *Chosen Hanto no Seikimatsu – Fin de siecle in the Korean Peninsula*, Toyo Keizai Shimposha, 1992
110 Leon V. Sigal, *Disarming Strangers – Nuclear Diplomacy with North Korea*, Princeton University Press, 1999
111 Robert A. Manning, 'United States-North Korean Relations', Edited By Samuel S. Kim and Tai Hwan Lee, *North Korea and North East Asia*, Rawman & Littlefield, 2002
112 Robert A. Scalapino, 'Korea – The Options and Perimeters', Edited by Tsuneo Akaha, *The Future of North Korea*, Routledge, 2002
113 Lu Xun, *Aqiu Zhengchuan – The Real story of Ah Q -*, Translated in Japanese by Yoshimi Takeuchi, Iwanami-Shoten, 1955
114 Thucydides, *History of the Peloponnesian War*, Translated by Rex Warner, Penguin Books, 1972
115 John W. Dower, *Embracing Defeat*, Allen Lane, 1999

Bibliography

116 Fumito Kanda, *Senryo to Minshu-Shugi – Occupation and Democracy*, Shogakukan, 1988
117 Haruhiro Fukui, 'Electoral Laws and the Japanese Party System', *Japan and the World*, Edited by Gail Lee Bernstein and Haruhiro Fukui, Macmillan, 1988
118 Ian Neary, *The State and Politics in Japan*, Polity Press, 2002
119 Saukichi Tsuda, *Nihonjin no Shisoteki Taido,* The Japanese Philosophical Attitude, Chuo Koron, 1948
120 Stephen S. Large, *Emperor Hirohito and Showa Japan*, Routledge, 1992
121 Masanori Nakamura, *The Japanese Monarchy – Ambassador Joseph Grew and the Making of the 'Symbol Emperor System,' 1931-1991* Translated by Herbert P. Bix, Jonathan Baker-Bates and Derek Bowen, M.E. Sharpe, 1992
122 Klaus Antoni, *Der Himmlische Herrscher und Sein Staat – Essays zur Stellung des Tenno im modernen Japan*, Iudicium, 1991
123 John W. Dower, *Japan In War And Peace*, HarperCollins, 1995
124 Anthony H. Birch, *The British System of Government*, Unwin Hyman, 1990
125 John Stuart Mill, *On Liberty and Other Essays*, Oxford University Press, 1991
126 William De Lange, *A History of Japanese Journalism – Japan's Press Club as the Last Obstacle to a Mature Press-*, Japan Library, 1998
127 Ben-Ami Shillony, *Politics and Culture in Wartime Japan*, Clarendon Press, Oxford, 1981
128 Hajime Karatsu, *Nihon Keizai no Sokojikara – The Potential Power of the Japanese Economy*, Nihon Keizai Shimbunsha, 1997
129 Kenichi Omae, *The Omae Report*, Kodansha, 1993
130 Keitaro Hasegawa, *Ikkyoku Shihai de yomigaeru Nihon-Keizai – The Recovery of the Japanese Economy under Mono-polar Dominance*, Bijinesusha, 2002
131 Terumasa Nakanishi, *Dai-Ei Teikoku Suiboshi – The History of the Decline and Fall of the British Empire*, PHP Kenkyusho, 1997
132 Ronald Dore, *Stock Market Capitalism: Welfare Capitalism – Japan and Germany versus the Anglo-Saxons*, Oxford University Press, 2000, Translated into Japanese as *Nihongata Shihonshugi to Shijyoshugi no Shototsu,* Toyo Keizai Shimposha, 2001

BIBLIOGRAPHY

133 Brian Reading, *Japan – The Coming Collapse*, Weidenfeld Nicolson, 1992
134 David Vogel, *Kindred Strangers – The Uneasy Relationship between Politics and Business in America*, Princeton University Press, 1996
135 NKDR, *Katsuryoku to Miryoku afureru Nihon o mezashite – Seeking for a Japan with Vitality and Charm*, NKDR Press, 2003
136 Ernest Satow, *A Diplomat in Japan, An Inner History of the Critical Years in the Evolution of Japan*, Charles E. Tuttle Co., 1983
137 Peter B.E. Hill, *The Japanese Mafia – Yakuza, Law, and the State*, Oxford University Press, 2003
138 Leon V. Sigal, *Fighting to A Finish – The Politics of War Termination in The United States and Japan, 1945*, Cornell University Press, 1988
139 James Babb, *Business and Politics in Japan*, Manchester University Press, 2001
140 Yoshihisa Tak Matsusaka, *The Making of Japanese Manchuria, 1904-1932*, Harvard University Press, 2001
141 Kiyohiko Nishimura, *Nihon no Jika no Kimarikata – The Way to Value Land Price in Japan*, Chikuma Shobo, 1995
142 Tony Kosuge, 'Fudosan-Toshi-Fukkatsu no Jyoken' – 'The Conditions for Regenerating Property Investments', *Financial Business Review*, Toyo Keizai Shimposha, April Issue 2000
143 Giichi Miyazaki, *Fukugo Fukyo – A Complex Depression*, Chuko Shinsho, 1992
144 Kazuo Hiramoto, *Rinkai Fukutoshin Monogatari – The Story of the Waterfront District*, Chuo Koron Shinsha, 2000
145 Shigeto Tsuru, *Jika o kangaeru – Thinking of Land Price*, Iwanami Shoten, 1990
146 Akira Noguchi & Hideomi Tanaka, *Kozo Kaikakuron no Gokai – Misapprehensions of the Structural Reform Theory*, Toyo Keizai Shimposha, 2001
147 Kazuhide Uekusa, *Nihon no Sokessan – Japan's Final Settlement*, Kodansha, 1999
148 Masaru Yoshitomi, *Nihon Keizai no Shinjitsu – The Truth of the Japanese Economy*, Toyo Keizai Shimposha, 1998
149 Hiroshi Kato, *Zashite Shi o matsu noka Nihon Keizai – Is the Japanese Economy Sitting and Waiting for an Eventual Death?*, Bijinesusha, 2000
150 Naoki Tanaka, *Nihon Keizai Fukkatsu heno Jyokyoku – A Prelude to*

Bibliography

Japan's Rebirth, Nihon Keizai Shimbunsha, 2003

151   Ron Chernow, *The House of Morgan, An American Banking Dynasty and the Rise of Modern Finance*, Touchstone, 1990

152   Norio Tamaki, *Japanese Banking, A History, 1859-1959*, Cambridge University Press, 1995

153   Jack Welch, *Jack – What I've Learned Leading a Great Company and Great People*, Headline, 2001

154   Motoshige Ito, 'Risona no Ura no Kajyo Saimu' – 'The Excessive Debt Behind Risona', *Nihon Keizai Shimbun*, 02/06/2003

155   Tetsuo Furuya, *Nitsu-Chu Senso – The Nippo-Chinese War*, Iwanami Shoten, 1985

156   Peter Tasker, *Nihon wa yomigaeru-ka – Will Japan be Ready in Time for the Coming Second Golden Age of Capitalism?*, Kodansha, 1994

157   Alex Kerr, *Dogs and Demons – The Fall of Modern Japan*, Penguin Books, 2001

158   Toshihiko Mori, *Okubo Toshimichi – Toshimichi Okubo*, Chuo Koronsha, 1969

159   Suguru Sasaki, *Okubo Toshimichi to Meiji Ishin, Toshimichi Okubo and the Meiji Restoration*, Yoshikawa Kobunkan, 1998

160   Simon James, *British Cabinet Government*, Routledge, 1992

161   Hiromitsu Ishi, *The Japanese Tax System*, Clarendon Press, Oxford, 1989

162   H. Clark Johnson, *Gold, France, and the Great Depression, 1919-1932*, Yale University Press, 1997

163   Thomas E. Hall and J. David Ferguson, *The Great Depression – An International Disaster of Perverse Economic Policies*, The University of Michigan Press, 1998

164   Dietmar Rothermund, *The Global Impact of the Great Depression, 1929-1939*, Routledge, 1996

165   Kichiya Kobayashi, *Ichiryu no Ridaa – Niryu no Bosu, – First-Class Leaders and Second-Class Bosses*, Futabasha, 2000

166   Kazuhiko Togo, *Hopporyodo Kosho Hiroku – ushinawareta Godo no Kikai – The Inside History of the Negotiations on the Northern Territory – Five Lost Windows of Opportunity*, Shinchosha, 2007

167   Hisahiko Okazaki, *Nihon Gaiko no Bunsuirei, – Diplomatic Strategy*, PHP Kenkyusho, 2000

168   Naoki Inose, *Doro no Kenryoku, – The Power of the Road*, Bungei

Shunjyu, 2003
169 William Shakespeare, *The Merchant of Venice*, Penguin Books, 1967
170 Shigeki Hakamada, *Puchin no Roshia – Ho-Dokusai heno Michi, Putin's Russia – The Road to a Legal Autocracy*, NTT Shuppan, 2000
171 Jean Grugel, *Democratization*, Palgrave, 2002
172 Francis Fukuyama, *The End of History and the Last Man*, Penguin Books, 1992
173 Shinji Ono, *Jinmin Chugoku heno Michi – The Road to People's China*, Kodansha, 1977
174 Sun Yat-sen, *The Three Principles of the People*, Translated by Frank W. Price, China Cultural Service, 1981
175 Gentaro Matsumura, *The Emperor's Islands*, Lotus Press, 1977
176 Hollington K. Tong, *Christianity in Taiwan: A History*, China Post, 1961
177 David Chung, Edited by Kang-nam Oh, *Syncretism – The religious Context of Christian Beginning in Korea*, State University of New York Press, 2001
178 Katsuhiro Taniguchi, *Oda Nobunaga Kassen Zenroku, The Details of All Oda Nobunaga's Battles – From Okehazama to Honno-ji*, Chuo Koron Shinsha, 2002
179 Luis Frois, *Historia de Japam*, Biblioteca Nacional Lisboa, 1982, Translated into Japanese by Kiichi Matsuda and Momota Kawasaki: *Froisu Nihonshi* 2 'Oda Nobunaga III', Chuo Koron Shinsha, 2000
180 A. Hamish Ion, *The Cross and the Rising Sun, volume 2, The British Protestant Missionary Movement in Japan, Korea, and Taiwan, 1865-1945*, Wilfrid Laurier University Press, 1993
181 Thomas Hobbes, *Leviathan*, Oxford University Press, 1996
182 Benedict de Spinoza, *A Theologico-Political Treatise*, Translated by R.H.M. Elwes, Dover Publications, 1951
183 Ruth Benedict, *The Chrysanthemum and The Sword – Pattern of Japanese Culture*, Routledge & Kegan Paul, 1967
184 Yukichi Fukuzawa, *Fukuou Jiden – The Autobiography of Yukichi Fukuzawa*, Iwanami Shoten, 1978
185 Michael Grant, *The Fall of the Roman Empire*, Weidenfeld & Nicolson, 1996
186 J.H.W.G. Liebeschuetz, *Continuity and Change in Roman Religion*, Oxford University Press, 1979

BIBLIOGRAPHY

187 Peter S. Wells, *The Barbarians Speak – How the Conquered Peoples shaped Roman Europe*, Princeton University Press, 2001

188 Arther Ferrill, *The Fall of the Roman Empire – The Military Explanation*, Thames and Hudson, 1987

189 Shinjiro Kodama, *Nishi Azia no Rekishi – The History of West Asia*, Kodansha, 1977

190 Elspeth Davies, *The Years of the Barbarians – A survey of the World of the Roman Empire in the First Centuries A.D.*, The Pentland Press Ltd, 1988

191 Peter Lasko, *The Kingdom of the Franks – North-West Europe before Charlemagne*, Thames and Hudson, 1971

192 Gregory of Tours, *The History of the Franks*, Translated with Introduction by Lewis Thorpe, Penguin Books, 1974

193 Russell Chamberlin, *Charlemagne – Emperor of the Western World*, Grafton Books, 1986

194 Henri Pirenne, *Mahomet et Charlemagne – Byzance, Islam et Occident dans le haut Moyen Age*, Jaca Book, 1986

195 Else Roesdahl, *The Vikings*, Second Edition, Translated into English by Susan M. Margeson and Kirsten Williams, Penguin Books, 1998

196 Hristo Hristov, *A History of Bulgaria*, Sofia Press, 1985

197 Geoffrey Hosking, *Russia and Russians – A History from Rus to the Russian Federation*, Allen Lane, 2001

198 Marvin Kantor, *The Origin of Christianity in Bohemia – Sources and Commentary*, Northwestern University Press, 1990

199 Niall Ferguson, *The Cash Nexus – Money and Power in the Modern World 1700-2000*, Allen Lane, Penguin Press, 2001

200 J. M. Roberts, *History of Europe*, Penguin, 1997

201 Keith Robbins, *The Eclipse of A Great Power – Modern Britain 1870-1992*, Pearson Education, 1994

202 Eric Hobsbawm, *The Age of Capital – 1848-1875*, Abacus Books, 1997

203 Charles Maurice de Talleyrand-Perigord, *Memoirs* concerning The Commercial Relations of the United States with England, Thomas B. Watt & Co, 1890

204 Carl N. Degler, *Out of Our Past, The Forces That Shaped Modern America*, Third Edition, HarperPerennial, 1984

205 William R. Brock, *The Evolution of American Democracy*, The Dial Press, New York, 1970

Bibliography

206 Max Weber, *Confucianism and Taoism*, Abridged by M. Morishima, Translated by M. Alter and J. Hunter, London School of Economics, 1984

207 Max Weber, *The Protestant Ethic and the Sprit of Capitalism*, Translated by Talcott Parsons, Introduction by Anthony Giddens, Counterpoint, 1985 and for the German original version, *Die protestantische Ethik und der Geist des Kapitalismus*, area verlag gmbh, 2005

208 William Urban, *The Teutonic Knights – A Military History*, Greenhill Books, 2003

209 Karin Friedrich, *The Other Prussia – Royal Prussia, Poland and Liberty, 1569-1772*, Cambridge University Press, 2000

210 Joseph Perez, *Histoire de L'Espagne*, Fayard, 1996

211 Sebastian Haffner, *The Rise and Fall of Prussia*, Translated by Ewald Osers from *Preussen ohne Legende*, Phoenix, 1980

212 Martin Brecht, *Martin Luther – Road to Reformation 1483-1521 – Sein Weg zur Reformation*, Translated by James L. Schaaf, Fortless Press, 1993

213 Gerhard Benecke, *Germany in the Thirty Years War*, Edward Arnold, 1978

214 Martin Kitchen, *Germany*, Cambridge University Press, 1996

215 A.J.P. Taylor, *The Course of German History, A Survey of the Development of German History since 1815*, Methuen, 1961

216 Henri Troyat, *Catherine the Great*, Translated by Emily Read, Phoenix Press, 1979

217 Translated by Hajime Nakamura, *Budda no Kotoba* – Suttanipata, (Buddha's Teachings), Iwanami Shoten, 1984

218 Yoshiki Hidaka, *Nihon ni Daitoryo ga Tanjyo suru Hi – When Japan has the Presidency?*, Shueisha, 1998

219 J. Mark Ramseyer & Frances M. Rosenbluth, *The Politics of Oligarchy – Institutional Choice in Imperial Japan*, Cambridge University Press, 1995

220 Kenneth J. Ruoff, *The People's Emperor – Democracy and the Japanese Monarchy, 1945-1995*, Harvard University Press, 2001

221 Herbert P. Bix, *Hirohito and the Making of Modern Japan*, Duckworth, 2001

222 Michael Dobbs, *Down with Big Brothers – The Fall of the Soviet Empire*, Alfred A. Knopf, 1997

223 John B. Dunlop, *The Rise of Russia and the Fall of the Soviet Empire*,

Princeton University Press, 1993
224 David Satter, *Age of Delirium – The Decline and Fall of the Soviet Union*, Alfred A. Knopf, 1996
225 Maurice Meisner, *Mao's China – A History of the People's Republic*, The Free Press, 1977
226 Tetsuo Furuta, *Nichi-Ro Senso, The Nippo-Russian War*, Chuo Koronsha, 1994
227 Trevor Royle, *Crimea –The Great Crimean War 1854-1856*, Abacus, 1999
228 J.N. Westwood, *Russia Against Japan, 1904-05 – A New Look at the Russo-Japanese War*, Macmillan, 1986
229 Constantine Pleshakov, *The Tsar's Last Armada – The Epic Journey to the Battle of Tsushima*, The Perseus Press, 2002
230 V.I. Lenin, *Imperialism: The Highest Stage of Capitalism*, Introduction by Norman Lewis and James Malone, Pluto Press, 1996
231 Peter Pulzer, *Germany, 1870-1945 – Politics, State Formation, and War*, Oxford University Press, 1997
232 Martin Gilbert, *The Churchill War Papers*, Volume I, 'At the Admiralty, September 1939-May 1940', Heinemann, 1993
233 Alan Bullock, *Hitler and Stalin – Parallel lives*, Fontana Press, 1998
234 Manfred Zeidler, 'German-Soviet Economic Relations during the Hitler-Stalin Pact', in *From Peace To War – Germany, Soviet Russia and the World, 1939-1941*, Edited by Bernd Wegner, Berghahn Books, 1997
235 Oleg A. Rzheshevsky, *War and Diplomacy – The Making of the Grand Alliance*, Translated by T. Sorokina, Harood Academic Publishers, 1996
236 Martin Kitchen, *Nazi Germany at War*, Longman, 1995
237 *Der Bombenkrieg – Feuerstrum Über Deutschland*, Edited by Christian Zentner, Otus Verlag, 2005
238 Robin Cross, *The Battle of Kursk – Operation Citadel 1943*, Penguin Books, 1996
239 Shotaro Tamura, *Biruma Dashutsuki – On the Escape from Burma*, Tosho Shuppan, 1985
240 Yosuke Matsuoka, 'Economic Co-operation of Japan and China in Manchuria and Mongolia, Its Motives and Basic Significance', Translated from a pamphlet published by the Chunichi Bunka Kyokai (The Sino-Japanese Association of Manchuria), Dairen, 1929

241 F.C. Jones, *Manchuria since 1931*, Royal Institute of International Affairs, 1949
242 Jean-Marie Bouissou, *Le Japon depuis 1945*, Armand Colin, 1997
243 Charles de Gaulle, *Memoires d'espoir*, Plon, 1999
244 Mitsuo Arai, *Shingaporu Senki, – Records on the Singaporean front*, Tosho Shuppan, 1984
245 John Maynard Keynes, *The General Theory of Employment, Interest and Money*, Macmillan, 1936
246 Naoki Komuro, *Shihonshugi Genron – The Principles of Capitalism*, Toyo Keizai Shimposha, 1997
247 N.J. Higham, *The Death of Anglo-Saxon England*, Sutton Publishing, 1997

Index

Abe, Shinzo 239–240
Acheson, Dean 136
Adalbert, Slavnik 296
Adams, William 354*n.205*
administrators, elite 49, 50–54
agrarian economy: areal limitation
   93; Chinese communists 102, 105,
   107, 272; Chinese New Year link
   46; Confucian principles 56, 58;
   departure from 97; economic cycles
   101; historic roots 14, 32, 33, 35,
   44–45, 333; Japan 71; traditional
   farming 115; Vietnam 132; Yin-Zhou
   revolution 42, 43
Akechi Mitsuhide 281, 282, 283,
   355*n.208*
Akiyama, Saneyuki 323
Akutagawa, Ryunosuke 75–76, 235
Alexius I 303
Altaic tribes 60, 345*n.31*
Ama-terasu-o-mi-Kami 273
Amakudari 54
Amakusa Shiro-Tokisada 74
anti-communism 107, 138
Antoni, Klaus 176
Anyang 38
Aoki, Mikio 239
Arabs: Abbasid 29; Umayyad 294, 296
Arai, Mitsuo 333
Araki Murashige 354*n.206*

arch-bureaucracy:
   China 49, 50–54, 57, 58, 72, 87,
      162–163, 265, 272;
   Japan: banking system 216–218;
      business 54, 189–190, 218–221;
      class system 87; financial policies
      216–221, 227, 229, 231, 334–
      335; lack of opposition 197; legal
      system 51; media restrictions 183,
      188; political decision-making 72,
      87–88, 90, 91, 169–173, 175–
      179, 200, 203, 219, 227; political
      reforms 53–54, 283, 315–317,
      332, 337, 346*n.52*; public sector
      reforms 219, 257, 258–259; and
      religion 275
   modern China 112, 112–117;
      North Korea 161, 162; socialist
      revolutions 319–320
Argentine 230
Aristotle, political ideology 21–22
Armitage, Richard 239
Asahi Shimbun 182, 243
Asai Nagamasa 279
Asakura Yoshikage 279
Ashikaga Shogunate 73
Ashikaga Yoshiteru 353*n.204*
Asoka, Emperor 312
Assumption Cathedral, Vladimir 295
Attlee, Clement 152

INDEX

augury 38, 39, 42
Australia 297
Austria, annexation 325
Austrian-Habsburg 297
Azuchi 281, 282

Babb, James 199
bad debts, Japan 12
Baltic region 304–305
Bank of International Settlement (BIS) 208
Bank of Japan 211, 227
barbarian tribes 59
Beidaihe 115
Beijing University 270
Benecke, Gerhard 306
Benedict, Ruth 287
Berlin, WWII 328, 329–330
Bielenstein, Hans 52
'Big Bang' reforms 222–223, 225–226, 235
Birch, Anthony H. 178
Bix, Herbert 316
Bogolyubsky, Andrey 295
Bolshevism 330
Bongwan system 62
Book of Changes 42, 47
Book of Rituals & Ranks 42
Book of Songs 42
Borneo 130
Botaihou 194
Bouissou, Jean-Marie 332
Boxer Rebellion 321
Brecht, Martin 306
Brentano, Lujo 303
Brezhnev, Leonid 238
Britain: Big Bang reforms 222, 225; Christian philosophy 284–285, 297; economic expansion 298; empire 297–298; financial policies 227–228; Hong Kong 121, 122; and Japan 78–79, 177, 321, 322–323, 324, 334; opium trade and war 77–78; Satsuma-British war 223–224; Singapore 124, 126, 127; WWI 79, 80; WWII 325, 326, 327, 331
British East India Company 124
Brock, William 300
bronze 36, *37*, 38, 39, 45
Brookings Institute, Washington 223
Buddhism: China 28, 48, 58, 60, 313, 358*n.252*; Christianity conversion analysis 338; Japanese 67, 168, 184, 286–287, 287–288, 313–314, 358–359*n.252*; Nobunga conflict 278–279, 354*n.205*, 354*n.206*; spread from India 312–313
Bulgaria 294–295
Bungei Shunjyu 184–185
bureaucratic officials: examinations 47, 48, 50, 62; financial policies 227, 228; France 169–170; Hong Kong 121–122; Japan 51, 53–54, 72, 87, 89–91, 169–171, 178–179, 216–217, 229, 315–316; Korea 62, 66; modern China 112; Zhou dynasty 42; *see also* arch-bureaucracy
Burma (Myanmar) 132, 156, 330
Bush, George W. 159
business: arch-bureaucracy 54, 189–190, 218–221; ethos 307; leaders, Japan 188–191; organised crime 192; 'privatisation' 12, 250–253, 257–259

Cabinet Planning Board 24
Calvin, Jean 303
Cambodia 132, 264
Canada 297
Canton 30, 78
capitalism: business ethos 307; China 97, 98, 107, 115, 320; expansion, effect on East 12–14, 233–234, 236, 265; global, dangers 233–236, 263–264; Hong Kong 122, 133; Japan 220, 221, 226, 228, 234–235, 260; Taiwan 117–118; technology impact

Index

263; United States 156, 190, 299
Caracalla, Emperor 288
Carter, Jimmy 157
Catherine the Great 296, 307
Catholicism 305, 306, 308, 357*n.241*
CCP (Chinese Communist Party) 103, 104, 270, 271
Celestial Empire 70
Chaebol 144
Chamberlin, Russell 293
Chang Myon, Prime Minister 139
Chang-an 60, 67
Chao Wendou 114
Charlemagne, Emperor 294
Charles, Carolingian king 294
Chen Shou 59
Chen Shui-bian 119
Cheng-Zhou-Cheng 39
Cheong, Sung-hwa 142
Chiang Ching-kuo 118
Chiang Kai-shek 117, 270, 276
China: areal limitation 93; boat people 132; capitalism 97, 98, 107, 115, 235, 308, 320; centralised power 25–26, 40, 114; Chinese name for 20–21; Christian political philosophy 336; Christianity 276; communism 98, 102–107, 109–110, 272, 276, 317–318, 320; decentralisation 114; democracy 97, 112–113, 124, 308, 318, 320; divided states 25, 26, 28, 114; economic decline 35; economic growth 260–261, 301; expansionist policies 44–45, 53, 93, 98, 261, 333; factionalism 103–104, 114, 116, 162–163, 333; first political system 38–40; foreign investment 108, 110–111, 118, 133–134; global capitalism 234, 235, 236, 260, 265–266; as global power 20, 92, 235; historic expansion 25–30, 33, 40; historic values 14, 21; Hong Kong 121–124; industrialization 96, 101–102, 105, 106, 107; invades Japan 72–73; and Korea 64, 142, 153, 156–157, 159–161; Korean War 148–149, 150–153; Manchuria 331; May Fourth movement 270; modernisation 19–20, 101, 104–107, 115–117, 269–272, 337; Mongolia, People's Republic 353*n.198*; national identity 43; national pride 20, 35; Nippo-Chinese War 219, 333–334; nuclear weapons 158, 159, 261; People's Republic formed 102; political core 44–49, 87; political ideology 20–24, 26, 27–29, 43, 98, 302–303; political protest 109, 162, 317–318; private sector growth 260; relations with Japan 241–243; relations with Taiwan 118, 119, 120; religion 277, 320; revolution 31–33, 40, 97–98, 109, 269–272, 318, 320; rift with Soviets 104, 106; Singapore links 124–125, 126; Sino-Japanese War (1895) 79, 101, 323, 324; socialist market economy 108–112, 123, 160, 260; Sun Yat-sen 21, 80, 269–272; support from Russia 102, 104, 147, 148–149; territorial waters 261; trade with Japan 82–83; trade with United States 123–124; unification 33; Vietnam invasion 106; Westernisation 13, 14, 200; WWI 270; Yasukuni Shrine 241–244
Chinese Communist Party (CCP) 103, 104, 270, 271
Chinese language 38, 39, 46–47, 60, 359*n.252*
Chinese Nationalist Party (KMT) 102, 270
Cholla province 143
Chollima economic policy 155
Chosen Chisso plants 148
Choshu clan 78, 168, 322
Chosogabe Motochika 282

INDEX

Christianity: Bulgaria 294–295; Catholicism 305, 306, 308, 357*n.241*; China 276; Europe 293–295, 296, 306–308; Japan 73–74, 277–278, 280–281, 283–284, 287–288, 312, 337, 338, 353*n.204*, 354*n.207*, 358*n.252*; Korea 135, 277, 336; and legal system 307, 309; Lithuania 304; Philippines 130; political philosophy influence 284–285, 336–338; Protestantism 297, 303, 305, 306, 307, 308, 338; Roman Empire 288–292, 293, 294, 296; Russia 295, 296, 307; and social science 310, 312; Taiwan 276–277; United States 299
Chronicle of Wei 59
Chronicles of Japan, The 70
Chuche policy 155
Chun Doo-hwan 141, 142
Chung, David 277
Chungchong province 144
Chuo Koron 184–185
Church, Clive 52
Churchill, Winston 326
civil service 48, 49, 51, 87, 179, 199, 227
clan system: China 55, 56, 57, 62, 64, 271; Japan 78–79, 85, 359*n.252*; rules 86
Clark Johnson, H. 236
Clausewitz, Karl von 97
climate change 98, 263
Clinton, Bill 158, 195, 230
Clovis, King 293
Cold War 155
colonisation 26–27, 29, 30, 33, 129–130
Comintern 103, 270, 353*n.198*
Commonwealth of Independent States 319
communism: and bureaucracy 319–320; Chinese 98, 102–107, 109–110, 272, 276, 317–318, 320–321; introduction in China 35, 102, 270; North Korea 148, 154, 156; Russia 156, 318–319; Zhonghua name kept 21
Confucianism 40–41: agricultural communities 56–57; banned 57; China 302–303; creative 24; immigration impact 129; Japan 68, 70; Korea 62, 65, 66, 143; restored 58; Taiwan 276
Conrad of Masovia, Duke 304
Constantine the Great 288–292
Constantinople 292, 295
Copenhagen, battle of 79
Cordoba, Caliphate of 296
Cotterell, Arthur 101
crime syndicates, Japan 191–194
Crimean War 321
Cross, Robin 328
crusades 303–304, 305
Cuban Missile Crisis 19
cultural differences, Western ignorance 20
Cultural Revolution 103
Czechoslovakia 326

Daewoo 144
Daoism 58
Datsu-A Nyu-Ou 199
Davies, Elspeth 291
Dayitong 25
De concept 86
de Gaulle, Charles 363*n.285*
De Lange, William 182
Degler, Carl 299
democracy: China 97, 112–113, 124, 308; East Asia 264–266, 336; global 263, 264–265; Hong Kong 122, 124; Japan 138, 168–172, 174, 176, 185–186, 193, 195–196, 201, 213–214, 248–250, 308, 315, 332, 339–340, 350*n.146*; North Korea 153–154; Pericles' principles 163–164; Singapore 128; South Korea 137, 140, 141–142, 143–144; Taiwan 117–121
Democratic Party of Japan (DPJ)

Index

196–197, 247, 248–249, 256
Democratic People's Republic of Korea *see* North Korea
Democratic Progressive Party 118, 119–120
Deng Xiaoping 103, 106–107, 109, 110, 122
diplomatic protocol 76
Dobbs, Michael 318
Donaldson, Gary 136
Dore, Ronald 188
Dower, John 167
DPJ (Democratic Party of Japan) 196–197, 247, 248–249, 256
dynastic regimes 28–30, 31–33, 40, 101
East Asia: Buddhism spread 312–313; China as historic power 26, 28–29; 'Chinese' ideology 43, 260–262; Christian political philosophy 336; democracy 264–266; economic dynamism 24; economic problems 11, 12–13, 301–302; export markets 261–262; factional politics 333; global capitalism 234, 236, 260, 263; nationalism 93–94; passive stance 14–15; political reforms 161–163, 321, 337; US role 300–302; Westernisation 13–14
Eastern Europe 35, 59, 108, 112, 118, 162, 305–306
Eastern Zhou dynasty 28
Economic Finance Consultative Conference 249
economic problems: 'Big Bang' reforms 222–223, 225–226, 235; China 98, 105–106; global capitalism 233–236, 261–262; global financial bubble 123, 205, 207, 213; Great Depression 11, 202, 208, 236; implosion 11, 101, 236; Japan 22–25, 96, 138, 185–187, 189, 199, 203–214, 218–221, 334–335; South East Asia 143, 144
economy: cycles 30–36, 97, 101; dynamism 24; growth 33; Hong Kong 121–122, 133; modern developments 113–117; North Korea 153, 155–157, 158, 160–162; politics link 21–23, 31; post-WWII Japan 177; reforms and management 336; Singapore 127, 133; socialist market economy 107–112, 123–124, 160; South East Asia 133–134, 138; South Korea 136, 140–145; United States 299–300; Vietnam 132
Eden, Anthony 301
Egami, Namio 66
Eigen-an 353*n.204*
Eisenhower, Dwight 152–153
Elvin, Mark 33
energy consumption 98
Enryaku Temple 279, 359*n.252*
enterprise zones 108
Estonia 304
Europe: Americas, economic influence 305; Christian political philosophy 284–285; empires 34–35, 75, 76, 92–93, 129, 261; European Union (EU) 233–234, 235, 261–262; expansion 92–93, 101, 292–298, 306; political evolution 337–338; Roman Empire 288–292
expansion: capitalist 12–14, 76, 101; China 25–30, 44–45, 98; Chinese immigration 129–130; European 92–93, 101, 292–298; Roman Empire 292; towards Japan 59, 60
Export Finance Corporation 215
Exxon 301

factions: Chinese agricultural expansion 333; Communist China 103–104, 114, 116, 162–163; Japan 84–85, 114, 169–171, 176, 222, 237, 239, 250, 252–253, 256, 332, 335; North Korea 154, 155; South Korea 143; Taiwan 114, 120

INDEX

faija 57
Fairbank, John K. 44
family values/networks 55, 56–57, 62, 64, 129
fanaticism, Japan 83–84
'Far Eastern' civilization 44
farmland, family asset 57
Federal Reserve Bank 228
Federation of the Japanese Economic Groups (FJEG) 191
Fedorenko, Nikolai 152
feng shui 38
Ferguson, Niall 297
Ferrill, Arthur 290
feudal (*fengjian*) principles 39, 42, 175
Fewsmith, Joseph 110
Financial Business Review 205
Financial Function Resuscitation Act (1998) 258
Financial Investment Fund 227
Financial Services Agency 216, 227
Financial Times 248
Finland 304, 327
Five Barbarians, Sixteen Kingdoms of 345*n.32*
Five Canons/Classics 41–42
Five Dynasties period 27
Five Kings of Wo period 60–61
Former Han dynasty 28
France: bureaucratic officials 169–170; Great Depression 236; historic expansion 293–294; Japan 78; National Employers' Federation 127; post-WWII politics 333; reasons for war 363*n.285*; revolution 51–52; Roman Empire 290–291; support for US independence 19; WWII 325–326
Franklin, Benjamin 300
Frederick of Prussia, King 307
free market, US 189–190, 228
freedom: China 109; Japan 168, 179, 181, 184, 274–275; North Korea 153–154; Roman Empire 292
French Indochina 331, 361–362*n.282*
Frois, Luis 281
Fujian province 118
Fujii, Haruho 251–252
Fujiwara clan, as the origin of Japanese aristocracy 359*n.252*
Fujiwara-no Kamatari 67
Fukuda, Takeo 189, 237–238
Fukuda, Yasuo 239
Fukui, Haruhiro 169
Fukuyama, Francis 265
Fukuzawa, Yukichi 181, 199, 287–288, 350*n.146*
Furuya, Tetsuo 219

Gansu Province 115
Gao Zianzhi, General 29
Geming 31
General Electric 217
Genghis Khan 30
George, Alexander 152
Germany: Clovis conquers 293; economy 188; historic expansion 303–306; industrial power 325, 328; Japanese army modernisation 322, 360*n.264*; Nazis 325–330; political terrorists 193; post-WWII politics 333; religion 303, 305, 306; Roman empire 290, 293; Sword Brothers 304; Teutonic Knights 304, 305; WWI 236, 357*n.240*; WWII 88, 89, 198, 242, 324–330
Gernet, Jacques 28
Giddens, Anthony 303
global economy: capitalism in danger 233–236, 263–264; Chinese role 111, 120, 123–124, 260; climate change 263; effect on politics 272; European emigration 298; financial bubbles 207–208; oil prices 141, 189; technology impact 263, 264; Western control over 13–14

INDEX

global power: Chinese advances 20, 28, 29, 92; European empires 34–35, 75, 85, 92–93; universal values 264
global warming 98, 263
Goebbels, P.J. 327–328
Goering, Hermann 326
Goh Chok Tong 128
Gokuraku Jyodo belief 278
Gorbachev, Mikhail 107, 318–319
government business, 'privatisation' 12, 250–253, 257–259
Grant, Michael 288
Great Depression 11, 202, 208, 236
Great Leap Forward 105–106
Great Wall 57
Greece 12, 291–292
Grew, Joseph 174–175
Grugel, Jean 264–265
Guangdong province 27, 114–115, 118
Guizhou Province 115
Gutoff, Reuben 217

Hamaguchi, Osachi 201
Hamashita, Takeshi 82
Han dynasty: capital destroyed 32; Chinese ideology 41, 43; expansion 27, 28; foundation 102; political power 30, 43, 48; stagnation 59; takes power 58; Vietnam 132
han-zi characters 38, 43
Hara, Takashi Davide 135–136, 168, 349 *n.103*
Harries-Jenkins, Gwyn 52
Hasegawa, Keitaro 187
Hashimoto, Ryutaro 212, 222, 237
Hatoyama, Ichiro 243
Hayami, Yuu 211
Hayashi Razan 312
Hegel, Georg 201, 285
Heisei Ishin 186
Hidaka, Yoshiki 315
Higham, N.J. 337
Hill, Peter 194

Himiko 59
Hindenburg, Paul von 357 *n.240*
Hirohito, Emperor 174, 175, 199, 244–245, 316, 351 *n.162*
Hiroshima 198
Hitler, Adolf 89, 325–328, 330, 357 *n.240*
Hobbes, Thomas 284
Hobsbawm, Eric 298
Hojyos, Japanese warlords of 280
Hokke-shu 283, 353 *n.204*, 354 *n.206*
Honda, Soichiro 177
Honen 359 *n.252*
Hong Kong 97, 118, 121–124, 133
Hongan-ji 354 *n.206*
Honno-ji 283, 356 *n.208*
horse-riding tribes 60, 66
Hosokawa, Morihiro 195
Hristov, Hristo 294
Hu Jintao 115, 116
Hu Shih 13, 270, 272, 343 *n.2*
Hu Yaobang 103, 107, 109
Huabei plains 39, 42
Huawai 43
Hungary 294
Huntington, Samuel 40–41
Hwanung 154–155
hyperinflation 31–32
Hyundai 144, 145

Iemitsu, Shogun 74
Ikeda, Hayato 229, 243
Ikko sect 278–280
Imai, Takashi 251
immigration: boat people 132; China 30, 55, 129–130, 344 *n.29*; Japan 66, 74, 132, 245; New World 297–298, 300; Singapore 124–125; to South East Asia 128–134
imperial system 26–27
Inchon 150
India: Buddhism 312–313; historic contact 26, 27, 28; Islamic expansion

INDEX

128–129; Myanmar immigration 132; opium trade 77; US Arms Lending Act 127
individualism: Japan 191, 337; North Korea 154
Indonesia 129, 131, 132–133, 348*n.98*, 361*n.282*
industrial revolution 33–35, 76, 297
industrialisation: China 96–97, 101–102, 105, 106, 107, 133; eastern nations 98; Germany 325; Japan 79–82, 96, 101, 176–180, 215; Korea 66, 96, 140, 144; South East Asia 133; Taiwan 96, 117–118, 120, 133; United States 299
Industry Resuscitation Scheme (IRS) 220
Inose, Naoki 251, 253
Inoue, Kiyoshi 314, 358*n.252*
intelligence: Japan 88, 89, 202; North Korea 148; Russia 88, 89; South Korea 139, 141; United States 246
interest rates, Japan 211–212, 230–233
Inukai, Tsuyoshi 81
Iraq 196–197, 264, 351*n.161*
Ireland, debt crisis 12
iron: agriculture 58; ships 34, 282; technology development 26, 28, 30, 34, 274, 313; weapons 66, 274, 279, 280, 354*n.205*
irrigation systems 58
Ise shrine 243, 273
Ishihara, Nobuaki 252
Ishihara, Shintaro 252
Ishii, Hiromitsu 228–229
Ishii, Koki 193
Ishiyama-Hongan Temple 278
Islamic influences 55, 128–129, 130, 133, 294, 296
Istanbul (Constantinople) 292, 295
Italy, WWII 326, 329
Ito, Hirobumi 78,172
Ito, Kazunaga 351*n.157*
Ito, Moroshige 218

Itochu 352*n.177*
Ivan IV, Tsar (The Terrible) 19
Izanagi and Izanami 273

James, Simon 227
Japan: Anglo-Japanese Alliance 321, 322, 324, 334; army modernisation 322, 360*n.264*; banking system 211–218, 227, 231, 234, 238, 254–259, 352*n.177*; 'Big Bang' reforms 222–223, 225–226, 235; Buddhism 67, 168, 184, 286–288, 313–314, 358–359*n.252*; bureaucratic controls on business 189–191; business leaders 188–191; calendar 179–180, 356*n.208*; canons 70; capitalism 220, 221, 226, 228, 234–236, 260, 308; Chinese History Studies 343*n.7*; Chinese ideology 66–76; Christian political philosophy 336, 337, 338; *Chronicle of Wei* 59; civil war 72, 73; clans 78–79, 85, 359*n.252*; class rankings 86–87; Confucianism 68, 70; defence spending 247–248; deregulations 250; economic depression 232; economic growth 177, 189, 203, 234; economic reforms 222–226, 238–240, 249–253, 256; emperor 67, 70, 72, 167–168, 172–176, 286, 316, 336–337; employment market 255; exports 177, 189–190, 209, 214, 231, 238; fanaticism 83–84; financial bubble bursts 207–214, 218, 232; financial policies 226–230, 231; foreign currency reserves 123; foreign economic aid 324; foreign influence rehabilitation 95; Genji clan 72, 85; Heiki clan 85; historic links with China 28, 29; historic values 14, 21; Land Standard 204–205, 209–211, 218; language 60; legal system 91–92, 180–181, 183, 192, 194, 220, 309;

388

INDEX

management systems 216–218; post-WWII politics 167–179, 186–187, 194–197, 203–205, 236, 332; public sector reform 257–259; public spending/debt 221, 226, 230–233, 251, 257, 259; railways 201; regional government 259; relations with China 82–83, 241–243, 261, 269; relationship with Russia 238–239, 262; religion (*see also* individual religions) 272–285, 312, 336–337, 353*n.204*; renaming 339; Road Corporation fiasco 250–253, 258; Russo-Japanese war 79, 95, 321–324, 334; Satsuma-British war 223–224; seclusion policy 74; shadow cabinet 248–249; Sino-Japanese war 79, 101, 323, 324; and social science 309–312, 317; and South Korea 135–136, 138, 140, 142–143, 145, 241–242; stagnation 231; Sun Yat-sen exile to 269; sword carrying 349*n.131*; Taika Reform 66–67, *69*; taxation 228–229, 258; technology 68, 73–75, 84, 176–177, 185, 187, 309; territorial waters 261; Thai immigration 131–132; trade with US 78, 177, 184, 189, 190, 209; trading networks 82–83; unification 283; US relationship 25, 78, 152, 170, 173, 194–197, 203, 239, 247, 301; Westernisation 13–14, 73–74, 78–79, 81, 84, 200; WWI 79–80; WWII 82, 89–92, 94, 102, 198–199, 240–241, 244, 324–325, 330–332, 346*n.53*, 361–362*n.282*, 362–363*n.283*; Yasukuni Shrine 240–245; *see also* arch-bureaucracy
Japan Development Bank 215
Japan Export Import Finance Bank 215
Japan Socialist Party (JSP) 194, 196
Jiang Zemin 103–104, 109, 111, 115, 116

Jiji news agency 182
Jiji-Shimpo 181, 199
Jin Guantao 31
Jing Huang 114
Jiyu (Liberal) Party 195
Jodo-Shin (*Ikko*) sect 278
Johnson, Chalmers 24–25
JR East Japan 251
JSP (Japan Socialist Party) 194, 196
justice system: China 51, 57, 86; Japan 91–92

Kaesong industrial park 145
Kaikaku to Tenbo 249
Kamakura Shogunate 72, 232
Kan, Naoto 196, 247
Kanemaru, Shin 157
Kanmu, Emperor 358–359*n.252*
Kantogun 201
Kaoshung Export Processing Zone 117
Karatsu, Hajime 185
Kato, Hiroshi 213, 257
Kato, Koichi 351*n.157*
Kawai, Eijiro 169
Kawamoto, Hiroko 251
Kaya states 61, *63*
Keju 50
Kennyo 278
Keynes, John Maynard 231, 335
Khalkhin-Gol, Undeclared War at 88–89, 90, 346*n.51*
Khrushchev, Nikita 19, 150
Kido, Takayoshi 224
Kiev 295, 327
Kikan Sagyo 189
Kim Dae-Jung 141, 143–145, 246
Kim Il-sung 147–151, 153–155, 157–158, 319
Kim Jong-il 144–145, 154–155, 158, 159, 161–162, 245–248
Kim Jong-un, 145–146, 161
Kim Yon-nam 160
Kim Young-sam 142, 143

Index

Kinyu-cho 216
Kishi, Nobusuke 139, 243
KMT *see* Chinese Nationalist Party
Kobayashi, Kichiya 196
Kodama, General Gentaro 322
Kodoha 82
Koei-Kigyo-Kinyu-Koko 258
Koeki-Hojin 199
Kofuku-ji temple 359*n.252*
Koguryo 45–46, 60, *63*, 261
Koizumi, Junichiro: Iraq question 196, 197; political reforms 237–240, 249, 259; Postal Corporation 240, 254–257; Pyongyang visit 245–248; Road Corporation fiasco 250–253; Yasukuni Shrine 240–245, 351*n.157*
Kojiki 70, 273
Kokusaiha 95
Kokutai ideology 168, 176, 362*n.283*
Kokutai ni awanai 284
Komatsubara, Lt. Gen. Michitaro 88
Komura, Jutaro 321
Komuro, Naoki 335
Konishi Yukinaga 345*n.36*
Konoe, Fumimaro 362–363*n.283*
Konoe, house of 359*n.252*
Konoe Sakihisa 355–356*n.208*
Korea: Buddhism 313, 358*n.252*; Christianity 135, 336; Confucianism 62, 65, 66; Democratic People's Republic of 153; factionalism 114, 143, 154, 155; historic development 59–66; historic links with China 28, 29; independence 66; industrialization 96; Japanese invasion 64–65; Japanese protectorate 66, 79, 135–136, 148, 324, 330; language 60; Manchu invasion 65; map *63*; political ideology 44, 85–86, 336; political influences 61–62; political reforms 337; Silla 60–62, *63*, 358*n.252*; Soviets 1945 advance 102; Three Kingdoms 45–46, 59, 61; *see* *also* North Korea; South Korea
Korean War 136–137, 138, 149–153, 276
Koryo dynasty 64
Koya-san 279, 354*n.206*
Krugman, Paul 211
Kuala Lumpur 133
Kubilai Khan, Emperor 72–73
Kukai (monk) 358*n.252*
Kumarajiva (monk) 313
Kumazawa Banzan 358*n.252*
Kumgang, Mt 145
Kuomintang 102, 104–105, 118, 119, 276
Kursk, battle of 328–329
Kusunoki Masashige 286
Kutuzov, Mikhail 327
Kwangtung Army 201
Kyodo News Agency 160, 182, 220
Kyongsang province 144
Kyoto: Nobunga 278, 279, 280, 281, 283, 355*n.208*; religion 353*n.204*, 358*n.252*, 359*n.252*; University 84, 316
Kyushu 74

Land Standard, Japan 204–205, 209–211, 213, 218
Landsberg, Conrad von 304
Lasko, Peter 293
Later Han dynasty 28
Latvia 304
LDP (Liberal Democratic Party): anti-American feelings 194–196; economic policies 212, 229, 238; manifesto 248–249; political reforms 240, 241, 314; Postal Corporation 240, 254, 256; Road Corporation 252–253
Lea, Arthur 284
League of Nations, Japan 202
Lee Hsien Loong 128
Lee Kuan Yew 110, 125–128

INDEX

Lee Teng-hui 118, 119
legal system: China 51, 57, 86, 111, 318, 320; Europe 307, 309; Hong Kong 122; Japan 91–92, 180–181, 183, 192, 194, 220, 309
Lenin, Vladimir 107–108, 320, 325
Leninism 35
Li Dazhao 270
Li Lisan 103
Li Peng 103 109, 111–112
Li Rusong 65
Liao (Khitan) 64
Liberal Democratic Party *see* LDP
Licinius, Emperor 291
Liebeschuetz, J.H.W.G. 289
Liji 42
Lin Biao 106
Lin Zexu 77, 78
literacy 47, 71
Lithuania 304–305
Liu Bang 102
Liu Qingfeng 31
Liu Shaoqi 106, 115
Long March 103
Lowe, Peter 153
Lu Xun 47, 163
Lugouqiao incident 219
Lunyu 41
Luoyang 39
Luther, Martin 297, 303, 306

Ma Ying-jeou 120–121
Macao 76, 160
MacArthur, General 150, 152, 169
Magadha 28
Magellan, Ferdinand 92–93
Mahayana 313
Mahon, Captain A.T. 323
Mainichi Shimbun 182
Malacca 129, 348*n.94*
Malaysia/Malaya 125, 126, 129, 133, 348*n.98*
Mamizu 213

Manchu dynasty 33, 65
Manchuria: expansion into 33, 65, 98, 330; Japan 89, 91, 139, 174, 201–203, 219, 330–331; Nomonhan incident 88–89, 346*n.51*; Russo-Japanese War 321, 324; WWI 80, 353*n.198*; WWII 102, 198
Mangyondae 154
Mansfield, Mike 25
Mao Zedong: Chinese writing change 47; comes to power 270; Korean War 151; policies 35, 102–106, 114, 116, 265, 271, 319; visits Soviet Union 147
maps: Korea *63*; Yin-Zhou Revolution *37*
Marubeni 352*n.177*
Marx, Karl 21, 202, 319, 320
Marxism 35, 103, 107, 320
Maryknoll magazine 276
Matsuda, Masashi 251
Matsumura, Gentaro 273
Matsunaga Hisahide 353*n.204*, 354*n.206*
Matsuoka, Yosuke 89, 202
Matsushita, Konosuke 177
Mauryan empire 27
Maxentius, Emperor 289
May Fourth movement 270
McCartney, Lord 76
McKinsey & Company 251
Meckel, Major Klemens 322, 360*n.264*
media, Japan 171, 179, 181–185, 244, 286
Medvedev, Roy 104
Meiji government 84–85, 89, 95, 169, 172, 181, 193, 199, 201, 223–225, 275, 330
The Merchant of Venice 256
metallurgy 34, 38, 39
Mie, northern 279
Mieno, Yasushi 211
Mikasa, Japanese flagship 324
Milan, edict of 289

INDEX

militarism policy 48
military capability: and agrarian economy 48; Britain 326, 328; China 20, 26, 29, 38, 48, 97, 106, 148–149, 151–152, 247, 261; Chinese communists 102, 103, 104; Germany 322, 326, 327, 328; Japan 88–89, 90–91, 94, 196–197, 202, 247–248, 322, 330, 351*n.161*, 360*n.264*; mercenaries 55, 59; North Korea 145, 147–149, 150, 247; nuclear weapons 97, 346–347*n.59*; People's Liberation Army 103; Russia 88–89, 102, 323–324, 329; South Korea 138–139, 196; technology impact 262–263; Zhou dynasty 39, 343*n.14*
military regimes: Japan 156; North Korea 158–159, 161; South Korea 138–142
Mill, John Stuart 181
Minamoto-no Yoritomo 72
Ming dynasty 28, 30, 34, 48, 65, 75
Mingdi, Emperor 59
mini-Zhongua-ism 65, 70, 75, 94
Ministry of Finance (MOF), Japan 11–12, 209, 216, 222, 226–230, 232, 238
Minjiang River 58
Mishima, Yukio 286
Mitchell, David 53
Mitsubishi UFJ 352*n.177*
Mitsui Sumitomo 352*n.177*
Miura Anjin 354*n.205*
Miyauchi, Yoshihiko 250
Miyazaki, Giichi 208
Miyazaki, Ichisada 84–85
Miyazawa, Kiichi 215, 216, 229, 233, 351*n.157*
Mizuho 352*n.177*
MOF *see* Ministry of Finance
Moltke, Helmuth von 360*n.264*
Mongol invasions: China 30; Japan 72–73; Korea 64; Russia 295

Mongolia: Chinese expansion 33; language 60; Nomonhan incident 88–89, 346*n.51*; People's Republic 353*n.198*
Moravia 296
Mori clan, feudal states of 282
Mori, Yoshiro 238, 239, 253, 254
Motoori Norinaga 75, 84
Mukden 322
Murai Sadakatsu 355*n.208*
Murayama, Tomiichi 243
Muromachi Shogunate 353*n.204*
Musashi battleship 330
Musashi Institute of Technologies 251
Myanmar 132, 156

Nagakute, battle of 64
Nagasaki 198
Nagashima 279
Nagashino, Battle of 280
Naijyu Kakudai 209
Naito, Konan 27
Naka-no Ooe, Prince 67
Nakajima, Lt-Gen. 334
Nakamura, Hideo 251
Nakamura, Kikuo 202, 346*n.53*
Nakanishi, Terumasa 187
Nakasone, Yasuhiro 241, 351*n.157*
Nakatomi-no Kamako 67
Namamugi incident 223
Nanjing 333–334
Nanjing Treaty 78
Nanyang Sing Pao 126
Nara 67, 69, 359*n.252*
National Emergency Council (NEC) 339–340
National Employer's Federation, France 127
national pride 20, 35, 125
nationalism 93–94, 133, 265, 275, 284, 339
Nationalist Party (Taiwan) 118, 119–120

INDEX

Natsume, Soseki 180
natural disasters 32
Nazis, Germany 325–330
Neary, Ian 170
Negative Gross National Public Debt 12
Negoro Temple 354*n.205*
Nelson, Admiral 323
Nerchinsk, Treaty of 75
Netherlands: historic expansion 23, 74, 75, 132, 297; shipping technology 297; trade with Japan 354*n.205*, 361*n.282*
Nevsky, Prince Aleksandr 295
New Year's Day, Japan 272–273
New Zealand 297
newspapers, Japan 171, 179, 181–183
Nicaea, council at 291
Nichiren (Monk) 359*n.252*
Nihon Keizai Shimbun 244
Nihon Koku 339
Nihon-Shoki 70
Nikkei 182
Ninigi-no-Mikoto 273
Nippo-Chinese War 219, 333–334
Nippon Steel 251
Nish, Ian 80
Nishimura, Kiyohiko 204
Nogi, General Maresuke 322
Noguchi, Akira 211
nomadic tribes 55, 59, 344*n.29*
Nomonhan Incident 88–89, 90, 346*n.51*
North Korea 147–164: Democratic People's Republic of Korea 153; economic implosion 260; economy 153, 155–157, 158, 160–162; industrialisation 148; invades South 136–137, 147, 148–150; and Japan 157, 245–248; joins UN 142; Kim Il-sung's reforms 153–155; Korean War 149–153; northern boundaries 261; nuclear weapons 145, 157–158, 159, 160, 246, 247; political ideology 161–162, 319; Rangoon terrorist attack 156; Russia/China relationship 155, 156, 159–161; sanctions 160–161; South Korea diplomacy 144–145, 159; threat to South 145–146, 159; US diplomacy 157, 158, 159, 160
Northern Wei 345*n.32*
Northern Zhou 345*n.32*
Novgorod 295
nuclear weapons: China 97, 104, 158, 159, 261; East Asia, future 25, 97; Korean War 152, 153; North Korea 145, 157–158, 159, 160, 246, 247; Russia 147, 148, 152, 159; South Korea 157; United States 152, 153, 155–156, 157, 198

Obuchi administration 212–213
Oda Nobunaga 74, 277–283, 354*n.205*, 354*n.206*, 355*n.208*
Oda Nobutada 355*n.208*
OECD (Organisation for Economic Co-operation and Development) 11, 143
Ohgimachi, Emperor 278, 281
Ohira, Masahiro 229, 243
Ohya, Eiko 251, 253
oil: China 261; Japanese WWII embargo 331, 361*n.282*; prices 141, 189; refineries, Singapore 127
Okazaki, Hisahiko 247
Okinawa 170
Okubo, Toshimichi 78–79, 223–226
Okuda, Tadashi 191
Okuma, Shigenobu 80
Okura-sho 226
Olympics, Seoul 142
Omae, Kenichi 186–187
Operation Barbarossa 89
opium trade 77
Orix Group 250
Ota Gyuichi 356*n208*
Ottoman Empire 296, 305

INDEX

Owen Haley, John 91–92
Oyama, Field Marshal Iwao 322
Ozawa, Ichiro 157, 195, 196

Paekche 46, *63*
Paektu, Mt 154–155
Pan-Germanic League 306
Park Chung-hee 110, 138–141, 157
Parkinson, C. Northcote 50
Patna (Pataliputna) 28
Patten, Chris 109
Paulus, Marshal 327
Payrefitte, Alain 76
Peabody, George 215
Peng Dehuai, General 106, 151
People's Action Party 126
People's Liberation Army 103, 104, 109, 151, 317
Perestroika 35
Pericles 163–164
Perry, Commodore Matthew 78
Persia 27, 28, 42
Peter the Great 296
PetroChina 301
Peyrefitte, Alain 76, 93
Philippines 129, 130–131, 134
pinyin characters 47
Pohang Steel Company (Posco) 140
Poland 296, 304–305, 306, 326
police forces 48, 153, 162, 191–194
political analysis, need for 15, 22–25
political ideology: China 20–24, 26, 27–29, 43, 98, 302–303; Christianity influence 314, 336; communist system 101–107, 110; dynastic regimes 31; East Asia 14–15, 21, 161–164, 260–262; economics link 21–23, 31; expansionism 44, 54, 55; fragmentation of power 87–92, 114; Hong Kong 122; Japan 23–25, 29, 44, 66–68, 70–71, 75, 90–92, 186, 199–200, 275; Korea 29; modern China 112–117; North Korea 153–154, 155, 156, 161–162; Philippines 130–131; political core 44–49, 81–84, 87; social science role 308; South Korea 136–144, 348*n.105*; United States 299, 300; Yin-Zhou revolution 36, 40–41, 43
political system, first 38–40
population: Chinese single child policy 106; economic cycle impact 31, 32, 33; Japan 75; racial/tribal amalgamation 39, 43, 55; rapid expansion 106; urban/rural balance change 115, 272
Port Arthur 322
Portugal: historic expansion 19, 92–93, 296; Japan 73–74; Macao 76; Malacca 129, 348*n.94*
Postal Corporation 240, 254–257, 258–259
Potemkin, Grigory 296
Potsdam 198
primordial characteristics 24
private-sector enterprises 50, 53–54, 191, 219, 249, 260
privatisation: government businesses 12, 257–259; Postal Corporation 240, 254–257, 258–259; Road Corporation 251–253, 258
propaganda, Japan 184–188, 199
Protestantism 297, 303, 305, 306, 307, 308, 338
Prussia 304, 305, 306, 307
public corporations, Japan 199, 216, 219, 220, 250, 254, 335
Public Financial Coffers for Governmental Enterprise 258
public sector reform, Japan 257–259
publishing industry, Japan 185–188
Pulzer, Peter 325
Pusan 150
Pyeoktchegwan, battle of 65
Pyongyang 64, 245–248
Pyongyang Castle, battle of 345*n.36*

INDEX

Qin empire 20–21, 26–27, 28, 32, 57–58
Qing dynasty 28, 33, 34, 65, 75, 101, 130, 269

Raffles, Thomas Stamford 124
railways: China 270; Japan 201; Manchuria 324
Ramseyer, Mark 315–316
Rangoon 156, 330
Reading, Brian 188
Reagan, Ronald 118
Reformation movement 297, 303, 305, 306
religion: China 58, 277, 320; Christianity conversion proposal 337, 338; Japan 67, 70, 73–74, 168; Korea 67, 135; and politics 307, 336–338; Russia 320; state 274; *see also* individual religions
revisionists 23, 24
revolution: anti-communism 107; China 31–33, 40, 97–98, 109, 269–272, 318, 320; communism 102–103; defeatism 161–164; historic cycles 31–33, 97; Japanese economy 213–214; North Korea 161, 162; Russia 320; United States 300; Yin-Zhou 36–43
Rhee Syng-man, President 136, 137, 148, 151
Ridgway, General Matthew 152
Rig-Veda 313
Rihabiri 95
river systems 45, 58
Road Corporation, privatisation 250–253, 258
Roberts, J.M. 297
Roh Moo-hyun, President 242
Roh Tae-woo 141–142
Rokokyo incident 219
Roman Empire 288–292, 293, 294, 296
Roosevelt, Franklin D. 361*n.282*
Roosevelt, Theodore 324, Rosenbluth, Frances 315–316
Royal Confucian Academy 62
Royle, Trevor 321
Rozhestvensky, Admiral 323–324
Rumania 327
Ruoff, Kenneth 316
Russia: capitalism 233; CIS formation 319; communist system 105, 110, 156, 318–319; historic expansion 19, 295–296, 305; Japan relationship 238–239, 262; Korean airliner attack 156; Korean War 148–153; Manchuria 321, 353*n.198*; Mao Zedong visits 147; name change 21; and North Korea 159; nuclear weapons 147, 148, 152, 155, 159; Perestroika 35; political reforms 107–108, 110, 112, 162, 318–319; religion 295–296, 307, 320; rift with Communist China 104, 106; Russo-Japanese War 79, 95, 321–324, 334; Soviets advance to Manchuria 102; support for China 102, 104, 148–149, 270; trade with China 76; Treaty of Nerchinsk 75; Undeclared War at Khalkhin-Gol 88–89, 346*n.51*; US relationship 152–153, 155–156; WWI 357*n.240*; WWII 89, 90, 198, 326–330

Saga, Emperor 358*n.252*
Saich, Tony 105
Saicho (monk) 358–359*n.252*
Saito, Admiral 135
Sakai 354*n.205*, 355*n.208*
Sakaiya, Taichi 213–214
Sakakibara, Eisuke 249
Sakhalin 198, 324, 330
Sakuma Nobumori 354*n.206*
Sakura-jima Island 223–224
Samurai 84, 85, 86, 278, 349*n.131*,

Index

354 n.205, 355 n.208
Sangyo Saisei Kiko 220
Sankei Shimbun 182, 259
Sasaki, Suguru 225
Sassanid dynasty 28
Sato, Eisaku 170, 194, 243
Satow, Ernest 193
Satsuma clan 78, 237, 322
Satsuma-British war 223–224
Satter, David 319
Saxer, Carl 144
Scalapino, Robert 159
Schroeder, Gerhard 242
Sejima, Ryuzo 94
Seljuk Turks 303–304
Seoul 142, 144, 149
service industry 116
Seven Years War 130
Shaanxi province 39
Shakespeare, William 255–256
Shandong province 269
Shang period 36
Shanghai 97, 108–109, 115, 271, 333
Shanrang 33
Sheldon, Charles 174
Shenzhen, Special Economic Zone 108
Shepherd Law 361 n.282
Shi Huangdi 32, 57–58
Shibata Katsuie 282
Shibusawa, Eiichi 200
Shijing 42
Shikoku 283
Shillony, Ben-Ami 183
Shimazu clan 78
Shimazu, Hisamitsu 223
Shingon sect 279
Shinran (Monk) 359 n.252
Shinsei (Rebirth) Party 195
Shinsin (New Progress) Party 195
Shintoism: and Buddhism 313, 358 n.252; Christianity conversion analysis 337, 338; Ise Shrine 243, 273; New Year 273; political scope 286–287; resurgence 272–275; state 67, 70–71, 168, 175, 176, 241, 244, 274–275, 337; Yasukune Shrine 241
Shiokawa, Masajuro 239
ships: iron 34, 282; Japanese 323–324, 330; navigation development 296–297; Viking 294
Shoriki, Matsutaro 182
Shotoku, Prince 180
Shoup, Carl 228
Shu (Shu Han) regime 27
Siberia 80
Sichuan 27, 58
Sicily 329
Sigal, Leon 158, 198
Silla 60–62, *63*, 358 n.252
Singapore 124–128, 133, 234, 333–334
Sinic civilization 44
Sinicization 39, 43, 55
Sino-barbarian synthesis 59–60, 345 n.32
Sino-Japanese War (1895) 79, 101, 323, 324
Sixteen Kingdoms of the Five Barbarians 345 n.32
slavery 55, 155
SME *see* socialist market economy
Smith, Adam 33
social science 308–314, 317, 320, 335–336
socialist market economy (SME) 108–112, 123–124, 160
society: China 302; Confucianism 58, 302; East Asian networks 84–85; family units 55–57, 62, 64, 129; Japan, state control 285–287, 335; Japanese class ranking 86–87; revolution 31; socialist market economy 111; traditional farming 115
Soga clan 67
Soga-no Umako 67
Sogoshosha 216
Soken-ji temple 281

INDEX

Song dynasty 27, 28, 33, 73
Soong, James 119
soothsayers 38
South Africa 297
South East Asia, immigration 128–134
South Korea 135–146: constitution 139–140, 348*n.105*; coup d'etat 138–140; economy 138, 140, 141, 142, 143, 144; establishment 136, 142; invaded by North 136–137, 147, 148–149; Iraq 196; and Japan 135–136, 138, 140, 142–143, 145, 241–243; joins UN 142; Korean War 149–153; North Korea diplomacy 144–145, 159; nuclear weapons 157; political ideology 276; Rangoon terrorist attack 156; relations with China 261; religion 135, 277, 284; and Russia 142; threat from North 145–146, 159; and United States 136–137, 148; Yasukuni Shrine 241–244
Soviet Union *see* Russia
Spain: Alhambra captured 305; Eighty Year's War 297; historic expansion 296; Islamic period 294, 296, 297; Philippines 130; religion 357*n.241*
Spinoza, Benedict de 285
St James, cult of 357*n.241*
St Petersburg 296
St Sophia, Istanbul 295
Stalin, Joseph: and China 105, 106, 147; Japan 89, 175–176; Mongolia 353*n.198*; North Korea 148–149, 150, 152–153; WWII 328
Stalingrad 327
Sudetenland 326
Suharto, Thojib 133
Sui dynasty 28, 45–46, 67, 84, 345*n.32*
Sukarno, Achmed 132–133
Sumerians 36, 38
Sumitomo 352*n.177*
Sun Yat-sen 21, 80, 269–272

Sung-hwa Cheong 142
Sunzi 25, 48
Supreme Council for National Reconstruction 139
Susano-o 273
Suvorov, Russian flagship 324
Suzuki, Kantaro 198
Suzuki, Muneo 238
Sweden 213, 295, 296, 304, 305
Sword Brothers 304

Taaksin, King 131
Tachibana Muneshige 65
Taika Reform 66–67, *69*
Taiwan: colonisation 30, 75; democracy 117–121; economic problems 121; factionalism 114, 120; industrialization 96, 117–118, 133; Japanese influence 79, 117, 330; martial law ended 118; political ideology 276–277; political status 119, 120–121; relations with China 118, 119, 120; religion 276–277, 284
Takahashi, Korekiyo 82
Takamatsu Castle 282
Takano, Iwasaburo 174
Takeda Katsuyori 280
Takenaka, Heizo 218, 249, 257
Takeshima Island 137
Takeshita administration 219
Takigawa Kazumasa 280
Takushoku University 251
Tales of the Old Incidents 70
Talleyrand, Charles Maurice de 298–299
Tamaki, Norio 215
Tanaka, Hidetomi 211
Tanaka, Kakuei 238, 239
Tanaka, Kazuaki 251
Tanaka, Makiko 238–239
Tanaka, Naoki 214
Tanaka, Yasuo 249
Tang dynasty: establishment 60; expansionism 27, 28–29; fall 32;

INDEX

relations with Silla 46, 61; *Zhenguan* 67
T'ang Leang Li 343*n.2*
Tannenberg, victory of 357*n.240*
Tanigawa, Michio 29
Tasker, Peter 220–221
taxation, Japan 228–229, 258
tea 30, 76–77
technology: adoption of Western 34, 66, 73, 335; Bronze Age 36; dynastic regimes 32, 33; effect on politics 262–264, 272; historic development 26, 27, 30, 33–34, 57; India role 313; Islamic influence 296–297; Japan 68, 73–74, 75, 84, 176–177, 185, 187, 309; matchlock weapons 280, 354*n.205*; SME modernisation 111; treble ball concept 309–310
television, Japan 183–184
Ten Kingdoms period 27
Tenji, Emperor 67
Tenka-Fubu 278
terrorists, political, Japan 193–194, 351*n.157*
Teutonic Knights 304, 305
Thailand 121, 129, 131–132
Thatcher, Margaret 122, 222
The Times 249
Three Kingdoms dynasty 28, 45, 59, 61
Thucydides 163–164
Thurow, Lester 22–23
Tiananmen Square 102, 109, 162, 317–318
Tibet Autonomous Region 115, 317
Togo, Heihachiro 323
Tojo, Hideki 203, 360*n.264*
Tokugawa Ieyasu 64–65, 74, 85, 278, 355*n.208*
Tokugawa Shogunate 74–75, 84, 86, 163, 173–174, 312, 313
Tokuyama, Jiro 91
Tokyo University 169, 170, 174
Toseiha 82

Toynbee, Arnold 41, 44, 48, 68, 295, 317
Toyo Shiso 200
Toyotomi Hideyoshi 64–65, 85, 278, 282, 349*n.131*
trade: British exports 298; Canton emergence 30; Hong Kong 122, 123; Industrial Revolution 34; Islamic influences 128–129; Japan 73, 74, 82, 87, 354*n.205*; North Korea 156–157; opium 77; Shang period 36; Singapore 124–125, 127–128; socialist market economy 108, 110–111, 123–124, 160; South East Asia 129–130; South Korea 140, 141; Taiwan 117–118, 120; tea 30, 76–77
trade unions, Japan 194
transportation technology 33
Trotsky, Leon 104–105
Truman, Harry 117, 137, 152, 198
Tsang, Donald 121
Tsuda, Saukichi 172
Tsujii, Masanobu, Colonel 91
Tsuru, Shigeto 210
Tsushima Strait, battle of 323–324
Tumen River 148
Tung Chee-hwa 122
Tungusic tribes 60
Turkic tribes 55, 60, 98, 303–304, 344*n.29*, 345*n.31*

Ueda Akinari 75
Uekusa, Kazuhide 212–213
Uesugi Kenshin 279–280
Ukraine 319
Ulchi Mundok, General 45
Umayabashi Castle 280
Umayyad Arabs 294, 296
Umehara, Takeshi 200
UN (United Nations): global interventions 264; Human Development Report (2002) 264; North Korea 142; Security Council

INDEX

19–20, 111–112, 153; South Korea 142, 149, 150–151, 152, 153; Taiwan expulsion 119

United States: economic recovery 230; financial policies 228; global capitalism 235, 261–262; global economic power 127; Great Depression 11; historic growth 298–300; Korean War 149–153; management systems 216–217; and North Korea 158, 159, 160, 246, 349*n.128*; nuclear weapons 152, 153, 155–156, 157, 198; political ideology 299, 300; relationship with Russia 152–153, 155–156; religion 299, 307–308; role in East Asia 300–302; Russo-Japanese peace treaty 324; and South Korea 136–137, 139–140, 148, 149; Taiwan support 117–118; trade with China 123–124, 261–262; trade with Japan 78, 177, 184, 189, 190, 209, 215; US-Japan politics 25, 138, 167, 173, 203, 228–229, 239; war for independence 19; WWI 299; WWII 198, 299, 324–325, 327, 330, 331, 361*n.282*, 362*n.283*

universal principle 314, 336

vassalage system 29
Vietnam 44, 106, 132, 138, 140, 331
Vikings 292–293, 294, 295
villages 57, 102
Vladimir, Prince 295
Vladyslav Jogaila, Grand Duke 304
Vogel, David 190
von Manstein, Erich 329

Wa-Kon Yoo-Sai 200
Wado-Kaichin 68
Walesa, Lech 162
Wang Gungwu 35
Wang Hsuan-ts'e, General 28
Wang Hui 112

Wang Mang 58
Warring States period 48
weapons: China 34, 38, 39; iron 34, 66, 274, 279, 280, 354*n.205*; Japan 73, 323, 349*n.131*, 354*n.205*; Korean war 148–149, 150, 151, 152; Russia/Japan conflict 88–89; *see also* nuclear weapons
Weber, Max 302–308
Wei dynasty 59, 345*n.32*
Wei Zheng 67
Welch, Rev. Herbert 135
Welch, Jack 216–217
Wells, Peter 289–290
Wen Jiabao 115
West: capitalist expansion 12–14, 76, 78, 236; debt crisis 12; global capitalism 233, 234–236, 263–264, 266, 301–302; global interventions 264; Singapore's links with 127–128
West Asia: Bronze technology 36; dualistic theology 42; imperial system 27
Western Jin 345*n.32*
Western Wei 345*n.32*
Wilson, Harold 127
Wladyslaw II Jagiello 304
Wo, Five Kings of 60–61
Wo-ren 59
Wojciech (Slavnik Adalbert) 296
Wolferen, Karel van 23–24
World Trade Organization (WTO) 96
World War I (WWI) 79–80, 236, 270, 357*n.240*
World War II (WWII): Britain 325, 326, 327, 331; France 325–326; Germany 325–330; Italy 326, 329; Japan 82, 88–92, 94, 102, 198–199, 240–241, 244, 324–325, 330–332, 346*n.51*, 346*n.53*, 361–362*n.282*, 362–363*n.283*; Manchuria 102, 198; Russia 89, 90, 198, 326–330; United States 198, 299, 324–325, 327, 330,

INDEX

331, 361 *n.282*, 362 *n.283*
writing system: China 38, 39, 40, 46–47, 274, 359 *n.252*; Hittite tablets 313; Japan 71; Vietnam 132
WTO (World Trade Organization) 96
Wu (*Bu/Wakatakeru*), King 61
Wuchuangzhen clan 84

Xavier, Francisco 73–74
Xiamen, Special Economic Zone 108, 118
Xiangyu, General 32
Xianyang 32
Xin dynasty 58
Xuanzhuang 313

Yakuza 191–194
Yalu River 148, 151
Yamagata, Aritomo 168
Yamato battleship 330
Yamazaki, Taku 240
Yandi of Sui 84
Yangban 136
Yap Ah Loy 133
Yasukuni Shrine 240–245
Ye Jianying 103
Yellow River 38, 42
Yeltsin, Boris 108, 162, 318
Yi Sun-sin, Admiral 64
Yijing 42
Yin dynasty 35–38, 39, 45
Yin and *Yang* 42

Yin-Zhou 'revolution' 36, 40–43
Yixing 40
Yokosuka 237
Yomiuri Shimbun, 181–182
Yong Lu, Emperor 30
Yoshida doctrine 177
Yoshida, Shigeru 169, 170
Yoshino, Sakuzo 214
Yoshitomi, Masaru 212
Yuan dynasty 28
Yuan Shikai 269
Yuen dynasty 30
Yugoslavia 264
Yun Po-son, President 137, 139

Zagoria, Donald 155
Zaibatsu 82, 175, 216
Zaimu-sho 226
Zeidler, Manfred 327
Zeng Qinghong 115–116
Zhao Kuangyin, General 33
Zhao Ziyang 107, 108, 109–110
Zhebin, Aleksandr 155
Zheng Chenggong, Admiral 75
Zhong Shang Parks 269
Zhou dynasty 28, 38–43, 345 *n.32*
Zhou Enlai 103, 106, 107, 150
Zhouyuan 39
Zhu Rongji 110
Zhukov, Georgi 90, 328, 329
Zongfa system 41
Zoroastrianism 42